NATIVE AMERICANS
AND WAGE LABOR

Native Americans and Wage Labor

Ethnohistorical Perspectives

Edited by
Alice Littlefield and
Martha C. Knack

University of Oklahoma Press
Norman and London

Also by Alice Littlefield
La industria de las hamacas en Yucatán (México, 1976)
Marxist Approaches in Economic Anthropology (edited with Hill Gates) (Lanham, Md., 1991)

Also by Martha C. Knack
Life Is with People: Household Organization of the Contemporary Southern Paiute Indians of Utah (Socorro, N.Mex., 1980)
Contemporary Southern Paiute Household Structure and Bilateral Kinship Clusters (New Haven, 1982)
As Long as the River Shall Run: An Ethnohistory of Pyramid Lake Reservation, Nevada (Berkeley, 1984)

Native Americans and wage labor : ethnohistorical perspectives / edited by Alice Littlefield, Martha C. Knack.
    p. cm.
    Includes bibliographical references and index.
    ISBN 0-8061-2816-X (alk. paper)
    1. Indians of North America—Employment.   2. Indians of North America—History—Sources.   3. Indians of North America—Economic conditions.   4. Ethnohistory—United States.   5. United States—Economic conditions.   I. Littlefield, Alice.   II. Knack, Martha C.
E98.E6N37   1996
331.6'997—dc20   95-31899
                                                                        CIP

Text design by Cathy Carney Imboden. Text typeface is Goudy Old Style.

The paper in this book meets the guidelines for permanence and durability of the Committee on Production Guidelines for Book Longevity of the Council on Library Resources, Inc. ∞

1 2 3 4 5 6 7 8 9 10

CONTENTS

CONTENTS

vi

FIGURES

PREFACE

This book began at the November 1990 meetings of the American Society for Ethnohistory (ASE) in Toronto, Ontario. There we met for the first time and discovered a common interest in a subject we agreed had been neglected by anthropologists and historians: participation in wage labor by North American indigenous people. Each of us had encountered evidence of such participation, in both rural and urban settings, and over a period encompassing more than a century.

Out of this conversation came a plan to organize a symposium around the topic for the 1991 meetings of the ASE in Tulsa, Oklahoma. Later we agreed to organize one for the 1991 American Anthropological Association (AAA) meetings in Chicago as well. The chapters in this book were largely selected from those presented in the two symposia, with three (Chapters 5, 7, and 10) added later.

We wrote our introductory chapter after the drafts of the other chapters had been submitted, and we owe much to the theoretical and conceptual challenges posed by those chapters. We are also indebted to those symposium participants (J. David Damrell and Thomas Burgess) whose work does not appear here and to Patricia Albers and John H. Moore, who served as discussants for the two symposia (Albers for the ASE and Moore for the AAA).

We are thankful to Hill Gates, Larry T. Reynolds, and Brian Baker for their useful comments on our introduction and to C. Matthew Snipp and an anonymous reviewer for a number of constructive criticisms of the book manuscript. We are also indebted to our editor, John Drayton, for his encouragement and patience and to the staff at University of Oklahoma Press for their assistance with this project.

ALICE LITTLEFIELD
MARTHA C. KNACK

NATIVE AMERICANS
AND WAGE LABOR

1

NATIVE AMERICAN LABOR
RETRIEVING HISTORY, RETHINKING THEORY

MARTHA C. KNACK AND ALICE LITTLEFIELD

Studies of North American Indian economic life have largely ignored the participation of indigenous people in wage labor, even though for over a century such participation has often been essential for the survival of Native individuals and communities. Anthropological fascinations with the "traditional," or compulsions to salvage the "aboriginal" before it became hopelessly contaminated by the "modern," may account for part of this silence. These professional biases toward the past, coupled with the habit of studying the Indian community as separate from the non-Indian, have all too often led to constructions that treat Native life as an isolate. Such theories are too narrow to account for the phenomenon of Indian wage labor, which of historical necessity has existed along the contact zone between Indian and non-Indian communities and cultures. Without an interpretive framework sufficiently broad to explain this labor, raise questions about it, and demand answers to those questions, most ethnographers and ethnohistorians have chosen to ignore Indians' employment for wages.

Even when scholars have addressed Indians' relationships to the larger political economy of the United States, they have all too often concentrated on federal Indian policy and its political consequences rather than on empirical discussions of the reality of Native economic lives as they were and are being lived. A focus on government documents, federal intentions, espoused policies, and bureaucratic justifications has led too many researchers to a false sense of uniformity. In reality, policies are often modified to suit local conditions or to assuage regional power holders (Bee 1981; Knack 1992; Perry 1993). Without a highly sophisticated political interpretation, reliance on federal documents, laws, and judicial decisions can create a fantasia, a never-never land of political pronouncements, rather than a realistic analysis of what actually has happened and is happening to Indian people.

Another cause of scholarly silence about Indian labor has been the restrictive definition of Native American economics as an issue of natural resources, specifically land. Although the wholesale dispossession of land from the first Americans is a dramatic, visible, and emotionally powerful issue, and one that has great strategic importance to indigenous peoples in their claims for political sovereignty and financial redress, it should not be allowed to obscure another resource that Indians possessed and non-Indians came gradually to control—their labor.

It has become a historical commonplace to decry U.S. wealth as built on the theft of Indian land (e.g., Olson and Wilson 1984) and the enslavement of African labor. There is clearly a good deal of truth in these twin assertions, for both were important in the accumulation that underlay the development of capitalism in the United States. Both assertions also oversimplify by ignoring the diversity of local circumstances that led employers to seek out a wide array of labor sources and to subject laborers to varying degrees of coercion. For Native peoples, the regimes of labor control that emerged often had important consequences for continuity and change in their social and political lives.

In this book we differentiate labor from trade as separate components of an economic relationship. In trade surely a component of labor is involved, as raw materials extracted from the environment are processed into a finished product and offered in exchange for goods manufactured by other people. In wage labor, however, there is only one type of good offered for sale—the work, skill, time, and effort of the laborer. Even though trade was a widespread phenomenon in precontact North America and reciprocal labor exchange both within and between kin groups was common, the sale of labor alone as a means to subsistence for entire families was rare to nonexistent (Driver and Massey 1957, 371–382). The treatment of labor as a commodity within a cash economy, to be bought

4

and sold on the open market, surely existed nowhere in North America before the arrival of Europeans. Wage labor, then, was a historic product brought about by the interaction of Indians and Euro-Americans and stimulated along the interface between two major cultural and economic traditions.

When scholars have considered Indian labor in this sense at all, they have usually concluded that it was of little importance to the historical development of the North American economy (e.g., Cornell 1988; Jacobson 1984; Snipp 1986a). The large-scale importation of African slaves into the English colonies and the rapid incorporation of European immigrants have led authors to dismiss Indian laborers as biologically too susceptible to European disease and numerically insignificant. They were, authors have said, unable to meet the rapidly expanding labor needs of the burgeoning capitalist economy of the eighteenth and nineteenth centuries, and their labor therefore lacked economic or political significance. Stephen Cornell (1988, 30), for example, asserts, "With the exception of the early Southwest, only in the fur trade was Indian labor either critical to colonial, U.S., or trans-Atlantic economies or a foundation of Indian-White relations."

In looking at Indian wage labor, we must ask at least two distinct questions. One queries, What role has Native labor played in the development of the U.S. economy? Here the focus is, as for Cornell, on the Euro-American, national whole. The other question looks to Native societies and asks, What role has wage labor played in the economic and social history of North American indigenous peoples? These two questions have different answers. Regardless of whether Indian labor was crucial to Euro-American enterprises (and we hope to demonstrate that in certain times and places it was), wage labor certainly was crucial to the survival of Native individuals and communities. To discover the role of wage work within the complex and diverse dynamics of Indian lives, we must look to the empirical reality of specific cases and reach beyond and beneath simple national policy.

Prominent narratives of Native American history have described Indian participation in wage labor as a twentieth-century development, resulting from New Deal reforms, which "cause[d] Indians to go to work"

(Zimmerman 1957, 32); from urban migration in response to the industrial labor demands of World War II; or from the Bureau of Indian Affairs' (BIA) subsequent urban relocation program of the 1950s (e.g., Hagan 1961, 166; Tyler 1973, 122, 159). Such narratives have said wage labor participation was instigated by the benevolence or malevolence of federal policymakers, depending on the interpretation of the author (e.g., Prucha 1984). Discussions of wage labor itself have described it among Native Americans as recent, urban, unstable, and marginal (Brophy and Aberle 1966, 68–70). Many authors have not perceived Indian wage labor as a significant subject at all, failing even to have index entries for "labor," "wage labor," or "work" (e.g., McNickle 1973; Washburn 1975, 1988); others, while not indexing "employment," have had entries for "unemployment," choosing to see wage labor as a social problem and somehow a failure or weakness of Indian economies (e.g., Josephy 1984; Wax 1971, 70, 80). Contrary to these common portrayals, the chapters in this book bear testimony to Native Americans' involvement in wage labor long before the twentieth century, frequently at their own initiative, in rural areas, and as a critical portion of their economic lives.

Because of the general lack of consideration of Native American wage labor in the literature and because we want to prepare the reader for the more detailed case studies that follow, we begin with an overview of existing knowledge about Indian labor in postcontact America. We then turn to some of the implications of Indian wage labor for wider anthropological and ethnohistorical theory.

An overview of Indian labor shows that it is clearly premature to generalize about "Indian labor" as a single, aggregate, monolithic phenomenon (Albers 1991). Ethnohistorically and ethnographically, American Indians experienced dramatically divergent sites for their labor, types of jobs, means of acquiring employment, wages received, and age and sex distributions of workers. But strictly case-by-case, localized explanations would miss the scale of Native American involvement in the wage labor market. From both on reservations and off, from western tribes with well-established federal relations to unrecognized eastern ones, the common reality of group after group entering wage labor markets points to underlying causes that affected them all.

INDIAN LABOR IN THE NORTH AMERICAN COLONIES
Although Indians were rarely waged employees of the French and English fur companies, Native labor was essential in trapping, processing, and transporting the furs that provided the basis for colonial economies (Cornell 1988; Wolf 1982, 158–194).[1] It was Indian men who did most of the trapping and Indian women who processed the bulk of the furs and hides for market (Klein 1983, 147–157). In addition to furs, Indians produced a range of other items needed by Europeans. Trading posts such as Green Bay and Mackinac depended on neighboring Indian communities for fish, corn, maple sugar, wild rice, canoes, snowshoes, and other necessary supplies (McClurken, this volume; Cleland 1992, 103–104, 177–178). Furthermore, Indians such as the famous Sacajawea worked for European traders as domestics and guides. Sometimes for a single season, sometimes in long-term marriage, Indian women formed partnerships with French traders (Van Kirk 1980; White 1991, 60–75). As much political as sexual alliances, these unions provided Europeans with legitimacy and social entrée into Native communities in order to engage in a search for profits.

In the late eighteenth and early nineteenth centuries as the fur trade progressively fell under the domination of a few large companies, Indian trappers grew dependent on credit to buy European manufactures, such as steel traps and muskets. The terms of trade shifted, coming increasingly to favor the traders over the producers until, it has been argued, the credit was a disguised form of wage labor, "a putting-out system, in which the entrepreneurs advanced both production goods and consumption goods against commodities to be delivered in the future" (Wolf 1982, 194). In formal terms, however, Indian trappers largely remained independent petty producers of a commodity extracted from the natural resources of the land.

Indians not only volunteered labor via commerce but also were forced into slavery in both French and English colonies (Lauber 1913; Olexer 1982). The colonists seem to have had two major motives for keeping

7

Indian slaves. One was the direct need for their labor in agriculture, domestic work, and other menial tasks. The other, perhaps more important motive was political and military, for trade in slaves was a means to cement relationships with indigenous allies by encouraging them to attack tribes allied with European rivals.

The number of Indian slaves kept in colonial America was not small. South Carolinian Englishmen actively encouraged their Indian allies to attack other tribes, especially those in territories claimed by encroaching Spain or France (Moore 1989; Nash 1992, 130–142; Willis 1962). In 1708 about 1,400 of the slaves (nearly one-quarter of the total) in that colony were Indians. Louisiana Colony held 229 Indian slaves (along with 1,540 Negroes) in 1726. Well into the latter half of the eighteenth century French settlers at Detroit held Pawnee, Osage, and Choctaw slaves purchased from Indian military allies. The English preferred female slaves, especially if young, and assigned them both domestic and agricultural tasks (Lauber 1913, 74–75, 91, 102, 105–106, 242–243).

English colonists complained that Indians made unsatisfactory slaves, largely because of their knowledge of the country and ability to escape successfully by seeking refuge in Native communities. To inhibit escape, colonists sold captives to distant buyers living in unfamiliar territory (Nash 1992, 81–86, 118–123; Lauber 1913, 168–195). Nevertheless, fearing the repercussions of keeping Native slaves after the Yamasee War of 1715, in which the Carolinians found themselves almost driven out by their former Indian allies, the English colonies largely replaced Native slaves with those imported from Africa.

For Spanish settlements in the Southwest and California, labor control formed an important aspect of colonial policy. Unlike the French and English, the Spanish lacked easy access to the transatlantic trade in African slaves, and settlements on their northern frontiers did not attract large numbers of Spanish or other European immigrants. Consequently, their need for Indian labor remained significant throughout the colonial period and beyond.

In New Mexico the Spaniards subjected the sedentary agricultural Pueblo communities to systems of labor control previously developed in central Mexico: missionization, tribute extraction, and the *encomienda*

(Dozier 1970, 43–71). In California hunting and gathering bands were rounded up and brought into the missions, where they worked in a combination of agricultural, domestic, and skilled crafts, including winemaking and blacksmithing (Carrico and Shipek, this volume; Cook 1976, 91–101; Forbes 1969, 28–32). More mobile tribes, not susceptible to such techniques, were encouraged to take captives and sell them to the Spanish settlers. In the nineteenth century Comanches raided Apaches and Navajos, and Utes raided unmounted Paiute bands as far north as central Utah for the Santa Fe market (Bailey 1966; Forbes 1960, 120–155; Hall 1989b, 204–236; Malouf and Malouf 1945). Estimates of Indian captives held by both Hispanic and Anglo-American settlers in New Mexico at the end of Mexican rule range as high as six thousand.

Indians who did not produce commodities such as furs for sale, or provide unpaid labor as slaves were employed for wages in the northern English colonies at an extremely early period (Prins, this volume). Scattered evidence shows that Indians worked for wages in either cash or kind in Massachusetts Bay Colony from as early as the 1630s, only ten years after the landing of the *Mayflower*. Throughout the seventeenth century Indians were employed in farming, whaling, doing domestic service, and building roads and stone walls in this area (Lauber 1913, 292–293). Long Island Indians not only worked as day laborers in agriculture but also crewed whaling boats to such an extent that in the late 1600s employers were bidding competitively for their services (Strong, 1994, 566; Trelease 1960, 199–203).

THE ANGLO-AMERICAN EMPIRE EXPANDS

As the Anglo-American frontier moved rapidly westward in the years after the American Revolution, Indians increasingly found themselves engulfed by settlers. Historians have given considerable attention to Indian losses of land during this period and the destructive effects of the removal policy of the 1830s and 1840s but have focused little attention on the survival strategies that Natives selected as the frontier advanced.

There were enormous variations among the experiences of different tribes in different historical situations and environmental regions. Nonetheless, there were some commonalities in this process of adaptation. Where land was still accessible, Indians maintained previous patterns of foraging and gardening, often in attenuated form (Knack, Prins, and Sennett, this volume; Jorgensen 1990, 92–94, 107–115). They adopted and adapted some European livestock, crops, and cultivation methods for Native domestic, rather than market, production (Knack, McClurken, and Prins, this volume). When Euro-American settlers were interested in native fish, game, crops, crafts, or gathered products, Indians provided these through both barter and cash transactions (Carrico and Shipek, McClurken, and Prins, this volume). In some areas production of furs or buffalo hides continued to be part of the mix of activities increasingly attuned to the cash economy (Moore, this volume; Klein 1978; Shifferd 1976).

In addition to alteration of the Native production system and development of an exchange system that moved resources extracted from the land into the Euro-American sphere, the commodification of labor itself was a conspicuous feature of the Native American adaptation in postcolonial America. Indian men received wages working for farmers, lumbermen, and other rural enterprises; Indian women worked as domestics or field laborers. In few cases were these full-time occupations; rather, kin groups and communities deployed labor power in a complex and shifting round of seasonal activities, with the proceeds often distributed through networks of sharing and reciprocity. Crucial in Indian adjustment to the loss of subsistence resources, Indian wage employment appears to have been most important to newly developing Euro-American enterprises in those regions that still lacked any densely settled, potentially competitive laboring population. Paradoxically, even though Native mobility within former resource areas was often restricted by land loss to Anglo-American settlements, the settlers' own transportation system of roads, wagons, saddle horses, and eventually trains and automobiles enhanced Indians' movement as they foraged for wages (Knack, Peters, Prins, and Sennett, this volume).

In the northeastern United States wage labor replaced both land lost to Anglo-American settlers and the decline of the fur trade in the early nineteenth century. By the mid-1800s the Mi'kmaqs in New England

and the Maritime Provinces were working as loggers, river rafters, guides, and agricultural laborers. When northern Maine emerged as a major commercial potato producer in the 1870s, Natives became a regular part of the harvest labor force (Prins, this volume). Iroquois people likewise turned to wage labor in the early nineteenth century. Senecas worked in lumbering and on railroads, as craftsmen and farm laborers (Rothenberg 1980, 74–78; Wallace 1969, 235, 313–314). Soon after 1820 Caughnawaga Mohawks were cutting timber, quarrying stone, performing in Indian shows and circuses, piloting river boats, and working in construction (Mitchell 1959, 13; Katzer 1988, 39–41).

In the Southeast large landowners continued to rely on African slave labor until after the Civil War, precluding a significant market for Native wage laborers. In the aftermath of that war, however, hard-pressed Cherokees managed to hire themselves out to local whites. By the 1870s "the Indians had raised their rates to twenty-five cents a day in salt, corn, or pork" (Finger 1984, 128).

Unlike the far north, the fur trade had declined in the Great Lakes region by the mid-1800s (Peterson and Brown 1985). Indians there entered commercial extraction industries, such as fishing and farming, and sold such traditional products as maple sugar and wild rice. Many also sold their labor to non-Indians in logging, railroad construction, copper mining, farmwork, shipping, tourism, and domestic labor (Littlefield, McClurken, this volume; Hosmer 1991; Keesing 1987, 229; Shifferd 1976). Work as loggers was especially important to Indians in the upper Midwest and remained so into the twentieth century.

After the destruction of the bison on the Great Plains and the collapse of the hide trade, formerly equestrian hunting peoples were restricted to barren and unproductive reservations. Numerous Plains groups became dependent on federal subsidies. It was here that the stereotype of Indians as people on the dole emerged. Subsequently generalized to all Natives, this stereotype has persisted into the twentieth century. Plains Indians appear to have engaged in little agricultural wage labor before 1900 (Moore, this volume), but previously they had often been employed by the U.S. government itself—first to act as guides, scouts, and mercenaries for the military (Dunlay 1982) and later to build reservation infrastructure, haul freight, and perform other menial tasks for the very Indian Service sent to supervise them.

The Great Basin differed from other areas in the very speed with which subsistence foragers shifted to wage labor. In this region what few reservations there were failed to provide year-round subsistence resources. Settlers rapidly controlled the localized water sources and displaced game with farms and domesticated livestock. There were few natural resources that local Indians could market, such as other Indian groups had done through the fur or hide trades. Unable to support themselves through hunting, gathering, or trade, Natives rapidly adopted wage labor and became dependent on it for subsistence. By the 1890s, less than fifty years after first settlement, Southern Paiutes were relying on wages for over half their provisioning (Knack, this volume). Here, as elsewhere, the division of wage labor was engendered according to Euro-American, not indigenous, concepts of proper sexual allocation of tasks: Native men worked in agriculture and rail construction; women were employed in domestic labor, as well as in harvest and other agricultural work. Unlike in some parts of the Southwest, Great Basin Indians do not seem to have been extensively employed in mining, except in supportive surface operations (cutting timbers for mine shoring, housebuilding, or firewood; constructing roads; cooking and laundering for non-Indian mine workers; or providing sexual services [Knack 1986b]). Throughout the Basin wage labor became part of a seasonal round that continued to include a wide variety of foraging activities in marginal areas (Knack, this volume; Downs 1966, 72–88).

In southern Arizona Indian labor played a critical role in establishing an infrastructure that benefited burgeoning non-Indian development. In the 1870s and 1880s San Carlos Apaches hired out to neighboring farms and mining camps to collect wood and hay, make adobes, herd cattle, construct ditches, and perform other casual labor. Around the turn of the century Apaches were active in railway, road, and dam construction (Adams 1971). In 1901 the local agent reported, "[The Apaches] eagerly seek work on the railroad, among the white farmers, at the mines, and, in fact, anywhere they can hear of a job. They have established a reputation as good workers. . . . There are several who are capable of running and caring for stationary engines, and quite a number are familiar with the use of drills and dynamite in mining" (quoted in Adams 1971, 119). Similarly, Navajos worked on the railroads of New Mexico and southern Utah beginning in the 1870s (Weiss 1984, 68–69) and Lagunas in New Mexico entered railroad work in the 1880s (Peters, this volume). By the late 1800s some O'Odham (Papagos) in southern Arizona were working in the copper mines (Waddell 1969, 18, 52–53). O'Odham living near Tucson had earlier been drawn into domestic labor and other menial jobs in the Spanish colonial economy, and they continued similar urban work into the twentieth century.

Even in California, where Anglos' genocidal treatment of Indians was notorious, Captain John Sutter and other northern miners and ranchers depended on Indian labor throughout the gold rush period (Findlay 1992; Hurtado 1983, 1988b). In the Los Angeles basin Indian labor was recruited for work in vineyards and wine production as early as the Mexican period. In the 1850s Indians were often arrested for public drunkenness; then in payment for their fines civil authorities auctioned off their labor to local ranchers (Phillips 1980, 184–191). San Diego County Indians provided an important part of the local labor force from mission times until the Great Depression. Both the Luiseños and Kumeyaays engaged in a wide range of economic activities involving both wage relations and petty commodity production. Luiseños were the main source of skilled vaqueros for the cattle ranchers but also worked as sheepherders and shearers, ditchmen, road builders, and woodcutters. Along the coast Indians found work in whaling, shipping, urban construction, and domestic work, forming the dominant source of urban unskilled labor between 1850 and 1880 (Carrico and Shipek, this volume).

Euro-Americans came late to the desert lands of eastern California. In Death Valley the Timbisha Shoshones began to include wage labor in their economic strategies only in the late 1800s (Sennett, this volume). Soon, however, they too were working in the full gamut of now-familiar jobs in farming and ranching, doing domestic labor, hauling wood for mining camps, and constructing roads, railroads, and houses.

At the same time significant numbers of Indian people in the Pacific Northwest were working in commercial fishing. As early as the 1860s

Lummis had begun to work as coal miners, lumberjacks, and migrant farmworkers. After 1880, however, commercial fishing and cannery labor came to dominate the Lummi economy, with men working on the boats and women in the processing plants. It was not long before technological changes in fishing and competition from cheaper Chinese labor in the canneries pushed Lummis out of the industry (Boxberger 1988). Farther north Indian and Eskimo labor remained important to the whaling and fishing fleets and canneries until freezer ships and other twentieth-century technology eliminated the need for seasonal labor (Klein 1978; Knight 1978, 78–100; Jorgensen 1990, 57, 76, 135–137, 243; McDonald 1994, 163–172).

Agriculture was another source of employment for Northwest Coast Indians. Lummis, Yakimas, and other groups, many from Canada, worked in the hop harvests of eastern Washington between the 1880s and the Great Depression (Boxberger 1988; Carlson 1981, 120; Knight 1978). Indians of British Columbia worked in the major industries of that province; lumbering and rail construction. Rolf Knight (1978, 177) summarizes:

> Indian workers, men and women, did not become irrelevant upon the arrival of the steam engine and the disappearance of the fur trade, as some authors would have us believe. In BC [British Columbia], the numbers and range of Indian workers and producers increased massively during periods when the industrial infrastructure of the province was being laid. . . . From the viewpoint of Indian history, wage labour became increasingly important in the forty years following the completion of the CPR [Canadian Pacific Railway] in 1886.

It cannot be overstressed that Native American wage labor participation during the nineteenth century was largely self-motivated. Native people did not wait for government agents to direct them to wage opportunities; rather, they perceived those openings and sought them out. They did this as a necessary part of their survival strategies, developed in adaptation to the Euro-American presence. It may even be that commitment to wage employment can serve as an index of the extent to which Indians had lost control over the land on which they could practice their traditional subsistence activities of hunting, farming, gathering, and intertribal trading. Having lost the power to determine their own lives, but still faced with the necessity of feeding themselves and their children, Native American men and women employed the one resource they still controlled: the strength of their hands and the sweat of their backs. Seizing a cultural custom of the newcomers and turning it to their own uses, Indians engaged to sell their labor. They sold what had not in their own cultures been a commodity: their labor power. Both on reservations and off, whether their tribes were recognized by the federal government or overlooked by it, in the East and the West, Indians turned to employment for wages.

INDIGENOUS WAGE LABOR INCORPORATION IN THE TWENTIETH CENTURY

Significant changes took place in Native American wage labor after the turn of the century. American Indian residence shifted from over 90 percent rural in 1900 to 50 percent metropolitan by 1980 (Snipp 1989, 83). This was far from a linear progression but varied with the fluctuating employment rates and occupational opportunities created by wars, economic depressions, growth and decline of particular industries, mechanization, and shifting federal policies. Wages and salaries became the major source of income for Indians nationwide, contributing over 80 percent of all income for Indian males in 1980 (Snipp 1989, 254). Over the century dependence shifted from rural primary-sector employment characteristic of the nineteenth century to the urban industrial and service sectors, and Indian women participated more than ever in the formally recognized labor force. Nonetheless, American Indian employment retained many of its earlier characteristics—higher turnover of jobs than was generally true for U.S. workers, more dependence on temporary or seasonal work,[2] greater dependence on public employment, and below average incomes (Snipp 1989, 206–265).

After the Dawes Act of 1887 allotment of Indian lands created stagnation and, eventually, decline in Indian farming. Where allotment was accomplished, the number of Indian farms dropped, and their size and value lagged further and further behind those owned by whites (Carlson

1981, 133–162). By 1930, 64.5 percent of Indian men were still employed in agriculture, but nearly half of these were farm laborers rather than farm operators (Carlson 1981, 156, 197).

Although often self-motivated, Indian participation in wage labor in the early years of the century was also stimulated by certain Bureau of Indian Affairs policies, some passively providing opportunity and others actively pressuring Indians to enter wage labor. In 1905 the Indian Service established an employment bureau that connected several thousand Indians each year with dam and canal construction jobs, maintenance work for the Santa Fe Railroad, employment in cotton and sugar beet fields, and other temporary or seasonal activities (Hoxie 1984, 201–202; Leupp 1910, 151–172; Peters, this volume). Sometimes Indian agents threatened to withdraw rations to coerce Indians into agricultural or other wage labor (e.g., Northern Cheyennes; Campbell 1993).

Other motivations toward wage employment had nothing to do with the BIA. During World War I labor shortages nationwide drew many Natives into wage work. In Oklahoma Cheyennes entered seasonal farmwork in significant numbers as federal wartime policies to maximize food production increased the opportunities for harvest work at the same time that other sources of migrant labor were in short supply (Moore, this volume). In California several hundred Indians were brought to Torrance to work in the steel industry (Meriam et al. 1928, 715). In Arizona wartime labor shortages were made more critical by other concurrent developments:

> Dislodgment of the I.W.W. [Industrial Workers of the World] from the mines, the vastly increased demand for copper, and the beginnings of large-scale cotton cultivation and concomitant irrigation projects all offered the Apache opportunity to extend their participation in the unskilled labor market. . . . As a result of the war boom, there was an outpouring of San Carlos families to productive areas throughout east-central Arizona between 1915 and 1930. (Adams 1971, 121)

As in later wars, American Indians also enlisted in the armed forces in large numbers.

Particularly in the Far West, which remained less industrialized than the rest of the country until well into the twentieth century, largely rural forms of employment continued to be important for Indians. Farm labor, lumbering, mining, and railroad work were not replaced in the Southwest and the Great Basin until well into midcentury (Moore, Prins, and Peters, this volume; Adams 1971; Dobyns, Stoffle, and Jones 1975; Knack 1987; Waddell 1969; Weiss 1984).

Elsewhere Indian employment became significantly urban in nature by the 1920s and became dominantly so during the industrial boom of World War II (Littlefield, McClurken, and Peters, this volume; Mitchell 1959). In the years between the wars Indian youths were becoming increasingly attracted to urban employment in Michigan. As elsewhere in the U.S. economy, the displacement of agriculture as the primary locus of employment and the growth of manufacturing during the 1920s contributed to this trend (Littlefield, this volume). During the same period Mohawk ironworkers shifted from a specialization in bridge construction to skyscraper framing as high-rise architecture became the hallmark of New York City (Hill 1987; Mitchell 1959).

Although census officials recorded that only 10 percent of the country's indigenous population was living in cities by 1930, they documented small, identifiable concentrations already forming in Los Angeles, Albuquerque, Minneapolis–St. Paul, Milwaukee, Detroit, Chicago, New York, and other urban centers. Some of these clusters were clearly spin-offs of BIA boarding schools, as graduates settled in cities nearby. Others were the direct result of employment opportunities, such as the Mohawk neighborhood that grew up in Brooklyn. These urban Indians faced diverse economic situations, from that of day laborers living in squatter camps on the outskirts of Anglo towns, to that of skilled laborers with steady employment in railroad yards or the building trades. In Los Angeles a few Natives found jobs portraying Indians in the growing motion picture industry. Although the "Roaring Twenties" were boom years for the U.S. economy in general, the Meriam Report documented widespread, deeply rooted poverty among Indians in both urban and rural areas at the end of the decade (Meriam et al. 1928, 667–724).

Data on the economic activities of Indian women nationwide are scarce for the 1920s, but there are suggestions that their labor force participation changed significantly over the decade. Even the crude statistics of the national census show that, of Indian women counted as economically active, the percentages in agriculture declined from 47.2 in 1900 to 26.1 in 1930, those in manufacturing grew from 24.9 percent to 37.6, and those in private household service increased from 13.4 to 22.5 percent (Amott and Matthaei 1991, 48). As is true of BIA reservation surveys and even many early anthropological reports, much of Indian women's economic productivity was probably invisible to the census takers—not only women's unpaid labor in housekeeping, wild plant gathering, and gardening, but also their intermittent sources of cash income from craft production, domestic labor, and seasonal agricultural labor.

The financial crisis of the Great Depression piled additional hardships onto Indians as the agricultural and labor markets on which they now depended collapsed. They found themselves suddenly in competition for the few available migrant harvesting and other menial jobs with poor whites who, driven by necessity to accept lower wages than was their wont, displaced Indians from well-established, local, off-reservation labor niches (Carrico and Shipek, and Knack, this volume). Major droughts in the plains exacerbated the situation as widespread crop failures eradicated still more jobs (e.g., at Pine Ridge; Biolsi 1992, 111).

Paradoxically, the depression years also brought other reservation Indians into wage employment for the first time. To some extent this was the result of federal programs aimed at general economic stimulation. Across the nation, for instance, large numbers of Native youths (twenty-five thousand in 1933 alone) joined the Indian version of the Civilian Conservation Corps (CCC). By the time this program was terminated in July 1942, over eighty-five thousand Indians had participated on more than seventy reservations, which had benefited from over $72 million in CCC funding for reforestation, range development, erosion control, and other conservation measures (Parman 1971). How significant this single federal program was can be illustrated by the Rosebud Reservation: in 1935 CCC wages outstripped all other sources of reservation income, and by 1942, 85 percent of Rosebud males had worked for the CCC or in other federal relief work projects (Biolsi 1992, 113–116). Rosebud residents were not alone; Indians in many regions depended heavily on federal relief jobs during the 1930s (Weiss 1984, 115–117).

Other federal actions also affected Indian wage labor relations. During the depression the deportation of Mexican farm laborers from many parts of the country increased. The resultant shortage of seasonal labor opened up opportunities for Indians in some cases; Lakota workers, for instance, apparently moved into Nebraska potato harvesting in the 1930s in larger numbers than earlier (Mekeel 1936).[3]

By contrast, for the San Carlos Apaches the 1930s marked a turn away from dependence on wage labor. Federal conservation and Collier-inspired BIA economic investment programs facilitated the growth of a reservation-based cattle industry (Getty 1963). Deliberately withdrawing from the Anglo world and its values, the San Carlos Apaches participated in the outside labor market selectively after 1940, rejecting low wages and distant jobs (Adams 1971).

Conditions of labor scarcity returned with World War II, which also brought an end to funding for most New Deal relief and BIA reservation development programs. Large numbers of Indians were propelled into the urban industrial labor force; an estimated forty thousand left their home areas to work elsewhere between 1941 and 1945 (Bernstein 1991, 68; Holm 1985, 156). Lakotas built military depots and training centers, Apaches and Hopis worked on railroad gangs, O'Odham miners dug copper for Phelps-Dodge in Arizona, Navajos staffed the Fort Wingate munitions depot, and Washakie Shoshones did the same in Salt Lake City. Even as barriers of discrimination fell and Indians entered jobs from which they had previously been excluded, patterns of differential pay persisted. Navajos at Fort Wingate never received the same pay as whites, even though they joined the Congress of Industrial Organizations and paid the same union dues (Bernstein 1991, 70–76; Luebben 1964; Madsen 1980, 101).

As with the U.S. population in general, the war brought shifts in the Indians' division of labor by gender. As men left the reservations for military service or industrial employment, women took on more responsibility for farming, significantly increasing reservation production of crops and livestock (Holm 1985, 156). At Sherman Institute, a BIA school in southern California, women took sheet metal and welding classes and then went to work in Los Angeles aircraft plants as riveters, inspectors, and machinists. Pueblo women hauled freight. In the upper Midwest Menominee women worked the second shift in the lumber mills. Some eight hundred Indian women joined the Women's Army Corps or Women Accepted for Voluntary Emergency Service (Bernstein 1991, 73–80).

The postwar period brought widespread readjustments in national employment patterns. Some Indians, such as the Navajos, were faced with unemployment and poverty (Bailey and Bailey 1986), while Apaches to the south could still count on high labor demand (Adams 1971). Kickapoos benefited from the tightening of federal restrictions on Mexican bracero field-workers in the 1950s and expanded the annual migration pattern they had initiated during the war, now traveling from the Texas border as far north as Wisconsin to harvest a sequence of crops. A decade later migrant labor had become far and away their greatest source of income (Latorre and Latorre 1991, 90–95). According to the 1950 census, 46 percent of employed Indian males were either farmers or farmworkers; very likely this high proportion disguises much underemployment as Indian veterans and industrial workers, some laid off by postwar recession or displaced by Anglo veterans, returned to the land to make a living. Furthermore, Indian veterans often found it more difficult to obtain GI loans for college and businesses than did non-Indians with better basic educations and so were shunted into agricultural training programs instead (Vogt 1951, 102).

The 1950 national census also recorded that 17 percent of Indians were nonfarm laborers, 13 percent were operatives, and 11 percent were craftsmen (Kelly 1957, 74). These stark statistics only hint at the importance of nonagricultural wage sources for Indians during these years. Even though Navajos have often been considered slower to integrate into the off-reservation economy than other indigenous groups, a detailed study of Navajo family income in 1955 found that off-reservation nonagricultural employment accounted for 42.2 percent of income;

railroad employment alone brought in twice as much as farming and stock raising on the reservation (Kelly 1957, 74). Although speaking specifically of the Great Basin, Martha Knack (1986a, 578) describes a situation that was common to many Indian areas in this decade: "a marginal agricultural-ranching economy on large reservations, complete dependency on equally marginal off-reservation wage work on small reservations, poverty, weak community infrastructure, little cash and less credit."

By midcentury Native labor markets across the United States were threatened by mechanization in agriculture (Prins, this volume), mining (Waddell 1969, 58–61), and other industries. As incomes dropped and large numbers of Indians returned to reservations, federal bureaucrats estimated there were over twenty thousand "surplus" families living on reservations that could not be supported by the economy there (Kelly 1957, 76). BIA policymakers, like historians and anthropologists writing after them, found that the role of wage labor in the Indian economy could no longer be ignored. Casting aside John Collier's assumption that reservation economies could be improved sufficiently to provide a living for the resident population, the BIA began in 1952 to encourage Indians to relocate from reservations to urban areas for the presumed economic benefits of employment available there (Neils 1971). The bureau established placement programs in major cities and contracted for vocational training for relocatees in auto mechanics, welding, cosmetology, and many other skills. Between 1945 and 1957, partially as a result of BIA encouragement and partially as a result of economic necessity, an estimated one hundred thousand Indians left reservations for towns and cities, contributing to the rapid rise of the Indian urban population; by 1960 one Indian in three was living in a city (Officer 1971, 58).

The urban relocation program has often been criticized for inadequate support services to relocatees, such as insufficient help in finding affordable housing or training in the mazeways of urban transportation systems, coping with landlords, and becoming generally familiar with city living. The jobs in which Indians were placed frequently did not match their training (Weppner 1971). In an analysis of a nationwide sample of relocatees, Lawrence Clinton, Bruce Chadwick, and Howard Bahr (1975) found that vocational training was positively related to income but only weakly related to employment stability. Other studies found that Indians who stayed in urban areas longest and were financially most successful were married and had relocated as families, had a high school education, already knew someone in the urban enclave, and rapidly established ties to the growing Indian networks (Ablon 1964; Graves 1970; Graves and Lane 1972; Graves and van Arsdale 1965; Hackenberg and Wilson 1972; Price 1968; Snyder 1968; Weppner 1967, 1972). The BIA assumed that the large numbers of trainees who returned to the reservations (perhaps as high as 30–50 percent [Weibel-Orlando 1991, 22]) represented program "failures," although little actual information on the subsequent careers of returnees seems to be available. Studies of other populations suggest that return migration has significant social, economic, and political consequences for communities of origin (e.g., Rothstein 1992).

Employment in nonurban environments continued to be important in many cases. Although Arizona O'Odham villages had been largely self-sufficient in the 1920s, the federal job creation programs of the 1930s and the relocation programs of the 1950s were instrumental in increasing O'Odham involvement in wage work. In one of the first systematic anthropological studies of Indians in the labor force, Jack Waddell (1969, 41–42) documented that in 1959 O'Odham provided 10–20 percent of Arizona cotton field labor and one-third of the farm labor force in Pima County. At the Phelps-Dodge copper mine at Ajo, Arizona, some O'Odham were already second-generation mine workers. Their employment had increased during World War II, then dropped when a literacy requirement was introduced. By the 1960s Indians were providing less than 10 percent of the workforce at Ajo, although some of them had moved from unskilled into skilled or semiskilled positions, largely as the result of mechanization (Waddell 1969, 51–64). Closer to Tucson, San Xavier O'Odham alternated farm labor with railroad, construction, yard maintenance, and other jobs. Some O'Odham lived in an enclave of their own in south Tucson, a neighborhood characterized by rapid turnover of residents (Waddell 1969, 70–79; see also Adams 1971, and Krutz

1971, for a similar Apache situation; Hodge 1969, and Kelly and Cramer 1966, for Navajos; and Nagata 1971, for Tuba City Hopis).

In southeastern Oklahoma temporary, seasonal work in the timber industry continued to be a significant form of employment for Choctaws. Like O'Odham miners in the Southwest, the Choctaws were nonunionized, poorly paid, and lacked the employee benefits or job stability enjoyed by other workers on the timber company's payroll (Faiman-Silva 1993, 220–228).

As the predominant locus of Indian employment shifted from rural to urban areas, patterns of cyclical migration became a relatively common feature of the indigenous scene. This was as true in the highly industrialized Northeast (Guillemin 1975) as it was in the West. Employment patterns were characterized by low wages, high rates of unskilled labor, high job turnover, and frequent trips back to reservation areas, sometimes for months or years.

The 1970s were unusually prosperous years for reservation-based Indians. The War on Poverty and post–Vietnam War federal programs provided a steady stream of federal funding for reservation economic development, enabling Native Americans to make the greatest economic gains of all minority groups in the 1970s (Houghton 1973). Federal tax waivers, minority-owned business contract preferences, and liberal federal loans were extended to lure private enterprise to reservation areas and stimulate tribal enterprises. Tribal governments themselves expanded to join the BIA as major employers of reservation labor (e.g., Grobsmith 1981, 33; Jorgensen 1972, 111; 1990; Knack 1986a, 579). Increasingly independent political action by Arab nations created an unusually favorable market for energy resources, and many Western tribes with extensive coal, oil, and gas deposits found lucrative opportunities for large-scale leasing (Jorgensen et al. 1978). Growing wealth, political power, and legal sophistication enabled tribes to unite in negotiations with international energy extraction corporations (Jorgensen et al. 1984) and to protect the workers' rights of tribal members (Robbins 1978). Unlike much rural or reservation-based employment in the past, such new jobs were often full-time, permanent ones requiring a high school education and fluency in English. Despite such improvements in the reservation economic base, Indians remained among the poorest of all racial-ethnic groups (American Indian Policy Review Commission 1976, 81–84; Snipp 1989, 247–261; U.S. Civil Rights Commission 1973, 10–62).

Since the 1970s automation, the decline of the Rustbelt, the industrialization of the Sunbelt, the growth of the service sector (including tourism), and changes in federal programs have restructured the U.S. economy, causing major employment shifts both for indigenous peoples and other Americans. Deep cuts in federal social programs under the Reagan administration severely affected the reservation economies because of the great dependence on federally funded wages, both in BIA jobs and through tribal governments and programs (Morris 1992). Unemployment exceeded 50 percent for a number of reservations by 1985 (U.S. Dept. of the Interior 1986, 48). Exploiting the legal opportunity posed by the exemption of reservations from state law, tribes responded to their grim economic scene by building gaming facilities (over 150 by 1991), which succeeded in reducing unemployment rates for some reservations, especially those close to major urban centers (Lieberman 1991).

The years between 1960 and 1980 brought significant changes in Indian women's participation in the labor force. Service employment in private households declined from 17 to 1.4 percent. This was offset by increases in skilled jobs, as clerical occupations doubled to 27 percent, professional and technical occupations rose from 9 to 14.5 percent, and managerial, administrative, and official occupations tripled to 6.6 percent. Although both employment rates and median incomes of American Indian women remained lower than those for Euro-American or African-American women (Amott and Matthaei 1991, 48, 305, 310), a decline in domestic work and a rise in public employment also occurred for other women of color in the United States as social service programs expanded. In the 1980s and 1990s gaming also created significant new employment opportunities for Indian women, affecting political and social organization in tribal communities in ways that are just beginning to be explored in the literature (Albers 1985; Klein 1980; Knack 1989).

Although beneficial in many respects, the continued restructuring of the reservation economies also raises new issues. Internally the division of the tribal workforce into bosses and workers has led to a new process of class formation within Indian communities (Damrell 1991). Externally as tribes and tribal enterprises grew into major regional employers, and Indian youths gained the educational experience to assume managerial and specialist roles in those enterprises, Anglos began to work for Indians, radically restructuring larger patterns of interethnic relations in many localities.

The variations in the patterns of Indian wage labor summarized here can be seen in one sense as responses to local historical events that created particular regional labor markets and community conditions and needs. In addition, the lack of pan-Indian uniformity was partially an outgrowth of traditional Indian cultural differences, for indigenous sociocultural formations influenced both the ways Indians sought out wage labor and the impacts such participation had on their own lives and communities. But because wage labor appeared so generally, despite all its varying forms and appearances, we must ask questions of the historical causalities that affected all Native Americans—questions of land, resource loss, and federal policies that affected Indian people uniquely—and also of the social formation and economic system they sought to enter.

WAGE LABOR AND SOCIAL ORGANIZATION

Even this brief historical survey has shown that Native American wage labor occurred within a wide variety of social settings. In some cases people worked without leaving their native communities, either for federal agencies, tribal governments, local non-Indian employers, or other Indian people (Carrico and Shipek, Knack, Littlefield, McClurken, and Moore, this volume). The very characteristics of these native communities often provided a support structure that was congenial to wage labor participation while at the same time making it financially necessary. Elsewhere the entire community participated in wage work, traveling as a group to the employment site in a round of seasonal or migratory labor (Knack, Peters, Prins, and Sennett this volume). In still other and apparently rare cases wage workers left their communities alone to seek out distant jobs for more or less extended periods of time (McClurken, this volume).

Repeated studies in virtually all social contexts, from reservation and nonreservation, small town, and major metropolis, have shown that Indian participation in wage work was neither a total economic commitment nor one undertaken by isolated individual laborers. Long after one member had obtained wage employment, many Indian families continued to derive income and subsistence from a wide variety of sources: foraging, farming, craft production, temporary employment, veteran's or Social Security pensions. Households pooled these diverse resources and shared them with kin and community through networks of assistance and reciprocity (Burgess 1991; Guillemin 1975, 126–213; Jorgensen 1978, 66–69; Klein 1978; Knack 1980; Munsell 1967; Nagata 1970, 98–222; Robbins 1968; Uchendu 1966, 235–258; Waddell 1969, 76–79, 100–103; Weibel 1976). Extended kinship ties provided a network for child care, financial assistance, job recruitment, and welfare support (Prins, Peters, this volume; Grobsmith 1981, 33–34; Guillemin 1975; Knack 1980; Moore 1991). Ritual redistributions, whether strictly traditional in form or modified to meet new circumstances, served as conduits for sharing wage income among still larger sectors of the Indian community (Grobsmith 1979; Moore 1993). In all of these ways the income from wages sustained Indian communities, permitting a continuance that might otherwise not have been possible.

Native workers used varied methods to obtain jobs. Indian agents, those bureaucratic representatives of larger policy and power, occasionally arranged employment for men from the reserves they supervised. In some areas the boarding schools cooperated with employers in recruiting students (Trennert 1983, 1988). On the Navajo Reservation traders were paid to recruit men for railroad work (Adams 1963, 129–135). But not all middlemen were non-Indians. Where Indian leaders had customarily held considerable authority and recruited activity groups, such as war parties, traditional headmen and leaders often formed a recruiting conduit between non-Indian employers and Indian laborers; sometimes the leaders even went along to serve as foremen for Native work teams (Carrico and Shipek, and Prins, this volume). In cultural areas where traditional leaders were simply spokespersons for existing groups, individual laborers did their own job hunting without the intervention of Native authority figures (Knack, and Sennett, this volume).

Because adult Native women clearly participated in wage labor as early and perhaps even as often as men (Carrico and Shipek, Knack, Littlefield, Moore, and Prins, this volume), the impact of wage labor on Native communities was farreaching. Not only did it absorb the labor of the workers themselves, but it also demanded that the rest of the population take on those roles that the workers would otherwise have filled. Studies of Third World labor migrations where a higher percentage of laborers were single men have been more sensitive than have Native American studies to the significant realignments in the sexual division of labor and organization of production in the home communities resulting from prolonged male absence (Boserup 1970, 66–81; Gonzalez 1969; Rogers 1980, 166–170). Carefully controlled comparative analyses are needed to determine whether the American Indian tendency to migrate in family units has caused more or less disruption of traditional social structures.

In spite of the enormous potential for disrupting community structure, wage labor was sometimes instrumental in maintaining ethnic identity rather than eradicating it (Peters, and Prins, this volume; cf. Watson 1959). Waddell (1969, 137–140) maintains, for instance, that O'Odham identity, as expressed through participation in reservation social networks and ritual, was supported by residential segregation from Anglos and Mexicans with whom the O'Odham otherwise shared labor and union activities. Mohawks made employment in high steel construction a source of prestige within the home community and a continuing source of ethnic pride, as well as a source of income (Hill 1987). Certainly the financial contribution of wages, funneled into the reservation communities and circulated through kinship and ritual networks, has been an important support for these marginal economies.

Findings such as these suggest that a significant rereading of Indian historical and contemporary economic realities is clearly needed. We have been accustomed to a scholarly and popular discourse that examines on-reservation and off-reservation Indian lives as isolated from each other. Yet it should be abundantly clear from the studies in this book and other sources (Guillemin 1975; Waddell 1969; cf. Mitchell 1966) that this conceptual separation falsifies the Native American experience in important ways. It diverts our attention from the constant interchange of resources, information, and personnel between reservation and nonreservation locales. Furthermore, it disguises the extent to which reservation communities provide (though imperfectly) for the social reproduction of a labor force that flows into and retreats from the larger economy as need and opportunity arise.

Although these flows across reservation boundaries pose difficult methodological problems, we need to begin analyzing them. In ways similar to Mexican immigrant counterparts in the southwestern United States, American Indian workers in urban areas often have ties to a homeland that plays an important role in the continual renewal of ethnic identity through circular migration and flows of resources. Similar ties to a home base characterize immigrant labor in many parts of the world.

To what extent, then, do such ties limit the proletarianization of American Indian workers? In chapter 2 Harald Prins describes how reserves provided the Mi'kmaqs with a means to avoid full proletarianization, allowing them to maintain a way of life "on the proletarian edge." But perhaps we also need to reconsider what we mean by proletarian. Gavin Smith (1991, 220), in his discussion of Valencian households that have straddled industrial and agricultural production for two centuries, criticizes the assumption that to be proletarian means "part of a unionized labour force engaged in routine work with fixed hours and fixed days of the week in a large factory from the age of 18 to 65." By such a definition, few workers could be considered proletarian. Smith's critique of conventional definitions of proletarian seems pertinent to considerations of indigenous American workers, as well as to other ethnically distinct workers who have long participated in wage labor without losing ties to their homelands.

WHY WERE INDIANS HIRED?

So far we have looked primarily at Indian wage labor from the inside, as it were: how it benefited Indians, why they selected and utilized it as part of their historic adaptation to Euro-American presence, and what its form and place were within the dynamics of the Native communities. There is, however, another set of questions that should be asked. These focus on issues and social formations external to the Indian societies, specifically those relating to the larger Euro-American economy. Questions appropriate to this framework might be, Why did Euro-Americans offer employment to Indians? What was the benefit of Indian labor, not for Indians, but for the larger society? Why was Indian labor of sufficient importance to become in the twentieth century a persistent concern of national policy?

In most of the cases documented in this book, Indian laborers carved out for themselves and then dominated some unique labor niche. These specializations became known locally as "Indian jobs." In other words, Indians contributed uniquely to the local labor forces, fulfilling functions not met by other workers. Even in highly diverse regions and historical time periods these stereotypical "Indian jobs" shared predictable characteristics. They were often unskilled or at best semiskilled jobs. Some involved large-scale resource extraction, such as timbering and harvesting; others were simply heavy labor, as in farm-work and construction work; still others were clearly service work, such as domestic labor. Some were rural (Knack, Prins, and Sennett, this volume); others were urban (Carrico and Shipek, and Peters, this volume). Few, however, involved control of material or financial resources, highly paid skills, or decision-making control over the worker's economic future. In most cases there was explicit segregation of work crews and supervisory functions by ethnicity.

Not only were the jobs Indians obtained often different from those filled by non-Indians in a particular labor market; so too were their wages. Increasing evidence from empirical studies documents that in many labor markets Indians received wages below those of comparable non-Indian workers (e.g., Talbot 1981, 178–184). Whether wages were received in cash or kind (Knack 1987), the pattern of substandard remuneration was so frequent that we must ask whether this utilization of Indians as cheap labor was not part of a larger relationship of ethnic and class dominance.

By the late nineteenth and early twentieth centuries the general U.S. labor force, especially in the blue-collar categories, was increasingly structuring itself into unions. The primary impetus for unionization was to overcome precisely the low wages and high job insecurity so common in Indians' labor experience. Nevertheless, Native workers' relations with these labor organizations have been highly varied. In some cases Indians were active participants or even union leaders (Peters, this volume; Knight 1978, 186–188; Mitchell 1959, 20–21; Moore 1991; Waddell 1969, 120–122). In others they were excluded from membership or denied full benefits (Bernstein, 75–76; Luebben 1964; Weppner 1971, 257). In the case of San Carlos Apaches William Adams (1971, 120) concludes that

> in view of the mounting power of the unions, it seems probable that by the turn of the century the Apaches were left as the principal source of cheap, unorganized labor in southeastern Arizona. This condition, coupled with suspicion of the rapidly growing I.W.W. and a disinclination to hire union members whenever it could be avoided, goes a long way to explain the economic role of Apache labor during most of the next two decades. It suggests that there was probably little opportunity for Apaches to work in the mines and other better-paid occupations until late in World War I, when the power of the union was broken.

In chapter 7 Kurt Peters reports that Lagunas were first brought to northern California by the Santa Fe Railroad as strikebreakers. Were Indians elsewhere recruited as strikebreakers or used to undermine union organizing? We simply do not know, and the relationship of American Indians to labor organizations is one of the most poorly documented aspects of Native American labor history (see Talbot 1985, 83–86).

It could be argued that Native Americans constitute part of a reserve labor force that, because of its low wages and high rates of unemployment, allows employers to hold down wages for labor in general. Certainly in many of the cases documented in this book Indian labor was key to resource extraction and profit realization. It does not follow, however, that Indian labor specifically is, or was, essential to the growth and development of global capitalism. If there is any lesson to be drawn from the events of the late twentieth century, it is the remarkable flexibility of capitalism as a system and the expendability of any specific small segment of the global labor force. The restructuring of global capital in the 1980s and 1990s involved widespread automation within the industrialized countries and the relocation of many labor-intensive operations to cheap labor regions of the less industrialized world. Like other North American populations, the Indian labor force was redefined in the process. Labor in the large sense is necessary to the survival of capitalism, but particular localized groups of workers who are critical at one time may well become superfluous at another, able to be replaced by machines or by another ethnic or immigrant laboring class.

INDIAN LABOR AND THE
EVOLUTION OF FEDERAL POLICY

Analyses of federal Indian policy, like studies of Native communities, have often ignored issues of labor. Critics have been quick to point out how government actions helped separate indigenous peoples from their land, resulting in relocation, impoverishment, and diminished political power. Especially in the nineteenth century, acquisition of Indian lands was a dominant motivation behind federal policy. By the twentieth century, however, Indians had little land left; so, it is argued, most economic and political elites, lacking financial interest in Indian affairs, largely ignored Indians (Castile 1991). Indian labor, unlike that of ethnic minorities whose immigration was explicitly encouraged to supply labor needs, is considered to have had little national importance and therefore to have been unrelated to the ways public policies were developed and manipulated by power elites (e.g., Hall 1989a; Jacobson 1984; Castile 1993).

The BIA was equivocal and inconsistent regarding labor issues, especially after the turn of the century. In both administrative practice and abstract policy some BIA programs denied, while others embraced, wage employment as a solution to Indian economic problems. Francis Leupp (1910), commissioner of Indian affairs from 1905 to 1909, bragged of federal programs to increase Indian employment. Boarding schools designed curricula in "industrial" skills and served important economic interests by funneling students into menial labor (Littlefield, this volume, 1991, 1993; Trennert 1983, 1988). The Meriam Report, for instance, detailed how in the 1920s boarding schools provided child labor to the sugar beet fields of Colorado and Kansas, where children earned as little as $0.09 a day (Meriam et al. 1928, 524–526). Indian agents cooperated with Oklahoma wheat farmers and cattle ranchers to see that Southern Cheyennes were available for harvest labor (Moore, this volume). Even in the choice of sites for reservations, labor was a consideration, as, for instance, Southern Paiutes were intentionally kept close to their Anglo employers (Knack, this volume).

Another look at familiar legislative landmarks will quickly show that general Indian policies, although their explicit import lay in other spheres, often had major impacts on Native American participation in wage labor. Much federal policy during the nineteenth century was overtly designed, not to draw Indians into the growing wage sector, but to lure them into an older and increasingly obsolete economy: that of independent subsistence farming. Through acculturation policies Indian agents, model farmers, teachers, and missionaries set forth subsistence farming as the ideal for American Indians (Carrico and Shipek, Knack, and Littlefield, this volume).

Many commentators have observed that the Dawes Allotment Act of 1887, although justified as a mechanism to enable Indians to obtain this ideal, separated Native people from two-thirds of their remaining land-based resources within fifty years. Many allotments were sold, or lost through debt or fraud, within two decades; many more were leased to non-Indians, not always with their owners' consent (Jorgensen 1972, 91–109; Nybroten 1964, 9–22; Wilson 1985). The Indians thus displaced not infrequently became wage workers, sometimes even on lands that had been their own (Carlson 1981; Meriam et al. 1928, 469–482). The connection between land loss and wage employment was known to the BIA; even agents in the field were aware of it, and some viewed it positively. In 1919 after the Cheyennes and Arapahos had been defrauded of many of their allotments, the supervisor of farming there opined that the Indians were "probably better off now than they were before. . . . now that the land is gone and they receive no rentals, they are compelled to go to work" (quoted in Berthrong 1985, 49). Nevertheless, even in the late 1920s when large-scale agribusiness was already displacing non-Indian farmers (Jorgensen 1978, 42–50), the

Meriam Report stubbornly continued to advocate assistance for family-operated farming and stock raising as the solution to Indians' economic problems (Meriam et al. 1928, 430–546).

When John Collier became commissioner of Indian affairs in 1933, he assumed Indian tribes, as tribes, should develop reservation lands and resources for their collective good. He pushed for passage of the Wheeler-Howard Act (Indian Reorganization Act, 1934), which, even in its politically reduced form, contained a number of provisions critical for this discussion (Deloria and Lytle 1984, 55–153). Most importantly, it ended allotment as a federal policy. Instead of advocating the breakup of reservation lands, the Wheeler-Howard Act enabled tribes to form local governments whose legislated powers included management of tribal lands. In the guise of business corporations tribes were encouraged to borrow money from a federally created revolving credit fund, which poured $31 million into reservation areas before 1952 to consolidate fragmented land holdings, improve rangelands, build irrigation systems, and engage in other projects designed to make the land economically supportive for the people living on it (Jorgensen 1978, 18). A number of tribes began tribal cattle herds and agricultural cooperatives (e.g., Aberle 1983, 645; Getty 1963; Jorgensen 1972, 151–157). A capable bureaucrat, Collier saw to it that the new tribal governments qualified for CCC funding, creating both jobs and further land development. He applied for federal excess lands to be given to tribes under the Submarginal Lands Program and used various federal conservation and depression relief programs legislated for the general population to create jobs and economic opportunities specifically for Indians. It was unusually fitting that the publicity newsletter of the BIA during his administration was called *Indians at Work*.

Despite the commitment of federal dollars during the late 1930s, these programs were inadequate to overcome the monumental state of reservation underdevelopment. Even these funds were cut off all too soon, as World War II demanded top financial priority. In the postwar period the federal policy emphasis shifted from joint development of tribal resources to termination of tribal entities, relocation of individual Indians or families, and dismemberment of reservation land blocks. Although other sources of federal money to tribes evaporated, they did receive almost $500 million through successful land claims against the federal government before 1975 (Jorgensen 1978, 23), used in part to establish reservation-based tribal enterprises. At the same time, as an intrinsic part of the termination policy the BIA was encouraging Indians to leave the reservations for urban wage employment (Zimmerman 1957, 38–39). It especially wanted the young, better-educated males, precisely the elite that might have provided leadership for successful reservation growth. The agency subsidized this "brain drain," subcontracted training programs in various low-skilled and semiskilled fields, and even itself entered the vocational training business, but always in urban centers far from reservation communities.

The BIA justified this relocation policy on grounds of the lack of employment opportunities available on most reservations. The distance of reserves from both raw material sources and markets added costs for any industries that might locate there, whether non-Indian, individual Indian, or tribal. Dirt roads, lack of electricity, and other underdeveloped infrastructure inflated the initial cost to businesses. The local labor force was often undereducated and inexperienced and could not provide a pool of experienced managers, accountants, or other skilled workers; the same rural isolation and weak infrastructure would make it hard to attract non-Indians to fill higher-level positions. Unless there was some overriding attraction on the reservation itself, such as minerals to exploit or cheap, nonunion workers to hire for a labor-intensive industry, there was little to attract outside investment.

In the 1960s the BIA tried to create such an attraction. By offering temporary tax incentives, below-market federal loans, subsidized wages for local Indians being trained, customized building construction, and similar benefits, it lured over 270 non-Indian businesses onto reservations over the next decade (American Indian Policy Review Commission 1976, 119–121). Indian preference in hiring became a standard element in BIA-approved contracts, giving local residents a competitive edge, provided they were otherwise "equally" qualified. Nonetheless, the long history of poor educational opportunity and economic isolation meant that all too few Indians were considered equally qualified, and over 60 percent of the on-reservation jobs created by federal subsidies went to non-Indians (Jorgensen 1978, 62). Study after study showed that 90 percent or more of employed reservation Indians worked either directly for federal agencies or indirectly for federally subsidized tribal governments and enterprises, leaving reservation dwellers extremely dependent on a federal budget that could change with any election (e.g., Grobsmith 1981, 33; Jorgensen 1972, 111).

The civil rights movement of the 1960s generated political pressure for a series of minority benefit programs, which applied to both Indian individual entrepreneurs and Indian tribes. The Economic Development Administration, Manpower Training Program, Office of Economic Opportunity, Small Business Administration, and numerous other federal agencies created programs to encourage the creation of minority-owned businesses. Federal contracting gave preference to these fledgling companies, a boon especially during the high-spending Vietnam War years. Tribes tried a wide range of enterprises, from the Mescalero Apache ski resort (Opler 1983, 426) and Rosebud Sioux pottery factory (Grobsmith 1981, 33), to the more humble Washo roadside campground and Goshute cattle-guard manufacturing (Knack 1986a, 582–586), but few survived the period of initial federal subsidy. Although having the advantage of knowing the people among whom they worked, these businesses faced exactly the same economic limitations that an incoming non-Indian business would face. In addition to the disadvantages of remote location and underdeveloped infrastructure, tribal businesses also had to break into markets already occupied by knowledgeable firms with established clientele. Despite federal programs, by the mid-1970s most of the few businesses still operating on reservations were owned by non-Indians (American Indian Policy Review Commission 1976, 79). Even those were far too few to support the number of reservation workers. Unemployment and underemployment were often two to ten times higher than in the surrounding off-reservation non-Indian population (Aberle 1983, 642–657; Gilbreath 1973; Jorgensen 1978, 61–63; Stanley 1978; U.S. Civil Rights Commission 1973, 10–62; U.S. Congress 1969).

Proclaimed to be a policy to free Indians from federal restrictions, the Nixon administration's Indian Self-Determination Act of 1974 enabled tribes to subcontract community services previously provided by the BIA, such as schools, health clinics, and social work. By 1983, 325 tribes were holding 1,275 subcontracts under this program, placing $241 million into tribal budgets (U.S. Dept. of the Interior 1984, 11). Most tribes used these funds to hire tribal members, increasing the already high percentages of reservation workers whose jobs were dependent on federal funding. When the first three years of Reagan administration cutbacks brought a 30 percent decrease to the BIA budget, many of these jobs were cut, and reservation unemployment skyrocketed (Las Vegas Review-Journal 1983; Morris 1992).

This summary of hallmark legislation merely hints at the complex relationship between federal policy and Indian wage labor. A thorough examination is needed of the complex web of often-conflicting special interests that affect policy implementation at the local level, as well as in Washington (e.g., Bee 1981; Perry 1993). Also needed is a healthy skepticism toward the moral discourse employed by bureaucrats trying to justify the refunding of their agencies. Such an examination must include analyses of the labor regimes that developed in particular industries and the ways in which the needs of these industries influenced the implementation of policy.

TOWARD EXPLANATION

Describing the history and cultural contexts of Indian labor and debating the extent to which that history was molded by policy are insufficient to truly understand and explain Indian wage labor. Because commodity labor was an economic phenomenon alien to Native North America, and because, for at least four centuries, employers were consistently non-Indians, any theoretical framework for analysis must take into account the structures of both Indian and Euro-American societies. Furthermore, an explanatory theory must conceptualize the dynamic interactions that link those two traditions into a network of interethnic relations.

Early anthropologists tended to ignore the reality of the wage employment that they undoubtedly observed during their fieldwork because they were intent on recovering remnant memories of aboriginal Indian cultures. These were then reconstructed either as cultural compendia (historical particularism) or as self-contained systems (structural-functionalism). Neither of the major anthropological paradigms before the 1940s provided practitioners with any framework for explaining Indian wage labor, a phenomenon that did not exist solely within the context of the indigenous culture.

The first paradigm that actually attempted to account for modern Indian life as a systematic relationship with non-Indian culture was acculturation theory. Like all pioneering theories, it was both crude and flawed. Although paying lip-service to the bidirectional nature of diffusion (Redfield, Linton, and Herskovits 1936, 149), most acculturation studies pragmatically assumed that Indians were unilaterally borrowing non-Indian culture traits. Wage employment was often used as a visible measure of the degree to which an Indian individual was "acculturated," "assimilated," or "adjusted to urban environment" (Dozier, Simpson and Yinger 1957, 161; Graves 1974; Henderson 1979; Kelly and Cramer 1966; Kunitz 1977; Spindler and Spindler 1971, 5; cf. Chadwick and White 1973; Hackenberg 1972). Acculturation theory's simplistic assumption that cultural borrowing was the almost automatic mechanism for this transition was not the theory's only flaw. Whereas the distribution of European-derived traits within Indian society was studied through systematic fieldwork, the non-Indian communities or structures with which Indians interacted were never given comparable empirical analysis. Acculturation theory assumed either that we knew what non-Indian society was like or that sociologists would tell us. More damaging still, the theory assumed that as Indians changed, they would indeed become just like those unanalyzed non-Indians. Thus, Indian wage workers presumably would merge with their non-Indian peers, and wage employment would structure Indian communities in the same ways it did Euro-American ones. Neither of these expectations was supported by the empirical evidence. Although acculturation theorists acknowledged the potentially creative aspect of the web of intercultural contact on the abstract level (Redfield, Linton, and Herskovits 1936, 151), they did not translate this potential into research designs that could capture any new social formations that might be generated by the multicultural interface.

A second paradigm—those approaches based on Marxism—offered anthropologists a possibility for more coherent analysis of the bicultural situation of American Indian labor. These frameworks shared the assumption that economic relations, especially those of production, shaped the interrelationships between social groups. They viewed social relations, ideologies, and hence cultural differences as deriving from or heavily influenced by economic relations. The profit imperative, Marxists said, drove capitalist systems inevitably to exploit the laboring class, and whether those laborers were Indian was immaterial. In other words, class relations transcended ethnic relations, and conflict of interests between classes was inevitable. Such conflict found direct political expression in the manipulation of the legal structure by power-wielding elites to strengthen their own economic interests. Thus, the relationship between Indian labor and Indian policy became at once predictable and comprehensible within this theoretical framework.

Knight (1978) and Steve Talbot (1981, 175–193) exemplified such Marxist analyses of American Indian labor. Russel Barsh (1988, 203), however, counterargued that these authors exaggerated and romanticized a solidarity between Indian and non-Indian members of the working class. He believed that racial and ethnic identity overrode class in constructing social structures: "Proletarian solidarity is a myth, and refusal to confront this condemns Indians and other indigenous peoples to the unhappy status of serfs of the labor organizations of dominant ethnic groups and metropolitan powers." While agreeing with Marxists that the problem was fundamentally both economic and political, Ward Churchill (1983) challenged the priority they gave to class relations. He argued that the Indian situation in the United States was too unique to be described by the general terms of Marxism. The cultural values of Indians contradicted the solution to class conflict proposed by socialism and therefore, he said, negated the analysis.

Many critics, both Indians and non-Indians, have faulted the more classical Marxist theories for their relatively undeveloped treatment of precapitalist societies and have therefore challenged the ability of those approaches to address the interrelationship of tribal peoples with Europeans. Neomarxians such as Andre Gunder Frank (1966) broke free of analytical reliance on specifically capitalist systems of production by pointing to the simple fact that commercial relations between any units of differential economic power siphoned off resources from the weaker to the more powerful. This "metropolis" then grew even more wealthy and powerful at the expense of the weaker "satellite." Deprived of such resources as minerals, labor, or skilled personnel and unable to use them for its own development, the satellite progressively weakened relative to the metropolis. In other words, Frank argued, development and underdevelopment were not separate phenomena but inextricably linked, each growing with and causing the other.

Immanuel Wallerstein (1974) applied this fundamental concept in his analysis of the development of European capitalism now known as "world-systems" theory. Wallerstein proposed that the historical power of late-nineteenth-century Europe was not an autochthonous development; it did not "pull itself up by its own bootstraps" but rather benefited from centuries of systematic economic relations with every other part of the world, from Africa to Asia and the Americas. Wallerstein posited, as did Karl Marx, that profit was generated by the primary producers—the laborers—many of whom were outside of Europe. Through a series of legal, military, political, and economic mechanisms, however, European-based capitalists managed to extract a disproportionate share of that profit. This created, as for Frank, a distinction between "core" and "periphery." Wallerstein's proposals on the resulting labor relations were succinctly summarized by Eric Wolf (1982, 22–23):

The two are linked by "unequal exchange," whereby "high-wage (but low-supervision), high-profit, high-capital intensive" goods produced in the core are exchanged for "low-wage (but high-supervision), low-profit, low-capital intensive goods" produced in the periphery. In the core, goods are produced mainly by "free" wage-remunerated labor; in the periphery goods are produced mainly by one kind or another of coerced labor. . . . He argues that the growth of free wage labor in the core area arose in response to the high densities of population that made workers competitive with one another and hence willing to submit to market discipline, while in the periphery low population densities favored the growth of labor coercion.

Wolf (1982), 158–194) dramatically brought world-systems theory to the attention of anthropologists in his analysis of European mercantilism, which included an insightful discussion of North American Indian involvement in the fur trade.

In a neocolonialist model Joseph Jorgensen (1972, 5–12; 1978) applied this logic to non-Indian development and Indian underdevelopment; he declared each could be understood only by their mutual interrelationships. Just as African and South American colonies became economic and political satellites relative to European cores, so too Indian country became subservient to the loci of urban financial power and the powerful elites based there. The structural relations of extraction, underdevelopment, and dependency replicated those in external colonies, even though in the Indian case the satellite-metropolis relation was enacted totally within the national land base. These relationships were the same whether Indians lived on rural reservations exporting cheap energy minerals or in urban areas providing labor for substandard wages because the economic and political manipulations were structurally the same. Jorgensen, like Frank, declared that the poverty characteristic of Indian populations was causally linked to the larger economic system and could not be understood apart from those ties. Through this model the impact of wage labor on Native communities was seen, not just as a residual effect of employment, but as an intrinsic component of the bicultural system. Such issues as the voluntary or stimulated removal from the Native community of the brightest, best-educated, and most ambitious people in their prime years; the resulting bimodal age distribution; and the underdeveloped indigenous economy that both drove people into employment and required their wages to sustain itself were made comprehensible by this framework.

Approaches that have utilized the perspective of internal colonialism, together with others that have analyzed the global restructuring of labor relations in recent decades (e.g., Leacock and Safa 1986; Ong 1991; Rothstein and Blim 1992), suggest that Wallerstein's broad categorization of labor regimes as peripheral, semiperipheral, or metropolitan must be modified considerably to account for local diversity, ethnic and gender segmentation of labor markets, and new patterns of flexible accumulation. In the case of Native Americans the recent rapid spread of gaming enterprises is restructuring Indian reservation economies, the labor and class relations within Indian communities, and the articulation of reservation communities with global capitalism.

Regardless of whether one of these theoretical frameworks or others will eventually prove most satisfactory in explaining the phenomenon of American Indian wage labor, any such attempt must surely have two fundamental properties. First, because Indian wage labor has historically crossed, and continues to cross, the boundaries of Indian and non-Indian societies, any theory adequate to explain it must have sufficient scope to address the processes and structures of articulation of the two societies. Second, this theory must recognize that the issue of Indian wage labor is not solely an economic one. It is also related to the politics of federal Indian policy, regionally specific features of production relations and class formation, the efforts of indigenous peoples to seek greater autonomy in their social and political lives, the social structure of Indian families and communities, processes of ethnogenesis, and other broader social and cultural issues. In our search for understanding of Indian wage labor, we must not allow ourselves too narrow a focus on our subject and thereby lose sight of its human context, both on the immediate level of individual case studies and on the wider regional and national levels.

CONCLUSIONS

A compendium of philosophical thought asserts that the "great issues concerning labor seem to be moral and political rather than economic. ... The analysis of factors affecting the productivity of labor ceases to be merely economic when the hours, conditions, and organization of work are viewed in terms of the working man" (Adler and Gorman 1980, 925). It is precisely anthropology's unique ability to view labor as the working of a living humanity existing within a larger social and cultural context that enables the discipline to bring significant insights to the study of Native American labor.

The few existing analyses of Indian wage labor by anthropologists and ethnohistorians have raised a number of important questions, some specific to Native American conditions and others of general import to the social sciences. Perhaps first and foremost is the question of why Indians were historically willing to engage in wage labor. Evidence shows that wage labor was rather consistently widespread at a very early stage in Indian contact with non-Indians. It preceded the extension to Indians of tax obligations, such as motivated so much of African colonial labor mobilization (Powdermaker 1962, 97; Richards 1961, 23). In North American fur trade areas commodification of natural resources was a Native strategy to gain exotic goods. In other regions Indian labor was coerced through enslavement. But far more frequently Indians were driven off the land and forced into the wage labor market in order to survive. Wage employment, then, is a historical measure of the degree of resource loss and dependency.

Studies of Indian wage labor have also involved the nature of that labor itself. Throughout the nineteenth century most Indian jobs were unskilled, heavy labor. Even late in the twentieth century the proportion of Indians engaged in unskilled and semiskilled labor far exceeds that of the general population. Their jobs still do not often include high wages, control of natural or financial resources, or major decisionmaking functions.

The broader issues that surround the work itself have been less often investigated than these simple descriptive characteristics. Wherein lies the social utility of Indian labor? Does the primary benefit accrue to Indian society, enabling it to subsist, endure, and reproduce? Or does the benefit pass to others, who receive its value through relations of production or exchange, as argued by John Moore in chapter 5? Surely the history of Indian wage labor demonstrates that Indian employment did enable many Native communities to survive and continue after other means of subsistence had been taken from them. Nevertheless, Indian labor was accepted as a commodity by non-Indian employers precisely because it created value in their economic sphere.

Broadening the analysis, we can ask about the social context within which Indian labor appears. Anthropologists have often inquired about Indian familial and community environments and the networks of sharing that move cash income through those social spheres. But we should also raise questions about interethnic relations of labor; the identity of employers and employees, foremen, and management; and the segregation of Indian workers from those who hire them, from labor unions, and from coworkers. Such a perspective on the social context also invokes questions of class. Do class structures crosscut ethnic units, uniting people of diverse cultural backgrounds through their common class interests in labor-related structures? Or do common interests generate parallel class structures within isolated ethnic worlds, separate but mirror images of each other? This understudied set of larger questions demands that we treat issues of Indian wage labor as part of the web of dynamic historical relations that have inextricably linked Indian to non-Indian society.

More of the "great issues of labor" previously mentioned as "moral and political" arise when we turn from a description of Indian labor to an investigation of the relations between it and the wealth it produced. If we assume, as did Adam Smith, Karl Marx, and most Native Indian cultures, a theory of wealth in which labor produces value, then we enter issues of cause and consequence having profound moral and political implications. Here arise questions of justice: whether Indian workers have received full value, however defined, for the work they have done or whether their return is even equitable in relation to that received by non-Indian workers. The number of documented studies pointing to unequal wage scales tends to imply that Indian workers have not, even in the limited sense of price and marketplace. But we can also ask about larger benefits or losses—ties to Native culture, religion, identity, independence, quality of life, progress—many of which are intangible and unmeasurable and yet are of crucial interest. Because in the real world wealth has implications of political power, the relationship of Indian labor to the value received leads inevitably to issues of policy. Who has the wealth and therefore the power to influence politicians, bureaucrats, and court cases that place legal circumscriptions around Indian lives? The history of Indian policy shows that it has had implications for Indian laborers. In raising questions of labor and value, we are also led to ask whether there is also a reverse causality, one in which interests in Indian labor influenced policy.

Wage labor forms an intrinsic part of the study of indigenous affairs, both in the historical past and in the contemporary world. It involves general questions relevant to economic anthropology, the study of the nature of ethnicity and class structure, and the understanding of the dynamic relations along the borders between cultural groups. As such, wage labor is a part of both general anthropology and social history. We hope that the contributions to this book will be valuable to others in those fields but, perhaps even more important, will stimulate others to continue the investigation of this important topic.

2

TRIBAL NETWORK AND MIGRANT LABOR
Mi'kmaq Indians as Seasonal Workers in Aroostook's Potato Fields, 1870–1980

Harald E. L. Prins

When we conjure up images of Mi'kmaq tribespeople[1], we tend to think of woodland trappers, spearfishers in birchbark canoes, or, perhaps, basket makers. Not coming to mind, probably, are rows of potato pickers working on large white-owned farms in the rolling hills of New England or the Canadian Maritimes. Yet almost every Mi'kmaq alive either has worked in the vast potato fields during the fall harvest or has a family member who has.

I first became aware of the importance of seasonal wage labor in Mi'kmaq Indian culture in the fall of 1981 when I began working as a tribal researcher in northern Maine for the Aroostook Band of Micmacs—at the time an impoverished off-reservation Indian community seeking federal recognition of its "tribal" status. Since then I have explored the socioeconomic conditions that gave rise to the wage labor complex in this tribal society, in particular to the Mi'kmaqs' participation as migrant workers on Maine's potato farms. Somewhat to my surprise, I found that, although wage labor often functions in the disintegration of traditional communities (Engels 1972; Redfield 1953, 26–53), migrant work opportunities for widely scattered Mi'kmaq kin groups in northeastern North America have actually contributed to the recent articulation of modern Mi'kmaq nationhood (for more detail see Prins 1996; cf. Meggitt 1962, 333; see also Wolf 1982, 192, 323, 354–383).

Although some Indian communities in this region became involved in wage labor as early as the mid-1600s, this chapter focuses on the period since the 1870s.[2] During this era the Mi'kmaqs, like many other Native groups in North America, turned in considerable numbers to seasonal wage labor—picking potatoes, apples, blueberries, and so on and working as guides, lumberjacks, or river drivers "herding" logs downriver (see, among others, Abler and Tooker 1978, 514; Bock 1978, 119; Boxberger 1988, 169–172; Kelly and Fowler 1986, 387–390; Lurie 1978, 705; Radin 1963, 3–4, 33; Spindler 1978, 709; and Weaver 1978, 531). That the Mi'kmaqs made (and often still make) these temporary work choices in part to retain a measure of their self-ascribed identity as "freedom people" suggests an effort to resist a full commodification of their lives.[3]

Like the Iroquois, the Mi'kmaqs form a large cross-border tribe. Divided in twenty-nine bands, they now number about twenty-five thousand. They possess numerous small and scattered reserves located throughout Canada's Atlantic Provinces (Nova Scotia, New Brunswick, Prince Edward Island, and Gaspé Peninsula, Quebec). Focusing on Canadian Mi'kmaq bands living in the Chaleur Bay region (particularly Restigouche) and the nearby Miramichi River area, this chapter examines the social organization of Native labor gangs and their seasonal involvement in the potato-growing agribusiness across the international border in northern Maine. It compares the impact seasonal wage labor had on them with its effect on the off-reservation Aroostook Band of Micmacs in Maine.[4] Reserve-based Mi'kmaqs appear to have been able to withstand complete assimilation into the labor market and persist as a distinct tribal nation on the proletarian edge. In contrast, off-reservation Indians do not have recourse to such economic refuge areas and are thus fully exposed to the pressures of capitalism. In hopes of bringing this picture and analysis to life, I have included recollections and comments made by various Mi'kmaq workers and non-Indian farmers in interviews with Bunny McBride and me.

HISTORICAL BACKGROUND

Traditionally the Mi'kmaq were migratory hunters, fishers, and gatherers. Perhaps numbering ten thousand to twenty thousand people immediately before their first encounter with Europeans around 1500, they hunted inland areas during the fall and winter and spent the summer by the seashore (see also Nietfeld 1981, 390–393, 459). Even though their total aboriginal range is uncertain, early-seventeenth-century records note their presence throughout a large area stretching from Cape Breton to Gaspé Peninsula to coastal Maine (Prins 1986b, 264–267, 275). The basic social unit among these foragers was the extended family, or kindred. Based on voluntary association, several of these kin groups formed regional bands. Widely varying in size, from less than fifty to over four hundred individuals, these autonomous bands formed large seasonal encampments from spring through summer, dispersing into smaller hunting groups in fall and winter. Usually headed by male chieftains, known as *sagamores*, these widely scattered bands collectively formed the Mi'kmaq—an ethnonym that probably derives from *nikmaq*, their word for "my kin-friends" (Whitehead 1987, 20). As a people the Mi'kmaqs constituted an ethnic group, the social boundaries of which were maintained by a limited set of cultural features that included a distinctive Eastern Algonquian language, as well as certain shared beliefs and practices, but did not comprehend a common political allegiance (Bock 1978; Hoffman 1955; Nietfeld 1981; Prins 1988; Wallis and Wallis 1955).

By the early 1600s when small groups of white settlers first established colonies in Mi'kmaq territory, the Native population had already plummeted to about 3,000, due primarily to alien pathogens introduced by European fishermen, and before the century's end it had reached its nadir of about 2,000 (Nietfeld 1981, 390–395). Survivors became marginally involved in the emerging international political economy as fur trappers. They were gradually drawn into a dependency relationship with European nations—first primarily with the French (until 1759) and then with the English (Upton 1979, 31–78). The most serious blows to Mi'kmaq independence began in the late eighteenth century when the number of colonists settling on Mi'kmaq lands soared to tens of thousands. For instance, in 1782 and 1783, with the American Revolutionary War coming to its conclusion, more than 30,000 British Loyalists resettled in Nova Scotia, tripling its non-Indian population within one year (cf. Upton 1979, 78). By the time of confederation in 1867 the province's population had soared to 400,000. Neighboring New Brunswick province was also inundated by white newcomers, especially Irish refugees, and numbered about 300,000 inhabitants, while Prince Edward Island had become home to about 95,000 inhabitants (Prins 1996). Across the newly established international border Maine also grew rapidly in this time, from about 35,000 to 650,000 (Abbott 1875, 542).

Pushed from traditional fishing sites, driven from hunting grounds, and prohibited from assembling at favorite coastal camping places, the vastly outnumbered Mi'kmaqs faced profound constraints in pursuing their traditional way of life (Prins 1988, 212–222). Divided in numerous small bands usually no larger than a few hundred people each, the Mi'kmaqs represented only a fraction (about 0.4 percent at the most) of the total population.

Meanwhile, beginning in the 1780s the British colonial government occasionally set aside small tracts of land as Indian reservations (in Canada called reserves), encouraging the dispersed kin groups to settle down and abandon migratory habits (Upton 1979, 81–123). Despite Mi'kmaq military support for the United States' struggle for independence, no protected tracts were provided on the U.S. side of the new border (Kidder 1867, 297–298; Prins 1988, 311–314). The Unites States and Great Britain, aware that the newly drawn international boundary split the aboriginal range of the Mi'kmaqs and their tribal neighbors, agreed in Article 3 of the 1794 Jay Treaty that these border tribes were free to travel back and forth across the new border for hunting, visiting, and trading purposes (Indian Task Force n.d., 5).

PAUPERIZATION OF THE MI'KMAQS:
THE STRUGGLE FOR SURVIVAL

Unable to escape the rapidly expanding political economy controlled by white newcomers, the widely scattered Mi'kmaq communities were soon overwhelmed. Repressed and degraded by the dominant society, these indigenous tribespeople fell on hard times and struggled to survive in a hostile world. Marginalization affected all Mi'kmaq bands, but it was not a uniform process. Moreover, different groups did not always react to these outside pressures in the same way. No matter the particular responses, however, kin groups camping within immediate reach of the newly founded towns were usually the first to be upheaved. In the vicinity of Halifax city, for example, resided large numbers of Mi'kmaqs. Commenting on their squalor, one white settler noted in 1801: "Several of them are employed in the fisheries in different places, and a small number as labourers by the farmers but the greater part choose to follow their ancient mode of living, and make up the deficiency of their hunting by making small baskets and other small articles (which they barter for provisions) and by begging. They are so much addicted to drinking and suffer so much from their own indolence that I think their number must be decreasing" (Smith 1801–1974, 4; see also Plessis 1903, 187).

In the course of the nineteenth century when it became increasingly impossible to survive on hunting and trapping alone, many Mi'kmaqs turned to crafts such as baskets, brooms, butter tubs, barrels, and porcupine quill work (McBride and Prins 1991, 10–11; Whitehead 1980, 54–58, 66–71). Peddling from door to door, they sold their crafts for cash or bartered them for food, clothing, or other commodities. Those living along the coastal waters speared salmon, eels, and lobsters to sell to the local townspeople. Occasionally the Mi'kmaqs were hired for some odd jobs about the house and yard. In areas such as Restigouche they began to cultivate gardens, growing potatoes, peas, beans, and oats, among other crops. Some even kept cows and horses (Bock 1966, 14–21; Cooney 1896, 216–217). Too often Mi'kmaq families faced periodic starvation, particularly during the winter, and came to depend on government relief in the form of food and clothing.

Meanwhile, the white newcomers ventured deeper into the interior of the Maritime Provinces and New England to exploit the vast timberlands. Soon gangs of lumberjacks reached the wooded borderlands of northern Maine. Initially, economic activities in this extensive region centered almost exclusively on the immense forests, with local farms producing food for home consumption and for the countless scattered *chantiers* (lumber camps) (DuBay 1989b, 154). By the 1860s the white population in northern Maine, which had become organized as Aroostook County in 1844, had grown to twenty-five thousand. Still mainly woodland, Aroostook entails an enormous tract of territory measuring 6,453 square miles, larger than the states of Rhode Island and Connecticut combined (Green 1989, 73). In the mid-nineteenth century almost every available man in the area could be found living in the lumber camps during the long winter season—destroying the remnant traditional hunting grounds of the Native peoples in the area. The handful of Indians still pursuing a life based on hunting, fishing, and trapping appeared to be doomed (Nicholas, with Prins 1989, 30–32).

Driven by hunger and despair, the Mi'kmaqs came to understand that they had few survival options left. Increasingly dependent on cash, they faced two major alternatives: selling crafts to white communities or working for them as wage laborers (Canada Dept. of Indian Affairs 1881, 45, 51–52; 1882, 32). In all probability to enhance their success on the white-dominated labor market, they generally abandoned their distinct Indian dress and hairstyle during this period. By the 1880s the Mi'kmaqs were typically dressed in the same way as non-Indian workers, and most had abandoned their traditional birchbark wigwam dwellings for small frame houses or shacks (Gilpin 1878, 111; Canada Dept. of Indian Affairs 1881, 42, 45, 51–52; 1882, 32; 1884, 36–37).

Temporary Wage Labor and Crafts

The completion of Canada's Intercolonial Railway in 1876 linked the Maritime Provinces with the political economies of the rest of Canada and the United States. Trains reinforced and reshaped the migratory traditions of the Mi'kmaqs, facilitating quicker, more far-reaching travel to work opportunities (Canada Dept. of Indian Affairs 1881, 34). Mi'kmaq artisans, producing crafts such as baskets, brooms, and quill boxes, set up camps near railroad stations, hoping for buyers passing by (Canada Dept. of Indian Affairs 1905, 57–58). Mi'kmaq lumberjacks rode the rails to join the booming lumber industry. They were typically hired for temporary labor as loggers and river drivers, dockworkers on the wharves, and woodworkers in the saw mills (Canada Dept. of Indian Affairs 1881, 34; 1897, 50–52; 1925, 21). Others traveled to new tourist centers where sportsmen from the eastern seaboard cities hired them as hunting or fishing guides (Upton 1979, 129–137).

Most Mi'kmaqs pursued a seasonal subsistence strategy, changing activities according to the dictates of environment and labor market (Canada Dept. of Indian Affairs 1897, 50–52; 1912, 66). The seasonal nature of Mi'kmaq economic activity is well documented. For instance, the Indian agent at Restigouche (population 462) reported in 1883 that in addition to some trapping, fishing, and farming, "the majority of the male portion of the community work for lumbermen during the winter months. Many of these Indians also act as guides to sportsmen . . . during the summer season [making good wages]. Others are employed in the [saw] mills [making reasonable wages]" (Canada Dept. of Indian Affairs 1884, xxix).

In 1890 the agent reported that the Mi'kmaqs of Restigouche "are sought after for the making of logs in the winter. Several camps are composed entirely of Indians under an Indian 'boss.' . . . These same Indians, that is to say, all the men who can leave the village, are employed in spring taking rafts down the river, which affords them an important means of livelihood; and . . . they command high wages" (Canada Dept. of Indian Affairs 1895, 33). During the absence of the men the women "employ their time making snowshoes, baskets, and moccasins, and fishing for smelts and tommy-cods." In the summer the women cultivated the gardens and gathered wild berries for sale in the local town, while many men worked in nearby sawmills (Canada Dept. of Indian Affairs 1893, 30).

Commenting on the variety of work Mi'kmaqs were engaged in during this period, one Indian agent noted: "No class of people occupy themselves in more varied ways than the Indians of the Maritime Provinces. Beside work for which they seem naturally adapted such as hunting, trapping, coopering [and other manual labor] . . . in winter and early spring many of them are occupied in lumbering operations; in spring and summer a goodly number are engaged as fishermen; while quite a few work on railroads and in factories year round" (Canada Dept. of Indian Affairs 1912, 66).

STOOP LABOR IN "POTATO PARADISE"

Railways first linked the rolling hills of northern Maine to the large population centers in northeastern North America in 1870. Soon thereafter the recently settled fertile lands of Aroostook County, which are primarily located in a squash-shaped area about 120 miles long and from 10 to 30 miles wide, emerged as a prime area for potato cultivation (Wilson 1937, 12; York 1989, 54). The nutritious tuber was in high demand not only as one of the world's major low-cost food commodities but also as a cheap starch source for New England's growing textile and paper industries. During the 1870s dozens of potato starch factories cropped up in Aroostook, and in the next decade the railways were extended considerably, soon giving even remote farming towns in the region access to affordable transportation to the large urban markets of eastern Canada and the United States. Potato production soared from 86,500 bushels in 1860, to 5 million in 1890, to an astounding 80 million in the 1940s. With a total of 220,000 acres in Aroostook dedicated to this crop, the area had become the single largest concentration of potato fields in the entire United States, making up about 10 percent of the total national production (Dubay 1989b, 154–157; 1989c, 146; Wilson 1937, 12–13; Rowe 1965).

With a regional subsistence pattern based primarily on lumbering and potato farming, the economy in Aroostook County was highly seasonal. This is reflected in the fact that less than 15 percent of its farmworkers were employed year round (Fitzpatrick 1982; Goldfarb 1981, 16). Especially during harvest time, a four- to six-week period lasting from mid-September through October, potato farmers needed every available person, including women and children, to bring in the crop. Seeking cheap unskilled day laborers, farmers turned to, among others, local tribespeople, primarily off-reservation Maliseet and Mi'kmaq Indians living in small clusters on the margins of Aroostook's towns (Prins 1982a, 78–85; Wherry 1979, 62–86).

In the premechanized period farmers typically divided their potato fields in sections, which were assigned to the harvesting crews. On the average handpicking a 75–100 acre potato farm required forty-five to fifty workers. For their backbreaking work, known as stoop labor, these pickers were paid by the barrel. Even though a strong adult could pick up to 100 barrels in a ten-hour day, the average picker was lucky to fill half as many. For more than a century the primary tool for handpicking has been a big wood-splint basket. These half-bushel containers, usually made by the region's tribespeople, could be filled in about two minutes. Each basketful was emptied into cedar wood barrels placed at regular intervals across the field. Once full, the 165-pound barrels were hoisted onto a wagon, hauled to the potato house, and spilled into huge bins. From there the crop was shipped out by train (see also Bock 1966, 49–50).

The rapid growth in Aroostook's potato production, especially since the 1920s, created a demand for a temporary workforce well beyond local capacity. Consequently, recruitment of migrant laborers became necessary to sustain the region's economic expansion.[5] Too far removed from the southern states, which provided most of the migratory farm labor in the eastern United States, producers in northern Maine recruited workers from across the Canadian border, particularly from the economically depressed Maritime Provinces. Since the turn of the century this region had turned into a backward periphery and thus offered a large reservoir of cheap labor, including widely scattered Mi'kmaq communities that ranged in size from a few families to groups of five hundred people.

Although the Indian labor force in Aroostook's potato fields was composed of a variety of regional tribal groups (including hundreds of Maliseets and Passamaquoddies, as well as some Penobscots), the majority was Mi'kmaq, especially from the mid-1940s onward (Bock 1966, 28, 48–52; Prins 1986a, 128–146).[6] The growing need to recruit unskilled farmworkers from the impoverished reserves in Canada is also apparent from the fact that the U.S. federal courts determined in 1927 that "Canadian Indians" could be considered domestic labor for the purpose of agriculture.[7]

By this time the Mi'kmaq people had begun to recover demographically. Their population surged from about 3,400 in 1871 to almost 4,500 in 1889 and nearly quintupled in size during the next one hundred years. This increase is well illustrated by the Mi'kmaq community of Restigouche, which grew from about 300 in 1830 to 481 in 1900, 1,100 in 1962, and more than 2,660 today. Naturally whenever they experienced yet another downturn in their fortunes, the rapidly growing Mi'kmaq communities were forced to disperse, at least periodically, to prevent starvation.

From the beginning life on the Mi'kmaq reserves was marked by grinding poverty. Local resources were rarely sufficient to sustain the growing number of people surviving on the small tribal enclaves. In an effort to avoid destitution, many tribespeople ventured far beyond their traditional range to find temporary employment as unskilled workers (see also Guillemin 1975, 78–80). Once the railway system was established, they commonly traveled by train. Sometimes they moved about alone, but more typically they journeyed in small cohorts made up of close kinfolk and friends. Although the early Native labor gangs appear to have been made up exclusively of adult males, women and later children were included (see also Bock 1966, 52). Anxious to maintain ties to local communities, laborers returned home during periods when there was little or no work available (Braroe 1975). The reserve, as one observer noted, turned into "a place to which one retreats in hard times until opportunity beckons elsewhere" (Guillemin 1975, 82). After several weeks or even a few months on the reserve, spent visiting with family and friends and engaging in such activities as basketry, fishing, clamming, and hunting, migrant Mi'kmaqs would leave once again (Prins 1988, 37–53; Wolf 1982, 307).

Migrating in search of seasonal work opportunities, the Mi'kmaqs sometimes traveled more than two thousand miles. Some, for instance, found temporary employment in the northern plains region, where they participated in the wheat harvests of Alberta, Saskatchewan, Wyoming, and Montana. The majority, however, remained within a closer range; these people went only as far as Aroostook's potato fields and the wild blueberry barrens of neighboring Washington County, where temporary workers were in great demand during the harvesting period. This migratory pattern of seasonal labor is well illustrated by the personal work history of a Restigouche Mi'kmaq named Joe Martin, who first came to pick potatoes in Maine in 1925. He worked in logging camps in Maine and Minnesota during the winter, followed by trout and salmon fishing back at Restigouche River in the spring. Then he worked on the river drives in northern Maine, followed by wheat harvesting in Saskatchewan or Montana during the summer. Like other tribespeople planning to work out west, Martin was entitled to a special "Indian ticket," issued by Canada's federal government, which allowed him to travel by railway for just a few dollars to distant regions. Finally he would return to Maine for potato picking during the fall, before heading back home to Restigouche (Prins 1982b).

Not all the Mi'kmaqs maintained a home base on a Canadian reserve. Bear River chief Richard McEwan (1988, x) writes in his *Memories of a Micmac Life* that he worked more than ten years in New England (1926-1937) before returning to his reserve village in southwest Nova Scotia. His older half-brother Michael, however, moved to Maine and never went back home: "[He] lived up in potato country. He had a little place that belonged to the farmer that he worked for. He worked right through the potato growing operation. He'd be there for planting and looking after gardens or whatever, and then in the fall he would be one of the pickers. Winters, he used to work in the woods."

Although there were many other Mi'kmaqs settling (more or less permanently) in northern Maine, most stayed there only for the harvest before returning to their respective reserves. Especially between 1920 and 1965, picking potatoes in Maine played a vital role in the reserve economies (Prins 1988, 40-53; Wallis and Wallis 1953, 115). For instance, more than 40 percent of the large Mi'kmaq population at Restigouche traveled the almost one hundred miles each September to Aroostook (see also Bock 1966, 48, 52). Many Mi'kmaqs, like other migrants, operated as freelance workers, arriving independently on the potato farms of northern Maine. Others were recruited directly by farmers who personally drove to the reserves to recruit pickers for the coming season (see also Wallis and Wallis 1955, 115). As one farmer remembers: "We'd go up [to the reserves] to pick up the Indians in a truck and bring 'em down to work. And at the end of the harvest we'd take 'em back and drop 'em off. They always got a lot of service" (Fitzpatrick 1982). Another form of migrant labor recruitment involved a special contractor known as a "jobber," who served as a middleman between the farmer and his Indian workers (see also Goldfarb 1981, 19-24). These farm labor contractors, or crew leaders, were commonly Indians with established kinship ties to the local reserves targeted for recruitment. As Philip Bock (1966, 49), who conducted research at Restigouche in the early 1960s, explains:

> Some go individually, but most of them travel in crews recruited by an Indian "jobber" who has agreed to furnish a certain number of pickers, loaders, or drivers for a particular farmer. . . . Depending on the size of the farm, the crews may range in size from four or five individuals to twenty or more. . . . Kinship, friendship, and locality seem to be the major determinants of crew membership. This is hardly a surprising discovery, but one must note that the potato harvest is presently the only organized activity completely under the control of the Indians.

Indian jobbers not only served in recruiting migrant laborers from the Mi'kmaq communities but also mediated between the farmer and his Indian picking crews during work: "The leader of the crew may work in the harvest or act as coordinator, or both, assigning sections to the pickers, keeping accounts straight, shopping for supplies, and so on" (Bock 1966, 49). As one farmer recalls: "There were crews of 10–30 Indians that came right off the reservation, and one in the group would supervise. . . . The head of the group was the one you talked to. We had buildings for them to stay in. Bedding and utensils they brought. They also brought someone to cook. Never paid 'em till Saturday night" (Fitzpatrick 1982). Generally Mi'kmaq jobbers earned a few cents for each barrel their crews picked (Bock 1966, 51).

The following reminiscence, as told by elderly Mi'kmaq basketmaker Sarah Lund (1987), now residing in northern Maine, is fairly typical:

> How well I remember the harvest season down home in Eel River. Around the fifth of September, everybody was so anxious to come to Maine and pick potatoes. I first came when I was sixteen. We packed up our shacks and packed all our clothes for the trip. Everybody was so excited in anticipation of coming to good old USA and making some money. We boarded a branch train for 10 cents to go the 15 miles to Campbellton to wait for another train to take us to the Maine border. Oh, how we planned for a month just to get here in Maine. It was usually about 36 people . . . going from the reservation. We would board the [train] at 8 AM for the 40 cents 95-mile ride to St. Leonard. We had our babies

and children, too, and we would all try to stay together. It took us all day to get to the Maine border. The train was so slow. . . . When we got to St. Leonard about 7 PM, the potato farmers would all be waiting for us to take us to wherever they lived. And then began the work. It was a great time for us. . . . I picked potatoes for many years after that.

The Mi'kmaqs, like other potato pickers, did their work crawling on their knees or standing square on the ground straddling their baskets, bodies bent in half. When chilly October rains turned the vast fields into dark stretches of cold mud, the work became especially dirty. Further aggravations resulted from the lack of toilet facilities in the fields (see also Thomas-Lycklema à Nÿeholt 1980, 40). Indian migrant workers were usually put up by the farmer who had hired them. They customarily stayed for free in a small picker's shack or camp, several of which were placed in a row behind the farm. These shacks rarely possessed adequate facilities, and the hygienic conditions were usually poor. Occasionally small crews boarded with the farmers themselves (Bock 1966, 49). In other instances, however, they were forced to sleep in the barn. One old Mi'kmaq woman remembers a farmer she worked for who "put everybody up in an old school house, half loaded with straw. There were big hand-made tables there for us to put our stuff on. And there was an old stove. We made tea on it in the morning. For lunch, you just do the best you can" (Doody, in McBride and Prins 1983).

After the fall harvest, where the Mi'kmaqs not only worked but also exchanged information, made new friends, and even found spouses, many headed "back home" to their reserves, where federal relief was barely sufficient for them to scrape through the long winter. Those who could find work often remained in Aroostook, hiring themselves out as lumberjacks; working as day laborers in the local starch factories or dark, dank potato houses; or producing hundreds of sturdy potato baskets for farmers in exchange for very modest housing (shacks or camps), food and clothing, or cash (McBride and Prins 1991). During the summer months from mid-July to late August many Mi'kmaqs picked blueberries on the vast wild barrens of coastal Maine, in Washington and Hancock Counties, situated some 150 miles south of Aroostook's potato fields. Sarah Lund (in McBride and Prins 1983) recalls:

> Abe and I always moved about. From April to June we'd be living on the reserve [period of slack employment], digging clams in Dalhousie. June to July we'd make potato baskets, usually in Maine. August, we'd be in Maine to rake [blue] berries, and during September–October we worked the potato harvest. If we found a good rent after the harvest we'd stay in Maine from November to March [potato house work]. If not, we'd return north to the reserve. But in the winter months we just survived. . . . So, we went back and forth, back and forth for years, following seasonal work opportunities and sometimes just following the crazy whims of fate.

MECHANIZED HARVESTING: THE END OF AN ERA

In the 1940s, when potato farming reached its peak, a total of forty thousand pickers were needed to bring in the harvest. In addition to local white and Native workers, farmers hired recent Irish immigrants and bonded French Canadians (Wilson 1937). During the war years, when there was a real labor shortage, trainloads of men, too young or too old to be drafted, were shipped in from as far away as Oklahoma. Numbering in this multitude were even two thousand German prisoners of war (see also DuBay 1989b, 159; 1989c, 167; McBride 1983, 92, 114).

In the mid-1950s farmers started to mechanize harvesting, and the impact in the regional labor market was dramatic. Capable of processing up to one thousand two hundred barrels per day, two-row harvesting machines replaced about fifteen to twenty adult pickers each. During the next decade mechanization of farm labor increased rapidly. By 1968 growers were using more than one thousand one hundred harvesting machines, sharply reducing the need for migrant labor (see also Goldfarb 1981, 12–16). For instance, the number of bonded Canadian workers dropped from seven thousand eight hundred in the early 1960s to no more than five hundred in 1972, while the number of Native Americans migrating from their reserves in Canada to Aroostook's potato fields dropped from perhaps as many as two thousand five hundred to no more than a few hundred (Johnston and Metzger 1974, 3–12).

By the early 1980s barely 10 percent of the crop was still being harvested by hand. The mechanization of farm labor in Aroostook had numerous side effects on the region's social life, including the demise of the more rowdy weekend scenes in town during picking season (see also Bock 1966, 51). Several older Mi'kmaqs living in northern Maine vividly remember the "good old days." An elderly Aroostook Mi'kmaq woman born at Restigouche recalls:

> I first came to Maine in 1934 with [my husband] to pick potatoes. By then there was a lot of people comin' from the reserves down to Maine for the harvest. More men than women came because folks didn't always have money for the train so they had to hitchhike, and men could hitchhike safer than women. . . . We met up with all kinds of Indian folks in a beer joint in town. A place called Melissa's—run by a 350-pound woman. Boy was she a bouncer. All kinds of different people, Indians from all over Nova Scotia, New Brunswick and Maine packed into that place every night during harvesting season. . . . Some people didn't even have enough money to go home with after picking season. (Doody, in McBride and Prins 1983)

According to another aged Mi'kmaq woman, a basketmaker in Mars Hill: "Maine harvesting—that was supposed to mean having a good time and making money. And there was a kind of freedom . . . in making the money. I could buy nice clothes. That first year, I worked in Presque Isle [Aroostook's potato center]. That was before there were harvesters and we worked with horses. The place was so packed with pickers. We could pick hard all day long and then in the weekend we partied" (Paul, in McBride and Prins 1983).

Mi'kmaq basket maker Donald Sanipass of Chapman recalls the tail end of Aroostook's potato heydays: "Back in the sixties there were 'bout 20 camps here [in Chapman], because there were all different jobbers around these parts—loggin', potatoes, potato houses. It was a thriving place. Lots of jobs. Like I was tellin' you, during potato season [the city of] Presque Isle was something else—like Dodge City back in the 1800s. No elbow room. There were Indians all over the place here—working . . . for all kinds of farmers. Presque Isle was one wild place on the weekends during harvest time." His wife, Mary, adds, "You bet it was wild. During harvest the jail was full every weekend." Donald continues: "Back then, border police were all around, always checkin' potato fields and potato houses for illegal Canadian workers. Nowadays everything's modern and harvesters have replaced most pickers. So there's only a few [Indians] comin' cross border compared to what it used to be" (Sanipass and Sanipass, in McBride and Prins 1983).

Even though a small number of Mi'kmaqs continue their annual trek from the reserves to work in Maine's potato harvest today (participating in both mechanical and manual harvesting), the introduction of welfare programs on Canada's Indian reserves has also made seasonal farmwork largely unnecessary. Those Indians now working in northern Maine are mostly local off-reservation Mi'kmaqs and Maliseets. According to a 1982 survey of American Indian households in Aroostook County, about half of all resident Mi'kmaqs and Maliseets were still seasonally employed as day laborers in the potato fields and potato houses. Stricken with poverty, often living in shacks or trailers, most of these Indian families depended on food stamps and other welfare programs to supplement their irregular and inadequate wage earnings and income from selling crafts (Prins 1983). Usually hired only as a last resort, these marginalized tribespeople were victimized by anti-Indian racism and suffered from discriminatory labor practices (Cleaves 1980, 1–8; Prins 1988, 51–56; Wherry 1980, 1, 3).

Mechanized harvesting also spelled disaster for the local Indian basket makers, who witnessed a steep decline in demand for their craft. In contrast to the peak years, when perhaps as many as twenty-five thousand potato baskets were sold each year, demand dropped to a few thousand (see also McBride 1983). Reflecting on this change, one Mi'kmaq basketmaker comments: "Twenty years ago [in 1960], there were more than half a dozen families in [northern Maine] making baskets. Now from Caribou to Fort Kent, there's just Abe and me. All the rest died and their children didn't take up the business, because no one wanted baskets anymore" (Lund, in McBride 1983, 91).

Tribal Network as Communal Survival Strategy

The radical economic transformation among the Mi'kmaqs from a lifestyle based primarily on self-provisioning to one based almost exclusively on wage labor and federal government support (Mingione 1991, 82, 150–151) becomes abundantly clear when we compare demographic information pertaining to nineteenth-century subsistence activities with more recent data. Hunting, fishing, and trapping were still prevalent in the early 1800s, but this was by no means the case later in that century. According to the 1881 Canadian public census, which lists Mi'kmaq adult males by occupation, just 7 percent still subsisted on the basis of hunting and 4 percent on fishing. Most men listed were farmers (29 percent) or coopers (25 percent). Only 10 percent were laborers (Canada 1881).

A 1968 economic profile of the Restigouche band revealed the modern commodification process in one reserve community. By then there were no hunters or fishermen, and only 1 tribesman was still listed as a farmer. A total of 206 men (70 percent) were seasonally employed as day laborers, 24 were millworkers, and 30 were metalworkers. The remainder were on the government payroll as administrative personnel. All told, 88 percent of Restigouche's adult males depended at least in part on wage labor. Since few jobs were available on or near the reserve, an average of only 43 percent of the men aged between twenty and forty actually resided on the reserve at any given time. In contrast, most women (75 percent) in this age group lived on the reserve year round (Ross and partners 1974, 46–47).

Restigouche's demographic patterns are fairly representative for Mi'kmaq reserve communities in general. Only on rare occasions were these settlements fully occupied. During much of the year, particularly when there was ample demand for cheap unskilled labor, the reserves were inhabited only by those who were unable to compete for jobs in the labor market, especially mothers, children, and the elderly, as well as the sick or handicapped (Guillemin 1975, 82–92). From the 1950s onwards virtually all reserve-based Mi'kmaqs relied in some degree on federal welfare programs: unemployment security, housing subsidies, health care, and/or child welfare support. With the help of such benefits, the reserves continue to function as refuge areas, offering a measure of financial security and social solidarity (Battiste 1977, 3–13).

Obviously the frequently long absences of so many tribespeople have left an indelible mark on the social fabric of the reserve communities. Commenting on the communal strategy for economic survival and the importance of the tribal network among urban Indians, Jeanne Guillemin (1975, 130–131, 136–137, 146) notes in her discussion of Mi'kmaq industrial laborers in Boston:

> The kind of work history which a Micmac Indian accumulates over the course of a lifetime includes an enormous variety of jobs. . . . As an outsider the individual Indian is almost immune to the confusion of personal and institutional goals. When routinization threatens to make a machine out of him, he quits his job, even when, from a conventional point of view, he cannot possibly afford to. As more than simply an economic unit, his primary responsibility is to keep himself a viable member of the community. . . . The amount of time spent on a job and the interim between one job and another is determined by social imperatives. Kin must be responsible to kin and friend to friend. Socializing, contests and conflicts, and communications must continue. Out of the social activity of the community comes its solution to economic marginality. . . . It would be impossible for the Micmac to survive in urban society if money (like information on work, places to stay, and transportation) were not shared. A man or woman can obey the impulse to leave work, shifting attention from earning money to investing time and energy in the community, precisely because the basic economic strategy of the tribe is communal.

By contrast, the Mi'kmaqs who are out of touch with the tribal network and do not have access to reserves may be forced into becoming fully proletarianized. Such is the risk many Aroostook Mi'kmaqs and other tribespeople without such ethnic refuge areas confront. Their predicament is expressed by one old off-reservation Mi'kmaq woman in northern Maine as she sums up her long and difficult life: "You know, I get all mixed up about the dates of things because I moved so many times in my life. I moved around so much through the years that thinking about it makes me dizzy" (Copage, in McBride and Prins 1983). Yet even among these off-reservation Aroostook Mi'kmaqs, there is regular contact with other Mi'kmaq communities. According to a 1983 survey, about two-thirds of Aroostook Mi'kmaq households occasionally visited kinfolk and friends living in Canada's reserve communities (Prins 1986a, 195–198). By the same token, Mi'kmaq migrant workers from Canada, as well as others passing through, from, or to the Boston area, frequently stop off in northern Maine. One Mi'kmaq elder recalls:

> Came to Aroostook for the first time in 1940 and left in 1948. I've moved so many times, to so many places, in and out of Aroostook. We used to live in Loring Base Street [in Presque Isle, Maine]. A bunch of us all living together, working in the potatoes. One day in 1947, Frank just walked into our place. Him and his brother Simon. They were here for picking, and had come up from Canada. They stayed all winter, then left in the spring to go back to Canada. But Frank came back that summer, and in the second winter he was here with us. He worked in the woods, cutting pulp. Stayed till blueberry time. His father used to come off and on and stay with us, too. (Francis, in McBride and Prins 1983)

Sometimes, of course, this communal economic strategy can turn into a major burden for families residing at major stopping places. Having just been invaded by a party of transient Mi'kmaqs, one Aroostook Mi'kmaq basket maker complains:

> It's hard to stay ahead because after blue-berrying, people headin' back north pass through here [Mars Hill, Maine] need food and a place to stay, and need money to help them get back home. And then there's all the folks who stay on to pick potatoes. Last year we had about a truckload of Indians staying here with us. But many of them we didn't even know. We can't get ahead this way, and we should put an end to it. Our own we would take in. Our friends and family we would take in and help them out. But, you know, even farmers send their pickers over here to pick on us. And we haven't got the money. (Paul, in McBride and Prins 1983)

CONCLUSION

Forming an internal colony based primarily on small tribal enclaves scattered throughout the Maritime Provinces and northern Maine, the Mi'kmaqs have persisted as a distinct Indian people after nearly five hundred years of direct experience with European power. Theirs is a history of a struggle for survival in which flexibility and adaptability are some of the more salient features. Since the mid-nineteenth century the Mi'kmaqs have found themselves on the proletarian edge. When they could no longer pursue their traditional subsistence strategies of hunting, trapping, fishing, and gathering, they turned to crafts and migrant labor. The seasonal nature of harvesting, in particular blueberry picking at Washington County's wild barrens in the summer, followed by potato digging in Aroostook's fields in the fall, played well into the Mi'kmaqs' traditionally migratory way of life. These temporary wage-earning opportunities within traveling distance from the reserves not only earned them relatively good money (albeit for rather short periods of time) but also allowed them to maintain a vital linkage with their tribal communities (see also Battiste 1977, 3–13).

In this respect the survival of Mi'kmaq bands as federally dependent communities merits consideration. In Canada the government bureaucracy recognizes bands, not tribes, as the corporate groups entitled to the reserved tracts of land and as the administrative units eligible for federal services and funding (Upton 1979, 172–181). Clearly these protected ethnic enclaves have played a critical role in the Mi'kmaq struggle for cultural survival. Serving the Mi'kmaqs as "a haven in hard times and as a focus of sentiments, as a home," the reserves have allowed the mostly unskilled and semiskilled workers to avoid the more dreadful consequences of the cheap labor market (Guillemin 1975, 61).

The impact of migrant labor on the organizational structure of Mi'kmaq tribal society has been threefold. First, it played into the disarticulation of the autonomous bands as self-supporting corporate communities: "Aside from electing band council representatives, people from the same band might never operate as an organized group, though individuals meeting for the first time can use their common band affiliation as an excuse for developing friendship" (Guillemin 1975, 63). In combination with a growing federal dependency, migrant labor also subverted the social, economic, and spiritual authority of the traditional band chiefs (Wallis and Wallis 1953, 120; 1955, 171–175). Second, while economic pressure compelled participation in wage labor, political status as "Indians" entitled Mi'kmaqs to residence on reserve lands and enabled them to resist full proletarianization.

Third, and this is an issue explored further elsewhere (cf. Prins 1996), migrant labor contributed to the process of Mi'kmaq nation formation. Clearly the seasonal demand for large numbers of rural wage laborers, coupled with the availability of mechanized means of transportation, greatly increased the interaction among tribespeople hailing from remote and widely dispersed communities. Periodically associating in Maine's blueberry barrens and potato fields, they not only expanded their knowledge about one another but also shared a common treatment as a low-caste minority group (cf. Hechter 1975, 15–43). Furthermore, these annual occasions provided the Mi'kmaqs with the chance to encounter numerous other Native people, including Maliseets, Passamaquoddies, Penobscots, and Indians belonging to more distant tribes. The outcome has been a growing sense of collective consciousness among the transient Mi'kmaqs clustering in these temporary encampments: "The community is today quite knowledgeable about the extent of its own tribal boundaries. Each member in the course of a lifetime is likely to meet up with many other Micmac who are relatively difficult to place in an immediate kinship network and yet look, speak, and act Micmac and have to be accounted for" (Guillemin 1975, 75).

The issue of migrant labor in modern tribal societies reaches beyond mere economic survival and cannot be understood in terms of one-dimensional categories such as underemployment. Even though Mi'kmaq migrant workers do "sell themselves piecemeal," they do so more or less on their own terms. As members within a diffuse tribal network, with a right to retire to their respective reserve communities, they are not fully "exposed to all the vicissitudes of competition, to all the fluctuations of the market" (Marx 1972, 341). The pursuit of a communal strategy shields them against full-fledged proletarianization and allows them to retain at least a semblance of independence as "freedom people" (see also Guillemin 1975, 146; Mingione 1991, 152, 188–191). Paradoxically, while migrant labor contributed to the waning of traditional band organization, it reinforced the ethnic solidarity among the widely scattered Mi'kmaq people, who increasingly identify themselves as a tribal nation—the Mi'kmaq Nationimow.

3

WAGE LABOR
IN TWO MICHIGAN
OTTAWA COMMUNITIES

James M. McClurken

The nineteenth-century expansion of U.S. political jurisdiction into the upper Great Lakes after the War of 1812 produced great social, political, and economic change for Michigan Ottawas.[1] Each band, which was politically and economically autonomous, responded differently to the pressures of Euro-American advancement. This chapter describes the response of two Ottawa bands to the ecological, cultural, and political changes that U.S. control brought to their homelands.

The Little Traverse Bay Odawas live on the northern tip of Michigan's Lower Peninsula, the islands of northern Lake Michigan, and the south shore of the Upper Peninsula. They are historically composed of at least nine autonomous bands that traditionally made their living by intensive horticulture, lake and inland fishing, hunting, trapping, and trade. They have inhabited the region along the shores of northern Lake Michigan and Lake Huron from the seventeenth century until today without interruption.

The Grand River bands once lived in nine horticultural villages along the Grand River and in smaller settlements on the Maple, Thornapple, Muskegon, White, Pere Marquette, and Manistee Rivers in the central and southern portions of Michigan's Lower Peninsula. Their ancestors moved southward from the Straits of Mackinac to occupy these lands during the early eighteenth century. The modern Little River Ottawas are descendants of several Grand River bands that returned north during the 1850s to join kinfolk who already lived on the Pere Marquette and

Manistee Rivers beyond the line of Euro-American settlement. There these bands formed a new community on and around lands reserved by treaties they had made with the United States in 1836 and 1855. The Little River Ottawas, assuming different names over time, have lived on or along the Pere Marquette and Manistee Rivers in Manistee and Mason Counties from 1855 to the present.

By the time settlers came to the Great Lakes, the Ottawas already had two hundred years of experience in dealing with representatives of European civilization and their descendants. From 1615 forward they had done so by incorporating their traditional subsistence and economic pursuits into the broader regional and global economy (White 1991). The Ottawa bands and the Europeans who lived in northern Michigan adapted their economic activities to accommodate their mutual needs and desires (White 1991). These Indians sold tons of preserved horticultural produce, wild plant foods, meat, fish, and furs and traded their technology—canoes, traps, fish nets, and snowshoes—to European and Métis traders, soldiers, and adventurers (Blair 1911(1), vol. 1, 276–277, 281–282; Feest and Feest 1978, 772–775). Men and women also sold their labor to European immigrants who lived at the frontier posts of Mackinac, Detroit, and Green Bay and even to distant Hudson Bay Company operators in Manitoba; these Ottawas worked as voyagers, gardeners, craftspersons, and guides and in other professions related to the fur trade (Blackbird 1887, 24–30; Ritterbush 1990, 40–87).

Two hundred years of successful economic accommodation to European-style economy and culture caused many Ottawa leaders to hope that they could continue their successful accommodations in the U.S. era. The 1836 Treaty of Washington, however, ended the balanced Ottawa and European economic accommodation that had allowed Indian communities to thrive for so long (Kappler 1904, vol. 2, 450–461). The U.S. government acquired ownership of and political jurisdiction over the Ottawas' core territory and with it the control of many natural resources that had provided the Ottawas' economic base.

Whereas the Ottawas hoped to continue their mobile, kin-based, horticultural, gathering, fishing, and hunting way of life, Euro-Americans saw few roles for Indians in the developing Michigan economy. Unlike the French and British, the Euro-Americans sought to replace the Ottawa producers with non-Indian farmers and wage laborers who would transform Michigan into an agricultural and industrial state (Cass 1821; Dunbar 1965, 235–236; Gilpin 1970, 69–78, 114–119). Land cessions in the 1836 treaty forced the bands to create more sedentary, permanent rural communities. A subsequent treaty negotiated by the Ottawas at Detroit in 1855 ended a threat of forced relocation to Kansas and secured small reservations within their former estate (Kappler 1904, vol. 2, 725–735), but between 1860 and 1875 the Ottawas were outnumbered by non-Indians on and around these refuges.

By 1875, roughly forty-five years after large numbers of Euro-American settlers had begun making homes in Michigan, the Ottawas lived in isolated rural enclaves within the boundaries of their reservation. Title to much of their reserve lands passed to Euro-American claimants. The Ottawas had little capital, few manufactured tools, and an insufficient knowledge of Euro-American economic skills to compete with U.S. investors and settlers in retaining title to their land, developing farms and industry, or securing the wage labor positions that accompanied U.S. expansion. Until the mid-twentieth century those few Michigan Ottawas who eventually found cash-paying jobs filled the lowest-status wage labor positions in their localities (McClurken 1991, 18–72).

The divesting of the Ottawas' independent economic status did not happen instantly, nor did it occur at the same rate throughout the Indians' home territory. The transition from independent producers to low-status wage laborers was governed by a complex interaction of several key variables. The attitudes of the individual Ottawa bands themselves concerning the Americanization of their culture, their towns, and their labor activities set the tone for each community's response. While some Ottawa bands embraced the adoption of animal-powered agriculture, a cash economy, and wage labor, others did not. Some chose to move as far beyond the line of U.S. settlement as they could, maintaining their traditional economy and protecting their political autonomy.

Those bands that consciously chose to rapidly adopt Christianity, a U.S.-style economy, and the accompanying changes in material culture benefited most directly from federal policies designed to educate the Ottawas and facilitate their move into the expanding agrarian and industrial economy. More of their members attended government and mission schools than did the bands that continued to rely exclusively on gardens, gathering, fishing, and hunting. Educated band members, then, plied their trades in the construction and operation of their own towns between 1830 and 1870.

Those Ottawa bands that opposed the degree of culture change required to compete in the new economic context continued to rely heavily on harvesting and selling the natural resources of their former territories. In some regions of Michigan where non-Indians made few claims on these resources, small bands continued to live almost exclusively by gathering, fishing, and hunting through the 1860s. By 1870, however, few, if any, of the Ottawas' natural resources remained untouched by the effects of lumbering and agriculture. When diminishing resources made subsistence from solely traditional economic pursuits impossible during the 1890s, the highly mobile Ottawa bands continued travel throughout their historic range, mixing their traditional economic activities with seasonal wage labor in lumber camps and as farmhands. Even those Ottawa bands that actively pursued an economic plan favoring wage labor continued to rely on the natural resources, on and off their reservations, well into the twentieth century. Which resources they used and the importance of the income to each household's support depended strongly on the Ottawas' access to wage labor.

The critical variables in determining Ottawa access to cash-paying occupations were primarily demographic. Communities farthest from viable transportation routes and markets changed only slowly, no matter what the intentions of the federal government, missionaries, or band leaders. In regions where non-Indian populations formed viable markets within close range of Ottawa communities, historical documents and personal histories show that some Ottawa people found low-paying, seasonal wage labor during the 1870s. From that time until the 1940s the Ottawas became a pool of underskilled people who relied on all economic avenues—traditional gathering and wage labor—for their support.

Despite tremendous historical forces that combined to deprive the Ottawas of their political autonomy, their treaty-preserved properties, and their culture, they have remained a distinct people. This may be attributed in some part to continued reliance on resources that demanded traditional cultural knowledge of the lands and lakes of their homeland, dependence on kinship and reciprocity to forestall economic disasters, and the work of skillful political leaders throughout the last century. This chapter describes the economic transformation of the Little Traverse Bay Odawas and the Little River Ottawas as they entered the wage labor market and discusses the process by which the Ottawas became part of an underemployed labor pool. The text draws on the Ottawas' own accounts of mixing traditional subsistence activities with wage labor to preserve a way of life defined by themselves and those around them as distinctly "Indian."

WORK IN THE LITTLE RIVER COMMUNITY

The Little River Ottawas entered the U.S. wage labor economy more slowly than did the Little Traverse Bay Odawas. The process of incorporation into the cash economy was not fully completed until the mid-twentieth century. For all intents and purposes the Little River Ottawas made the greatest portion of their living by subsistence gathering, fishing, and hunting practices well into the 1940s. Only the massive changes in the U.S. economy during and after World War II proved strong enough to transform their economy.

That the Little River Ottawas historically preferred to continue their traditional economic pursuits is evident from decisions their leaders made during the treaty era. When given the opportunity to select reservation lands anywhere in the upper half of Michigan's Lower Peninsula, they first reserved land in Manistee County in 1836 and selected a second reserve in Mason County in 1855. All of these lands fell within their historic winter trapping and fishing range. From the standpoint of U.S. treaty negotiators, these lands were undesirable for non-Indian settlement. The very features that made the lands undesirable for Euro-American settlers enhanced their value to the Little River Ottawas.

From the earliest days of Euro-American settlement in Michigan, farmers avoided the sandy, pine-timbered lands of the Manistee and Pere Marquette River drainages in the central Lower Peninsula. The majority of Ottawas themselves historically avoided permanent residence on these rivers, with their large bayous and hordes of mosquitoes and black flies during the summer months. Rather, they traveled seasonally from their horticultural villages at Little Traverse Bay, Grand Traverse Bay, and Grand River to winter along the inland marshes on these and other rivers, where sheltered wetlands provided rich winter hunting and trapping (Blackbird 1887, 32–33). These locations were especially favored by the Grand River Ottawas (McClurken 1993, 1–33).

Only the band headed by Kewaygushkum (Striking Out Toward Home) had made Manistee its permanent home at the time of the 1836 treaty. This extended-family band never numbered more than ninety people (Schoolcraft 1839). A second band headed by Nahkonnokowag, or Good John, lived twelve miles up the Pentwater River, near the present-day town of Custer. Both bands maintained large gardens. Nahkonnokowag's people had cleared and used about "100 acres of good land" (Grand Rapids Daily Enquirer and Herald 1858). The Manistee band members maintained two favored garden sites a short distance from the Manistee River and a summer village site at the river's mouth (*History* 1882, 20–21). These indigenous bands were on hand to meet the Grand River bands that migrated north after 1855.

The 1836 and 1855 treaty commissioners and the Ottawas intended the land reserves stipulated in the agreements to allow the Indians permanent access to the riverain resources located both on and off the reservations (see Figure 3.1). The rich lands and long growing season in areas south of the Grand River, they believed, would accommodate the largest numbers of Euro-American farmers then immigrating to Michigan (Dunbar 1965, 376–378). Few, if any, influential legislators in the state or federal government believed that the sandy lands on or around the Ottawa reservations would ever be desirable for non-Indian settlement. The abundance of natural resources and isolation from the potential disruption of settlers induced seven bands, nearly one-third

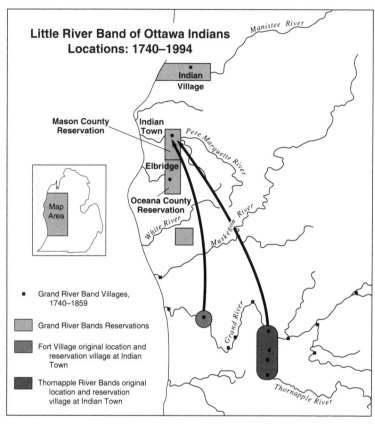

Fig. 3.1. Locations of the Little Traverse Odawas and the Little River Ottawas. (Map by James M. McClurken)

of the Grand River Ottawa population, to move north to the Manistee and Mason County reserves (McClurken 1993, 104–110).

The reservations created by the 1855 treaty were designed to concentrate the Ottawas in enclaves apart from non-Indian settlement. According to Commissioner of Indian Affairs George Manypenny (1880, xxi–xxx), who negotiated the treaty, reservation boundaries would protect Indian property from land speculators and squatters long enough for Indians to become proficient in the knowledge and skills necessary for life in U.S. society. Within five years adult Ottawas would receive forty- or eighty-acre farms. For another five years the remaining reservation lands could be purchased exclusively by Indians. Lands selected as allotments were to be held in trust for the Indians for at least ten years, and perhaps longer, depending on their success at adopting the skills of U.S.-style farming and economics (Kappler 1904, vol. 2, 727). On the reservation allotments the Ottawas were to draw on treaty-specified federal laborers, tools, and money to transform themselves into hard-working, productive, American, Christian agrarians. These treaty provisions were adopted with good intentions by the U.S. commissioners.

The removal of the Grand River bands north to their former hunting and trapping grounds did not mean that members of these bands intended to live solely by hunting and trapping. The Ottawas had never done so on the Manistee River or at any other village. Provisions of their 1836 treaty provided them with capital and tools to intensify production of their traditional corn, squash, and bean crops and to expand their agricultural repertoire with a variety of new fruits, grains, and vegetables. Potatoes and new varieties of apples were grown for the Ottawas' own use and for sale. At the same time, the combined Ottawa bands specifically maintained the right to continue gathering traditional subsistence crops of berries, maple sugar, fish, and wild game. In Article 13 of the treaty the Indians stipulated for "the right of hunting on the lands ceded, with the other usual privileges of occupancy until the land is required for settlement" (Kappler 1904, vol. 2, 454). The Little River Ottawas availed themselves of all these provisions, but they relied heavily on the right reserved in Article 13 (see Antoine 1915; Blackbird 1892; Dobson 1978, 23–24; Lee 1878a; Medacco 1930; Olson 1928; Porter 1855; Selkrig 1855; Turner 1857).

Although Euro-American settlers were not drawn to the Manistee and Mason County area, lumbermen were. By 1840 Michigan's non-Indian population already stood at 212,267—outnumbering the Ottawas nearly 200 to 1—and was growing rapidly (Dunbar 1965, 250; Schoolcraft 1839). The expanding settlements in Michigan and in the prairie states demanded thousands of board feet of durable, easily milled white pine to construct homes, barns, and factories. When lumber barons began cutting white pine on navigable western Michigan rivers during the 1820s, they believed the Pere Marquette and Manistee Rivers, with their easily dammed beds and large stands of virgin pine, offered great prospects for wealth. Lumber operations began on the Manistee River in the 1840s. When the timber was cut, the lumbermen intended to sell farmers the upstream parcels, where the sandy soil mixed with clay loams and where the growing season was lengthened by the warming lake effect (*History* 1882, 49–54, 73, 105–106). These lumbering operations could have provided the Little River Ottawas with opportunities for wage labor, but they did not. These small operations were run by small teams of non-Indians who cut the timber and ran all milling operations until the 1870s. The result of lumbering was a slow but constant move of non-Indians to the reservation.

The implementation of the provisions of the 1855 treaty soon left the Ottawas without title to the lands they had reserved and almost as dependent on the nonagricultural resources of their traditional range as they had been before the treaty was negotiated. Successive generations of Indian Office agents and administrators thoroughly mismanaged the allotment process. The selections that were to be completed in ten years took twenty. Non-Indian settlers and their state and federal legislators took every opportunity to clamor for the opening of the reservations to U.S. citizens. Congress acquiesced to their wishes in 1872 and passed legislation that allowed non-Indians to take claims on the Ottawa reserves (United States 1872). The continual erosion of the Ottawas' economic base and competition from U.S. immigrants compelled the Ottawas to accept any work available to them.

The number of non-Indians on and around the Ottawa reserves competed for what remained of the region's natural resources, leaving the Little River Ottawas on the brink of economic disaster. To compensate the Ottawas for lands lost to non-Indians and to further adoption of U.S.-style farming, the United States allowed the Ottawas to select homesteads under special legislation (United States 1875, 1876). This homestead right, however, did little to further the Ottawas' prospects toward becoming either self-sufficient farmers or wage laborers. Local officials interpreted terms of the homestead legislation to require permanent Indian residency on the selections. When Indians seasonally left their claims to gather, fish, or hunt, their homes were often declared abandoned and sold to non-Indians. Even when the homestead residency requirement had been met and titles issued, Indians often lost their homesteads for back taxes (Brooks 1878a).

In 1871 non-Indian speculators and sharpers quickly separated the Ottawas from their allotments and homesteads. Agent George Smith (1871, 510) reported that "the work of dispossessing those Indians of the title of these lands is still going on without let or hinderance." Federal agents were several times sent to the region to investigate claims of fraudulent taking of Ottawa homesteads and in many instances found sound evidence to substantiate the Ottawas' claims (Brooks 1877a; Lee 1878b). Had speculators and politicians allowed the Ottawas to hold their reservation allotments and homesteads, perhaps the Little River Ottawas would have more quickly entered fully into the U.S. economy as farmers and wage laborers, but this did not happen.

Even if the Little River Ottawas had been able to retain title to a land base sufficient to encourage agriculture and the development of wage labor, they still lacked the financial and technical means to do so in the 1870s. They had moved to the reservations carrying only those belongings that would fit—along with their family members—in birchbark canoes. The only cash in their isolated settlements came from their small treaty-stipulated annuities. In 1859 the annuity payment averaged approximately $3 per person (United States 1859). Not even the wealthiest Ottawa emigrants could afford to purchase tools or to hire anyone to work for them.

The few small landholdings that remained in Ottawa hands after the land frauds of the 1870s were often located on the edges of non-Indian towns on or near the Ottawa reservations. One forty-acre parcel might serve as a home base for an extended family of fifty to one hundred people. Relying on inadequate federal distributions of livestock and tools, each family collectively invested many hours and labor clearing one- to ten-acre swidden plots by hand and building log houses. Indian Office promises to provide draft animals to power the agrarian transformation rang hollow as agent after agent failed to deliver them (Paybame et al. 1869). Even when oxen were delivered, the Ottawas to whom they were entrusted sold them (Lee 1878b). The Ottawas relied entirely on the help of kinfolk to clear land and build their new houses.

Few, if any, Ottawa farms ever grew beyond the most incipient stages of single-family, animal-powered agriculture. After 1870 the Ottawas' annuities ended, leaving them almost entirely without cash. Even if they had invested money and made fine farms, there were no local markets for Ottawa produce, and they had no cost-efficient way to deliver their crops to market even if ready purchasers had awaited. There was little or no incentive for the Ottawas to change their former cultural patterns beyond what was necessary to survive in their new environment. In 1894 a federal agent reported that the Ottawas of Mason County were raising no produce for market. During his September visit three-fourths of the Ottawas were in the woods gathering ginseng for sale (United States 1894).

In their precarious economic position, the Little River Ottawas remained horticulturalists who relied heavily on gathering, trapping, and hunting for their living. One special agent who visited the Ottawas in 1877 described their continued practice of felling trees, burning the brush and smaller pieces, and planting between the large logs. When he asked why they did not clear their fields like white settlers, they were astonished and answered, "I want to save the timber so my children will have a place to make sugar" (Brooks 1877b, 93).

Little River Ottawa control of and access to natural resources steadily decreased in the 1880s as the non-Indian population of Manistee and Mason Counties increased. When the Grand River bands arrived in the Manistee area in 1858, the non-Indians at Manistee totaled only 974 persons, and Mason County had approximately 200 more non-Indians. By 1864 the non-Indian population of Manistee had risen to 1,674 and of Mason County to 846; by 1874 Manistee's population had increased to nearly 10,000 non-Indians, with Mason County's population growing to more than 5,000. Throughout these years the Ottawa population remained stable at 500 to 600 persons (*History* 1882, 16, 26–29; United States 1894). Each year the Indians returned from gathering, fishing, and trapping expeditions to find more and more of their homes declared "abandoned" and title conveyed to new owners. Those Ottawas who used land as collateral for loans could not repay them and forfeited their property. Throughout the 1880s and 1890s the Little River Ottawas gradually collected on the few small tracts of land still owned by relatives, forming summer villages on the outskirts of lumber mill towns and railroad centers at Fountain, Freesoil, Hamlin Lake, Custer, Eden, and Brethren (Campau 1975; Campau 1990; Chandler 1990; Koon 1975; Medacco and Medacco 1991; Micko and Micko 1975; Pego 1991; A. Sam 1990; Waitner 1990).

Little River Ottawas received their first opportunity to work as wage laborers in the Manistee region in the late 1870s. Manistee and Mason Counties are bounded by Lake Michigan on their west, and the effect of warm lake waters extended the local growing season long enough to shelter fine apple, peach, pear, and cherry orchards. The first orchards were planted by Euro-American settlers in the 1860s. Twenty years later fruit growing had become the predominant commercial agricultural activity in the region. Ottawa extended families moved from orchard to orchard working as migrant laborers. They trimmed trees, picked fruits and vegetables, packed them for shipping, and hauled the fruit overland to Manistee and Ludington, where ships made regular runs to the rapidly growing lake ports of Chicago and Milwaukee. The arrival of a railroad at Manistee in 1882 expanded the market for local commercial fruit production as well as for Indian-harvested berries (*History* 1882, 11–13). The fruit and berry industry continued to grow throughout the early twentieth century.

Lumbering provided a second important source of wage labor. Euro-American lumbermen cut white pine logs on the Manistee River even before the Grand River Ottawas joined Kewaygushkum's band and settled permanently in the region after 1870. During the 1850s and 1860s lumbermen believed that Indians were unreliable and incompetent workers. In truth, few spoke English and therefore could not follow instructions of foremen and bosses. Non-Indian men from southern Michigan farms left their families each year and traveled north to cut pine timber. By the 1870s, however, a number of Ottawa men could understand English and could translate instruction for their kinsmen who could not. In the late 1870s Indian crews joined in the seasonal felling of virgin timber.

When the Little River Ottawas commenced working for cash payment, all ages and sexes participated. Ottawa men, unlike non-Indian lumbermen, rarely left their families at homesteads through the winter while they worked in the lumber camps. They moved their wives, children, and often their entire extended families to the camps. Women cooked and washed for their families and for the non-Indian lumber crews. In the spring when non-Indian laborers returned to their southern homes, Indians remained in the forest to bring the winter's logs to sawmills (Dembinski, Dembinski and Fischer, 1991; Miller 1975; Peters 1975; A. Sam 1990). For nearly forty years the Little River Ottawas incorporated lumber-camp work into their seasonal economic cycle. In the 1920s when the virgin timber stands in the Manistee River drainage were gone, Indian men could occasionally work in the forest cutting second-growth pine and poplar into bolts for paper and cardboard manufactured at Manistee. But with the end of lumbering, the greatest opportunity for wage labor simply ended (R. Sam 1990).

Seasonal farm labor, lumbering, and production from natural resources demanded the cooperation and mobility of the kin-based band organization. The Little River Ottawas continued to live in and value their traditional communities and culture well into the twentieth century. In 1900 a band of seventy-five people lived in log cabins and wigwams deep in the woods near the present town of Fountain to remain as far from civilization as they could. There they practiced their traditional religion and healing rituals undisturbed by clergy (Brooks 1877b; Gribb 1981, 163–166; United States 1894). Accounts of Works Progress Administration (WPA) case workers who visited the Little River Ottawas between 1933 and 1936 found the way of life little changed from forty years earlier (Armstrong 1938).

From the 1890s to 1940 Indian Village in Brown Township on the Manistee River served as a center of traditional gathering, fishing, and trapping. Many Ottawas who lost their allotments and homesteads near Fountain, Freesoil, Manistee, Hamlin Lake, Custer, and Crystal gathered at the Manistee River estuaries each fall to fish, shoot game birds, and trap furbearing animals (Michigan County Atlas 1977, 111). The Indian Village site had already been stripped of timber even before the land was offered for sale on the public market (Mallett n.d.). This sandy, barren land was unattractive to local timber speculators and farmers alike and had been used primarily by the Manistee Boom Company for its timbering operations (Manistee County 1930, 29). By 1916 the land had reverted to the United States and was purchased by the nephew of band chief Pacquotush, who in turn divided the village among households of the band (Manistee County 1916).

There were no wage labor opportunities available to the residents of Indian Village in the early 1930s. As WPA case worker Louise Armstrong (1938, 200) explained:

> Our case-workers soon visited the camp [Indian Village], and of course reported that all the Indians were in great need. There was no question about their being underprivileged, or that they needed care and a chance to have at least a minimum of subsistence just as much as did the white men. In their case, however, it was not just a matter of the depression. Apparently they had always been kicked about, and there is no knowing how many of them had died from want and disease in the process.

Armstrong was impressed by the degree of separation between the Ottawas and their non-Indian neighbors in the 1930s. She (1938, 201–202) wrote:

> There were scattered families of Ottawas living in other locations in the county, but the majority of them lived together in this particular section [around Indian Village]. . . . Relatively few white citizens in the city [Manistee] have any idea where the Indians live, and even the few who might venture on the River Road and the adjoining woodland trails would be likely to pass within shouting distance of those interesting primitive little houses without even noticing that they were there. The Indians, shoved away from the white community like unwanted stepchildren, might be cheated of their just share of some of the more civilized blessings of the county; but in their poverty and friendlessness, at least they had selected a paradise in which to live. . . .

Fig. 3.2. Members of the Pacquodush band, Indian Village, circa 1930. This extended-family photograph includes all generations from the 1860s removal period to the present, standing in front of one of the original homestead cabins erected on the Manistee River. The oldest members of this group left villages on the Grand River in 1860; the youngest people are now tribal elders. All participated in the mixed hunting, fishing, gathering, and wage-labor economy of the Little River Ottawas. (Photo courtesy of Little River Band of Ottawa Indians)

Their little cabins were usually about a quarter of a mile apart, though some were nearer together, and there were no white inhabitants except on the outskirts of the settlement. There were probably not much over a hundred Indians in the county, including the children.

The cabins were of different types. Some were log cabins which had been there since the lumber days. No one knew just how old some of them were. Most of them, however, were crude little shacks built more recently, from odd bits of material. Some were covered with tar paper. One attractive young couple, whom we came to know very well, had a cozy little one-room shack. . . . Only one of these families owned the land on which they lived. . . . The men of the family had cleared a little plot of ground, and they had quite a successful garden in the sand. The cleared ground was neatly fenced off with a rustic fence of white birch. The house was built close to the edge of the cliff, as many of them were. It was about forty feet above the riotous little trout stream [the Manistee River], and they had a windlass rigged to draw up water.

Indian Village was a residential center for Little River Ottawas until approximately 1940. From this village on a high clay bank overlooking the Manistee River, the men hunted, trapped, and fished the river bottom and marshlands below just as their ancestors had.

Related men hunted in extended family teams. Each family at Indian Village received a share of the fish or meat taken and part of any cash received for pelts (A. Sam 1990; Waitner 1990). The hunting and gathering were income-generating occupations. Local non-Indians were content to purchase or trade their agricultural produce for the Indians' wild harvest. This cooperation intensified during the Great Depression, when even the rural non-Indian population in Mason and Manistee Counties was forced to rely on wild foods that the Ottawas had harvested.

From 1915 onward, however, state and local officials threatened the Little River Ottawas with arrest and fines for hunting and fishing without licenses. Indeed, in 1928, the year before the stock market crash, young men from almost every Indian Village family were arrested for trapping muskrats (Olson 1928). From that time on there were so many arrests of Ottawa hunters and trappers that one tribal member who owned a printed version of the 1836 Treaty of Washington was delegated by the band to attend court proceedings to defend Indian Village men. He would turn the well-worn pages of the treaty and read Article 13 to local magistrates (Bailey 1994).

In addition to hunting and trapping, picking wild berries in the summer and fall continued to be a viable moneymaking venture for the Ottawas throughout the 1930s. Whole extended families moved to the wild blueberry and huckleberry marshes each year for three weeks to a month of picking. As they did with wild meats, the cooperating Indian families peddled their harvests to non-Indians at local farms and rural general stores and shared the income.

Cooperation in these joint economic ventures united extended kin groups and strengthened cultural ties, as well as providing for the economic well-being of the bands. In the camps both men and women worked on traditional black ash baskets and other crafts. Cultural links were forged with the past as children and adults sat around campfires making baskets and telling stories. Although the Manistee region had no significant tourist market for the finest of the Indian arts and crafts, the Indians could sometimes sell "fancy work" to people traveling through the area by automobile. The sturdy black ash hampers, market baskets, and bushel baskets found ready buyers at local farms (A. Sam 1990; Chandler 1990).

Between 1880 and the 1940s few, if any, Little River Ottawas held wage labor jobs that required school-acquired education. The first Indian known to graduate from a school in either Manistee or Mason County did so only in 1890, and he continued to make his living just as his kinsmen did—through seasonal collecting and occasional wage labor (A. Sam 1990). After 1880 some families sent their children to Indian boarding schools at Holy Childhood of Jesus Indian School at Harbor Springs, on Little Traverse Bay, or to Mt. Pleasant Government Indian School on the Saginaw Chippewa Reservation at Mt. Pleasant, Michigan. At these schools children had the opportunity to learn skills that prepared them for low-paying manual labor jobs useful in the local economy. Girls learned techniques for sewing and housework, but living in isolated rural farm communities, they had few, if any, opportunities to earn cash with these skills. Boys learned simple mechanics, agricultural techniques, house and sign painting, and other manual trades. Men plied their acquired trades in bridge and house construction and many other temporary jobs. Indians and non-Indians alike relied on a few Ottawa women for medical attention. These women used traditional knowledge of plant medicines and midwifery to earn cash (M. Bailey 1975; R. Bailey 1975; Campau 1990; Medacco and Medacco 1991; Oliver 1990; Peters 1991).

Interviews with Little River Ottawas who attended Indian boarding schools seem to indicate that, with some exceptions, few of the children who went there stayed for more than one or two years before returning to their homes. Those who traveled to Holy Childhood of Jesus at Harbor Springs were less likely to remain in school than were those who attended the Mt. Pleasant Indian School (Tawney and Thomas 1975; Battice 1975; Peters 1991). In both instances students had to leave their homes for years at a time. They saw little need for the lessons schools could teach and were often homesick, and their families needed them to help make a living. After 1900 Ottawa children in the Little River community more frequently attended public schools near their homes. For some students, this was their first opportunity to learn to read and write in English. Nevertheless, the inability to buy school clothes, racial difficulties with non-Indian children, and home chores caused frequent absences (Dobson 1978, 46–58; Chandler 1990; Glocheski 1991).

Lack of education, coupled with the racist attitudes prevalent in the local towns throughout the twentieth century, helped lock the Little River Ottawas into a cycle of subsistence and low-paying manual wage labor. Consequently, the Indians had few, if any, opportunities for economic advancement. Contemporary Little River Ottawa men and women alike report racial discrimination (Battice 1975; Dobson 1978, 139–142). The effect of racism was particularly clear to Ottawa women after the men of Indian Village left to fight in World War II. One woman reports that if an Ottawa applied for jobs in any of the local industries and used an easily identifiable Indian name on her applications, she would not be considered for the position. After this woman married and assumed a Polish name, she had no difficulty finding a factory job (Waitner 1990).

The collapse of the U.S. farm economy in the 1920s and the Great Depression of the 1930s sent ever-larger numbers of Little River Ottawas outside of their rural settlements to work. Just as railroads opened new economic opportunities by encouraging fruit production, automobiles spurred migration to cities across Michigan. Indian men continued to work in projects such as building roads and laying sewers, but they also labored in downstate factories. By the mid-1930s Muskegon and Grand Rapids, the urban areas nearest to Manistee, each had small communities of Little River Ottawas who migrated to the cities to work in factories, especially in foundries and paper mills.

Michigan's urban industries offered a far more reliable source of cash income than did any other kind of work available to the Little River Ottawas, yet very few of these industrial migrants considered the "Indian town" sections of southern cities to be their permanent homes. Each fall families returned to Indian Village to hunt and trap, seemingly forgoing reliable cash incomes for less lucrative work. They did so for good reason. The urban Indian ghettos of the 1920s and 1930s were not pleasant places to live. The low pay of unskilled laborers assured that Indians lived in urban poverty, without their gardens and wild foods and without enough cash to replace these sources of food and income (Glocheski 1991). Several families often inhabited one house, and this overcrowding increased tensions among individuals. Once the Indians moved to the urban environment, the social controls that regulated their daily lives were gone. Alcohol use and physical violence increased in urban Indian settlements (Glocheski 1991). Children moving from rural to urban environments were targets for abuse by their non-Indian classmates, either because of their poverty or because of their Indian heritage. All of these forces brought early Ottawa urban dwellers back to their parent communities regularly throughout the early twentieth century (Chandler 1990; Lempke 1990; Medacco and Medacco 1991, Pego 1991; A. Sam 1990).

The 1940s saw a restructuring of the economic and social order in the Little River Ottawa community. For the first time since the Euro-Americans had arrived in Michigan, Ottawa men did not gather to hunt and trap in the Manistee River basin. They enlisted in the U.S. Army to fight on the European and Pacific fronts, until every able-bodied Indian man in Indian Village up to forty years old was gone (Lempke 1990). Many of these men returned to Michigan after the war and brought with them skills that qualified them for work in the postwar boom in Michigan's auto industry. Some settled in Detroit, where they found good-paying full-time employment. Others took full-time jobs in Grand Rapids and Muskegon. This generation of men and women is now returning to the Little River Ottawa community.

Several World War II veterans who returned to Manistee after the war did so as heroes whose deeds had been widely reported in the local press (Campeau 1990; Koon 1990). These few men could finally be "trusted" to hold jobs as milkmen, roadcrew bosses, or workers for the federal government in the Manistee National Forest, a newly established national forest that included much of the Little River Ottawas' reservation and hunting territory.

Wartime industries in Manistee and nearby Ludington had employed Indian women in wage labor occupations for the first time. Those who speak of factory work usually refer to jobs in local paper and cardboard factories. In some instances the Ottawa women continued working in local factories until retirement in the 1970s. In rare instances Ottawa girls received nurse's training at a Manistee school, but these professionals moved outside of the community. The entry of Ottawa women into the workforce completed the Little River Ottawas' transition to modern wage labor.

WORK IN THE LITTLE TRAVERSE BAY COMMUNITIES

The Little Traverse Bay Odawa community differs greatly from that of its relatives at Manistee. The forces that shaped this northern Michigan community were cultural, political, and geographical. When faced with the threat of removal, the Little Traverse Bay Odawas chose to transform their historic towns and economic system to meet the demands of the U.S. market. This feat required all the skills of able political leaders, who won support for new economic pursuits by interpreting change in terms of Odawa cultural values. The Odawas' northern location, above the line of most rapid Euro-American settlement, both protected their access to the Great Lakes fishery and gave the Little Traverse Bay community enough time to create a place for itself in the new Michigan economy. As the extractive frontier economy gave way to lumbering and, later, tourism, the Little Traverse Odawas received education in Catholic and government-sponsored schools, which allowed them to compete with non-Indian locals for jobs as blacksmiths, coopers, tailors, and seamstresses. As a result, the Little Traverse Bay Odawas continued to inhabit the towns that their ancestors had founded in the nineteenth century. This continuous habitation in the center of their traditional band territory afforded them greater opportunities for successful accommodations with the U.S. economic system than the Little River community enjoyed.

The Little Traverse Bay Odawas had selected the location of their homeland for the political and economic opportunities that it afforded. Their communities formed following the French and Iroquois peace of 1670. Odawa towns that had dispersed after the fall of Huronia first gathered from their exile on Lake Superior and Green Bay to reclaim their former townsite at modern-day St. Ignace on the Straits of Mackinac. Living astride the major water transportation route from Montreal to the west, the Little Traverse Odawas used their corn horticulture and fishing to provision the fur trade throughout much of the eighteenth century. Their women married or formed liaisons with French and Métis traders. The offspring of these unions and their Indian kinsmen served as boatmen and guides for traders who passed by, assuring their people access to the best available contemporary European technology and a secure living in the colonial economy (Petersen 1985, 37–71; White 1991, 42–47, 65–69, 99–104).

Between 1670 and 1740 the Little Traverse Odawas moved their principal fields and villages to the Lake Michigan shores west and south of the straits. By 1740 more than one thousand five hundred people occupied towns of longhouses stretching from Ahnumawatikomeg (Pray Tree Place or Cross Village) to Wagnagisi (or Crooked Tree, later called Aptawaing or Middle Village). They maintained smaller seasonal villages farther south at Weekwitonsing (Little Bay Place, later called Harbor Springs), at Mukwasibing (Bear Creek, later called Petoskey), and at

Shingwaksibing (Pine River, today called Charlevoix). Seasonal sugar camps and fishing-trapping settlements extended along the Lake Michigan coastline from the north shore of Lake Charlevoix in the south to Mackinac at the northern tip of the Lower Peninsula, to the Beaver Island archipelago, and along the south shore of the Upper Peninsula from Drummond Island to Bay de Noc.

During the French regime Jesuit missionaries lived in the Odawas' principal towns and helped link the Odawa and French peoples. They performed marriages between women of influential Odawa families and French traders, which cemented interethnic economic ties. Although Odawa economic and political influence lessened during the British regime (1761–1812), the Odawas continued to provision the traders who passed through the straits and to gather furs into the early decades of the nineteenth century (Petersen 1985, 37–72; White 1991, 214–215).

When the Euro-Americans arrived at Little Traverse Bay following the War of 1812, Odawa leaders there assessed their options for dealing with the new kind of Europeans. The fur trade alone would not support the large Odawa towns. The sources of local furs were exploited beyond their capacity, and forests in favored southern territories along the Kalamazoo and Grand Rivers were falling to Euro-American axes. Leaders who had participated in war campaigns from New York throughout Ohio country clearly understood the U.S. intention to replace Indians with Euro-American farmers. Indian leaders no doubt had many conversations with other tribes that had already been given the option of settling on reservations and becoming Christian farmers or moving westward beyond the line of Euro-American immigration. Faced with potential dislocation from the territory the community had inhabited for more than one hundred years, the Odawas adopted a political strategy that had worked for them in the past—economic change to match a changing political landscape (McClurken 1988, 127–160).

During the 1820s Odawa leaders joined their French Métis relatives in inviting Catholic priests to build a permanent church at Little Traverse Bay. The Odawas hoped that resident clergymen would provide them with cash and tools to intensify their regional horticulture and fishing for the U.S. market, with schooling for their children in the mathematical and language skills they would need to survive in the new political and economic climate, and with political advocacy to help the Odawas keep their homes and natural resources. In 1829 the Catholic Church, responding to the Odawas' requests, built a new mission at Harbor Springs.

Convincing the Little Traverse Odawas to abandon a way of life that had served them well for two hundred years was no small task. The success of their transition is directly attributable to skilled leadership. Men such as Assiginac (Black Bird/Starling), Apakosigan (Smoking Mixture), Muccatabenese (Black Hawk), Nawamashkotta (Center of the Prairie), Kishigobenese (Day Bird), Kanapima (The One They Talk About), and Pabamatabi (He Who Pulls) were directly responsible for setting examples and constant exertions to persuade their people to follow them. Four of these men—Assiginac, Apakosigan, Kishigobenese, and Muccatabenese—held considerable status in Little Traverse society based on their war experiences against the United States during the War of 1812 (Taylor 1986, 50–53). These men began the movement to convince the Odawas that rapid transformation of their economy offered the most viable opportunity to remain in their homes. These leaders persuaded their most reluctant constituents to support the agenda for economic change by reminding them of the great influence the Odawas had held the last time that Jesuit missionaries had lived in their villages— during the heyday of the Mackinac fur trade. Within five years more than half of the Little Traverse Bay Odawas claimed some affiliation with the Harbor Springs mission (McClurken 1988, 127–160).

Building towns after the Euro-American style required more capital than missionaries could provide. For the first few years government blacksmiths and carpenters at Fort Mackinac, on nearby Mackinac Island, lent their services to the tribe. In 1835, however, the federal government threatened to cut these vital services when the Odawas needed them most as a way to pressure the Little Traverse Odawas to sell their Michigan lands. The government hoped that the bands would accept new lands in Kansas in exchange for new capital to use in "civilized" economic pursuits.

Word of government plans for a treaty reached the Little Traverse community early in 1835. Leaders of the mission-affiliated Odawas at

Weekwitonsing quickly recognized the threat to their community and acted to forestall any attempt at removal. The Odawas immediately sent a delegation to Washington to make a counteroffer. They offered to sell the United States their interest in lands of the eastern Upper Peninsula and islands in Lakes Huron and Michigan in exchange for restored services. Secretary of War Lewis Cass would not negotiate for these lands without the presence of the Chippewas, who had a stronger claim to them. Cass proposed that the Odawas return home, gather a delegation of all the Michigan Odawa bands and the Chippewas of the eastern Upper Peninsula, and return to Washington to negotiate a treaty for all of their Michigan lands. The Odawas were made to clearly understand the limited range of their political options. In the winter of 1835 and spring of 1836 the Odawas and Chippewas returned east and negotiated the 1836 Treaty of Washington.

The 1836 treaty contained an ambiguous stipulation for the Odawas to move from their Michigan reservations to new lands in Kansas after five years if they chose to leave Michigan. These provisions worried Odawa leaders, who understood the dangers of clearing land and investing cash and labor in new towns to which they had weakened titles. Nevertheless, they and the other Catholic Odawas remained committed to the course of developing their towns, whose population still numbered about one thousand five hundred people. Between 1836 and 1855 these Odawas bought an estimated eighteen thousand acres of land within the boundaries of their reservation, including land in and surrounding their towns. They virtually ceased their involvement in the fur trade; increased the size of their gardens; planted new fruits, vegetables, and grains; built houses and outbuildings; greatly revised male and female work roles; and sent their children to school. Young people learned European-style carpentry, blacksmithing, and farming, as well as reading and mathematics (McClurken 1988, 90–91, 195, 220–285).

Although the annuities that the Odawas received under the 1836 treaty were small, the Little Traverse bands did not have to abandon the investments they had made from the 1820s through the 1850s and relocate, as had the Little River Ottawas. For the Odawas, the annuities from the 1855 treaty further enhanced the development of the communities they had built using their 1836 annuities. Although the Odawas enjoyed more stable village locations and had more disposable wealth, there is no indication that they entered into a wage labor economy until the late 1870s. As in the Little River Ottawa community, the Odawas' cooperative kin-based system of reciprocity remained the primary economic ethic that allowed the community to build stable and substantial homes without resorting to wage labor between Indians themselves. Indeed, the Odawas also continued their seasonal rounds well into the 1870s. Federal investigator Edward Brooks (1877b, 91–94) reported that the Little Traverse Odawas

lead a nomadic life, subsisting largely by hunting and fishing. When they leave their homes on an expedition of this kind or for the purpose of doing a few days work to supply their necessities, the whole family goes together, a temporary wigwam is erected in which they all live, and while the husband is at work the wife and children subsist the family by picking and selling berries, fishing, or making baskets. Their idea of a homestead is a place on which to make sugar in the spring, raise a few potatoes and sufficient corn to supply their bread during the year, and to have a home upon, to which they may at any time return. Most of them have small houses in the old Indian villages to which they repair during the fishing season for the double purpose of convenience, and in order that the women and children may be on hand to clean and cure the fish which are caught. During the winters as has been remarked they reside largely in the villages for comfort and social advantages and for the purpose of schooling their children. They are largely under the control of the Catholic priests, who have, as the Indians informed me, told them that it was not necessary for them to live on their lands during the winter, and have at the same time required them to send their children to school during the season. About the first of March such of them as have been in the villages return to their land to prepare for sugar making. Generally I think they remain on the land until about the first of June when the summer fishing commences. During the summer they alternate between the fishing grounds and their farms visiting the latter for the purpose of caring for their growing crops, and in the fall they return again to their land for the purpose of gathering their corn, digging and bringing their potatoes, and other work.

Wage labor at Little Traverse developed slowly. The Odawas produced and sold thousands of tons of maple sugar and continued to manufacture snowshoes and other Native technology for sale. These activities earned a great deal of cash without the involvement of wage labor. As early as the 1830s a few people found work at the U.S. Army post on Mackinac Island or labored as helpers at the government-sponsored blacksmith shop, school, or the Catholic Church, though there were few of these jobs available. The Little Traverse Odawas earned most of their cash by using new technology to intensify their fishing operations. In these activities Indians most likely paid Indians for their labor. The Little Traverse Odawas also became known for building plank boats that allowed some families to catch, salt, and sell their fish as far south as Chicago (McClurken 1991, 54–59).

Successful political and economic adaptation to the available niche in the northern Michigan economy continued in the Little Traverse Bay communities throughout the 1860s. In 1862 their principal town at Harbor Springs had two stores, a post office, and a hotel to accommodate the passengers of steamboats that regularly docked there (DeLaVergne and Graham 1981, 9). By 1870 their towns were boasting streets lined with both log and frame houses made of lumber cut by their own community members at their own sawmills. In 1855 the Indians of the Little Traverse Reservation reorganized Emmet County, forming a political entity that roughly followed their reservation boundary. The Odawas consciously added a second political tier to their traditional band organization, electing county officials from the most prominent families on the reservation. Community members who had been educated in Catholic schools became Democrats and filled county offices from postmaster to county clerk. Michael Keway, Paul Wasson, Francis Nabassaih, Andrew Blackbird, Amable Ettawageshik, and Joseph Payant served in a number of elected posts, placed there by an Odawa electorate composed of their own families (McClurken 1991, 77).

In 1875 the Odawas' successes in developing their own resources for themselves in the context of a largely Indian society ended. The 1872 Act for the Restoration to Market of Certain Lands in Michigan, allowed Odawas who had not yet received individual farms under the allotment clause of the 1855 treaty to select homesteads and receive fee-simple patents

Fig. 3.3. Harbor Springs, circa 1870. The Little Traverse Odawas at Wagnagisi constructed their own town of log and frame houses, with a store, mail carrier, blacksmith, school, and the church in the center of this image. Between 1872 and 1880 most of the dwellings were claimed by non-Indians. Many of the Odawa families moved to the hill, from which this image was made, and into the remaining woodlands behind the church. Holy Childhood of Jesus Church and Indian School remained a vital part of the Little Traverse community throughout the twentieth century. (Photo courtesy of Little River Bay Bands of Ottawa Indians)

to their land (United States 1872). Selectors had six months to make and register their claims. At the end of that time the land within the reservation would be open for settlement by non-Indians. The Indian towns situated on Little Traverse Bay were the region's prime real estate, the point of shipping, and the center of what would rapidly become a thriving tourist industry. In 1872 the Grand Rapids and Indiana Railroad opened a line that ran to Petoskey, only ten miles from Harbor Springs (Ruonavaara and Rodgers 1981, 17). Within a short time non-Indians outnumbered Odawas on the Little Traverse Reservation. Since Indians held patents to many of the town lots and surrounding lands, immigrants devised simple strategies for dispossession. Squatters abounded everywhere, and few Indians could protect their property from the non-Indians who simply settled in and began clearing forestland. A second method for dispossessing the Odawas, the familiar technique of declaring Indian homesteads "abandoned"—even if the Indian owner remained on the parcel—became a favorite tactic. Because Indians could not find justice in local courts or from the federal government, they almost always lost their homes (White n.d., 114–122; Brooks 1877b).

A third technique of dispossession used by non-Indians proved even more effective in gaining possession of title to Little Traverse Reservation lands and the buildings on them. By 1880 the non-Indian population of Emmet County had reached approximately 3,072. The Odawa population had probably grown little since the 1850s, so non-Indians outnumbered the Odawas by more than 2 to 1 (Ruonavaara and Rodgers 1981, 15). For the first time in twenty-five years the Odawas could not elect their own candidates to county government. Non-Indians won election over Indian candidates by a large margin and redefined the laws that governed Indian participation in the local political system. Non-Indians also controlled taxation, and shortly after 1880 tax assessments on Odawa lots in Harbor Springs rose to a record $38 per year (Ogabegijigokwe 1877; Brooks 1878b). Few, if any, Indians could pay this price to live in their own towns. The process of setting these taxes was perfectly legal. No matter how loudly the Indians complained of their mistreatment, federal officials paid little attention to the Odawas' problems.

During the first years of the settler invasion would-be non-Indian farmers faced difficult times. It took settlers much time and effort to clear lands.

They had to supplement what they could grow with berries, greens, fish and game, and especially passenger pigeons. The Odawas provided settlers with some of these provisions but also faced direct competition with settlers who used whatever wild crops they saw fit wherever they found them (Ruonavaara and Rodgers 1981, 11–16).

Within one short decade, between 1872 and 1882, the Odawas found themselves living in small enclaves on the outskirts of the towns that they themselves had built. Six realtors at Harbor Springs alone provided lots for a rapidly expanding non-Indian business community there. By 1878 Harbor Springs had two general stores, a meat market, a bakery, and a confectionery shop, in addition to stores specializing in liquor, jewelry, hardware, and millinery. Two doctors and three attorneys set up office in the town. A barber, a blacksmith, a photographer, and a newspaper joined the local businesses. Three hotels stood along the main street, and three ferry lines ran between Harbor Springs and Petoskey (Baker and Graham 1981, 17–18).

For the first time in history, the Odawas made the greatest share of their living by laboring for non-Indians. The arrival of train service from Grand Rapids in 1873 and its extension to Harbor Springs in 1881 spurred the cutting of Emmet County's hardwood timber for the burgeoning furniture business. Lumber camps operated year round and by 1900 supported nearly 75 percent of the Emmet County economy (Baker and Graham 1981, 24). The pattern of lumber-camp life that Little River Ottawas experienced in the 1870s was repeated in the north. Little Traverse Odawa families left their homes to live for long seasons in lumber camps. Some men also formed crews to make extra money by collecting hemlock bark for local tanneries.

Regular passenger train service from Chicago and Grand Rapids delivered tourists, lured to the blue waters and fresh cool breezes of Little Traverse Bay. The number of large resort hotels in Harbor Springs grew from three in 1878 to eleven hotels and seventeen rooming houses in the early 1920s (Baker and Graham 1981, 24). The Odawas staffed many maintenance and service jobs. Women worked as laundresses, maids, and cooks. Men also cooked, but their jobs included building, construction, maintenance, and groundskeeping as well. Odawa men crewed on the ships carrying passengers between other lake ports and the resorts. Indian fishermen supplied sumptuously set tables with fresh whitefish and lake trout. The Odawas found a ready market for their traditional basketry and porcupine quill embroidery and even entertained resorters with Hiawatha plays (McClurken 1991, 88–111). The resorts, together with fishing and hunting, provided regular but low-paying seasonal employment that the Odawas could count on year after year.

Unlike the Little River Ottawas who had to leave their villages to attend school, the Little Traverse Bay community hosted its own boarding school at Harbor Springs. The Franciscans opened Holy Childhood of Jesus Indian School in 1884 and continued to educate Little Traverse children for nearly one hundred years. Like all other late-nineteenth-century Indian boarding schools, Holy Childhood operated on a strict schedule, with the children attending classes half the day and then working on the school farm, in shops, in bakeries, in laundries, or in training for manual labor jobs. Because Holy Childhood served primarily Odawa children, few former students reported alienation like that experienced by Indian children who attended public schools at Manistee. Training at Holy Childhood taught Little Traverse boys and girls useful skills that they could later employ in the towns they lived in, especially among the wealthy seasonal resorters. Although not all children enjoyed the rigid school program, they could at least see a reward for their learning. Occupational training at Holy Childhood, coupled with seasonal wage labor near home, provided the Little Traverse Odawa communities with a stability not equaled among other bands living elsewhere in Michigan.

The Little Traverse Odawas entered the downstate wage labor market later than did the Manistee Ottawas. A small number of the hundreds of Odawa students who attended Carlisle, Haskell, Hampton Institute, or Mt. Pleasant between 1890 and 1940 used their advanced training in places as far away as Oklahoma and California. Many, however, returned to their homes within a few years. As at Manistee, the post–World War II economic opportunities, especially in the auto industry at Flint and Detroit, began to lure community members from Petoskey, Harbor Springs, Middle Village, and Cross Village. The larger, more permanent population at Little Traverse

Bay, however, assured that emigrants could regularly return to a core community that continues to live in Odawa historic towns today.

The evidence of Odawa cultural continuity is greater on Little Traverse Bay than in any other Michigan Indian community. Pageants and, later, powwows; arts and crafts; the political actions of their leaders; continued affiliation with Catholic Indian churches; and an often-told history have clearly marked the distinctiveness of this Indian community. From 1870 through the 1940s and beyond the Odawas have also been distinct in their role as low-paid, seasonal wage laborers in a local economy.

CONCLUSION

This chapter has described the transition of two Ottawa communities from independent bands that earned their livings from direct exploitation of natural resources in their home territories to wage laborers in the larger U.S. political economy. The decline in Ottawa status from self-sufficient producers to lower-class wage laborers began in 1836 when Indian people throughout western Michigan lost control of the natural resources in their territories. It continued as they were divested of the greatest part of their resources during the nineteenth century. We have seen, however, that different communities selected particular resources in their former estates to incorporate into new economic patterns.

The options open to these two communities in selecting culturally satisfying accommodations to the expanding U.S. economy rested on many variables beyond the Indians' immediate influence. At Manistee the early and effective efforts of settlers to acquire title to Ottawa homesteads and allotments ended any hopes that federal officials or the Indians themselves had of creating a class of Christian Indian farmers. The Indians, however, continued to defend and use their treaty-preserved rights to hunt, fish, and collect on public lands.

Exploitation of wild plants and game throughout the Manistee River drainage allowed the Little River Ottawas to make a living in a reduced portion of their tribal estates, harvesting resources that non-Indians thought of as unimportant. The increased availability of seasonal work in lumber camps in the 1870s and as farm laborers after 1880 combined with the older Odawa subsistence pursuits to provide an adequate living to the bands until the 1920s, when the entire Michigan farm economy collapsed. The seasonality of wage jobs and race-based discrimination prevented Little River Ottawa children from attending local schools to learn new living skills—though there is no evidence that doing so would have enhanced their status in the local class structure. The resulting marginalization may have played a major role in the community's dispersal when higher-paying jobs became available during and after World War II.

The Little Traverse Odawas enjoyed several advantages that their southern kinfolk did not. In their position north of the line of primary Euro-American agricultural settlement, the Little Traverse communities retained control of their key resources far longer than did the Manistee people. During the years between the major land cession in 1836 and dispossession in the 1870s, these Odawas intensified production of their historically important natural resources, including horticulture, fishing, and production of maple sugar. They built towns that rivaled other frontier settlements throughout the state, they educated themselves and their children in the ways of the Euro-American political and economic system at their own pace and on their own terms, and they even created a county government that mirrored those of the non-Indians around them. Throughout this process the Little Traverse people viewed these changes through their own cultural lenses, building a sense of social and political consensus that bound their community.

Dispossession from their towns and natural resources was no less devastating for the Little Traverse Odawas, however, than it had been for their Manistee relatives. They too became marginalized as large numbers of settlers transformed the landscape and assumed local economic and political control. Nevertheless, many Little Traverse Odawas were able to remain in their own towns. They occupied a vital niche as low-paid workers in the lumber and resort industries that dominated the regional economy into the 1930s. Catholic institutions in their community provided vital support to Indian families. The proximity of education and work formed a viable, secure base for the local Indian community.

The effects of wage labor patterns established in the late nineteenth and early twentieth centuries and the availability of modern economic resources remain relatively unchanged today. Surveys conducted in the Little Traverse and Little River communities since 1990 indicate that temporary, seasonal wage labor or low-paying service employment is still the rule within these communities. The net effect in both the Little River and Little Traverse communities has been continued poverty.

According to the *1990–1991 Biennial Report* of the Michigan Commission on Indian Affairs (1992), the median income for Indian families in Michigan was $15,916 per year. Statewide figures, including both urban dwellers and rural communities such as Little River and Little Traverse, indicated that 49 percent of all Native American families lived in poverty. This poverty was exacerbated by a Native American unemployment rate of 54 percent in Michigan. The median age of death was sixty-three years, nine years earlier than that of other Michigan residents. Statewide, 58 percent of all Native American households headed by women lived below the poverty line (Michigan Commission on Indian Affairs 1992, 25, 43).

Michigan Indian poverty is greater in northern and rural areas such as Emmet, Charlevoix, and Cheboygan Counties—the home region of the Little Traverse Bay bands. The Little Traverse Odawa community is at least a three-hour commute from any major manufacturing or urban center. Those Odawas who seek good-paying jobs often live away from their parent community. Most of those who remain in the community throughout the year hold seasonal service-oriented jobs associated with the modern hospitality industry of tourism, yachting, and resorts. The Little Traverse Bay Bands Tribal Council estimates that 75 percent of their members live below the poverty line (Michigan Commission on Indian Affairs 1992, 25, 43).

The Little River Ottawas, with their closer proximity to larger towns and industrial centers at Muskegon and Grand Rapids, have a greater opportunity to benefit from wage labor than do the Little Traverse Odawas. It is a historical irony that the band that lived in the greater poverty throughout the nineteenth century today enjoys a higher standard of living than the band that enjoyed a higher standard of living in the early days of U.S. expansion into Michigan.

A survey conducted by the Little River Ottawas in 1992 showed that the average income in this community was approximately $17,184 per year. Thirty-seven percent of the Little River Ottawas who were employed worked of living than the band that enjoyed a higher standard of living in the early days of U.S. expansion into Michigan.

A survey conducted by the Little River Ottawas in 1992 showed that the average income in this community was approximately $17,184 per year. Thirty-seven percent of the Little River Ottawas who were employed worked in factories, 6 percent had "professional" jobs, and 27 percent worked in service jobs. Approximately 30–35 percent of the Little River Ottawa households fell below the poverty line (Confederated Historic Tribes 1992, 3–7).

Many Michigan tribes are currently enjoying an economic boom brought about by on-reservation casino gambling. The gaming industry has provided seven federally acknowledged Michigan tribes with capital to create their own economic development programs and employ their own people. The Little River and Little Traverse communities have not shared in this economic development. Administrative termination by the Bureau of Indian Affairs in the late nineteenth century interrupted their government-to-government relationship with the United States. As "unacknowledged" tribes these bands have not been able to use federal resources to generate tribal economic programs until recently. On September 21, 1994, President Bill Clinton signed legislation that reaffirmed the government-to-government relationship between the United States and the Little Traverse and Little River peoples. The governments of these tribes have now accepted the task of reversing more than one hundred years of economic adversity.

4

INDIAN EDUCATION AND THE WORLD OF WORK IN MICHIGAN, 1893–1933

ALICE LITTLEFIELD

Vocational education was one of the explicit concerns of the Bureau of Indian Affairs (BIA) boarding school system throughout its history. From the time Colonel Richard Henry Pratt (1964) opened the doors of the Carlisle Indian School in 1879 until World War II, training in agriculture, blacksmithing, carpentry, domestic science, and other "trades" was a central part of the curriculum in these schools and explicitly promoted as a major key to successful assimilation.

Toward this end most students divided their day between the classroom and vocational training or work assignments, with the latter activity contributing substantially to the maintenance of the schools. School farms and livestock provided substantial quantities of food for school kitchens. Students did much of the cooking, cleaning, and laundry necessary to school operations. Girls made sheets and towels, as well as their own clothing. Boys learned carpentry, masonry, and other skills by carrying out routine maintenance of school facilities.

In addition to vocational training on school premises, some of the schools used the "outing system." Under such arrangements students were placed with non-Indian families for the summer or for longer periods of time. Students did domestic and agricultural labor for such families in return for their keep and a small stipend. This experience was intended to enhance students' vocational skills, as well as foster the assimilation process. Robert Trennert (1983) has described the role of the outing system at the Phoenix Indian School in funneling Indian labor into the Arizona economy.

Over time, however, it became evident that there was a lack of congruence between the specific kinds of vocational training provided in the BIA schools and the economic opportunities available in the areas from which the students were drawn. Critics complained that the students had few opportunities to practice the skills they had learned once they returned to their home communities, nor were they prepared to compete for jobs in the non-Indian world (Szasz 1974, 2). The Meriam Report (Meriam et al. 1928, 383) concluded; "Very little of the work provided in Indian boarding schools is directly vocational in the sense that it is aimed at a specific vocation which the youngster is to pursue, or based upon a study of known industrial opportunities, and vocational direction in the form of proper guidance, placement, and follow-up hardly exists at all."

Elsewhere, I (Littlefield 1991, 1993) argue that the BIA schools played an important role in helping channel Native Americans into the wage labor force. The policy statements of bureaucrats and educators, the content of the curriculum, the outing system, and the placement services for graduates all indicate that gainful employment of Indian people in the cash economy was a significant goal of the system (Hoxie 1984; Kvasnicka and Viola 1979; Leupp 1910), but the outcomes were not always the ones envisioned. There were complex motivations at play among those involved, including students and their families, and there were built-in structural contradictions that broadened the gap between intentions and results.

In part, the BIA failed to develop appropriate vocational programs because most government bureaucrats and educators misunderstood the cultures and economic systems from which their charges were drawn. They failed to recognize or systematically devalued the survival strategies that had kept indigenous peoples alive in spite of the loss of resources many of them had experienced. Bureaucrats and educators downplayed or ignored altogether indigenous horticultural and subsistence skills, developed over centuries and often finely tuned to local environmental variations, and attempted to replace these with agricultural methods that were sometimes environmentally unsound and often out of reach for people with little access to capital (Carlson 1981; Hurt 1987). Bureaucrats, in their assumptions of Indian laziness and their eagerness to instill values presumed to be lacking, appear to have been ignorant of the long history of American Indian involvement in the cash economy as fur traders, lumbermen, commercial fishermen, sugar producers, and even plow agriculturalists (Feest and Feest 1978; McClurken 1991; Moore 1989).

Although the heavy emphasis in the boarding school curriculum on skills related to agricultural production may have been poorly attuned to the economic opportunities students confronted, the schools nonetheless played a significant role in preparing their charges for entry into the wage labor force. Along with basic literacy and vocational instruction, the BIA educators sought to instill punctuality, industriousness, honesty, obedience, and orderly habits. In doing so, what they achieved was not so much assimilation as proletarianization—the formation of subjectivities and dispositions appropriate to workers in the surrounding capitalist economy.

THE MT. PLEASANT INDIAN SCHOOL

The interplay of contending forces and motivations is evident in the case of the Mt. Pleasant Indian School, one of the boarding schools in the BIA system. Located in Mt. Pleasant, Michigan, on land originally part of the Isabella Reservation,[1] the school was in operation from 1893 to 1933. Over this forty-year period residential industrial schools dominated the education of indigenous peoples in the United States. In the same period a significant proportion, perhaps as many as half, of all Michigan Indian children attended the Mt. Pleasant School for some of their schooling.

The curriculum and other practices at Mt. Pleasant were very similar to those of other federal Indian schools. The school provided eight (and, later, nine) years of instruction. Except for children in the early primary grades, all students spent only half the day in class; the other half they worked in the kitchen, laundry, dairy barn, or other assignments regarded by BIA educators as part of preparation for adult life. Some of these activities were specifically designated as vocational classes; others were referred to as work details and consisted of the routine cleaning and other activities needed to maintain the schools.

As in the other BIA schools, daily schedules at Mt. Pleasant were highly regimented. The students rose and went to bed on signal and marched in military style from one activity to another. Although the amount of required marching was reduced in the late 1920s and early 1930s, disobedience, tardiness, and infractions of rules were still systematically punished, usually with extra work assignments or denial of privileges and occasionally with beatings with a strap or rubber hose.

"FOR EACH BOY A FARM OF HIS OWN"

From the time the school was founded in 1893, there was a heavy emphasis on training in agriculture. In 1895 the school superintendent expressed the goals of the curriculum as follows:

> When the pupils leave this school they must return to agricultural communities. At their future homes, either upon small farms belonging to themselves from allotment or as employees of white farmers, these Indians must make their living. They need then first and most important of all a practical and working knowledge of agriculture as carried on in this State, then a sufficient intellectual training to enable them to transact the business of a small farm, and finally development of such habits and characters as will make them industrious, frugal and reliable citizens. The girls need the training that will make them good and saving housekeepers, faithful and worthy wives. (Cited in Bureau fo Indian Affairs n.d., 2)

The school began operations on a 200-acre farm site and then expanded to 360 acres a few years later. On these lands policy goals were pursued as students raised potatoes, corn, wheat, and hay; kept vegetable gardens, apple orchards, and vineyards; and cared for chickens, pigs, dairy cows, and draft horses.

In discussing vocational training for boys, the school's annual report for 1912 reiterated the goals of the curriculum: "The great fact which this department tries to impress upon the minds of the boys is for each boy to have a farm of his own when he leaves school and to work it

Fig. 4.1. Mr. Pleasant Indian School students with team of horses. The school curriculum stressed training in agriculture and other manual trades. (Photo courtesy of Clarke Historical Library, Central Michigan University)

himself and thus to be self supporting and to have a home garden and thus always to have plenty to eat" (Bureau of Indian Affairs 1910–1932, for 1912, 12–13).

In spite of such statements, the emphasis on agricultural training appears to have had a limited relationship to the home circumstances from which the students came. Aboriginal subsistence systems in the Great Lakes region had long involved a combination of maize horticulture and fishing, hunting, and collecting. For climatic reasons there was somewhat less reliance on crops in the northern than in the southern parts of Michigan. The southern bands (largely Potawatomi, Odawa, and Huron) lost most of their lands in the years between 1814 and 1840 through treaty concessions, removal (both forced and voluntary) to the west, and strategic retreats to locations more northerly and hence less desired by Anglo-American settlers. Because reservations in Michigan were largely phased out under the terms of removal treaties, Indians could retain land in the late nineteenth century only as allotments or privately owned holdings. Although some adopted plow agriculture during this period, many Michigan Indians became involved in other ways of producing both food and a cash income, such as commercial fishing, maple sugar production, and lumbering (Clifton 1978, 736–740; Feest and Feest 1978, 777–780; McClurken 1991).

Data from the annual reports filed by the Mt. Pleasant School suggest that many of the students' families depended on lumbering or itinerant fruit harvesting for cash income. The following excerpt from the 1912 annual report is revealing, both of the economic conditions of Michigan Indians and of the judgments of those conditions made by the superintendent:

> There are about 10,000 Indians in this state. . . . Some are very progressive, own property, pay taxes . . . are marine captains and engineers, firemen, railroad men, lumbermen, farmers, and fishermen, and all of these with very few exceptions, send their children to the public schools. But still another class of our Michigan Indians are the poorer ones, who . . . are found in the Indian villages or settlements adjoining some lumber camp, town, or summer resort. This is the class of Indians with whom we have most of our dealings and from which the great majority of our pupils come. They are a nomadic people like their forefathers, and are continually moving from place to place, at the different seasons of the year, where ever [sic] they can find work and make a living. During the winter a great many are employed in the lumber camps and take their families with them to those forsaken out of the way places. (Bureau of Indian Affairs 1910–1932, for 1912, 4–5)

Later reports summarized similar conditions:

> The Michigan Indians, many of them having sold or traded away their land for a mere nothing forty or fifty years ago, are now wretchedly poor. (Bureau of Indian Affairs 1910–1932, for 1916, 12)

> They [Michigan Indians] live wherever there is work for them to do, in logging camps in the winter and in the berry and beet fields and fishing

sections in the summer; in fact, anyplace where they can secure employment, temporary or otherwise. There are special cases where some own good-sized farms, are doing well, and are on equal standing in their communities with the white people. But the roving life of the majority naturally puts the children far behind their white brothers. (Bureau of Indian Affairs 1910–1932, for 1917, 9)

The 1930 report made the following comment about the nearby Indian population of Isabella County: "The Indians earn their living mostly by labor among the farmers and in the local industries, especially the oil fields of late. . . . A considerable number of baskets are made. . . . The local sale is small and the price obtained is not as remunerative as it should be" (Bureau of Indian Affairs 1910–1932, for 1930).

Some of these statements may reflect the Indian Service educators' negative view of nomadic lifestyles, as well as their desire to justify the need for a residential school by emphasizing the rootlessness of the Michigan Indian population. Recent oral histories conducted with former students and other data tend to qualify, as well as confirm, the notion that a large part of the Michigan Indian population was dependent on seasonal wage labor in the early twentieth century.

I have interviewed thirty-five former students who attended the Mt. Pleasant School in the 1920s and early 1930s.[2] Of these, less than half came from families that owned land, and those that had land usually did not farm it. Much of the land seems to have been marginal, in plots too small to provide a living, or shared with several relatives. Only six of those interviewed grew up on farms, and all but one of those farms were operated by relatives other than the speaker's parents. In four cases the landowning families did not live near their land. Several of those from landless families mentioned that their grandparents had owned land but that it was no longer in the family when they themselves were children.

Former students were also asked about their fathers' occupations. Eliminating non-Indian fathers, duplications resulting from interviews with siblings, and missing data, I have occupational information for twenty-two Indian fathers (see Table 4.1). Of these, one was primarily

Table 4.1. Occupations of Twenty-two Indian Fathers

Occupation	Number Employed
Lumberman	6
General laborer	5
Construction worker, road worker	3
Farmer (owner-operator)	3
Farm laborer	2
Fisherman	2
Factory worker	2
Carpenter	1
Tailor	1
House painter	1
Baker	1
Miner	1

Note: Some fathers were reported as having more than one occupation.

a farmer on his own land. Two of the fathers had operated their own farms for a time but left farming for urban jobs in the 1920s while their children were still young. Two fathers (both located in communities on the Great Lakes) were commercial fishermen. All of the others were wage laborers, including six who worked in lumber camps or sawmills, four in skilled trades, and two in factories. Only two of the wage laborers worked primarily in agriculture, although some of the five men reported as general laborers occasionally did agricultural work.

Additional information about the students' families comes from surveys carried out by Lela Cheney (1933), a social worker employed in 1932–1933 to assess the effects of closing the Mt. Pleasant School on the children and their families. She made visits to several counties and submitted reports, some of which are available in the National Archives. These reports indicate that in the depths of the Great Depression, the majority of rural Michigan Indians were living in considerable poverty. Most had little or no land, and few had jobs (see Table 4.2). The data

Table 4.2. Survey of Indian Families, Four Michigan Counties, 1933

Family Characteristics	Leelenau	Mason	Oceana	Muskegon	Total
Families visited	50	13	30	25	118
Family members	274	64	154	110	602
School-age children	78	17	43	42	180
Children enrolled at Mr. Pleasant	22	3	20	14	59
Families owning land [a]	25	6	6		37
Families on relief [b]	0	12	3	25	40

Source: Data from Cheney (1933).
[a]Land holdings varied from 3.5 to 75 acres. In Muskegon County all of the families surveyed were living in the city of Muskegon.
[b]Public relief services varied from work programs in Muskegon County to no relief services at all in Leelenau County.

suggest that agricultural opportunities for Michigan Indians were very limited by the 1920s and 1930s.

Available evidence indicates that even in earlier years few of the Mt. Pleasant graduates pursued agricultural careers, contrary to the hopes of school administrators. Documents listing occupations of former students are few but mention mostly nonagricultural forms of wage work, including employment in the Indian Service for some. The 1912 annual report summarized the previous year's graduating class:

> Three of the boys have attended high school this past year. . . . One of the boys is in Sault Ste. Marie at work on the locks, and the other boy was given the position of assistant carpenter here at the school. . . . One of the girls was married and now has a home of her own, three have been working in the homes of the best families in Mount Pleasant and are very well thought of, and the fifth girl was offered the position of assistant seamstress here. (Bureau of Indian Affairs 1910–1932, for 1912, 6–7).

In 1917 Superintendent Robert A. Cochran was apparently feeling some frustration with the opportunities available to the school's graduates:

"The greatest trouble with the pupils going out to make their livings, is that the white people place them on the same level which the negro holds in the south, they want them as servants and not as associates" (Bureau of Indian Affairs 1910–1932, for 1917, 10). By 1925, however, Cochran's views had shifted:

> A goodly number of our graduates are doing well, earning good wages.
> . . . A few have settled on farms, but the majority have gone to the city and have secured good jobs with the various automobile companies. Others, unfortunately, have turned out rather poorly, have not married well and have reverted to old conditions and become idlers, worthless to themselves and to every one else (Bureau of Indian Affairs 1910–1932, for 1925, 1–2)

Even though few Michigan Indians maintained their own farms, the school's emphasis on agricultural training continued through the 1920s. An analysis of the school's semiannual report for 31 December 1926 (Bureau of Indian Affairs 1926) indicates that a total of 136 out of 210 boys were assigned to instruction in a trade or industry during the fall quarter (see Table 4.3). Thirty-one of these were assigned to the farm or garden, work that would likely have occupied a larger number of boys during the spring. Another 18 boys were assigned to the dairy or poultry shed. A group of 33 boys, mostly fourth and fifth graders, were assigned to the boys' residences, presumably to do routine cleaning.

Forty-one boys, most of them in the sixth through ninth grades, had assignments classified as engineering or carpentry. Interviews with former students indicate that these assignments included such activities as powerhouse operations, routine plumbing and wiring repairs, and the making of storm windows. Although these activities could be considered more related to the industrial jobs available during the period under discussion, few of the men I interviewed worked as adults directly in the fields in which they had been trained at Mt. Pleasant.[3]

Among the 15 men interviewed, only 2 reported working in farm labor as adults. Most held more skilled jobs than the men of their fathers' generation, including such occupations as welder, electrician, accountant, truck driver, first mate on a dredge, and substance abuse counselor. Several reported receiving useful vocational training at Haskell Indian

Table 4.3. Work Assignments, Mt. Pleasant Indian School, December 1926

Work Assignment	Boys	Girls
Bakery	4	
Carpentry	17	
Cooking		34
Dairy	14	
Dining room		43
Engineering	24	
Faculty club		2
Farm	29 [a]	
Garden	2 [a]	
Gymnasium	2	
Hospital	2	15
Kitchen	1	22
Laundry	2	6
Office	2	
Poultry	4	
Residences	33	5
Sewing		26
Other		3
Total	136	156

[a]These numbers were probably larger in the spring and summer quarters than in the fall.

School or in the military, though not at Mt. Pleasant. Five of the men (33.3 percent) completed high school, 1 as valedictorian in a rural school, and 3 also spent some time in college. In general, these men were more successful economically than those who did not finish high school. Those who did not continue their education at all after leaving Mt. Pleasant were most likely to have been dependent on seasonal labor in agriculture or other fields.

In spite of the lack of congruence between the specific vocational skills taught at Mt. Pleasant and the kinds of employment held by its graduates, several men mentioned the ability to get a job as the major advantage of having attended an Indian boarding school. This was especially true for those who had continued their schooling elsewhere. These men felt that their education at Mt. Pleasant had given them the foundation to successfully pursue additional training.

"Good and Saving Housekeepers"

Although vocational training for boys bore little specific relationship to their later occupations, the picture for girls is somewhat different. Their training in "domestic science" was more closely related both to their mothers' occupations and their own later participation in the labor market.

Mt. Pleasant educators stressed training for girls as a preparation for the housewife role but also saw this training as linked to possibilities for wage employment. This excerpt from the 1911 annual report suggests one such link:

> In the laundry the work is done mostly by machinery, so, in order to teach the girls to do laundry work with the most limited outfit, for when they return to their homes they will have few facilities for doing laundry work, they are encouraged to wash for the employes [sic] using tubs and rubbing the clothes on wash boards, and the employes pay them for the work. In this way girls become expert laundresses and make good wages doing this work when they return to their homes especially during the vacation months working in the summer resorts near their homes. (Bureau of Indian Affairs 1910–1932, for 1911, 5)

Although most of the mothers of the people I interviewed were primarily housewives, a number of them worked at least for a time in the paid labor force. Of the twenty-four Indian mothers for whom data are available (see Table 4.4), occupations included cooking, cleaning, or laundering for restaurants or tourist hotels; domestic service in private homes; production of traditional crafts for sale; sewing; and seasonal labor in food processing plants. Several of the mothers are represented in more than one of these categories. Ten of the mothers had been students at federal boarding schools, including Mt. Pleasant, Carlisle,

Table 4.4. Occupations of Twenty-four Indian Mothers

Occupation	Number Employed
Housewife	12
Restaurant or hotel worker	5
Private domestic service worker	4
Craft producer	4
Seamstress	2
Seasonal food processor	2

Note: Some mothers were reported as having more than one occupation.

or Haskell, compared with only four of the fathers. Perhaps female graduates viewed their experiences more positively and were therefore more likely to seek similar schooling for their children.

In the fall of 1926 work assignments were reported for 156 of the 204 girls at Mt. Pleasant (Table 4.3). The largest number, 56, were assigned to cooking or other kitchen work, such as doing dishes. Most of these were in grades five through seven. Forty-three third and fourth graders were assigned to the dining room to set tables and clean up. Twenty-six girls in grades four through eight were assigned to sewing and mending, and 15 girls, mostly ninth graders, were assigned to the hospital as nurse's aides. Only 6, all fourth graders, were assigned to the laundry. Apparently their work consisted mainly of folding clothing. The records indicate that boys, rather than girls, were assigned to clerical work in the school office. Only in a few cases were boys and girls assigned to the same work areas (see Table 4.3).

In the official lists of work assignments little mention is made of the work the girls did in cleaning the rooms and baths of their own residences. Although only 5 girls were specifically assigned to the girls' residences, 33 boys were assigned to the boys' residences. For girls, such routine cleaning must have been done in addition to the assignments listed in the reports. It is also worth noting that, at least in 1926, girls were more likely than boys to have a work assignment and at lower grade levels. The value of the work performed by the girls could be consider-

Fig. 4.2. Advanced sewing class, Mt. Pleasant Indian School. (Photo courtesy of Center for Cultural and Natural History, Central Michigan University)

able. In 1922–1923 the sewing room produced $2,684 worth of items, including 274 dresses, 186 towels, 13 dozen tablecloths, and 21 dozen sanitary napkins (Bureau of Indian Affairs 1910–1932, for 1923).

The available documents, as well as interviews with former students, indicate that girls from the Mt. Pleasant School often worked in private homes during the summers, either before graduation or soon after, cleaning or taking care of children for families in Mt. Pleasant and other parts of Michigan. When the school closed in 1933, Mary Foley, the girls' adviser, arranged for several of the older girls to stay with non-Indian families in Detroit and suburban Royal Oak, doing domestic work in return for their keep and the opportunity to attend public high schools. Although some of these placements did not last long, those involved still describe themselves as "Miss Foley's girls."

The women I interviewed were more likely to work outside the home as adults (fifteen out of eighteen, or 83.3 percent) than were the women of their mothers' generation (twelve out of twenty-four, or 50 percent). Most began their wage-earning careers as domestics, but only one remained in this occupation for much of her adult life. In contrast to the men, the subsequent occupations of the women were often related to the skills emphasized in the Mt. Pleasant curriculum: waitressing or other restaurant work, hospital or nursing home employment, and sewing. One woman worked most of her adult life in a home for emotionally disturbed children. The continuities between vocational training and later employment for these women may simply reflect the greater sex stereotyping of women's occupations in general during the early twentieth century and the consequently greater ability of educators to anticipate relevant fields of training.

Of the former students interviewed, a slightly higher proportion of the women (eight of the twenty, or 40 percent) than of the men (33 percent) finished high school, and one of these was valedictorian of her parochial school class. A few pursued postsecondary training. In general the high school graduates were able to secure better jobs than those who left school earlier. Two women who pursued secretarial training at Haskell eventually secured office jobs after facing some discrimination by employers. One of these women later held a responsible accounting position with the state of Michigan.

Among the women interviewed, most report that the training they received at Mt. Pleasant was useful, even when they did not use the training directly in the labor force. They applied their knowledge of cooking, sewing, and nursing in their homes, and some mentioned these skills as the most valuable things they learned at Mt. Pleasant.

LAND, LABOR, AND EDUCATION IN MICHIGAN

The Mt. Pleasant School was established with the stated goal of training Indians in those skills necessary to operate their own farms and compete on an equal basis with Euro-American settlers. From the school's inception, however, this goal was seriously at odds with the conditions facing the Michigan Indian population. The land retained after the removal era had been largely allotted in individual holdings after the Civil War. By the 1890s many Indians in Michigan were landless, having lost both allotments and other kinds of holdings in a variety of ways (McClurken, this volume; Rubenstein 1974). In the early twentieth century they survived primarily through a combination of wage labor (much of it seasonal), craft production, gardening, and subsistence hunting and fishing.

Among those families that retained land, many apparently did not farm it. Some lacked capital to compete with white farmers. Some had moved to urban areas to take advantage of more lucrative job opportunities. Others were apparently driven off the land by the agricultural depression of the 1920s and 1930s. In 1933 nearly all of the Indian landowning families in Leelenau County were in arrears on their property taxes and safe from the auctioneer only because of a statewide moratorium on tax sales (Cheney 1933).

In Isabella County Indian allotments were commonly leased to Euro-American farmers who used them for planting annual crops. In 1932 the annual report included the following comment about the allotments on the Isabella Reservation: "There is very little farming done by the Indians upon their own land. Their work is mainly among the neighboring white farmers. The last two years have not been very good for this kind of labor and our Indians, in consequence, are in poor circumstances. The tracts still owned by the Indians are small, ranging from five to forty acres each" (Bureau of Indian Affairs 1910–1932, for 1932, 2).

There is reason to believe that leasing may have been less common elsewhere in the state. In most of the Upper Peninsula a short growing season left few opportunities for farmers of any ethnic group. In the western Lower Peninsula where Odawas and Potawatomis were concentrated, commercial fruit farming had developed. Such farming demanded substantial long-term investment in orchards or berry fields, and the Euro-American fruit farmers may not have been interested in annual leases. For the Odawas in such areas, leasing land to Anglo farmers was apparently uncommon (McClurken, 1992a).

In spite of many obstacles, there were some Indian families that farmed successfully. Paradoxically, Cheney's survey and my interviews with former students suggest that the children of successful farmers were the least likely to attend the Mt. Pleasant Indian School. Farm families often kept their children at home and sent them to local public or mission schools, either because they could afford to do so or because the children's labor was useful on the farm. Both former students and documentary evidence indicate that by the 1920s Mt. Pleasant was in large part an institution emphasizing care for orphans and the children of the poor. In this respect it may have differed from some of the western Indian schools.

> The necessity for the Mt. Pleasant Boarding School is . . . in reaching those whose home conditions are such that they cannot attend a public school. It is more in the nature of an orphan institution than that of probably any other school of its kind in the Service. There is considerable poverty and distress in certain sections and this, with the orphans, the children from broken homes, almost constitute our enrollment. (Bureau of Indian Affairs 1910–1932, for 1930, sec. 3)

Among the former students I interviewed, loss of a parent was a common and often the major factor precipitating the decision to send the child to Mt. Pleasant. The high proportion of orphans at Mt. Pleasant was also mentioned in the Meriam Report (Meriam et al. 1928, 405). In the school's later years, at least, parents or guardians requested admittance for many more children than could be accommodated. The decision to accept students was based largely on material need: "The desire of the Office was closely followed in the enrollment of children, in that the most needy who asked for enrollment were accepted only. . . . Many of the children now here would be charges of the State if there were not this school" (Bureau of Indian Affairs 1910–1932, for 1931, 4).

As I have already pointed out, the annual reports indicate that Mt. Pleasant educators knew their students were not headed for careers as independent farmers. Yet the inappropriateness of the vocational program was not confronted directly until the school's last few years. When Superintendent Louis E. Baumgarten took over the administration of the school in 1926, he requested sums for upgrading vocational instruction but by 1930 had this to say:

> After spending nearly 4 years in Michigan, I am coming more and more to the conclusion that this school is not giving the Indian children of Michigan all the education they should have. Michigan is primarily an industrial state. There should not be much else taken into consideration for the Michigan children, except training in some industrial course. (Cited in Bureau of Indian Affairs n.d., 5)

Acting on this assessment and in response to the currents of reform then sweeping through Indian education, the superintendent hired a full-time manual training instructor for the 1931–1932 school year, and fewer boys were assigned to the farm and dairy operations (Bureau of Indian Affairs 1910–1932, for 1932).

The agricultural training curriculum survived at Mt. Pleasant for as long as it did for both practical and ideological reasons. As Trennert (1988, 150–181) points out for the Phoenix Indian School, funding for the BIA schools remained relatively constant in the 1910s and 1920s in spite of the inflationary process set off by World War I. To balance the books, the schools had to maximize internal production of food and other goods and rely on student labor for routine maintenance. These were the conditions that led to widespread criticism of the schools in the 1920s, including charges that the schools provided inadequate diets, were unhealthful, and exploited child labor (e.g., Meriam et al. 1928, 314–340, 388–391).

BIA educators justified the curriculum partly in ideological terms. Rigid discipline and the routine performance of menial tasks were seen as useful in instilling desired work habits and character traits, such as diligence, punctuality, and obedience. This ideology was absorbed not only by the educators but also by many of the students themselves. Former students ranked academic skills as the most useful things they had learned at Mt. Pleasant, but some also mentioned discipline, self-reliance, respect for others, and good work habits as skills that had helped them adjust to adult life and survive the difficult years of the Great Depression. These comments from former students represent opinions shared by many of them:

> You learned to do a lot of things, which has helped me through the years up 'til now: sewing, cooking—well, work. . . . We had work to do and I learned to do it well. (Church 1992)

They were Army-regimented. But it did you some good; you learned discipline, taking orders. . . . And one of the most important things: you learned to work there. That's why, later in life, most of these people weren't lazy, 'cause they learned to work there. (Spruce 1992)

We had routine, you know, bedtime and our meals and discipline. . . . And of course your schooling. You went to school every day; you didn't miss one day. (Shorten 1992)

THE MAKING OF AN INDIGENOUS WORKING CLASS

In spite of the many contradictions within both statement and practice, it could be argued that the Mt. Pleasant Indian School contributed significantly to the educators' goal of assimilation. Although the students did not become farmers or farm wives, they were largely incorporated into the increasingly industrialized wage labor force. Most spent their adult lives working and living among non-Indians in urban settings, and several married non-Indians. In large part their lives have been similar to those of the urban working class in general.

However, it is also clear that most of the former students I interviewed have not lost their sense of Indian identity. Several have been active in urban Indian centers or in tribal organizations; a few have held elective or appointive positions in tribal government. Most of those belonging to unrecognized tribes have been supportive of efforts to gain federal recognition. Several have chosen to return to reservations or historically Indian communities in their retirement years. Some are active in Indian churches, although they are divided on the question of incorporating "traditional" Indian spirituality into the Christian framework.

A few of the interviewees have been involved in teaching indigenous languages or crafts; others have enrolled in such classes. Some have worked with the public schools to introduce elements of Indian tradition, one as a coordinator for a federally funded Title IV program. Most take considerable pride in children or grandchildren who are active in Indian affairs. In the course of interviews I was often shown examples of baskets or other craft items they or members of their families had made or photographs of offspring in powwow outfits. At least two of the former students follow the powwow circuit as part-time traders.

With a few exceptions, their indigenous origins are clearly an important source of identity for these people. But it is an identity that is largely compatible with living in an urbanized, English-speaking society with a capitalist economy. They have joined the working class, but they have not left all of their heritage behind. In this sense proletarianization may better describe the effects of the boarding school experience than does assimilation. Michigan's indigenous population was drawn into a process of class formation affecting not only the region but also the United States and the rest of the globe during the period of rapid industrialization in the late nineteenth and early twentieth centuries. For several decades the majority of Indians in Michigan have lived in urban areas. Can my research subjects be described, then, as part of an indigenous proletariat?

Michigan's industrial labor force has long been ethnically heterogeneous, drawing significant numbers of Eastern European, Mexican, and Arab immigrants; former sharecroppers, largely African American, from the South; and Anglo-American farm youths from Michigan and Appalachia. Many of these workers have maintained ties with their home countries or communities through visits, ownership of property in the home area, and return migration when laid off or pensioned. For Michigan farmers within commuting distance of the automobile plants, simultaneous employment in the factory and continued production on the farm were facilitated for many years by seasonal layoffs, which often coincided with periods of agricultural work. In the "rural" area of southern Michigan where I spent my childhood, simultaneous or alternating involvement in agriculture and industrial employment was common.

With the "deindustrialization" of the Midwest, including plant closings and increased automation in the Michigan automobile industry, there has been an accelerated process of return migration to home areas affecting both indigenous and nonindigenous workers. For Michigan Indians, this process has also been stimulated by the economic development programs of the federally recognized tribes, especially by the development of the gaming industry during the 1980s. Some of the tribal communities are now in a position to provide jobs, medical care, and housing to members. For those Saginaw Chippewas living on or near the Isabella Reservation today, for example, jobs in gaming and other tribal enterprises far outnumber those in nearby factories. The rise of gaming activities and tribal bureaucracies has also significantly expanded the employment opportunities for reservation-based women.

The process of reconstitution and revitalization of tribal communities has also resulted in a resurgence of identification with the indigenous cultural heritage. The process of reverse migration has not, however, reversed the proletarianization process. Rather, the home communities themselves have now become sites of a new process of class formation involving divisions between workers and managers within tribal enterprises and bureaucracies, divisions that are reconciled to some extent through appeals to a common cultural heritage and common interests vis-à-vis the outside world.

If many Michigan Indians are part of an indigenous working class, to what extent did the federal system of Indian education contribute to this end? Clearly it was only one factor among many. Efforts at Christian conversion and participation in the global economy had been part of the Indian experience in the western Great Lakes for two centuries. One could argue that proletarianization was already well under way when the Mt. Pleasant School opened in 1893 and that it would have continued in any case, given the inexorable economic pressures facing an increasingly landless indigenous population.

Nevertheless, the boarding school experience facilitated the process of proletarianization, not necessarily by imparting specific vocational skills (which, as already pointed out, were often irrelevant to the emerging labor market), but by imposing the behavioral routines, patterns of social interaction, and personal dispositions necessary for adapting to an industrial economy. To an extent the schools were also successful in instilling the consumer tastes of the mainstream society and in convincing Indian youths that traditional ways were backward and inferior. As one former student explained: "I liked getting into an environment where we had modern plumbing. . . . We didn't have this up north, see. And we had regular meals. It was a good balanced diet." (Spruce 1992). Electricity, several kinds of labor-saving machinery, and medical services were among the other boarding school amenities that many students lacked at home.

The boarding schools also contributed to the increased use of English. At Mt. Pleasant, as in the other schools, English was the language of instruction and of daily communication. By the 1920s Mt. Pleasant educators were no longer imposing harsh punishments for "talking Indian." Most of my sources reported that they had never experienced or even observed any punishment for indigenous language use. This relaxation of discipline was probably due less to enlightened policy than to the reality that many children already knew English when they arrived at the Mt. Pleasant School. Some were second-generation boarding school students; others had learned English from a non-Indian parent.

The boarding schools thus served in part as instruments for imposing cultural hegemony. This process was neither smooth nor totally successful, and it occasionally led to the creation of new forms of Indian identity (Littlefield 1989; McBeth 1983). In spite of these contradictions, however, the Mt. Pleasant School was able to position its charges to make the transition from rural to urban wage labor, a move that often brought them significantly better incomes and living standards than their parents had enjoyed. It is this process of facilitation that former students refered to when they insisted that the boarding school experience had prepared them to earn a living.

5

CHEYENNE WORK IN THE HISTORY OF U.S. CAPITALISM

John H. Moore

We might suppose from reading the standard ethnographies of the Cheyenne Indians that they contributed very little to the economy of the United States. The image of Cheyenne men presented in standard ethnographic sources is much the same as that evoked by James Earl Fraser's famous sculpture *End of the Trail*, which stands in the Cowboy Hall of Fame in Oklahoma City. In this enormous sculpture, bronze copies of which occupy places of honor on wealthy ranchers' desks all around Indian country, a windblown Indian warrior sits, head bowed, on his horse, defeated and dejected, deprived of his freedom to wander the plains, and apparently anticipating a future in which he will mainly sit around the Indian Agency waiting for his rations. Early reports of Indian agents also sound this same theme of demoralization and inactivity, with their constant references to Cheyenne men as "coffee cooler Indians" and "blanket Indians," unwilling to work and unable to adapt to sedentary life. Cheyenne women, who have received relatively little attention from artists, ethnographers, or Indian agents, are seen stereotypically as shy but chaste souls who might be persuaded to sell beadwork if they need the money but who otherwise are creatures of the camp and teepee.

These are only the Cheyenne examples of some very general stereotypes about Native Americans that have been part of Anglo-American ideology for a long time. The purpose of this chapter is to subject at least this example to a "truth test" concerning the nature and extent of the Cheyennes' work in the pre- and postreservation period. Here I consider three examples: (1) the buffalo robe trade from 1815 to 1864, (2) seasonal wage work as it developed from 1890 to the present, and (3) craftwork, especially moccasin making, as it has existed from aboriginal times to the present. My methodology is partly economic and partly ethnographic: I look at the dollar values of commodities, and I report field observations of Cheyenne work and emphasize the opinions of living Indian informants about their history and culture. This chapter is part of a developing tradition that already comprises Rolf Knight's study (1978) of Indian labor in British Columbia and Lawrence Weiss's analysis (1984) of Navajo economy.

THEORETICAL CONSIDERATIONS

Although Marxists are committed to the kind of analysis that gives priority to a labor theory of value, calculations are expressed more often in money values than in hours. The reason for this, of course, is that capitalism generates its data predominantly as dollars rather than as hours worked. Marxist economists would be operating at a severe disadvantage if they had to convert dollars to hours at every step of their analyses. Nevertheless, Karl Marx (1906, 45) was very clear in saying: "A use-value, or useful article, therefore, has value only because human labour in the abstract has been embodied or materialized in it. How, then, is the magnitude of this value to be measured? Plainly, by the quantity of the value-creating substance, the labour, contained in the article. The quantity of labour, however, is measured by its duration, and labour-time in its turn finds its standard in weeks, days, and hours."

Anthropologists, however, have less opportunity than economists to take their measures in money. When exchange is informal, takes place within the family, or is done by barter and delayed reciprocity, as is normal among American Indians even now, no dollar values can be easily attached. However, it is also unusual for ethnographic fieldworkers to collect the kind of time-and-motion data necessary to calculate the values of goods and products in terms of their labor value. One of the few examples is John Roberts's monograph *Zuni Daily Life* (1965), in which five households were recorded for their minute-by-minute activities for one day each. Roberts, however, published his database as it was, without subjecting it to further analysis.

French Marxist anthropologist Maurice Godelier (1977) has attempted to quantify labor values in a tribal economy, in this case in New Guinea. After examining the amount of labor needed by the Baruya to produce bars of salt, he then studied the rates of exchange of salt for other commodities, such as axes, machetes, dogs, feathers, and shells. Unfortunately, Godelier was overcome by an attack of structuralism before he published his analysis, and so he concluded that salt was valuable, not so much because of its labor content, but because it embodied various psychological sentiments, such as scarcity, expertise, and association with certain rituals.

There is also the issue of the immortality of labor value once it is created. This issue has often been raised as a moral one in regard to the contribution of slave labor to the economy of the United States. According to this view, labor, once it is converted into use value, continually circulates in a national economy, multiplying and reinforcing the labor of the generations that follow. That is, as use value is consumed, it replicates and diffuses in the economy, enriching the lives of unborn generations. Therefore, the slave ancestors of black Americans created a sizable proportion of the present wealth of the United States, even though they were not paid a fair wage for their labor, and even though their descendants do not own a fair share of present resources. In this chapter I argue that the same is true for Native Americans.

THE TRADE IN BUFFALO ROBES

Treaties written with Indian nations continue to confound the U.S. legal system, creating many unsolvable dilemmas and contradictions. Historical writers continue to wonder why these treaties were written in the first place since they have done so much to impede monopoly capitalism in its desire to exercise complete control over Indian land and resources in the United States. The original reasons for these treaties are transparent, however, if we conceive of early political interactions with Indians, not as nation to nation, but as Indian nations to particular sectors of U.S. capitalism. Marxists recognize that the U.S. state represents the class interests of capitalists almost exclusively, but we also recognize that there are competing sectors within the capitalist class that can rise and dominate the other sectors for a time, giving the class, and the state, a particular character within a particular historical period.

Among the most problematic treaties written with Indians, from the standpoint of the industrial capitalists of a later period, were those written in the early nineteenth century to ensure the success of the fur trade by formally recognizing Indian nations and assigning them discrete and exclusive territories within the area claimed by the United States. These treaties continue to haunt U.S. capitalist interests to this day, especially the energy and mining companies that wish to further annex the Indian land guaranteed by the treaties.

On the Great Plains, the source of buffalo robes in the nineteenth century, two early expeditions were especially designed to collect information and write treaties that would expedite the fur trade. These were the Lewis and Clark Expedition of 1803–1806 and the Atkinson Expedition of 1825. Thomas Jefferson's instructions to George Clark included the charge to collect some specific information about the numbers and disposition of the Indians. Jefferson wrote, "The commerce which may be carried on with the people inhabiting the line you will pursue renders a knowledge of those people important." Specifically, Jefferson asked them to investigate the "articles of commerce they may need or furnish, and to what extent" (Hosmer 1917: xlviii–xlix).

General Henry Atkinson's expedition up the Missouri to the Yellowstone in 1825 also had as an explicit purpose the protection of the fur trade (Nichols 1965, 49). The treaty written between Atkinson and the Cheyennes in 1825, for example, is almost entirely about the fur trade. In Article 1 the Cheyennes "admit the right of the United States to regulate all trade and intercourse" with them. In Article 3 they agree further to trade in places "designated and pointed out by the President of the United States." And finally in Article 4 they agree to arrest and deliver to U.S. authorities "any foreigner or other person" not legally authorized to trade (Kappler 1904, vol. 2, 232–234). It was stipulations like these that ensured the success of the fur trade in the newly acquired

Louisiana Territory and ensured that certain influential persons would have monopolistic control over the trade as it developed.

The total extent of the trade in buffalo robes is difficult to estimate with great precision. It was just one part of the fur trade and did not develop until the beginning of the nineteenth century. The beaver trade, which began much earlier and was also more extensive geographically, produced much more wealth, as compared to buffalo robes or deerskins (Phillips 1961; Chittenden 1935).

One methodological problem in estimating the trade in buffalo robes is that some sources do not distinguish between "hides," which were merely raw buffalo skins dried and folded, and "robes," which were the tanned, softened, and finished buffalo skins produced by Indian women and used as lap robes in carriages. Another analytic problem is whether the robe totals appearing in documents of the New Orleans trade constituted a separate supply from the southern plains or whether the New Orleans traders were merely reselling robes shipped down the Mississippi River from St. Louis. To avoid the possibility of counting some robes twice, I have counted only the Missouri River robes, which were mostly shipped from St. Louis by the American Fur Company and some smaller operators.

Beginning with a "few hundred" robes in 1790–1800, the robe trade grew to a peak of about 110,000 robes per year in 1848. As the herds diminished and Indians were confined to reservations iduring the years from 1864 to 1878, the number of robes produced annually declined and finally ceased altogether about 1884. These figures indicate that Indian people continued to produce fine robes for several years after they had been confined to reservations.

I estimate that for the entire period of the robe trade 5.5 million robes were produced by the tribes of the Missouri River valley (Chittenden 1935, 807; Gregg 1970, 141; Hornaday 1887, 437; Roe 1951, 448–503). If we estimate further that approximately ten thousand to thirty thousand Indian women were involved in producing robes, the approximate number of adult women in these tribes, then each woman was producing roughly five to ten robes per year. The total value of these robes, as sold in eastern cities, was $6 to $25 each, with an average price of about $9

(Hornaday 1887, 437; Hurd n.d., 55; Wurttenberg 1822; Hart, Taylor, and Co. 1876). The total value of the buffalo robe trade from the Missouri Valley in the nineteenth century was therefore roughly $50 million.

The Cheyenne Indians were among the most diligent producers of buffalo robes on the plains. Compared to the territories of the southern tribes, the Cheyenne territory was rich in buffalo, especially the forks of the Platte, which they occupied in the early eighteenth century. As buffalo populations diminished in that area, the Cheyennes moved to eastern Colorado and finally to the upper Republican and Smoky Hill Rivers in the 1850s, where the last of the central herd was killed about twenty years later. The tribes south of the Cheyennes, the Kiowas and Comanches, had difficulty preserving robes and skins because of the warmer climate, and they also had more difficult access to traders. By contrast, the Cheyennes had close relations to Bent's Fort in Colorado, where early in the century William Bent had married the daughter of the most prestigious Cheyenne leader, Gray Thunder (Lavender 1954). The Cheyennes were similarly proximate to and intermarried with the traders on the south fork of the Platte River (Moore 1987, 186–187; Lecompte 1978).

My estimate of the amount of labor required to make buffalo robes is aided by James Mooney's (1903) step-by-step ethnographic description of the tanning process. To this I add, based on my own research, an estimate of the labor involved in training buffalo horses, making equipment, and hunting buffalo. I was fortunate to interview three of the last Cheyenne horse trainers, members of the "horse lodge," and I incorporate their information in the following analysis. My consultants were Edward Red Hat Sr., Roy Bull Coming, and Henry Mann.

To make calculations possible, I have estimated the useful life of hunting horses and equipment. Of course, my results are only as good as my estimates, which are as follows. I assume that a horse is ready for training at age eighteen months, in the fall of its second year. During that time the horse has been "gentled" almost daily by the boys who herd the horses, as well as by the owner. After the training period the horse hunts for four years, killing 200 buffalo. I am assuming that the saddle and tack also last for four years and that three bows and eighty

Fig. 5.1. Unidentified Cheyenne women scraping buffalo hides near Fort Keogh, Montana, circa 1878. (Photo by Stanley J. Morrow, courtesy of Smithsonian Institution National Anthropological Archives)

arrows are used in this period. The labor time for all these activities, according to consultants, is as follows:

Gentling	600 hours
Training	200
Making saddle	80
Making tack	30
Making 3 bows	120
Making 80 arrows	320
Finding buffalos	800
Total	2,150 hours, or 10.7 hours per buffalo

Considerably more time is required for women to scrape and tan a buffalo hide, according to Mooney (1903). The steps include several

Fig. 5.2. Unidentified Cheyenne woman scraping a hide preparatory to tanning, near Colony, Oklahoma, circa 1915. (Photo by Mrs. E. C. Grinnell, courtesy of Museum of the American Indian, Heye Foundation)

wrappings and soakings, several scrapings, and several applications of tanning solution, followed by a lengthy process of graining and dressing whereby the skin is made supple. The women observed by Mooney were tanning cow hides, which are about 30 percent smaller than buffalo hides. Therefore, although Mooney's process required 55.7 woman-hours per hide, about 70 hours should be needed for a buffalo robe. When the figure is added to the 10.7 hours of men's work, the result is approximately 80 hours of Cheyenne work to produce a dressed buffalo robe suitable for trade. That is, each buffalo robe presented to traders for exchange represented 80 hours of necessary labor done by a Cheyenne family. So what did the producers get in exchange for their labor?

Although the robes were sold in the East for $6 to $25, depending on decoration and condition, the Indian producers did not receive nearly that amount. In fact, the Indians received no money at all but were paid in trade goods. The usual payment for a robe was from $1.50 to $2.50 in goods, depending on size and condition (Wurttenberg 1822; Hart, Taylor, and Co. 1876). But the trade goods were usually marked up 80–2000 percent over the price the trader had paid in St. Louis

(Sunder 1965, 36). The most frequent markups, however, were on the order of 400–500 percent (Papin 1831). So although the Indian producers might be paid $2.00 in trade goods, the cost of these goods to the trader was about $0.50. Even if we add the labor of transport from St. Louis for the trade goods, to make $0.80, we can still see, if we roughly transform this petty commodity production into wages, that the wage paid to the Indian workers was only about $0.01 an hour.

Before we condemn this kind of payment as terribly exploitive, we should first determine the wage rate paid to eastern laborers in these years. Looking first at the most comparable industrial jobs, in leather manufacturing, we see that the average wage was $9.50 per week for a sixty-hour week, or about $0.16 per hour. In 1870 the average yearly wage of a leather currier was $438 (Simonds and McEnnis 1887, 676). Calculating a rate of exploitation as the eastern wage divided by the payments to Indian producers for their robes, we see a rate of 1600 percent. If we calculate on the basis of the value of the robe divided by the value of the goods exchanged for it, the rate of exploitation is somewhat less, about 1000 percent. With rates of exploitation like this, it is no wonder that the Astors, owners of the American Fur Company, were among the first millionaires in U.S. society. They became millionaires off the sweat and skill of Indian women and off the courage and knowledge of those Indian men who hunted buffalo.

Seasonal Farmwork in Oklahoma

The Civil War saw the rise to prominence in U.S. capitalism of the railroads and of certain manufacturing concerns, such as Dupont and Procter and Gamble, which had become prosperous from war production. After the war there were enormous giveaways of public land and public money for the further development of railroads and mining. The sector of capitalism that had been oriented toward the Indian trade was unable to stand up against these new tendencies, and so the lands guaranteed to Indians by treaty were invaded between 1864 and 1877, often over the objections of trading interests, and were distributed among the newly dominant interests (Moore 1987, 193).

The negation of these treaties caused the creation of some of the most contorted legal arguments and convoluted logic in the history of U.S. jurisprudence. These peculiarities continued through the early reservation period, as the Dawes Act (1887) was passed, which gave small parcels of land to individual Indians instead of preserving large commonly owned tracts of reservation land under special status. This enabled white farmers, ranchers, and mineral speculators to buy or lease land from individual Indians. Typical of the legal logic of this period was the Supreme Court's infamous "Lone Wolf Decision," which established that any kind of fraud perpetrated against Indians was legal if it was ratified by Congress (Prucha 1975, 202–203).

The steady attrition of Cheyenne land in Oklahoma has been well documented in the work of Donald Berthrong (1976) and Robert Nespor (1984). Although allotted five hundred thousand acres in severalty in 1892, the Cheyennes retained less than 20 percent of their land by 1910. But contrary to the established myth, the Cheyennes in Oklahoma were successful farmers both before and after allotment, although they preferred to work as extended, rather than nuclear, families. Nevertheless, Cheyenne farming was continually undercut by the meddling of Indian agents, the failure of seeds and equipment to arrive on time, and the machinations of local bankers and businessmen. Consequently, by the time of World War I most Cheyennes constituted a rural underemployed proletariat, sharing small amounts of lease money and diminishing government rations.

The loss of land was a double-edged sword to the Cheyennes. Not only did they lose their land, but they also were forced into the wage labor market. Ironically, many Cheyennes ended up working on land that they nominally owned but that was leased through the Bureau of Indian Affairs (BIA) to white ranchers. And here we have the genesis of the myth of the lazy Indian. For the indignation of local whites against Indians was not merely that the Indians were slothful and refused to work on their own land. Their real objection was that Indians often refused to work for white farmers on the land owned or leased by white people! That is, the criticisms were intended, not to make Indians more responsible in their own affairs, but to get Indians out of their houses and into the fields harvesting white people's crops for wages. Apparently white people did not mind Indians being "lazy" as long as there was no wage work for them to do. No document better illustrates this kind of thinking than the following exchange of letters between farmer J. M. Rapp and W. W. Scott, the superintendent of the Indian Agency. The letters were written in September 1918 and are now preserved in the archives of the Oklahoma Historical Society. Rapp's request appears under the letterhead of the Blaine County "Council of Defense," a local vigilante group that was organized ostensibly to protect white people from Indian attack. But we will see that the council had other functions.

Dear Sir:

You may know that some of your Indians are encamped south of Watonga. Today one of the farmers there, Mr. E. L. Whisler, complained that he has trouble with the Indians' horses breaking into his fields and destroying crops, and there seems to be no redress for it. Of course, the sheriff could see about this, but we think it would be better if you would come up and see to the matter. Another matter the Council would like you to consider, and that is whether the Indians could not be induced to do some work at least in an emergency case like putting up hay or taking care of some fodder crop. We mean with pay, of course. One of our men had two Indians hired at $3 per day and board, but when the Camp began they quit the job and are idling now. We know, Mr. Scott, this is somewhat of a ticklish job for you, or for anybody else, but it would be a good thing if the Indians could be brought to do some work in the present emergency.

The Council ordered me to send this communication.

Very respectfully yours,

J. M. Rapp, Secretary

Superintendent Scott's response was as follows (I have corrected some spelling and punctuation):

Mr. J. M. Rapp, Secretary
County Council of Defense
Watonga, Oklahoma

My Dear Sir:

I have your letter of yesterday in regard to the Indian camp near Watonga, and agree heartily with you that action should be taken in regard to it.

I am enclosing a carbon copy of a letter which I have asked our Farmer, Mr. Goss, to have read to them. If they do not move immediately I will go out next week. I am obliged to be in Oklahoma City until Monday, but will phone our Watonga office immediately on return and see what has been done. Mr. Goss was directed some days ago to deliver no money to the bunch until camp is broken.

I believe good results could be obtained if your Council could visit the camp and explain to them the necessity of getting to work. I have done that so often that it may have lost its effect, but they have a wholesome respect, or fear, of officers of the law.

I would be delighted if arrangements could be made under which able bodied Indians could be offered work—then if they persisted in idling away their time drastic action would be in order. Many of these Indians would work if a job were offered them, but they will not look for it—and there are many who will not work under any circumstances.

There are a good many young men who have received deferred classification [from the military draft] on account of dependent families—that they do not support—who should be advanced [on the draft list], and we will furnish the names if it is desired to advance them.

Very sincerely,
W. W. Scott
Superintendent

In these letters we see all the elements of the system of seasonal wage work that was developing in those years and that continues to the present time. First, there is the coercive element, in which armed ranchers intimidate Indians to get access to land, water, and timber or to get them to work. The Cheyennes are still harassed and intimidated in this manner. In recent years scores of Cheyennes have been physically attacked by semiofficial groups of local farmers and ranchers, and two have been killed. Second, there is the political factor, by which the farmers and ranchers press the BIA to manipulate Indians so that the workforce is available when it is needed. Ideally, there should be enough income available to Indians in the off-season to keep them in the area but not so much that they will refuse to work when the time comes. Although the form of payments made to Cheyennes has changed grad-

Fig. 5.3. Indian men harvesting wheat in western Oklahoma, circa 1915. (Cunningham-Prettyman Collection, Photo Archives, Western History Collections, University of Oklahoma Libraries)

ually since 1918, welfare and per capita payments instead of rations and annuities, the effect is about the same.

According to elderly Cheyenne consultants, seasonal employment has been available to the Cheyennes since World War I. Wheat production boomed in western Oklahoma during the war and continued unabated until the farm crisis of the 1970s (Hale 1982, 56–57). Seasonal work created by the harvesting of wheat, hay, and other crops usually lasted about four months, from May until September. During these months, according to consultants, every Cheyenne man who wanted to work was able to find employment. Unemployment in the off-season among the Cheyennes was, according to government statistics, the highest among all Indian people and in fact the highest of any group in the United States, over 80 percent (Bureau of Indian Affairs 1980). But this situation has worked to the advantage of local farmers and ranchers since the greater the unemployment in the off-season is, the greater is the Indian desire to work in the wheat harvest.

Agricultural wage work by Indians in this part of Oklahoma, however, is statistically invisible. Farmers do not wish to report the work so that they can pay less than the minimum wage. Current wages, according to my consultants, are from $20 to $30 per day for an eight- to ten-hour day. For their part, Cheyenne workers do not want their wages reported for fear that it will disrupt their payments from welfare programs such as food stamps and Aid to Families with Dependent Children. Indian consultants estimate that the employment rate during the wheat and hay harvest in western Oklahoma is about 90 percent for Cheyenne and Arapaho men who live in that area. This rate of employment was constant from the beginning of intensive wheat cultivation, during World War I, until about 1985, enabling us to make some rough calculations for the contribution of Cheyenne labor to the economy for that period. The population of Cheyennes in western Oklahoma (who are combined with Southern Arapahos in official figures) rose from about three thousand in 1920 to about eight thousand five hundred in 1985, according to tribal enrollment figures. If we assume that approximately one-fourth of the population has been employable men, which is reasonable given the age-sex structure of their population in this period, and if we assume that 70 percent of them have been involved in seasonal farmwork (90 percent less 20 percent employed elsewhere), we calculate a total of 416,500 man-months of work from 1915 to 1985. If we figure 200 hours per month at even the minimum 1985 wage of $3.38, we get a total of about $281 million, the approximate value of the contribution of Cheyenne and Arapaho labor to the wheat harvest, in 1985 dollars. Of course, if we calculated the real value of the wealth produced by Indian workers in terms of the value of the wheat harvested and sent to market, the amount would be much more. But the price of wheat is so distorted by the machinations of grain elevator operators and other middlemen that it is difficult to calculate on that basis.

In any event it is clear that the Cheyennes have realized very little of the value of the wealth they have produced. For them, it did not become capital but was immediately turned into food for subsistence, leaving them just as poor as they had been before. But the wheat farmers, middlemen, and food companies have prospered from the timely annual labor of the Cheyennes, just as the capitalists of the buffalo robe trade profited a century ago.

It is not clear to me whether or how many other American Indian groups on the plains serve as seasonal laborers. The Cheyenne case may be somewhat unusual in that the Cheyennes actually live in communities dispersed among the farms and ranches of western Oklahoma. On northern plains reservations, such as the Crow Reservation in Montana, it is more difficult for Indian men to travel to locations where agricultural work is available. Therefore, their contribution may be less. But it is also the case that some northern reservations, such as Pine Ridge in South Dakota, comprise large areas of land leased or owned by non-Indian farmers and ranchers. In these cases work may be as readily available as in western Oklahoma.

THE CHEYENNE MOCCASIN TRADE

Cheyenne women have been specialized moccasin makers for a very long time. Even at the time of the Lewis and Clark Expedition in 1804, the Cheyennes were reported as the suppliers of moccasins to other tribes (Tabeau 1939, 158). This situation continues to modern times, and

Fig. 5.4. Unidentified Cheyenne woman smoothing her beadwork in Lame Deer, Montana, circa 1915. (Photo by Mrs. E. C. Grinnell, courtesy of Museum of the American Indian, Heye Foundation)

Cheyenne women of my acquaintance are often amused to visit museums and see moccasins beaded in a uniquely Cheyenne style labeled as "Kiowa Moccasins" or "Sioux Moccasins" because they were obtained by the museum from members of those other tribes. Among Cheyenne women each pattern of moccasin design is owned by individual women, often inherited from their mothers, and cannot be used by other moccasin makers. These singular designs occur on moccasins collected by museums back through the last century.

The database presented here on the current Cheyenne moccasin industry was collected by my student Charles Hilton, who devoted a summer of fieldwork in 1983 to interviewing Cheyenne moccasin makers

Fig. 5.5. Aurelia Black Bear of Watonga, Oklahoma, making moccasins in her home in 1993. In addition to her beadwork, she works full time in an Indian health clinic. (Photo by Eugene Black Bear Jr.)

and the traders who sell their moccasins. Among the surprising things he discovered was this continued specialization of Cheyenne women as moccasin makers. The women of other tribes are specialized in making other kinds of crafts for trade. The Otoes, for example, specialize in ribbon work, although they also make beaded necklaces and key chains, as well as some moccasins. All tribes make several kinds of crafts or trade commodities, although they are more intensively interested in certain items.

Another surprising aspect of the moccasin trade is that most moccasins are sold, not to white tourists, but to other Indians, especially Navajos and Pueblo Indians. But here again the pattern is very ancient since the Cheyennes have attended the Taos trade fair in New Mexico for nearly two hundred years (Kenner 1969, 74–76). At present Cheyenne moccasins are marketed largely through eleven "Indian stores" in western Oklahoma. The total number of pairs of moccasins sold each year in these stores is one thousand two hundred, of which "over 90 percent," according to traders, are made by the Cheyennes. The moccasin trade, however, is only one fragment of the total market of Indian craft products, accounting for approximately 15 percent of the whole. The Cheyenne moccasins are produced by about fifty Cheyenne women, many of whom are related to one another and have relationships of master-apprentice among themselves.

Until recently the moccasins were produced at home by a farm-out system in which a trader visited the moccasin maker and supplied her with leather, beads, and other raw materials with the understanding that she would provide a certain number of pairs of moccasins at a certain price at a later date. Nowadays, however, the maker usually produces her moccasins and then visits various Indian stores to negotiate a price for her finished moccasins, with the payment to include a supply of new raw materials. Traders in stores therefore keep such materials on hand so that they can exchange these, along with money, for the finished moccasins.

The selling price for moccasins depends on whether they are "partially beaded" or "fully beaded." Partially beaded moccasins, which only exhibit a few strips of beaded designs, sold in the Indian stores in 1983 for between $40 and $90. Fully beaded moccasins, which are beaded all over the top from toe to heel, sold for $135 to $300. In fancier stores in New York City, Boston, and Toronto, however, fully beaded moccasins in this period sold at an average price of $700, and partially beaded moccasins were marked at an average of $210.

For a pair of partially beaded moccasins priced in an Oklahoma Indian store at $90 in 1983, a Cheyenne woman could expect to receive $35 in cash and $30 in materials. Of course, the trader exchanges at his retail price for the materials, not his wholesale price, a tradition that goes back to the trade in buffalo robes. So the trader was actually paying about $35 in cash and $20 in materials for this pair of moccasins. His markup, then, was from $55 to $90, or about 40 percent.

According to Charles Hilton's fieldwork, the time required to make moccasins is highly variable among different workers. He observed that the time required to make one pair of partially beaded moccasins ranged from seven and one-half hours to fifty-six hours, with a mode of about eighteen hours. If we consider that the average wage for a pair of partially beaded moccasins was about $40, counting the wholesale value of materials received in exchange, the hourly wage was about $2.22. Women who took more pains with their work earned less than a $1.00 an hour.

According to old-time traders interviewed by Charles Hilton, the extent of the moccasin trade has not changed very much since the turn of the century, although the method of sale has changed considerably. Early in the century Indian crafts were sold at railroad stations in Oklahoma City, Clinton, and El Reno. After that trading posts sprang up along Route 66 for the tourist trade, which has now shifted to Interstate 40. The sale of moccasins to other Indians has been stable all along primarily at the Indian stores in Clinton and Anadarko.

If these oral accounts are accurate, we can calculate the approximate value of the moccasin trade in this century. Of the one thousand two hundred pairs sold each year, about two hundred pairs are fully beaded, and one thousand pairs are partially beaded. In eighty-five years, approximately eighty-five thousand pairs of partially beaded and seventeen thousand pairs of fully beaded moccasins have been sold. When we calculate money values for this century, however, we must allow for inflation, so using 1983 prices, we can calculate the total value of the Cheyenne moccasin trade up to 1983 at about $10 million if we price the two kinds of moccasins at $65 and $250. As with the other two kinds of work previously discussed, however, making buffalo robes and harvesting wheat, the Cheyennes creating the value have not received much benefit from it. In this case they received about half of the sale price for their labor, money that was quickly spent to survive rather than to build a capital or land base for themselves. By contrast, Indian traders in western Oklahoma are among the wealthiest people in that area, once again from the sweat of Cheyenne brows.

CONCLUSION

Although we have looked only at three examples of Cheyenne work over the last two hundred years, the Cheyennes have clearly made a considerable contribution to the U.S. economy. At the peak of the buffalo robe trade in the 1860s, it amounted to over $1 million a year, at a time when total U.S. manufacturing was about $4 billion and annual national imports amounted to about $250 million (Simonds and McEnnis 1887, 695, 703). On the scale of the times, the fur trade as a whole, of which the robe trade was only one part, was a significant fraction of the U.S. economy. And let us not be fooled into believing that the fur trade had anything to do with the exploitation of beavers or buffalos, as the classic sources would have us believe (Gregg 1970, Chittenden 1935, Phillips 1961). As far as I know, neither beavers nor buffalo have contributed any labor at all to the U.S. economy. The fur trade was a system for mobilizing and exploiting the labor of Indian people. The pelts, furs, and hides that were traded east were valuable for one reason only; because thousands of Indian people had worked for millions of hours to produce them.

The agricultural work of Cheyennes in the twentieth century exemplifies a different system for putting Indians to work and extracting their labor. In this case we see a finely tuned social apparatus that provides farmers with willing workers at a particularly crucial time of year, the harvest season. Here the farmers and the BIA personnel, who sometimes are the same people, provide just enough support at public expense to keep the labor pool viable but not enough to make laborers independent of the system. Although the Cheyennes are not migrant laborers like the Hispanic workforces of Texas and Florida, they function in the economy in just the same way and are just as important.

Cheyenne moccasin making, like Cheyenne agricultural work, is predicated on the sedentary nature of the Indian workforce. In this case traders set up networks of stable relationships with women who will provide moccasins, although these traders collude among themselves to depress the prices they pay to the makers, thus keeping rates of profit at a maximum. Like workers in other places, Cheyenne women sometimes see their situation in terms of what Marx calls fetish values. They wonder how much a pair of moccasins is "worth" or how much their labor is "worth." They often fail to see that their efforts are constrained within a total system of capitalism that is pervasive in its scope and massive in its ability to oppress and constrain their work to create profits, power, and leisure for other people.

But the sheer scale of Cheyenne efforts, as we have seen in these three multi-million-dollar examples, is impressive and helps put the lie to the myth of the lazy Indian. Even so, we have looked at only a few measurable types of work. Other, not easily measurable work is done by the Cheyennes in nearby cities—Tulsa, Oklahoma City, and Dallas. Young Cheyenne men, as well as many women, migrate to these cities in the off-season of agricultural work to earn some income for their families. But here the work is largely invisible; I do not know of any method for measuring the amount of work done by these Indian people and separating it from the amount of work done by non-Indians. In these cities no statistics are kept about how many Indians work for brief periods or how much money they make, although I suspect the amount is sizable.

Unfortunately we must also recognize that, despite the actual performance of Indians in the economy, the myth of the lazy Indian lives on. This is only because the myth is functional and convenient for the white majority. It allows a farmer in Watonga to pay an Indian man $20 a day because "you can't get no work out of them." Or it permits him to hold a man's wages for weeks at a time because "you know, they're unreliable, likely to run off on you anytime if something comes up at home or they have some big doin's." And if an Indian in fact "runs off," that provides a perfect excuse not to pay him at all. In short, it is the myth that allows the poverty and oppression to continue and that assures the successful continuation of the system—"successful," of course, for a white owner of a farm or an Indian store.

A curious inversion of the myth was related to me by a trader talking about moccasin makers. He said, "You know, it don't take them Indians no time at all to turn out a pair of moccasins." But when I asked the trader why the Indian women worked so fast, he said, "Well, it's because they're essentially lazy. They want to hurry up so they can get back to drinking or visiting or whatever it was they were doing before." So the myth remains secure. If Indians do not work hard, it is because they are lazy. And if they do work hard, it is only because they are anxious to finish so that they can go back to being lazy. But in this chapter I have tried to present some objective and quantitative measures of how hard some particular Indians have worked and how much wealth they have created historically for the benefit of all.

6

NINETEENTH-CENTURY GREAT BASIN INDIAN WAGE LABOR

MARTHA C. KNACK

Indians in the Great Basin engaged in wage labor from the first days of non-Indian settlement in their country. It soon became the dominant mode of subsistence for most groups between the Wasatch Front and the Sierra Nevada and, once established, remained stable for nearly one hundred years. The specific characteristics of their wage labor distinguished it from non-Indian work in the same area and determined its role within the Native community. Since theorists often declare lack of resources, especially landlessness, to be a key variable in driving a preindustrial population into the wage labor market, I consider two cases within the Great Basin to determine the extent to which possession of a land base influenced the adaptation to wage labor in this region.

The first area I discuss is southern Nevada and adjoining southwestern Utah, where Southern Paiutes lost control over native resources without the compensation of reservation lands. The second area lies three hundred miles to the north, where the ethnically unrelated Northern Paiutes had the large Walker River Reservation set aside for their use.

Throughout the Great Basin the traditional Native subsistence economy, like that of other hunters and gatherers, utilized a wide variety of plant and animal species from a number of ecozones, which required great mobility for seasonal and sequential collection. Base camps were made near reliable springs or along short and intermittent streams, with water carried to dry camps to enable hunting or the gathering of food plants in the desert. Bilateral kinship groups held resource areas in

144

common, but they shared these reciprocally with other camp groups in times of drought or other productive failure. Division of labor was by sex and age, with much overlap and sharing of tasks. Without occupational specialidation, the jobs of adult men or women were known and accessible to all, as were the resources necessary for their accomplishment. Each person's labor was free, with no chief or even household head to dictate the day's task or the distribution of the resulting product (Steward 1938, 230–258).

SOUTHERN PAIUTES

Essentially unchanged by Spanish travelers and early Anglo-American beaver trappers, this economy was altered significantly by the stream of gold seekers in 1849. The Old Spanish, or Mormon, Trail from Salt Lake to Los Angeles cut directly through the Southern Paiute study area, while the Overland Trail, to San Francisco across South Pass, came within a few miles of Walker River. Immigrants hired Indians living along these roadways to herd draft animals toward grass and water overnight. One greenhorn had the local custom explained to him by an old-timer:

> He told us that when we made our camp at night that two Indians were sure to camp with us . . . no matter whether we had seen an Indian that day or not. He told us that they would take care of our horses and bring them to camp the next morning, and all they would want was a camp kettle of mush, so on our camping that night we looked around for some Indians to herd our horses, but there was none in sight. No sooner had our camp been made and our fire lighted than two Indians appeared from whence we did not know. We asked them to "Pooney wooney" (herd our horses) and they consented. (Farnes 1920, 16).

The Church of Jesus Christ of Latter-day Saints, the Mormons, settled Salt Lake City in 1849. Two years later that church sponsored cohesive migrations to colonize southern Utah. Within a few years the Mormons had villages located on all flowing water sources (Arrington 1966, 84–95). In a matter of a few years precisely those few spots of greatest value to the Native economy were suddenly held as private property by white men.

Records of the Mormon church insist that Southern Paiutes invited its members to settle with them. The leader of an 1852 church-sponsored exploration of southwestern Utah wrote, "They [Paiutes at Toquerville] expressed great anxiety to have us settle among them, so they could 'manika' (work) for the Mormons, like the Pah Eeds [Paiutes] at Parowan" (Lee 1852). Twelve years later another church expedition contacted bands east of Las Vegas, Nevada, and reported, "They are anxious for us to settle the country, and are willing for our cattle to eat their grass, if we will employ them that they may have clothes to wear and food to eat when their grass seed is all used" (Call 1865).

These and similar statements suggest that Southern Paiutes well ahead of the settlement edge were familiar with the wage labor of their relatives and viewed it as a desirable means of acquiring rare goods, especially clothing. The records also assume that Paiutes experienced periodic hunger and saw labor as a means to access new food resources, especially when the wild plant cycle was unproductive. Native invitations to settle may not have been quite as innocent as church records imply, for some bands actively sought Mormon protection against mounted Ute raiders who seized children from pedestrian Paiute camps to sell in the slave market at Santa Fe (Malouf and Malouf 1945). Furthermore, Mormons aggressively used their highly efficient and tight social organization, along with their technological advantage of horses and guns, intentionally intimidating Paiutes and forestalling protest.

From the very first year of settlement southern Utah diaries mentioned Paiutes as providing much-needed supplementary labor for initial construction tasks—grubbing sagebrush before plowing, digging irrigation ditches, and snaking timber down from the mountains both for white cabins and forts intended to protect against the Indians! As early as 1854 Southern Paiute women found common employment washing clothes for unmarried white men. Although Mormon women rarely worked in the fields, hired Indian labor routinely included not only men but also women and children: "Dug up all my Potatoes. . . . 4 Squaws and some Indian Children & my wife assisted me. . . . I cannot help but remark, that when I am very busy, Indians come & assist me in my work, I feel to thank my Father in Heaven for putting it into the hearts of these poor fallen people to come & help me Labour" (Lunt n.d., entry for 21 October 1852). Indian women brought their own tools, especially large conical burden baskets, and they occasionally used traditional digging sticks for potato harvesting and other digging tasks. In their domestic economy Paiute women harvested wild plant products extensively, making many of the jobs non-Indian farmers offered appear as familiar parts of the Native female division of labor.

During the early years of Mormon entry settlers often admitted their dependence on Indian labor. "I will say this much concerning the Indians," wrote a Mormon leader at the principal southern town the year after its founding, "only for their labor, there would have been hundreds of bushels of produce lost, that could not have been saved by the white population. I consider myself a common hand to work but I must give up to some of the Piedes for quickness" (Adams 1852).

Soon the church sent out missionaries, both to convert and pacify the Paiutes around Mormon settlements. The missionaries considered that demonstrations of agricultural methods were of equal, if not greater, importance than preaching and so immediately opened farms, not incidentally for their own support. "Many of the Piutes came to see us throw the dirt as they call plowing," recorded one of the leaders. "They cut the sage brush & cleared the land fit for the plow. All things prospered exceedingly. Those Piutes that worked for us we fed. They considered it a privelege [sic] to eat a meal of victuals with us, and they had not much but yant [agave] to eat" (Hamblin n.d., 17). Here, as throughout cash-short nineteenth-century rural Utah, wages were paid in agricultural produce, usually flour. The worker got meals during the hours of actual employment but in quantity only enough for himself. Of course, this did not provide subsistence for the entire family unless each member had a job. Nor did it provide a surplus to store for winter use; it was literally a subsistence wage.

Hiring Indians was not only an economic policy but also a political one. Anticipating and encouraging the creation of a colonialist dependency, the secretary for the newly established Mormon fort at Las Vegas revealed this in 1855: "If we only had plenty to feed them for their labor, we could govern & control them to the very letter" (Jensen 1926, 188).

Long-term Mormon Indian policy involved not only employment but also trade with the Indians through a church-owned, centralized mercantile marketing system (Arrington 1966, 81–84, 293–314). The Paiutes disappointed such hopes, however. In late 1854 the missionary in charge of the trade program reported that exchange with the local Indians was "dull," in fact, nonexistent. He justified the failure by explaining that the Paiutes lived at a margin close to survival and did so on products unattractive to Euro-American tastes, so they had nothing to trade:

> The few that have been steady & regularly employed in the settlements have been clothed, those that still prefer an outside & offish course are fully engaged hunting our Small game—rabbits for their food. And the many almost naked we find on the Santa Clara & surrounding country have nothing to give in return for this clothing, at present, but they are very willing to work, and perhaps the days are not far distant when they will be taught & capable of producing more than they need to consume. (Brown 1972)

Both settler and immigrant accounts frequently disparaged the Native Great Basin diet. Wild plant products were labeled "weeds," and the eclectic search for meat, which did not eschew insects and amphibians, was called "loathsome." Paiutes were therefore blocked from capitalizing on the scant resources of their territory, in contrast to the way subarctic peoples, for instance, marketed beaver pelts. The only wild food resources favored by both Indians and non-Indians were fish and piñon nuts; Southern Paiutes attempted to retain control of both of these.

The Paiutes living near Panguitch Lake, long a favored gathering place for surrounding bands during the fishing season, "at first . . . would not let the settlers fish in the lake but would catch them and sell them to the settlers" (Chidester n.d., 5). When the mounted Utes to the northeast rebelled against increasing Mormon control of their lands in the Black Hawk War of 1866, settlers declared local Paiutes to be implicated, attacked their camp at the lake, and killed a leading shaman. Another Indian, baptized as a Mormon bishop, was made "chief" and the Indians "reconciled," to become "a friendly tribe ever after" (Chidester n.d., 6). Panguitch Lake became a resort for non-Indian fishermen.

The only resource over which Paiutes did retain control and could extract for their own profit was piñon nuts. These they were picking for commercial sale as early as the 1880s (e.g., Pioche Weekly Record 1885a). However, the growth of non-Indian towns required both construction and firewood, and the development of mining in southern Nevada in the 1860s demanded shoring timbers; this led to the strip cutting of many piñon groves and the decline of this resource (Thomas 1971; Klett et al. 1984, 105–134, 143–166).

Occasionally Paiutes cut grass for travelers' draft animals. As late as 1898 the federal agent for the Shivwits Paiutes in extreme southwestern Utah wrote: "One way in which a little money comes to them is by feeding the horses of travelers passing through, as they strike the Reservation after 25 miles of desert. . . . They feed 2 horses for .50 cts. and the regular wages for a man or woman is .50 cts. a day" (Work 1898a, 4).

Profit from purveying natural resources such as piñon, fish, and hay for the white market provided only periodic and minor income; the Paiutes had only one product left desired by white settlers—their labor. Indian men served as guides and retrieved lost men and stock (e.g., Jensen 1926, 211). Prospectors carried ore samples to show to Indians, and many mines were "discovered" when the Euro-American was led right up to the outcrop by a Paiute guide (e.g., Jensen 1926, 214, 266). Indian women were regularly washing clothes and helping harvest crops by the end of the first year (e.g., Brooks 1972, 67). Chemehuevi Paiutes gathered driftwood from the Colorado River for the steamboats that supplied the mining camps of southern Nevada (e.g., Pioche Weekly Record 1891a). Such jobs were short-term, contracts were ad hoc, and payment, in either food or cast-off clothing, was immediate at the end of the day (e.g., Jensen 1926, 175, 187, 273).

By 1860 Pioche had become the largest mining center in the southern half of Nevada, with a population of six thousand, which far outnumbered the Native population. There Paiute men cut firewood and built roads so that ore wagons could roll from the remote mines to the processing mills; Paiute women washed clothes and did "heavy charring" for the predominantly male mining community (Knack 1986b). In 1872 a federal exploring party reached the Mohave Desert mining camp of

Ivanpah and noted: "[H]ere there are quite a number [of Indians], who, for the most part, are employed by the miners to carry water to the mines. This idea of labor is not applicable to the men, as they as a general thing are perfectly contented to enjoy the fruits of the labors of their squaws. . . . They belong to the tribe of Pi-Utes" (Lockwood 1872, 74–75). Indians, it appeared, performed virtually all tasks except the lucrative mining itself. For their labor they received considerably lower wages than did non-Indians; the 1870 financial report by the primary mining company in Ivanpah specified that Indian laborers were paid $15 per month and white miners, $60, four times the Indian wage (*Piute* 1870, 18).

Paiutes were not only willing to work for non-Indians in their immediate areas but also were actively seeking out wage labor opportunities by the 1870s. Well before a reservation was established for them, the Shivwits Paiutes had established a commuting cycle in southern Utah. "Each Sabbath most of them come to St. George," their first agent wrote, referring to the Mormon town twelve miles east. There "the women wash Mondays + Tuesdays, going home Tuesday p.m. or Wednesday a.m. . . . Some of the men are excellent cowboys, and have work much of the time with neighboring cattlemen, while others hoe and do other small chores while in St. George, or take care of the pappooses [sic] while the wives are washing. The braves are excellent nurses, and very gentle and affectionate with the children as a rule" (Work 1898a, 2; see also Work 1906, 2, for the distant and little-known prereservation San Juan Paiutes). Both the men and women had regular clients. By the end of the century a pattern had emerged of men doing agricultural and construction work, which was seasonal, while women did washing and cleaning, a far more reliable employment that often earned more than their husbands'. An agent at the Nevada reservation praised the women: "The squaws are very industrious and are better to work than the men, and earn quite an amount making baskets, washing, and working for ranchers" (Sharp 1904, 244–245).

Not only was the Anglo-European sexual division of labor imposed through selective employment (with the continued exception of harvest labor), but so also were other sexual standards. The memoirs of a young schoolteacher in the Muddy Valley of southern Nevada recalled of 1881: "An indian came and asked me to sell him a dress for his wife as she could [then] go to a family and get work. My wardrobe was too slim entirely but I gave him one of the three dresses and he paid me a dollar. The Indians did nearly all the work in the valley. A good set of people these Piedes, better than most of the white population" (Cox ca. 1928–1930, 159).

Continued growth of irrigated subsistence farming, mining towns, and the cattle ranches that supplied them increasingly restricted land for Native hunting and gathering. Ethnohistorical evidence and oral history agree that Paiutes continued foraging in remote areas to a diminishing degree for another one hundred years, although it is unclear whether some bands retreated totally into remote areas to avoid contact or whether most groups engaged in wage labor seasonally as part of a modified, eclectic subsistence cycle that partially retained indigenous food sources as well. Evidence is equally abundant, however, that by 1870 many groups were either forced to seek the resources of towns or did so voluntarily. In 1875 the Indian agent at the tiny 1,000 acre Moapa Reservation, founded to house all Southern Paiutes from three states, estimated that 25 percent of the local Paiutes' subsistence was earned through wage labor (Bureau of Indian Affairs, 1875, 632–633). By 1880, a mere thirty years since the first significant contact, that estimate had risen to nearly 60 percent, the rest coming from hunting, gathering, and government or church distributions (Bureau of Indian Affairs, 1880, 708–709). In 1898 their first federal agent estimated that 50 percent of the Shivwits Paiutes' subsistence came from wage labor, compared to only 20 percent from hunting and gathering and the rest from government rations, charity, and women's sale of baskets (Work 1898b).

Agricultural jobs, the source of much Paiute employment, were necessarily seasonal. The extensive account books of the first large ranch in the Las Vegas valley disclose an employment pattern of heavy spring and fall hiring, with layoffs occurring during the scorching summer (Knack 1987, 45–46, 50–51). A rather haphazard sample of 133 specific citations of Paiutes hired in the larger southern Utah–southern Nevada area between 1851 and 1891, encompassing the broader economy of

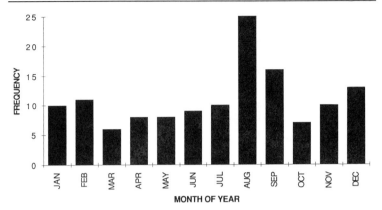

Fig. 6.1. Southern Paiute seasonal wage labor, 1851–1891. (Data were compiled from Ashworth n.d.; Bean n.d.; Bleak n.d.; Bradfute 1886; Brooks 1972; Carvalho 1857; Cleland and Brooks 1955; Cox ca. 1928–1930; Cutler n.d.; Farnes 1920; Foote n.d.; Hamblin n.d.; Ingalls 1874a; J. A. L. 1957; Jensen 1926; Johnson n.d.; Kelly 1948–1949; Kimball 1867–1889; Lee 1853, 1854; Little 1945; Lockwood 1872; Lunt n.d.; Lyman 1857–1863; Mangum 1939; Pioche Daily Record 1875; Pioche Weekly Record 1885a, 1889, 1891b; Smith 1970; Smith 1852, 1855; Steele n.d.; Stewart n.d.; Streeper 1867; Wheeler 1872.)

agricultural, mining, and village employment, shows a similar, although less marked, seasonality (see Figure 6.1).

An 1880 letter by the Moapa agent converted such impersonal numerics to a human reality in its grim description of the Southern Paiute marginal, mixed economy in the early spring, the hardest time of year for Great Basin hunters and gatherers. The Indians, he wrote,

are here now constantly asking for work + grub[.] they have no money to buy with + then there is none [nothing] to buy in the valley + no work among the farmers and Miners, the poor things are living on Roots, Lizards, frogs + snakes as they [the animals] are beginning to show themselves now. Some of the men are returning from the Mountains say they cant find any thing to kill or to pick, as the winter has been so cold, the vegetation [sic] has not commenced yet at this Season of the year they usually find mescal, an herb they eat. There is none this spring as yet. (Bradfute 1880, 1).

We have little sure knowledge of Paiute motives for engaging in wage labor. Perhaps, as settlers would have liked to believe, it was the attraction of new goods and escape from periodic starvation, perhaps necessity caused by displacement from food production areas and water sources by the settlers themselves, perhaps a combination of these. Little mystery, however, surrounds white motives for hiring Paiutes, for these were clearly stated in the historical documents. First, although white labor was nearly always preferred when available, there was simply little of it to be had. Furthermore, those few non-Indians available had higher expectations than did Indian workers. They demanded "room and found," expected a monthly wage, and insisted on being kept on the payroll regardless of whether there was work for them to do; otherwise, they would drift to other jobs. In the cyclical agricultural economy they were expensive. Indians, in contrast, could be "turned loose" when there was no work to do and left to subsist at their own expense until needed again.

In addition, until well into the 1920s Southern Paiute wages were frequently one-third to one-half of those paid non-Indians (see Figure 6.2). The crassness of the economic motive became apparent, for instance, in 1885 when a Pioche Indian woodcutter attempted to profit from a seasonal labor shortage, according to his clear comprehension of the law of supply and demand. He unilaterally escalated his wages from $1 per day to $5; the local newspaper observed, "Pioche capitalists concluded to continue amusing themselves with the saw" (Pioche Weekly Record 1885b, 3). Indian labor was a convenient luxury as long as it did not cost too much, and equal wages were considered too much. Even the Indian agent at the new Kaibab Reservation in Arizona supported this local opinion in 1910: "The trouble with these Indians," he wrote,

is they have been given rations, which has made them feel that they do not have to do a day's work unless they can get their price for it, instead of being willing to work for what they can get. I know men that would employ Indians at $1.50 per day when they can get white labor for $2.00,

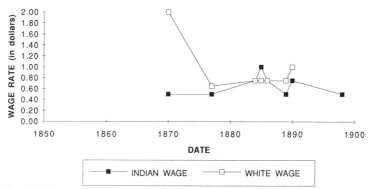

Fig. 6.2. Comparison of Southern Paiute and non-Indian daily wage labor rates, 1851–1900. (Data were compiled from *Piute* 1870; Bradfute 1886; Pioche Weekly Record 1885a; Stewart n.d.; Work 1898a.)

but the Indians consider their labor equal to that of the whites, therefore they complain. On the average I think the Indians are well compensated for their labor. (Ward 1910, 1)

Paiutes disagreed. One of the earliest Paiute-written letters I have found was a protest against the wage situation. "Is there any more slaves should be held in the states any more?" a Kaibab man asked the Indian commissioner. "That mine Father is working like a slaves of states Utah, only for eat. . . . I could not hardly stand that workes. he not got any money from. Because my Father doesn't know anythings about the money, and getting old now. He has worked about 7 years, only Just for eat and many other Indians do that at Mormon towns. . . . That slavery working" (Pikyavit 1909, 1–2). In a remarkable percentage of the extremely rare Paiute killings of non-Indians after the initial settlement period, at least one source declared the cause to be the victim cheating the Indian out of or withholding wages gainfully earned (e.g., Cox 1911, for Queho case of 1897; Lincoln County Record 1903, for Seegmiller case; Las Vegas Review-Journal 1931, for Tecope case). Although protesting perceived injustice, sometimes to the point of violence, the

Southern Paiutes were not successful in establishing any sort of control over their wage scale or pay practices.

Paiutes obtained jobs individually; Native leaders in this area did not control access to employment. In the traditional economy the headman was expected to be very knowledgeable about food sources and often directed hunting and gathering activities, but nowhere did he have the power to forbid or deny any member of his group access to subsistence resources. Nor did such authority develop in historic times.

Neither did federal Indian agents ever become labor bosses, as they did in some northeastern areas. "I have no way of knowing the amount of money they receive," wrote the Shivwits agent in 1898, "as they attend to their own affairs, which I think is better than if I tried to do it, and I have not interfered unless they asked me to do so" (Work 1898a, 4). Although there was a well-known and stable Indian wage rate in the region, slightly higher in towns than in farming districts, those salaries were actually paid in kind until well after 1900 (Knack 1987, 46–57). Furthermore, the value set on those goods was set by the non-Indian employer and could vary with person-to-person negotiation. "These Indians [at Moapa] dont need pecuniary assistance from the Government," the subagent declared in 1886. "[T]here is work for them at from 50 cents to $1.00 per day whenever they will work. They get their pay in money clothing or horses just as they can make their bargain with their employer" (Bradfute 1886, 4).

Sometimes a farmer sent a message to the agency asking for a particular Indian, and the message was forwarded, but usually the Paiutes, both men and women, established their own contacts and had their own network of clients. A rancher from the Koosharem area of west-central Utah recalled how the system worked:

They'd just pull into our place & never say a word to anybody. They had a regular sort of campground out back. They would pull through the yard and open the gates that needed to be opened and unhook [their teams]. They would go out on the haystack & throw down enough hay to feed their stock. They just made themselves at home. After dark father would go out to their camp and talk a while. They would stay there several days. They always came three or four times a year. (Buchanan 1974–1975, 43)

Despite such seemingly personalized labor relations, whites in this same area refused to allow off-reservation Indian children into the public schools until 1935 (Farrow 1935), and the federal agent commented that the only relationship Paiutes had with the white population was a purely commercial one.

Within ten years of initial settlement many whites were expressing dependence on Southern Paiute labor, such as the early farmer who considered Indian workers a divine gift. By the 1880s non-Indians were objecting when Native subsistence commitments interfered with their labor supply. During the piñon harvest of 1885 the newspaper in Pioche bemoaned:

> The scarcest article in this section, and the greatest in demand, is "Lo, the poor Indian. . . . "Yes, an Indian is a rare thing in Pioche, and . . . is greatly missed by many of our residents. Those who wish his services cutting wood and doing chores miss him, and the poor house wife, having dislocated her back bone bending over the washtub, wearied and tired at night, heaves a heavy sigh and wishes the nasty squaws would return, and can't see the use of them remaining out in the mountains for a three months' feast. . . . The usefulness of the Indian, as it cannot now be obtained will hereafter be appreciated. (Pioche Weekly Record 1885b, 3)

This dependence grew to such an extent that when the federal government finally became interested in establishing reservations for the Paiutes at the turn of the century, it met resistance from local whites. The investigator sent to buy land for the Kaibab Paiutes of northern Arizona in 1907 found, "[A]s soon as it was noised about that my errand was to confer with Indians, I was waited upon by a number of the principal people of Kanab, who objected strenuously to the Indians being removed from their vicinity, as it was stated to me that they relied upon both the men & women as laborers" (Churchill 1907, 4).

The Paiutes too knew the value of wage labor and the freedom it gave to live without governmental restriction. The first Bureau of Indian

Affairs (BIA) agent to visit the Paiute community at Cedar City in 1907 found:

> They make their living by doing odd chores for the whites in the town. . . . They have always lived on the Public Domain & have never received any benefits from the Government, nor do they want anything whatever to do with the Government now. When I informed them that they were wards of the government & that I was Indian Agent in charge they refused to have anything to do with me, whatsoever. The chief of the band Captain Pete replied that they were no government Indians, but Mormon Indians, meaning by that . . . as far as any submission on their part to any authority was concerned they subjected themselves to the Mormon community about them and not to the Indian Department. (Runke 1907, 1–2)

Without federal encouragement, the Southern Paiutes had established a wage labor adaptation that not only resulted in but also required coresidence with the Anglo-American population. Both the Indians and local non-Indians saw wage labor and reservation life as antithetical. All BIA discussions whether to found, maintain, or abandon reservations for Paiutes of necessity included discussion of access to day labor jobs. The inspector sent to allot and dissolve the one existing Paiute reservation at Moapa in 1887 wrote to the Indian commissioner:

> The total number of the tribe I am unable to learn, as they are scatered [sic] over the surrounding country for 200 miles in all directions from the Reserve, making their own living, some among the Mormon farmers others in the Mines, where they will remain unless some effort is made by the Govt to collect them on the reserve, which is not supposed to be your desire. But rather that they should continue to be self[-]supporting and remain in small, desireable [sic] numbers among the whites. (Welton 1887, 1)

However, another agent argued *for* establishing reservations on the grounds that wage work was *not* available in the countryside:

> The Indians properly belonging to this agency do not have the opportunity to labor for white settlers in farming and mining as the Shoshones and Utes [do], as there are no mines requiring their services; and but little farming land, save in Utah, and there the people are too poor, or too

numerous, to need their labor. . . . I believe the chiefs or captains should all receive a small salary and be requested to give special attention in seeing that all their people work, as directed by the agent and farmer. (Ingalls 1874b, 283)

A number of small reservations were eventually established for the Southern Paiutes, beginning with the one at Moapa in 1872, then Shivwits in 1891, Kaibab in 1907, Las Vegas in 1912, and others through the 1920s. Many were located directly on the fringes of established non-Indian towns, clearly following the advice of the inspector who argued that reservations should not be made "remote from civilization where work is scarce, where they are compelled to go anywhere from fifteen to even sixty and seventy miles to secure work. . . . in the future should other superintendencies and schools be established for these small bands of wandering Paiutes, it would, in my opinion, be well to acquire good land near white settlements" (Norris 1910a, 20, 21).

Although reservation sites were selected in part for agricultural potential, every Indian agent reported a land base completely insufficient to support the number of Indian families expected to make their homes there. For instance, although Shivwits in southwestern Utah appeared physically to be quite a large reserve, enclosing nearly 28,000 acres, only 80 of those acres were irrigable, a necessity for agricultural production in this region. One hundred twenty Paiutes were enrolled there, resulting in only about two-thirds of an arable acre per person, a totally inadequate amount for subsistence production. The BIA expected to settle more than one hundred Paiutes on each of the ten-acre residential locales in Cedar City, Utah, and Las Vegas, Nevada. The richest reservation was Moapa, along the Muddy River in the southern Nevada desert. Its 1,000 acres, half irrigated, still allowed only a 2.5-acre allotment per family.

Wage labor, already part of the Native economic adaptation when these reserves were founded, had to continue to be so out of sheer necessity. At no time did more than one-half of the Southern Paiute population live on reservations, and it was not until the 1930s that the majority was even enrolled. As early as 1879 the Moapa agent reported: "As to the Indians, they are doing well. *None* of them live on the

Fig. 6.3. Southern Paiute men and women harvesting radishes in Logandale, Nevada, a few miles from their Moapa Reservation homes. They were paid $0.03 for every dozen radishes bundled and crated at the side of the large fields. (Photo by Rothstein, 1940; Photographic Division, U.S. National Archives)

reservation now. . . . The young men work out at times and get clothing and other articles for their families" (Bradfute 1879a; emphasis added). Such emigration resulted in an uneven residential population composed primarily of the elderly and their dependent grandchildren. During the winter of 1879 at Moapa the only resident Indians were "the old men and Squaws that never go out to work. . . . the young men will continue to live out and earn their own living[.] the old men and women take care of home matters" (Bradfute 1879b, 4). Twenty-five years later a newly assigned agent arriving at this same reservation in the depth of winter observed, "Upon my arrival I found about 1/3 of the Indians gone from the reservation hunting work in different parts of the valley from the ranchers to make a living for their families. The Crops as Saved the past year would not Support more than 1/2 the Indians that belong here. *Consequently* the seeking for labor" (Sharp 1903, 1; emphasis added). This pattern was repeated on all Paiute reservations virtually from their foundings, especially during the agricultural season.

While admitting the inability of the reserves to support the population, most agents had an ambiguous reaction to Paiute wage work. The Kaibab agent recommended against a reservation housing project because the Indians had not "given up the nomadic spirit nor shown that they will settle down and live here" (Maxwell 1913, 1). "At white ranches and at and near the towns and mining camps," another scolded paternalistically, "good wages can be earned and a more free life can be led. They are practically unhampered in their habits, left almost absolutely free to do as they please, to indulge in immoral practices & gratify their desires for gambling and the use of intoxicating liquor" (Norris 1910b, 8–9). Other agents criticized the Paiutes for treating labor like subsistence, stopping when their needs were satisfied, and not having developed the infinite wants that drive a consumer economy: "There is nearly always work for them to do but they are naturally indolent & do not care to provide for more than their immediate necessities. They will work until they get a few dollars & then quit" (Goodall 1913, 16).

Such objections were unrealistic, because the employment that the Paiutes could get, in both mining and agriculture, was by its nature short term; therefore mobility was required as workers shifted flexibly from one job to another. For instance, in 1911 when "[m]ining in the Search-light and Eldorado districts [was] dull," there was "little demand for the Indians' labor in boating, . . . catching drift wood for fuel and work about the mines, so they have gone to the interior for work on the railroads and ranches. When work opens up again along the river they will seek their old occupations and homes" (Ellis 1911, 5).

Inspectors repeatedly found only a handful of Indians resident on reservations that carried one hundred or two on their census rolls. Paiutes had always pursued their subsistence round together as family units, and traditional ethics strongly emphasized the value of family cohesion, so when they sought off-reservation labor, men, women, and children all traveled. The first supervisor of Shivwits Reservation commented that he "encouraged the Indians to work for wages among the farmers and a great many are now engaged in this way but when they go from the [reservation] farm to work they take their families with them and this reduces the attendance at school" in violation of federal policy (Ivins 1893, 2–3). As with earlier debates over whether wage-working Paiutes needed reservations at all, some argued against construction of schools for Paiutes because of their mobility: "[S]ending their children to a boarding school will not be dependent on where the parents make their home or whether they have a permanent home. The advantages of the day school are of course plain and recognized, but unless these people are fitted out so that they can have a permanent home it would be inadvisable to supply them with a day school" (Runke 1908, 3–4). Agents were forced to justify low school enrollments and embarrassing service delivery statistics. Their own careers threatened, they began to lure Paiutes back to the reserves in the 1910s and 1920s by creating jobs— digging irrigation ditches, constructing roads and school buildings, fencing range, and repairing flood damage. Smart agents expended their limited day labor funds in winter, when competing jobs were fewer and Indians would work for the lower federal rates. Then families would return home to their elderly relatives, put their children in school for the winter, tend a few cattle at Kaibab or plant a small garden at Shivwits, and in the spring depart again, in a classic "base camp wandering" settlement pattern.

In the 1910s the BIA began a program of reimbursable loans to increase individual Paiute farm productivity by enabling the Indians to purchase wagons, draft horses, and sets of harness. Agents were appalled when Paiutes took the increased mobility thus achieved and used it for more efficient off-reservation job seeking. At the same time, the arrival of the railroad to southern Nevada had allowed specialized crops to be taken rapidly to urban markets, and non-Indian farmers in the lower Muddy River Valley quickly converted their operations. Wages for cantaloupe pickers rose to $9 a week, and Moapa became a mecca for Paiutes from other areas. The frustrated agent ranted that Indians who did not "belong" to the reservation were living there and that Moapa men were working as harvest hands on other people's land to such a degree that they neglected their own farms (Sharp 1907).

But Paiutes' decision in favor of wage employment was rational. Alfalfa remained the only crop practical on the Moapa reservation without expensive machinery beyond either the BIA's or the Indians' budgets; with its price standing at $15 per ton, the average two-and-one-half-acre allotment could produce a maximum of $75 for a season's work. If a man's whole family picked cantaloupes for non-Indians down the valley, they could earn the same amount in two weeks. Wage work *was* the rational choice, and Paiutes made it; at Moapa in the cantaloupe and radish fields, at Richfield in the sugar beet fields, they became migrant harvest hands. Seizing Model T pickups as soon as they were produced, Paiutes eagerly hit the new highways, again increasing their range for seeking seasonal wage labor.

They also provided nearly all regional construction labor until the Great Depression. Then huge federal construction projects such as Boulder (now Hoover) Dam lured floods of poor Euro-Americans into the area: "Their [Paiutes'] chance for employment has grown increasingly less with the great influx of people from all over the country seeking jobs at Boulder City and Hoover Dam" (Lindquist 1933, 20). Paiutes continued, however, to be the backbone of the migrant harvest labor pool until the late 1940s, when they were replaced first by Navajos and later by Hispanics (Salt Lake Tribune 1951; Magleby 1953, 2).

WALKER RIVER NORTHERN PAIUTES

It is reasonable to ask whether the retention of a land base, as envisioned by federal reservation policy, improved or changed the economic situation for Great Basin Indians in any significant way. Unlike the essentially landless Southern Paiutes, the Northern Paiutes had the 320,000-acre Walker River Reservation set aside for their use in 1859, enclosing the lower Walker River, its terminal lake, and a fringe of surrounding land. Because of the lake, perennial water flow, arable bottomlands, and rich delta, this was a valuable piece of real estate, much coveted by non-Indian neighbors. A comparison between these two cases reveals that not the preservation of land title, nor the use of a portion of Native homeland, nor the presence of BIA programs and policies significantly affected Great Basin Indians' embrace of wage labor.

In 1859 the first BIA representative, sent to northern Nevada simply to discover what tribes lived there, found that Northern Paiutes had already been regularly employed by non-Indian ranchers and farmers for nearly ten years. He reported, they "will make excellent men to work. Some of them can take hold of a scythe, and mow, drive oxen or a four-horse team, equal to a white man" (Dodge 1859, 373). Two years later, actually during the only open fighting between Northern Paiutes and incoming settlers, the founder of the first non-Indian settlement confirmed the agent's assessment:

> I have lived in the Carson Valley ten years. . . . I established a store there and opened an extensive trade with the Indians. I sold my stock & finding the Indians friendly and disposed to work I opened a farm and have since followed farming and stock raising Indians being my principal laborers of whom I have often had as many as twenty five to work for me at one time. They are fine Indians and are very much inclined to labor. They will work at my kind of employment faithfully. (Reese 1861, 1)

In the same year that the reservation was set aside, silver was discovered forty miles to its west. This Comstock Lode brought a flood of miners, along with supporting cattle ranches and farms. Throughout the 1860s the Walker River Paiutes turned increasingly to wage labor, and in 1866 the agency farmer described them as "extensively employed throughout the country as farmhands, especially during the harvest season. For the purpose of securing employment they resort to the towns and mining camps in large numbers, and by their industrious habits and orderly behavior have gained praise and good will from our citizens" (Campbell 1866, 119).

The reservation itself provided a permanent home for few Northern Paiutes. Traditionally it had been a major winter campsite, highly valued for its rich fishery, but little used at other seasons when the people moved to other resource zones. When non-Indians were prevented by the federal reservation from seizing this bountiful fishery, as they had from the Southern Paiutes in Utah, the state of Nevada moved to block the Northern Paiutes from developing the resource into a commercial asset with a series of restrictive laws (Knack 1982).

Despite the reserve's location in an arid zone so far north that agriculture would never be a successful element of the regional economy, the BIA, in accordance with its standard policy of the era, insisted that the lakeshore become an agricultural base, which would require irrigation in that climate. The Walker River, heading in the Sierra Nevada, flowed across seventy miles of sandy, level valley floor before terminating in the lake. Spring thaws and major rains caused the river to jump its shallow banks and flood extensively. Early BIA irrigation constructs were simply piles of brush with a few rocks, all that could be done within the scant appropriation by the single agent with a horse team. Adequate during normal flow, these barriers promptly deteriorated in the face of seasonal flooding. The soft alluvium provided no footing for dams or irrigation diversions; floodwaters simply surrounded such structures and dragged them away. Irrigation reconstruction became an annual item in the reservation budget requests.

The agency farmer reported that the Indians "have manifested much interest in my first efforts at farming and voluntarily offered to assist in any way they could, but having neither provisions to feed them nor tools for them to work with, I was obliged to decline their assistance" (Thomas 1866, 121). Because of inadequate federal financial commitment to overcome these technological difficulties, agency farming policy at Walker River was not a success in the nineteenth century. Even had the Northern Paiutes, who, unlike the Southern Paiutes, lacked a tradition of horticulture, been interested in developing farming for either subsistence or commerce, they were never realistically presented with the opportunity. There was insufficient arable land along the stream banks, and the northerly climate and unreliable water source stood against them. The Paiutes, meanwhile, did not sit idly by but busied themselves to find self-support elsewhere.

As early as 1868 some Indian agents were using the Paiutes' wage labor to justify abandonment of the reserve on the grounds that they did not need it (and mining interests did). "The Indians are well fixed this fall as regards food and clothing. Their labor is in good demand, and at good wages," wrote the Nevada superintendent. "The reservations they have in this superintendency are at the present time of no use or value to them whatever. It would benefit them vastly more if they were abandoned and allowed to be settled by the whites, for there would be so many more farms for them to work on." With utterly fallacious logic he continued: "I have demonstrated the fact that these Indians will not farm for themselves; at the same time, they are good hands to work for white men" (Parker 1869). As in the Southern Paiute case, many BIA personnel saw wage labor and reservation life as economic alternatives rather than as complements.

An inspector arriving in 1870 warned the Walker River Paiutes about Euro-American best-use theory of land rights: "Unless these lands are improved around here, the white men will want to get the lands as the Indians won't work them. Now I want to know whether you will work the land so I can prevent white men from getting the land." Immediately assuring him of the importance Paiutes placed on the land and their willingness to work, the Paiute headman also inquired: "If my boys go outside of reservation, away from it—does it make any difference?" The agent responded, "If they do they can't get anything from me. . . . Indians who want to work for others away from reservation, all right, they can look out for themselves, buy their own clothes, food" (Douglas 1870, 16). BIA policy disclaimed any responsibility for Indians not living on reservations. Meant as a threat, this disclaimer did not worry the Walker

River people. They knew and realistically accepted that the reservation was an insufficient economic base for their population.

The economy that the Walker River Paiutes had developed by 1870 was complicated and involved Native foraging, wage labor, and market sales. "No part of the Reservation is under cultivation," observed the same inspector:

> [T]here are no . . . agricultural implements, nor in fact any thing of use for the purposes of agriculture *or for any other purpose* as far as Indians are concerned. There are but few Indians on the Reserve. . . . The Indians at present attach no value to the Reservation except as a fishery. They congregate in the summer, catch and cure their fish and after the fishing season betake themselves to the mountains, mines, and towns, working for what they can get selling their fish, and making such a living as they can. They make money enough to obtain food and clothing by working at small jobs such as chopping and sawing wood, tending stock, shooting ducks for which they find a ready market, and other transient occupations. They appear to be well fed and comfortably clothed by their own efforts without any assistance from Government. (Douglas 1869, 2–6; emphasis in the original)

At least as early as 1870, a mere twenty years after initial non-Indian settlement, there were already well-documented bands, often of mixed tribal origins, living around white towns. Whether these were distinct town-dwelling groups or simply the urban phase of an economic cycle utilizing both foraging and wage resources, I do not know. They did eventually develop a stable population, although, again, at what point I do not know.

As in southern Utah, both non-Indians reliant on Indian labor and off-reservation Paiutes often resisted reservationization. In 1888 a letter by the headman of the band living on the edges of the town of Paradise, north of Walker River on the Humboldt, defended the Natives' right to live where they chose:

> My people are well and happy and good and never take anything from the whites. My people help the whites to cut wood, grub sagebrush, pack water, sheer sheep and all the work that white people do. . . . We want

to be left as we now live and not be sent to a reservation. My people go into the mountains and hunt the deer but we never drive any cattle or horses away nor harm them. We work for the white people and with the money buy our flour, tea, coffee, sugar and clothing. We do not want any of our people in this valley taken away . . . but want them left here to work, and help the white men. (George 1888, 1–2)

Again, as in the Southern Paiute case, northern Nevada non-Indians soon came to rely on Northern Paiute labor. By the early 1880s, "nearly all of the extra farm work near the reservation [was] being done by these hired Indians" (McMaster 1882, 117). A BIA agent specified the types of jobs Northern Paiutes found:

They largely work for the whites in nearly every department of labor. . . . Quite a number are fair workmen at carpentering, at blacksmithing, horseshoeing, irrigating, building ditches, fences, stables, and small frame houses; at least one-half the men can talk English sufficiently to be understood in ordinary work. They have done a large amount of the farm labor in Mason Valley,[1] Humboldt Valley, Surprise Valley, and the other neighboring valleys this season. . . . Quite a number have places that they live on outside the reservation and get their living by working for the whites, as do laborers elsewhere, appearing no different but in color from white laborers (McMaster 1884b, 126)

Paiute wage labor was not steady employment. Like the Native subsistence economy, the new wage labor was carefully scheduled into a balance of multiple resources. "In addition to doing their ranch work," the Walker River agent described,

several Indians find employment during the winter at a Soda factory or Marsh near the reservation. Oftentimes as many as thirty are employed during two months of the winter at a borax factory near the southern boundary of the reservation. . . . After curing their own hay in summer many of them take employment with the white ranchers in the neighboring valley during the remainder of the hay season. . . . This with a small amount of fish, game and Government freighting are their resources. (Ellis 1894, 4–5)

Walker River agents in general approved off-reservation wage labor. It seemed to accomplish the acculturation desired by BIA policy; the agents' reports frequently approvingly documented Paiutes' knowledge of English, dress, and hair length. Wage employment eased tight reservation budgets by reducing the number of Indians for whom agents were responsible. However, after a day school was constructed, wage employment also lowered enrollments by taking entire families away from the reservation and generated embarrassing statistics.

The agents tried to counterbalance the wage labor that drew so many Paiutes away from the reservation by creating jobs for them on the reserve. From the early 1870s onward the agents employed "a small force of Indians putting in spring crops and making ditches for irrigation" (Bateman 1871, 1). But farming was not even mildly successful before the 1880s. Trying to supplement the shortage of irrigated land, the agents hired Paiute men to haul government supplies from the railhead, build bridges, supply construction timber, dig irrigation ditches, and grade roads—in short, construct the infrastructure of the reservation itself. By the end of the decade the Walker River agency had become a major employer of Indian labor.

As early as 1865 a standardized wage of $1.00 per day was established in western Nevada for Indians to do farm labor, $1.50 to grade railroad bed, and $2.50 to dig in the borax and salt mines. At first the agency argued that, like non-Indian farmers, Indians on the reserve were really working for themselves and should not expect any wage. Laborers were supported with enough food for the day they worked. This practice, however, ignored the availability of off-reservation wage jobs and the Paiutes' grasp of market dynamics. As hay harvest approached in 1887, the agency farmer complained: "I expect to cut, haul, and stack from 120 thousand to 200 thousand pounds of Hay at this Reservation, and the old men who work for rations can do but little at harvesting, and as the young able bodied men can find employment on ranches at wages ranging from $1.50 to $2.00 per day and board during harvesting, therefore I cannot get them to work for rations" (Gibson 1887, 1).

The agency began to offer what it called wages, comparable to $1.00 per day, paid, not in cash, but in an equivalent value of government-issue goods. One agent explained how this system worked: Paiute workers were "given rations and feed for their teams and credited on their wagons

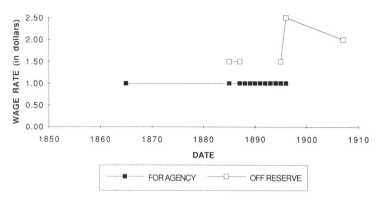

Fig. 6.4. Walker River Northern Paiute daily wage rates, 1850–1907. (Data were compiled from Campbell 1865; Gibson 1885, 1887, 1888; Jones 1907c; Sears 1889, 1890; Spriggs 1906; Warner 1891, 1893; Wootten 1894, 1895, 1896.)

and harness +c. After they had earned these they were credited on Blankets clothing +c" (McMaster 1884b, 2). Because of extensive precious metal mining, western Nevada's was a hard-currency economy. The Paiutes were accustomed to receiving salaries in cash off the reservation and resented government payment in kind. To attract any men with wagons and teams, who had the mobility to work elsewhere, the agency broke down in November 1884 and paid these workers in cash. Nevertheless, it resisted outside pressure on labor rates, continuing to pay only $1.00 per day for manual labor until the end of the century.

The reservation labor pattern did not change significantly until 1902, when a professionally engineered irrigation system was funded in anticipation of allotment. Competition between the irrigation project and the agency soon developed for the fixed number of Paiute laborers. There also happened to be a mining boom in progress just south of the reserve. A narrow-gauge railroad was under construction, and its owners preferred Indians to grade track bed: "Indian labor is much more satisfactory than whites in the same capacity" (Spriggs 1906, 271). Not only did the railroad absorb the labor of many Walker River men, but, perhaps worse, it also began paying $2.50 per day to attract them, inflating the traditionally stable regional wage rate (see Figure 6.4).

In the spring of 1907 the Nevada superintendent for Indian affairs anticipated a shortage of workers for reservation projects. "[O]ur Indian laborers," he wrote, "will be in demand in the hayfields through July and August and if we cannot give them definite promise of work the probability is that they will get scattered and we will be able to do but little before September" (Asbury 1907, 1). July proved him correct. The engineer in charge of the Walker River irrigation project wrote:

> [I] have had a streneous [sic] time getting started, as the shovel-men did not like to go to work for $1.75 per day, and the teams were at work in their hay-fields. . . . Some of the ranchmen from Mason Valley came over here and offered as high as $3.00 per day for hay pitchers, and a bunch started over, but Mr. Lovegrove [the BIA farmer in charge of Walker River] sent the [Indian] Poliece [sic] after them and brought them back, in fact the "big stick" has been brought into play occasionally to get anything done. (Jones 1907a, 1)

In October the haying season and agency road construction siphoned off men, and by midmonth the off-reservation potato harvest started. The irrigation project innovated in order to entice Indian labor back by paying wages in chits for the local white-owned general store, which carried a better line of goods than the agency-issued ones. Nothing seemed to work; Paiutes continued to seek employment off the reservation.

Competition soon came not only from alternate white employers but also from the Native subsistence cycle. Despite project delays, the agency refused to bid for labor by offering higher wages. The engineer grumbled, "[W]here the Indians gain on the wage proposition is from the fact that the whole families are given employment, squaws, and children included, therby [sic] being able to gain in the agregate [sic] more than as though the men were working alone on the ditch work" (Jones 1907b, 1).[2] After the potato crop was in, the piñon harvest and the fall rabbit drive kept the Paiutes off the reservation.

Fig. 6.5. Northern Paiute women work in the wheat fields near the Pyramid Lake Reservation in northern Nevada. In the Great Basin one of the earliest forms of wage employment was to hand-harvest wheat and other grains (this was before machinery was generally available for this purpose). Workers were nearly always women who brought their own traditional basketry equipment, formerly used for nearly identical harvesting of wild grass seeds. (Photo by Samuel A. Barrett, 1916; Photographic Collections, Milwaukee Public Museum)

By late October the irrigation project had been stalled four months for lack of laborers. The engineer in charge broke down and recommended

> that an increase for team wages to $3.50 per day might help owing to the high prices of forage, but cannot recomend [sic] any increase in the wages of the shovelmen, as we are paying more now than they are realy [sic] worth, but have to to [sic] meet the cost of living at this place, which is high for them, but where the indians are employed outside the reservation the wages are $2. per day, and in some instances board with it, but since the recent financial flurry a great many employers of indians have been obliged to close their work. (Jones 1907c, 1–2)

Late in the month the agency farmer was forced to agree: "I really think the Govt ought to pay $2. per day for Shovel labor. And 3 1/2 for the teams. The squaws are making more at picking up potatoes than the Govt pays a man for working on the ditch. The Indians pay one another more than the Govt offers. There are several men now working on the Res for other indians at $2 1/2 per day. and $2 per day and board" (Lovegrove 1907a, 1).

At the same time, the irrigation project had a job paying $75 a month for a man with a horse team but could find no white man to take it at that rate. "Several Indians," the agent observed, "would be glad to get the white man's chance at $75 to look after a team, and glad to get it. But no it is not for the Indian. *They know these things and do not like it*" (Lovegrove 1907a, 2; emphasis added). Paiutes were rejected for this job, not because of inability, but because of race. The agency itself was practicing wage discrimination, and the Paiutes knew it.

The agency farmer then complicated matters for the irrigation engineer by finding a lucrative short-term contract for a few Paiutes to haul firewood to the new boomtown of Rawhide at the then-unheard-of rate of $10.00 per day. Not only were the irrigation men annoyed by this, but also the off-reservation non-Indian freighters were outraged that *Indians* should benefit when they had hoped to profit themselves. "[T]hey are trying their best to get a union started at Rawhide among the teamsters to boycott the Indians as freighters," protested the Walker River farmer. "[T]hey are working against the Indians as much as they can and trying to get shelter for their own benefit at the same time" (Lovegrove 1907b, 1). "They are giving the Indians *Hell* at the other end of the line," he noted later, without elaborating on the means non-Indian teamsters were using (Lovegrove 1907c, 2). A full-scale regional, inter-ethnic labor war was in progress, and one of the issues was whether the substandard Indian wage would continue.

The Walker River agency did finally increase general wages, "on account of the high prices for labor prevailing around here," to $3.50 per day for a man and his horse team and $2.00 for manual laborers (Jones 1907d, 1). This was still below the going rate for off-reservation Indian labor.

Not only had the Paiutes gained concessions on wages, but they had also forced the BIA to expedite its notoriously slow accounting procedures and wage payment. Amid this labor shortage, they went elsewhere. "Uncle Sam is so blamed slow to pay," complained the agent, "that they can get out and make more in the same time at this time of the year than working on the ditch" (Lovegrove 1907c). In addition, regional inflation was driving up the price of hay, and Walker River Paiutes were withholding all they raised on their allotments for their own teams and in anticipation of future profits (Jones 1907d). The Paiutes were clearly learning the lessons of market capitalism.

By November the irrigation engineer was so desperate for workers that he brought in Pyramid Lake Paiutes as "strikebreakers." Even so, in December he was still short and reported in relief, "I had a letter from Capt. [Paiute headman] Ben who went to Fallon or Carson Sink to the big Rabbit hunt, and he stated that all of the Walker River indians were going to return here Saturday" (Jones 1907e, 1). Not until mid-December did the Indians return from subsistence hunting and the engineer get twenty-three horse teams working and full manual crews (Jones 1907f). Despite such struggles, during fiscal year 1908 the Walker River irrigation project paid Paiutes over $16,000 in wages, a significant contribution to the Native economy.

By the turn of the century the Walker River Northern Paiutes were clearly in the habit of deciding economic issues on the basis of financial maximization, sometimes to the discomfiture of the agency. They were juggling a complicated economic cycle that included wage labor for both men and women as an essential component. They were very much integrated into the overall economic development of the region, both on the reservation and off.

CONCLUSION

Although wage labor was a radically new way of living for the Northern and Southern Paiutes in the mid-nineteenth century, it shared many characteristics with the Native economy that enabled compatibility with continued hunting and gathering. Wage labor could therefore become absorbed as a part of a mixed system utilizing a diversity of economic resources, which also included continued foraging, some reservation farming, and the running of a few cattle. Like the use of native resources, wage labor was seasonal and short term, nearly always by the day or week. It demanded high mobility. Both men and women participated significantly.

Wage labor in the Great Basin began surprisingly early and before the turn of the century created social patterns seen in few other areas until the mid-twentieth century, although they are now all too familiar in reservation and urban Indian populations (Jorgensen 1971; Stanley 1978; U.S. Congress 1969). Lacking sufficient arable land to support the registered population despite federally-financed irrigation development, all Paiute reservations within ten years of their founding became refuges for the old and infirm, burdened with large numbers of dependent grandchildren. The middle-aged and able were drained off by the white economy and Indians' own need to seek income elsewhere. Jobs were of a distinctive type: overwhelmingly unskilled and manual, carrying low prestige and low pay, not involving extensive training, and not leading to promotion or occupational specialization. Jobs became stereotypically agricultural for men and domestic for women. Wages were stratified, with Indian labor paid significantly less than non-Indian labor. What little employment did exist on the reservations was primarily infrastructural construction, heavily dependent on fickle federal subsidies. There was virtually no private enterprise, either Indian or non-

Indian, on the reserves. The Paiutes themselves lacked the capital or skills in capitalist resource management and decisionmaking to guide the group in economic development.

The presence or absence of BIA personnel and programs made no apparent difference in the economic history of Great Basin groups. Because of the inadequate lands reserved, it seemed to have made very little difference whether Indians were assigned a reservation, as were the Walker River Northern Paiutes, or not, as in the case of most nineteenth century Southern Paiutes; the end results were the same. Precontact economies had been predicated on the sequential seasonal utilization of a wide range of wild resources harvested from lands far more extensive than Euro-Americans ever considered necessary to set aside for Indian support. Within one generation of initial Euro-American contact Great Basin Indians lost control over those extensive natural resources and were left, at best, with only a segment of their land base; they were consequently denied large portions of their annual round. Development of reservation resources, such as mining or ditch irrigation systems, required capital far beyond the means of the Paiutes, and federal funding was wholly inadequate until well into the twentieth century. Thus, with no new resources opened on the reserves to compensate for those lost beyond their boundaries and facing water shortages, very limited agricultural production, and crippled growth, Great Basin reservations, where they did exist, were chronically unable to support the Native population—either through traditional or horticultural subsistence or through commercialized cash cropping or fishing (Knack 1982).

Native groups with lands, like their off-reservation-dwelling relatives, were forced to fill the resulting economic void by any means they could; Indians throughout the Great Basin had virtually no option but trade and no marketable commodity except their labor (see also Malouf 1966, 18, 29, for Goshute Shoshones; Knack 1992, 72–73, for Washakie Shoshones; and Rusco 1991, 80–81, for Yomba Shoshones). That Indian labor, however, was avidly sought by the explosively growing and labor-short Euro-American settlements; where reservations existed, this labor market was simply supplemented by agency jobs. Within a single generation of Euro-American settlement both the Northern and Southern

Paiutes had become integrated into the wage labor economy, albeit at a distinctive, low stratum in that hierarchical system. Not only did they rely on wages but also regional agriculture and construction relied on them, until mining expansion in the north and federally subsidized development projects in the south brought in competitive non-Indian labor between 1905 and World War II.

Such, indeed, are the characteristics of many reservation and urban Indian economies in the second half of the twentieth century. One hundred years earlier Indians of the Great Basin may have had the very dubious distinction of developing one of the first "modern" Indian economies.

7

WATERING THE FLOWER: LAGUNA PUEBLO AND THE SANTA FE RAILROAD, 1880–1943

KURT M. PETERS

The government's twin assimilation strategies of tribal termination and urban relocation between 1950 and 1970, which offered employment and vocational training as incentives for change, are often cited as responsible for twentieth-century Native American migrations. The myth that Native American urban migration stemmed only from mid-century termination and relocation policies has persistently obscured historical reality. Between 1900 and 1945 significant numbers of people of color migrated to the San Francisco Bay area, principally as laborers for the expanding empires of the automotive, railroad, and shipbuilding industries. As a result of these movements, the region near Richmond, California, along San Francisco Bay north of Oakland, became heavily infused with migrant laborers. One such group of people came from Laguna Pueblo in New Mexico, arriving at Richmond in 1922 as employees of the Santa Fe Railroad.

Standard rhetoric concerning twentieth-century Native American urban experience ignores the fact that Laguna Pueblo Indians began migrating from New Mexico to the bay area at least thirty years prior to the introduction of the government's paradigm for urban assimilation. Furthermore, it was not termination of the tribe that instigated Laguna movement but the motivating power of a specialized agreement with the Santa Fe Railroad, coupled with a changing economic structure at Old Laguna. The historical source of the Laguna migration lies wrapped in layers of relationships with other Native people, Spanish intruders, and, later, Anglo-American invaders. Land tenure conflicts in New Mexico had plagued the Lagunas for generations, and their economy was slowly shifting away from an agrarian base as early as the 1880s. There is evidence that long before the move to California, declining agricultural success forced the Lagunas to look outside their traditional structure for subsistence.[1] The arrival of the steam locomotive in the Southwest offered alternative employment, which led directly to the departure of many Lagunas from the pueblo to areas hundreds of miles distant.

In 1880 a dispute resulted from the government's proposed taking of a portion of the Laguna lands near Albuquerque for westward expansion of the Atlantic and Pacific Railroad lines, later to become part of the Santa Fe Railroad. According to Laguna historians, a compromise was struck between the pueblo and the railroad involving the guarantee of Laguna railroad employment on a yearly renewable basis. This annual contract renewal came to be known among the Laguna people as "watering the flower." There is a disparity between Laguna remembrances and corroborative data as to whether the agreement with the railroad was ever set out on paper.[2] Aalthough no written agreement has been discovered, the Lagunas involved believe strongly that an oral contract was made and continues in force.

Indeed, in 1922 belief in the certainty of this mutual obligation led a contingent of Lagunas to Richmond in response to a nationwide railroad crisis. The operations of the Santa Fe were being crippled by a national strike. A substantial number of Lagunas met the railroad's needs: they watered the flower, their contract, and migrated to the Richmond Terminal to bolster a depleted workforce.[3] During the workers' lengthy sojourn a set of boxcars, completely enclosed by the railroad yards, constituted their housing. Within this enclave they replicated traditional cultural practices, forming a microcosmic extension of their distant pueblo.

Subsequent waves of migrant Lagunas, buttressed with members of neighboring Acoma Pueblo, left New Mexico, passing in and out of the terminal at Richmond between 1922 and the mid-1980s, when the "Indian village," as it had become known, was disbanded. They adapted themselves to surrounding non-Indian functions but clung to tradition, returning often to the pueblo for nurturing celebrations and rituals. Children were born in the village, some later referring to themselves as "boxcar babies," while others migrated from Laguna with their parents. Scores of Lagunas were raised in the village and educated nearby, and at one point over twenty Laguna children attended a local elementary school. Some of the Catholic village residents participated in masses celebrated at a local church. Tribal members working for Santa Fe learned to value their own worth, joining railroad craft unions when the workforce at large voted to organize.

During the workers' employment at Richmond the village functioned as a de facto satellite of the distant Laguna Pueblo. Sociologically and psychologically the village remained inextricably a part of the home pueblo, much as if it were situated nearby, along the railroad right-of-way west of the Rio Grande River in New Mexico. The shared experience of those who intermittently occupied the village is a tribute to both cultural persistence and pragmatic accommodation by those who watered the flower of the Santa Fe contract. In the process the participants not only extended the vitality of the Laguna Pueblo community but also expanded significantly their people's rich cultural tradition. The effect of the Laguna–Santa Fe relationship on the lives of the laborers involved is notable even today.

Eighty people are gathered in the Laguna Indian Reservation Recreation Hall for a sit-down dinner on the evening of 14 November 1992. A white-haired man, 102 years old, is surveying a collection of old photographs on an otherwise bare wall. The 1880 agreement was just thirty years old when he began service nearby as a laborer, working on a section gang from a now-vanished railroad junction called "Suanee." The old man's Santa Fe experience can be recalled through the nostalgic photographs. All the dinner guests are among the 7,103 enrolled members of the Laguna Indian Tribe of New Mexico.[4] The symbolism of this night is purely Laguna: there is evidence of historic events that remain forever just at the edge of the participants' reality.

This year is the eve of the 125th anniversary of the founding of the Atchison and Topeka Railroad Company, ancestor of the Santa Fe Railroad Company and inheritor of the Atlantic and Pacific Railroad in New Mexico (Daggett 1981, 127; Duke and Kistler 1963, 11). Those present have been somehow connected, if even peripherally, to the Santa Fe during their lifetimes. Retirees, wives, children, grandchildren, great-grandchildren, and widows and orphans of deceased Santa Fe workers are sitting down together. It is the first time in the 112 years since the Atlantic and Pacific, now the Santa Fe, contracted to employ the Lagunas as laborers that a gathering of this kind has taken place. Many express their pleasure, commenting repeatedly, "We thought the company had forgotten about us." Although there are no Santa Fe representatives present, the dinner guests are nonetheless surprised and happy that their former employer has sponsored this reunion dinner.

The reunion has been eagerly awaited by most of the participants. Working for the Santa Fe brought many alliances, experiences, and memories that are now only partially recalled by fading photographs and news clippings: the Santa Fe All Indian Band, powwows in Golden Gate Park, children playing at night under the dim security lights of the train yards, a first communion dinner in a boxcar meeting hall at the Richmond Terminal. The reunion is a chance, hoped by most to be the first of many, to grasp at threads of experiences that are now woven into that seamless cloth of awareness: the persistent sense of being Laguna. Those experiential strands emanate from the post–Civil War foundations of railroad expansion.

A group of investors met on the frontier in 1858 with a plan for capitalizing on the flood of immigration and federal grants for railroad construction (Duke and Kistler 1963, 10).[5] The Atchison and Topeka Railroad Company was born at this meeting in Atchison, Kansas, and chartered by the state of Kansas in 1859. Four years later the name was changed to Atchison, Topeka and Santa Fe Railroad Company (Duke and Kistler 1963, 10; Daggett 1981, 127). A congressional land grant was subsequently made in 1863 allowing a route from Atchison, Kansas, to the Colorado state line. During July 1866 congressional debates ensued over the morality of proposals to invade Indian Territory for the proposed track routes and whether title could be legally obtained at all. Concurrently, the Atlantic and Pacific Railroad was authorized to build a line from Springfield, Missouri, to Albuquerque, along the thirty-fifth parallel to the Colorado River at the Arizona border, and then "by the most practicable . . . route" to California and the Pacific Ocean (Duke and Kistler 1963, 11). Congressional allowances for easements along the right-of-way were given with relief from "taxation within the Territories of the United States" for the grounds so granted (Duke and Kistler 1963, 11).[6] A specific grant of land in excess of thirteen million acres was made to the Atlantic and Pacific in 1866 for a line between Albuquerque and the Arizona-California border at the Colorado River (Armitage 1948, 204).

Laguna territory lay squarely in the path of the railroad surveys favoring a route from Colorado through New Mexico to California.[7] Thus, after years of warring with marauding tribes; continually resisting invaders of Spanish, Mexican, and Anglo-American ancestries; and accommodating squatters of all types, the Laguna Pueblo people found themselves under new pressure regarding their land: at least two railroads would now vie for use of their living space.

The Atlantic and Pacific entered New Mexico in 1880 and began laying track south and west of Isleta Pueblo. Reports that "the hard labor of building the grades . . . took all available and willing men from Laguna, Acoma and Zuni" (Minge 1991, 65) corroborate narratives claiming the railroad crossed Laguna lands during that year. The Lagunas seized on the arrival of the railroad's construction crew to set a precedent, however. According to modern narratives regarding the 1880s, a war chief named Lorenzo was away actively pursuing parties of Apache and Navajo raiders.[8] His son, Hiuwec, secretary of the Tribal Council, took responsibility for halting the crews of the Atlantic and Pacific Railroad preparing to lay track across Laguna land. In stopping this extension of the rail line, Hiuwec set in motion a visit from eastern railroad authorities, which resulted in another accommodation of outsiders by the Laguna Pueblo people. This time there was a peculiar innovation. The railroad would be allowed through the Laguna territory unmolested, with a single stipulation: it would forever employ as many of the Lagunas to help build and maintain the system as wished to work so long as the governor of their pueblo granted the workers his approval. This oral agreement in 1880 gave the Laguna people a guarantee of jobs and the railroad a guarantee of unhindered right-of-way. The event is recalled more than eighty years later during interviews with an elder Laguna:

> A. When the railroad first came through here, the old people . . . they had some understanding [with] the railroad about coming through here . . . about the lands of the village.
>
> Q. . . . When did the railroad first come through here?
>
> A. The railroad came through here, which was the Atlantic and Pacific Railroad. Came through here . . . came through Albuquerque about 1880.
>
> Q. Right to California?
>
> A. Yeah, to California in 1881. . . . It came through here, through the Laguna Reservation . . . was the first one out west. . . . Since then the Santa Fe Railroad has run clear from Chicago to west coast . . . San Francisco. (Husband 1969, 1)

The bargain of 1880 was sealed by a handshake, according to the narratives, referred to as "the gentlemen's agreement of friendship" (personal interviews). Subsequent railroad negotiations with Laguna Pueblo for other privileges were made, especially for the use of resources.

> A. . . . The railroad had to have water, just like the coal. . . . They had to have water and . . . we had water right there. . . . Every so far they had water. . . . You can see the water tank down here . . . real big. There used to be a couple of those big tanks right down in Laguna, just east of where the depot used to be . . . and . . . they have a spring, northeast of Laguna. Do you know where that railroad crossing is?
>
> Q. Yeah.
>
> A. I don't know how many billions of gallons of water the Santa Fe has pumped out of that spring.
>
> Q. And the railroad paid for that water?

A. I don't know. Railroad . . . I couldn't tell you . . . if they paid anything for that[9] . . . but they [the Atlantic and Pacific] lost the contract[10] . . . and that is where they [the Atchison, Topeka and Santa Fe] agreed to come in.

Q. Hiring a man . . .

A. Giving the man a right to work . . .

Q. Anybody?

A. Yeah, anybody that wants a job they can work. . . . There used to be a lot of them working there. . . . You see that contract was written forever.

Q. Forever?

A. Yeah. (Husband 1969, 9)

Laguna men began their employment laying track, with some eventually becoming section maintainers, on the portion of the rail line passing through the 458,933-acre Laguna Reservation (Reddy 1993, 1036). The latter work was done from fixed locations on the reservation known as New Laguna, Mesita, Casa Blanca, and Las Lunas. Laguna maintenance workers and their families were housed in permanent structures built by the railroad at these points along the right-of-way. The primary negotiator of the original agreement, Hiuwec, was working as a section maintainer on the reservation during the early 1900s. Other men accepted Santa Fe work at Albuquerque, Gallup, and other locations along the rail line outside the reservation.

A. . . . When I was just a boy . . . they used a lot of coal. . . . They had coal shutes here and there and every . . . few miles . . . and they had one here at Laguna . . . one in Albuquerque and Belen and . . . one in Grants . . . and Gallup and all. . . . A lot of our people work in the coal shute and around here and there. . . . Different towns furnish for boilers, make a lot of work, laying pipelines. (Husband 1969, 8)

On 29 June 1897 the lines established by the Atlantic and Pacific were purchased by the Atchison, Topeka and Santa Fe, and the "way to the Pacific began to open" (Duke and Kistler 1963, 10). The Laguna Pueblo and its relationship to the railroads using its lands are not mentioned in the documents of sale, and there are no Laguna signatures (Santa Fe Pacific Railroad Co. 1897).

Preparation was being made by railroad companies for a move into the lucrative transoceanic mercantile business of San Francisco Bay, with a link to the profitable eastern commerce of Chicago. A real estate developer named Augustine S. Macdonald contacted other investors with railroad connections, and in 1899 the town of Richmond, California, was created as a rail terminus (Duke and Kistler 1963, 161; Scott 1985, 88). The Santa Fe purchased rights to the San Francisco and San Joaquin Valley Railway to complete the rail lines to Richmond. As a bridge connection between Richmond and San Francisco, across the bay, would not be contemplated until well after the turn of the century, the first San Francisco–Chicago direct railway service began in July 1900, when cargo in a Santa Fe–owned ferry left China Basin in San Francisco for the rail head at Point Richmond (Bryant 1974, 180; Look 1946, 107).

Of all the areas on the Santa Fe system, none was more difficult to recruit for than the Southwest. According to some sources, track crews were mostly Irishmen in the 1870s, as the heat and seemingly inhospitable desert kept away all but the least employable unskilled white workers. Santa Fe paid higher wages and was less harsh with strikers in response to these difficulties and recruited heavily among people of color as laborers for the area. Accounts mention that Mexicans were recruited for track crews in the early 1880s, that they were in use throughout the system by 1910, and that they continued to numerically dominate the southwestern crews through the end of the century. Use of black Americans from the early days, and Japanese immigrants beginning around 1900, has been documented (Bryant 1974, 87, 101, 322; Ducker 1983, 27). Although track crews in the more desirable locations at the eastern end of the system received less pay than their counterparts in the desert, the Japanese apparently undercut them all by a willingness to work for as little as $1 per day (Ducker 1983, 28). In 1928 the Meriam Report noted the Santa Fe's attitude that as common laborers the "Mexican is slow and easy-going" and that "Indians compare very well with white men doing the same class of work" (Meriam et al. 1928, 703).

The recruitment of local Indians started as the Atlantic and Pacific began to lay track west of Albuquerque. Near the Santa Fe's large western land grant lay several reservations, including the Laguna, Navajo, Hopi,

Zuni, and Walapai, and local merchants and traders who had connections within the tribal communities were often relied on to supply Native American labor to the railroad. These workmen began to swell the numbers of nonwhite employees already on the railroad's track force and are cited as occupying "nearly a hundred [jobs] in the lower positions in the shop at Needles" (Ducker 1983, 28). The activities of one labor recruiter were reported in 1906 by *The Indian's Friend*, a monthly assimilationist newsletter targeted for a largely non-Indian audience:

> C. E. Dagnette, outing agent for the Indians in the southwest, arrived in the city last night from a trip to Los Angeles and Phoenix, where he has been completing arrangements with the Santa Fe coast line people for the supplying of Indian labor to the Santa Fe. Mr. Dagnette said that contracts had been signed with the Santa Fe people for all the Indian laborers that could possibly be supplied. The laborers will compose Navajos, Moquis, Hopis and Apache Indians, and will work west of Albuquerque. (National Indian Association 1906, 7)

In addition, the Meriam Report noted that "the Santa Fe railroad company seems to favor Pueblo Indians in its employment policy and has Indian employees in the cities it serves in Arizona and New Mexico" (Meriam et al. 1928, 705).

During the early years the Santa Fe took every precaution to assure its employees' health, comfort, and "proper" distractions from the relative isolation of life on the road. Company-run hospitals, to which employees donated a small amount of pay, were touted by the Santa Fe as having "no superior in the country." A system of "reading rooms, recreation rooms, lodging-houses, bath-houses, lunch places and audience rooms for religious and other gatherings" were in full operation under the direction of S. E. Busser by the early 1900s. Samuel Busser was responsible for utilizing the extensive facilities to avoid "the various dissapations [sic] which once brought grief to so many railroad men and their families" (Gleed 1912, 25). There is no indication in the documentation of this era that the Santa Fe facilities were not available to the people of color employed by the railroad, but a random survey of photographs taken at the popular reading rooms and recreation facilities does not reveal anyone of other than Anglo-American phenotype.[11]

Pay was distributed to the Santa Fe worker as "a full recognition of his services as measured by the prevailing rates" (Gleed 1912, 25). The wages of Santa Fe employees in 1900 averaged just less than $700 annually, as compared to $548 for all railroads. By 1915 all-railroad earnings had advanced to an average of $815 annually, as compared to $854.81 for Santa Fe employees. According to railroad historian Lawrence L. Waters (1950, 328), "The average employee of the Santa Fe received 27.2 cents per hour and worked a little over 60 hours per week." Waters also notes that between 1900 and 1915 the employees' "status was relatively unchanged as far as purchasing power was concerned." The onset of World War I accounted for a dramatic increase in wages resulting from shipments of war matériel. Piggybacked bonuses based on war production brought sharp increases in pay; so that average earnings had doubled by 1920. One retired Laguna summarized his attitude about Santa Fe employment in an interview conducted at Laguna during the 1960s:

Q. Good boss?

A. Very good, I enjoyed working for them. . . . Well it all depends on how you feel about your job. . . . A lot of them work for the railroad and they get tired . . . and of course other things that would keep them from holding this jobs . . . liquor . . . and . . .

Q. Yeah, I'll bet that was bad, wasn't it?

A. Well otherwise if you do the job right, they don't bother you. . . . At least that is the way that I have experienced it. . . . Nobody bothers you when you work. . . . I go ahead and do my day's work, do it like it should be done . . . to the best of my ability. . . . That's the way I served the [Santa Fe]. . . .

Q. They must have fired a lot of Indian people.

A. Oh yeah, they did. (Husband 1969, 7)

The classic *The Problem of Indian Administration* (Meriam et al. 1928, 7) devotes dozens of its pages to the social, health, and employment conditions of so-called industrially housed Indians. One significant focus of Lewis Meriam's study is the Indians who migrated to southwestern cities in response to railroad employment with the Santa Fe. The study particularly notes that "five Indians now with the company have been *granted the privilege* of a course in the railroad apprenticeship school; two of these have already completed their courses" (Meriam et al. 1928, 703; emphasis added). The possibility of advancement to be gained by the apprentice system was not lost on the Laguna employees:

Q. How did the men learn their jobs?

A. Well, they had apprentice. . . . They kind of like, go to school for a few weeks. When they started to work for Santa Fe they trained them how to do different kind of jobs.

Q. When someone signed on to come out here [Richmond], then Santa Fe decided who would get what job?

A. Right.

Another former Santa Fe employee intercedes in the interview:

A. Let me tell you about that. I'm with Santa Fe thirty-nine years. Want you to know about this. Men that finish high school, they hire them. They put them on Apprentice for four years, but mostly are White people. After your four years finished and then you're a welder, and they test you, take you back to Chicago for the testing. They pass, they're a welder, or an electrician, lathe machinist. But our [Laguna] people, the men, when they finish here at school, they go to school for their training around here [New Mexico] somewhere to learn the welding and all that stuff. When they finish, the welder and the electrician, they go to the Santa Fe job. They just hire them right away.

Q. They were good for you?

A. Yeah, but before, a long time ago, when they are set to strike in 1922, we [Santa Fe] don't pay much because they don't have union. (Personal interview)

Railroad and government animosity toward labor unions, resulting partially from the wage gains granted during the emergency needs of World War I, had erupted during a series of railroad strikes when management tried to roll back wartime wage gains. One such confrontation, the Shopmen's Strike of 1922, strangled the operations of the railroads nationally, and service disruptions were commonplace. Near Needles, California, over three hundred passengers had been put off the train and left stranded by striking Santa Fe workers loyal to the unions. The loyalty of the non-union Laguna workers to their employer, based on their forty-two-year-old verbal agreement, is equally clear: "You come up something like the strike, you always call us and need help, we'll help you, you know. They take good care of us, and that's a good company, the railroad" (personal interview).

The flower of the Laguna Pueblo agreement was watered by a request from the Santa Fe management. The Laguna governor responded, and more than one hundred men were moved from the pueblo in New Mexico to the Santa Fe Terminal at Richmond, California, to replace striking workers. Lagunas were transported from their home and through the picket lines in coach cars. Once in the railroad yards at Richmond, they were housed and fed for the duration of the strike in the assembly hall, one of the several maintenance buildings at the terminal (personal interviews). As the strike continued, some railroads signed the "Baltimore Agreement," essentially putting the control of terms of rehiring strikers in the hands of railroad management. The Santa Fe continued to hold out and did not initially sign onto the negotiations, instead injecting the diminished labor force with nonunion workers, including the Lagunas.

When the pueblo responded to this emergency need, the company found a shortage of available Laguna men and called on neighboring Acoma Pueblo to fill the ranks. Animosities based on historic friction over New Mexico land tenure were revived by this arrangement and would continue as the Acomas later became permanent residents of the village in Richmond.

A. The Acoma people did not have a verbal agreement with the Santa Fe.

Q. How did they get involved?

A. Well, during the time, in 1922, that was the first railroad strike. That was when the Acoma people came about because the Governor of the Pueblo did not have enough Laguna people to send out to the Bay area. It just so happened that the President [a Santa Fe executive] that was sent to Laguna hired some of the Acoma people to go out there. That's how the Acoma people got there. (Personal interview)

The role of the Native Americans called on during the 1922 strike was, prima facie, the dangerous one of strikebreaker. Interviews with sons and daughters of the Lagunas sent to Richmond in 1922 are revealing about their parents' knowledge of their role in the strike:

A. My father-in-law, he was out there. A lot of the men, these old folks, they were out there in California. My father was out there in 1922. He works around Oakland, and down as far as to Bakersfield, for the Santa Fe. He was a fire builder for the engines. That was in 1922 when the railroad was on a strike, was when the Laguna people first had gone out there to work for Santa Fe.

Q. Did the first group come out here with families?

A. No, they [the men] just come up because it's such a danger, you know. They said that [strike] was . . .

Q. A lot of trouble?

A. Yeah. (Personal interview)

In September 1923 the Shopmen's Strike was settled. According to Laguna narratives, some of the men remained at the Richmond Terminal or at least remained with track crews using the facility as their base. Other Lagunas returned home, and still others transferred to Santa Fe centers such as Barstow, Winslow, Calloway, and Needles. Santa Fe has had relatively few labor disputes of importance since the 1922 strike, and these have been cast in the mold of national struggles (Waters 1950, 325).

The railroad brotherhoods eventually drew the Native American workers into their ranks as part of a general employee vote to organize the shops. Laguna recollections are not clear as to exactly when the vote to organize the Richmond shops occurred.[12] However, the attitude of the Laguna laborers remained loyal to the spirit of the 1880 agreement, making annual visits to the Santa Fe regional office in Los Angeles to water the flower. A former Laguna governor recalls that the demeanor of each group, Santa Fe and Lagunas, was one of friendship and accommodation during the ritual meetings.[13] When asked how the union officials felt about such unilateral negotiation on the part of Laguna employees, he replied that "the union knew there was a prior agreement and felt it was in everyone's best interest to honor it" (personal interview). The Laguna workers at Richmond reciprocally honored the intent of their union membership. One retired man recalls his union relationship:

Q. They paid good, paid you on time and took care of your medical?

A. Yeah, after the union came in.

Q. Everybody belonged to the union?

A. After that we belonged to the union. You don't belong to the union you have to get out. You don't work with the railroad no matter if you have agreement with the railroad. Union really did good for us, went along with us. Our wage goes up when we asked, and medical stuff, and all those things. One time they decided to strike, all of them, engineers, mechanics and shop. So they all agreed because some they don't get any raise much, you know. They want to get everything raised good. So he [the Santa Fe management] wasn't going to go along but they told him that this time we going to stop all the working men on the road. Santa Fe lost all a lot of vegetables. You know the freight cars? They got a refrigerator on it for the meat, all kinds of potatoes, everything vegetable. But they had to all rot somewheres because nobody don't touch them. When it happened they lost a lot of meat and stuff. So, they agreed after that and we start back. After that no more strikes, they don't strike anymore. They give us raise, whatever we asked for, what we need. It was a good union. The union did pretty good. (Personal interview)

Prior to 1940 the Richmond area, described by historian James Gregory (1989, 176) as a "dull industrial suburb," had a population of about twenty-four thousand residents. The introduction of the Kaiser Shipyards to meet wartime needs, added to the Santa Fe shops, the Standard Oil Refinery, and the Ford Assembly Plant, brought Richmond the distinction of being the "quintessential war boom town," with a population exceeding one hundred thousand in three years of rapid growth. The Santa Fe shops at Richmond employed increasing numbers of the railroad's workforce, which grew as trackage increased and the southwestern lands became more settled. A second wave of Lagunas came to live in the terminal yards sometime in the late 1930s. As the Santa Fe system expanded after 1940, the migration of Native Americans to other points of employment along the railway continued, with major concentrations of Indian labor occurring at the growing junctures of the railroad and urban populations.

By World War II there were six historic villages on the Laguna Reservation and four new settlements elsewhere along the lines of the Santa Fe between Albuquerque and Richmond. The presence of major settlements of workers is reported at Gallup, Winslow, Barstow, and Los Angeles. The communities at Gallup, Winslow, Barstow, and Richmond applied to the governor at home for formal recognition as "Colonies of the Laguna Pueblo in New Mexico" and were granted this status. The Santa Fe eventually adopted the same designation for the village at Richmond.[14] Noted anthropologist Edward Spicer (1962, 554) considers such colonies to be "extensions of the reservation communities, wholly dependent on the general economy and constituting to some extent a source of subsistence for the people remaining on the reservations."

A daughter of Lagunas living at the Richmond village during the war years recalls that her father came first, with the "second group" of men, and her mother later. Initially her father was bunked in the Santa Fe's firehouse, but when the family arrived from New Mexico, the company provided more permanent housing in boxcars set in rows on sidings. Her mother recalls the influx of Laguna families migrating just prior to World War II:

Q. And about how many people were in the village at that time?

A. At that time the families weren't out there yet; it was just the menfolks that went out first. There was over a hundred men that were working with Santa Fe.

Q. And then the families came on later?

A. Yeah, and then the families came on later, and there were twenty-nine families besides the bachelors that were out there.

Q. Do you remember the housing?

A. Well, the houses were set up . . . at first they were boxcars sitting on the railroad tracks . . . and each family had a house, a boxcar . . . you know, a regular boxcar, but made into duplexes. . . . [The railroad added] a kitchen and the bathroom. (Personal interview)

A former forty-year resident of the Richmond village remembers that the homes were two boxcars connected in the middle by a passageway constructed to form the cars in an "H" shape. The passageways held the kitchens, which used wood-burning stoves for both cooking and heat. The early arrangement had the sanitary facilities located in the train yard.

Q. When the village was first set up . . . did they have water inside?

A. No. There were three rows of boxcars, and the middle set was washrooms. There was one for the ladies and then one for the men themselves, a men's washroom and a ladies' washroom. (Personal interview)

Eventually the company had each boxcar "duplex" fitted with a shower and commode, one for each family. The boxcar living quarters, with their all-wood interiors and wood-burning stoves, are remembered fondly by the residents (personal interviews).

The role of Native Americans, women, and others changed between the early years and World War II with regard to responsible jobs on the lines. In 1874 Caroline Prentis, the Santa Fe Railroad's first female employee, served as a clerk at the Topeka station. Later more women were engaged in stenographic and clerical work, with some eventually employed as telegraphers, station agents, and car cleaners, probably as a result of the male labor shortage during World War I. The number of women employed by the Santa Fe, including many Native Americans, grew from two thousand in 1925 to three thousand five hundred by World War II (Bryant 1974, 322; Waters 1950, 327). Sharply increased demands on labor pools during wartime found women railroad workers filling such diverse jobs as signal tower operators, agents, freight handlers, turntable operators, yard clerks, track sweepers, drill press operators, sheet metal workers, engine wipers, fire builders, and timekeepers.

Margaret Irwin Hauke, director of the Women's Personnel Division, came in 1943 to the Richmond shops to review some problems specific to the employment of women. Hauke (1984, 5, 10) remembers one incident unique to the temporary wartime employment of some Navajo Indians:

When I got over to the roundhouse, up on top of it was a very colorful, pretty thing—I'll always remember it—there three Navajo women on the top of this steam engine, cleaning it. They were polishing and cleaning it, and they had all their Navajo skirts on and their velveteen blouses and all this wonderful Indian jewelry. And the head of that division said, "We can't get these women to wear pants at all, so I don't know what we're going to do but we just let them work like that. . . .

We had a large safety department [and] the women . . . were not to have any flowing garments. Well, this worked very well, except for the Indians— they didn't want to do this, so they drifted away to some other position. They just didn't want to stay with us—that is in the Bay Area, because we wouldn't let them come with those big skirts.

Among the Laguna families retired from the Richmond yards are many women who began their first employment away from the reservation during World War II. Like the men, they have retained photographic reminders and other memorabilia from their years on the Santa Fe. One woman proudly recalls the attention given her Santa Fe employment:

Q. Oh, you worked for them, too?

A. Yes, she [the speaker's daughter] has a picture of me that came out in all the newspapers all over the United States. It was about the railroad. . . . It was in the Santa Fe Magazine, too. (Personal interview)

Nevertheless, for all the confidence of identity with the employer at Richmond, the Lagunas maintained their village as an extension of the home pueblo. In reflecting on the "Permanence of City Residence," the Meriam Report claimed that many Indians view the city as a temporary residence and that they hoped to return to the homelands as soon as they were economically able, noting that "love for the lands of their forebears is often expressed" (Meriam et al. 1928, 737). But Meriam did not take into account, probably because of a mandate to measure the Indians' acculturative "progress," that the symbiotic homelands of reality and remembrance were no longer the same.

A. These freight trains go by here every day, little trains go by here 24 hours. . . . And then some trains . . . they are not really making enough to satisfy them. That is why they are trying to cut out the train. . . . They just can't make people believe there is no money in passenger trains. They know that people want them. . . .

Q. Do they stop here?

A. Well they cut out this depot here. There were a lot of people here where the train stops. You can't get on here, it doesn't stop unless you get a stop order here. . . .

Q. Well, are . . . people from here still working for the railroad?

A. They call for people when they want men to work, but . . . our people get out of the reservation. . . . That is why they are moving out . . . go out to work. . . . Railroad is good job and they pay good.

Q. What do people want to do?

A.. . . They want jobs right here on the reservation. . . . There aren't any. . . . There aren't any jobs . . . anywhere. (Husband 1969, 9)

Michael McGerr (1993, A48) observes that, while being structurally relevant to the economy, corporations "have had a surprisingly limited impact on individual Americans' attitudes and behavior." The paradox follows, according to McGerr (1993, A48), that

> For all their scope, corporations and other bureaucracies have failed to remake their own workers, let alone American culture. To understand the 20th-century United States, we need to go beyond our faith in the power of organizations to transform people and culture. Our nation may well be exceptional not for the power of organization, but for the persisting sense of human agency. We need to explain why.

One reason for this inconsistency may lie in the fact that corporations are created by, and are therefore agencies of, the state. For Native Americans, such as those at Old Laguna and the Richmond village, their communities have always remained just slightly at the margins of the larger, statebound, socioeconomic structure. Some of the marginality, however, may be self-imposed and maintained, wittingly or unwittingly, as an act of resistance to real and imagined hardships filtered through the lens of historical hindsight. According to Spicer (1971, 798), "An identity system . . . develops independently of those processes by which a total culture pattern, a set of particular customs and beliefs constituting a way of life, is maintained. The continuity of a people is a phenomenon distinct from the persistence of a particular set of culture traits."

The relevance of the Santa Fe experience to the continuity of the Laguna people becomes important when measured against the role it has played in their persistence as Lagunas. The railroad's employment of the Lagunas, with its origins in the flower, received vitality because it was absorbed into the sense of being Laguna. A new singular entity of Laguna essence was not thereby created, merely one that was different from all the other configurations of Laguna identity.

The impact of Santa Fe employment on Laguna life can be discerned at the November reunion. The old man is resplendent in his baseball jacket, the coat is a remnant of days when Native American railroad laborers were called on to display their tribal being for corporate profit. Indian employees assisted the Santa Fe in marketing its services, using advertising almost totally dependent on southwestern themes. The red jacket is one of three remaining that were specially designed by a fellow Laguna to wear as they toured on company business. On the back is a large embroidered profile of a stereotypically war-bonneted Indian. When the old man turns to have his surface features recorded on film, a round blue-and-white Santa Fe logo flashes from the left side of the jacket, from over his heart.

Belief in an enduring Laguna–Santa Fe relationship is apparently not pervasive throughout the Laguna Pueblo population, however. During a break at the reunion dinner an elderly veteran of railroad life points up the slope of the nearby mesa toward the ever-present Catholic Church. The site near the church where the Santa Fe wished to place railroad cars as mementos of the persistence of loyalty by each entity to the other is bare to this day. The Laguna Tribal Council voted to refuse the offer. Whether this was an act of resistance to further industrial intrusion on tribal lands is unclear. However, the elder relating the story is clearly skeptical about the wisdom shown by the council: "Those guys are crazy. If we had let the railroad do that then we could have worked with them on other things. Maybe they would have said, 'Well, those Indians don't have a baseball field or a good recreation hall, so let's put one up for them.' " The narrator appraises the hard, lifeless exterior of the recreation building as he returns to the dinner, then exclaims dismissively with a laugh, "Them guys don't know nothing. They're crazy."

None of the Laguna Tribal Council is in attendance at the dinner, save for a latecomer, the tribal interpreter. He is a college-educated World War II veteran who wears as his proudest badge of honor the fact that he has remained at home on the reservation. Others succumbed to the lures of urban life, to the material lifestyle that would come with spending the years away, only returning for the obligatory meetings and ritual events. He is proud as he rises and asks through a family member for the opportunity to make some remarks. A few opening words are in English, but none is in Spanish, which until two generations ago was the "second" language on the reservation; the rest of the address is made in Laguna. As the words pour forth, everyone is silent, though many of the younger people may not fully comprehend the phrases. Later, when asked to outline the interpreter's comments, an older Laguna tribal member explains:

> He says that this dinner is a good thing, that we need to remember our past and our responsibility to the agreement we made in the early days with the Santa Fe, when it first come through here. Our women have been reminding us for a long time now, he says, that we should do what we used to, that we should go to the Santa Fe and renew our verbal agreement, like we did every year since Hiuwec stopped the train from coming through in 1880. We need to water the flower again. It is the way our people have survived, and it is the way we can provide for our children and for the tribe to continue (Personal interview with Kurt Peters)

This dinner gathering has been a ritual for renewal, a celebration of continuity. The ritual, the watering of the flower, originated in 1880 as a recognition of the accommodation of each entity, Laguna and Santa Fe, to the other. Intervening years have added experiential depth and texture to the ceremonial design, and the annual remembrance of the event has served to intertwine the Santa Fe experience with the mesh of Laguna lifestyle. Today that employment experience is indistinguishable from any of the other threads that constitute the weave of Laguna life. The absence of that thread there would not destroy the weave, but the present essence, the continuing, persistent sense of being Laguna, would be unavoidably altered.

8

INDIAN LABOR IN SAN DIEGO COUNTY, CALIFORNIA, 1850–1900

RICHARD L. CARRICO AND FLORENCE C. SHIPEK

Documentation of Indian wage labor in California has focused largely on the Central Valley, northern California, or metropolitan areas, particularly Los Angeles (Hurtado 1982, 1988b; Phillips 1980). With the exception of passing mention in the historical literature or as a section within a larger study, Indian labor in San Diego County has been neglected (Carrico 1990; Carrico 1985; Shipek 1977). The region comprising pre-1907 San Diego County embraced more than sixteen thousand square miles, with more acreage than Connecticut and Massachusetts combined. The role of Indian labor over such a large area warrants more detailed study.

The experience of San Diego County Indians varied from those Indians affected by the fur trade of the Great Lakes, the land rushes on the Great Plains, and the gold rush in northern California. Despite a U.S.-era population decline from about ten thousand in 1850 to about one thousand five hundred in 1900 (Shipek 1977, 1986), the Indian tribes of San Diego County played a varied and complex role in the economic structure of the county during that period. San Diego County included large portions of what are now Riverside and Imperial Counties and encompassed four distinct tribes: the Takic-speaking Luiseños, Cahuillas, and Cupeños of the north county region and the Yuman-speaking Kumeyaays, who were more southerly. As laborers tribal members continued to be the primary supply of labor to the Anglo-Americans, just as they had been earlier for the Spaniards and Mexicans. To a large degree it

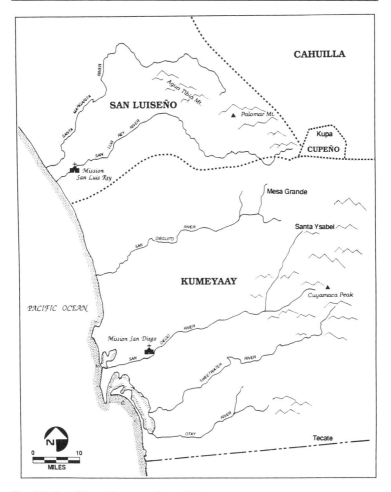

Fig. 8.1. San Diego County tribes, 1800

was the entry into the wage labor economy that allowed many Indians to persevere and persist. Their exchange of labor for food, supplies, and cash was a well-devised survival mechanism, not a sporadic activity.

By the time of California statehood in 1850 the Indians of San Diego County who had been in contact with the missions had developed a variety of adaptive mechanisms for dealing with the growing Anglo-American population of the region. Unlike most of the Spanish California missions, both San Diego and San Luis Rey Missions lacked sufficient land and water for agriculture near the missions and were unable to congregate the converted Indians (Shipek 1977, 1982). Instead, members of each band were brought to the mission for training and baptism. They then returned to their home villages, coming back to the two missions as a rotating labor force and for special ceremonies. The initial Spanish need for a large Indian labor force to construct the San Diego Mission and the Presidio (and later, Mission San Luis Rey) gave way to a reduced workforce. The Native people kept at the mission were those trained as craftsmen, unmarried girls and women, the sick and elderly, and those whose home territory had been occupied by these missions (Shipek 1977, 1982). At San Diego the Presidio also kept a Kumeyaay labor force, often drawing from a pool of imprisoned people. In the rugged mountains the southern Kumeyaays kept the Spaniards out of their homelands and close to the coast so that few southern inland Kumeyaays spent time at the mission (Shipek 1982, 1986).

In northern San Diego County the Luiseños and Cupeños had undergone a more benign experience with the Spaniards than that of their southern counterparts, the Kumeyaays at San Diego Mission (or even of the northern section of their tribe at San Juan Capistrano; Shipek 1977). In the seven decades following the founding of Mission San Luis Rey de Francia, members of traditional Luiseño leadership families served as the midlevel managers or middlemen between the mission and Luiseño bands. Pablo Tac, a Luiseño born at Mission San Luis Rey in about 1822, wrote in 1835 that the Spaniards appointed leaders "from the people themselves that knew how to speak Spanish more than the others and were better than the others in their customs" (Hewes 1952, 103). By learning the language of the intruders and accepting some elements of Spanish culture, the Luiseños were able to accommodate the mission while retaining most of their culture.

After the end of the Spanish empire and the collapse of the colonial system with mission secularization under Mexican control, both the Luiseños and Kumeyaays were effective in keeping the Mexicans from using the interior of southern California. Both tribes refused to be unpaid laborers for the Mexican rancheros and townspeople, and most abandoned the coastal strip. Both tribes also resisted the efforts of the rancheros and corrupt officials to control them and take their land. The tribes continued their long tradition of plant husbandry combined with cultivation of corn, beans, and squash in the mountains (and for the Kumeyaays, the desert also). To these foods they added wheat, watermelons, olive and Spanish fruit trees, and grape species, as well as domestic animals (dairy cows, cattle, sheep, horses, burros, pigs, and chickens).

The Kumeyaays attacked whenever a Mexican ranchero attempted to use any of the interior valleys for grazing cattle. Only those who lived at the coast or those in the more open inland valleys of northern Kumeyaay territory had learned Spanish and been trained in animal husbandry. By contrast, the Luiseño leaders first sent petitions and wrote protests to Mexican officials about the more abusive Mexican *mayordomos*. The Mexican officials interpreted these protests as the start of a revolt, and for fear of an inland uprising the Mexican rancheros clung primarily to their coastal lands. Furthermore, of the twenty-one Indian land grants in Mexican California, seven were to Luiseños. The Cupeños, farthest inland of the Mission San Luis Rey jurisdiction, had the same treatment as the Luiseños and the same training. This training and the Luiseño petitions indicate that the Luiseño leaders had developed greater facility in dealing with the Mexicans as a result of unique training and treatment under Fray Antonio Peyri at Mission San Luis Rey (Shipek 1977). From this position the Luiseños and the Cupeños were in a more favorable position to deal with the entering Anglo-Americans.

With the entrance into California of the U.S. Army under Stephen Watts Kearney, followed by Anglo-American settlers, those bands along the emigrant trails began increasing their wheat, corn, and other plantings to sell food supplies to the emerging market of soldiers and emigrants.[1] For those bands living near or along these overland routes, there was a short period of prosperity as the Luiseños, Cupeños, and northern Kumeyaays marketed their produce to the travelers or brought it into the burgeoning towns (Shipek 1977). The ability of the Cupeños to take advantage of the economic opportunities offered by emigration was noted by Judge Benjamin Hayes as early as January 1850, when he reported that they had planted extra acreage of wheat, "induced probably by the demands of emigration" (Wolcott 1929, 59). In their efforts to supply a newly created market, the Luiseños and Cupeños were no less the entrepreneurs than the better-documented Pimas and Maricopas of Arizona, who developed a similar adaptive strategy to cope with the influx of emigrants across their lands (Harris 1960, 80–82; Hayden 1965). In fact, in 1849 would-be gold miner and argonaut Benjamin Butler Harris (1960, 95), having just passed through Pima territory, where he was fed and purchased foodstuffs, favorably compared the Cupeños to the Pimas.

The Indians of the inland southern mountain areas were not afforded such an opportunity at this time. Those mountains and valleys were not entered by settlers until about 1867, after the end of the Civil War. There was no road through the region until the stage road was built in 1869. The primary rush into these mountains began after the 1870 discovery of gold in the Cuyamacas (Shipek 1988, 1991).

Along the main roads and near the coast emigrants, dissatisfied with purchasing food and supplies from Indians, coveted the productive farms for themselves. Some asked to rent a piece, and the Indians, seeking further economic opportunity, obliged. After paying rent for a couple of years, some settlers filed a homestead document claiming all of the improvements as their own, including twenty- and thirty-year-old fruit trees and vines (Shipek 1988). In 1851 Congress passed an act creating the State Lands Commission which was c harged with examining Mexican land titles. This commission ignored its explicit instructions to seek out and determine Indian land rights, even though many papers concerning Indian land titles were sent to the commission (Shipek 1977, 1988). Another more direct method of acquisition of Indian land was outright appropriation, often by force. When Luiseño villagers left Pejamo, near Temecula, for their summer rounds, local whites entered the village, set fire to the homes, and took possession of the water supply and fields. In spite of protests from the Indians and their agent, William E. Lovett, the whites retained control of the land (California State Legislature 1866).

As the Luiseños and Kumeyaays lost their crop and grazing lands, and many of their central village areas, they turned to wage labor for sustenance.

Because the Cupeños were on a major inland Mexican land grant and had filed a case in court, they were able to hold their crop lands longer than many Luiseños and Kumeyaays. They turned to a combination of wage labor and running the hot springs as a spa for visitors. By contrast, land loss occurred almost immediately near the coast, and the loss gradually spread inland over the next thirty to forty years. When executive order reservations were established in December 1875, the Luiseños and northern Kumeyaays who had worked for and cooperated with ranch owners, and had become better known, received modest tracts of land (Shipek 1988). Luiseño and northern Kumeyaay leaders played an active role in securing lands by retaining attorneys and pressing Indian agents to make their case before the Bureau of Indian Affairs (BIA). These Indians subsequently received moderately sized tracts of land (Carrico 1990, 75–88).

In contrast with the Luiseños, Cupeños, and northern Kumeyaays, who had learned Spanish, viniculture, and animal husbandry at the missions, the southeastern mountain Kumeyaays consistently resisted the Spaniards, Mexicans, and earliest Anglo-American settlers and had not learned the language of either Euro-American group. Although these Kumeyaays would gradually learn the techniques of accommodation to massive numbers of intruders into their land, their entry to this new dominant society was at a lower level than that of the missionized Spanish-speaking bands. Their initial reaction to the Anglo-American settlers was one of resistance, as it had been to the Spaniards and Mexicans.

The Kumeyaays were also different from the Takic-speaking Luiseño peoples immediately north of them in terms of tribal organization. Gerónimo Boscana (1933, 19–22) notes that once the Luiseño captain (*noot*) and council decided on an action, it was announced, and all of the people obeyed. In contrast, neither the Kumeyaay captain (*kwaaypaay*) nor the tribal chief (*kuchut kwataay*) ever issued orders. They merely announced what they planned to do, and each family was free to follow or not as it pleased (Shipek 1982). In other words, the Kumeyaays were more individualistic and independent and were unaccustomed to being ordered to some action. The autonomy and individualism of the Kumeyaay significantly retarded the growth and viability of Mission San Diego de Alcalá in southern San Diego County. It never achieved the success of Mission San Luis Rey in crop yields, livestock raising, or Native baptisms. Kumeyaay resistance to the Spaniards was so strong that after six years of an uneasy stalemate, southern Kumeyaays attacked the mission in November 1775, burned it to the ground, and gave California its first Catholic martyr, Father Luis Jayme.

Kumeyaay resistance to missionization had been so strident and constant that in 1776, after destruction of the mission, Governor Pedro Fages noted what he called the Kumeyaays' "resistance to rational submission" (Englehardt 1920). From their mountain villages most southern Kumeyaays avoided contact with the Spaniards and thus with the acculturative processes. After the Mexican Revolution and the expulsion of Spanish rule, they were generally successful in resisting the Mexicans, who did not leave the coast without an army squad and did not actually use any of the inland rancho grants.

Even though these Kumeyaays had added wheat, watermelons, and fruit trees, among other Spanish crops, and domestic animals to their existing crop complex, they did not speak Spanish. They continued their resistance to encroachers on their lands during the U.S. period. But two smallpox epidemics in the 1860s and the overwhelming numbers of well-armed Anglo-Americans who moved into the area after the Civil War greatly affected the tribe. The population was reduced from over two thousand to about two hundred persons by 1890, when the tribe finally came to the attention of the government and land was reserved for it after 1892. As a result of inadequate reservations, incursions by non-Indian cattle, and the white practice of providing food only to laborers (Shipek 1991), only about one hundred Kumeyaay people were still alive by 1910. Except for foothill reservations in the south composed of the tiny Sycuan and the larger Capitán Grande tracts, no other Indian reservations were established at this time. With no land reserved for

Indians along the entire coastal plain and only two inland reservations, the southern people were further dispersed.

Given the differences in the ways that the northern people (including the Luiseños, Cupeños, Cahuillas, and northern Kumeyaays) and southern Kumeyaays were influenced by the Spaniards and Mexicans, the methods and timing of adaptation of the two populations varied. This was best reflected in the northern people's grasp of the importance of learning and conversing in non-Indian languages. Communicating initially through Spanish translators, and in later years by learning Spanish, Indian spokespersons retained power and status and came to gain even more through their roles as mediators and translators. With a well-developed system of middlemen who represented clans or villages, the northern groups traded with the Anglo-Americans, worked on their ranches as vaqueros, fit into households as domestics, grew and sold crops on the open market, and pursued myriad economic activities. In an attempt to retain Indian lands, Olegario Calac, a Luiseño leader, hired an Anglo-American attorney and, with Tomás, a northern Kumeyaay leader from Santa Ysabel, and possibly a Cahuilla leader, made a visit to Washington, D.C. (Shipek 1988; Carrico 1990, 83–84). In 1875 Olegario and other Indian leaders were successful in gaining formal executive order reservation lands. These leaders continued to file petition after petition on behalf of their people's claims, clearly understanding the power and necessity of written agreements.

AGRICULTURAL PURSUITS:
INDIANS WORKING FOR THEMSELVES

One of the ironies—or perhaps more accurately, hypocrisies—of Indian life on the reservations was that the tracts set aside for the Indians were most often the least desirable lands (Shipek 1988), while at the same time the BIA mandated that reservation Indians practice agriculture. Large traditional villages and farmlands were generally excluded from reservation tracts; the Indians were provided with hillsides and rough terrain. At least one reservation was totally mislocated and lacked water on its steep hilltop tract. Even when the land was suitable for agriculture, water rights were ignored by settlers and not protected by the BIA, which seemed more concerned with the supposed rights of Anglo settlers.

Often the executive order reserving the agricultural land was ignored. Settlers pushed in and filed claims stating that they had lived there and put in the improvements, when in fact the plowed fields, orchards, and structures were the result of decades of Indian labor. In the fifty years between 1850 and 1900 Indian people practiced agriculture when it was feasible but often found the economic rewards minimal. This is not to say that they did not attempt farming or stock raising but rather that wages paid for labor on other's farms and ranches often exceeded the economic return of working reservation land. For example, from 1893 to 1910, Gregorio Omish, a Luiseño of Rincón Reservation, raised wheat and barley for sale, raised and sold livestock, picked grapes, cut and sold wood, hunted and sold quails, and worked as a laborer. Omish's journals for these years provide valuable insights into his and other tribal members' economic activities (Omish 1893–1910). Ever the opportunist, like most Luiseños, Omish worked at these various tasks as the season or market dictated. In 1895 Omish reported in his journal receiving only $1.00 for 100 pounds of wheat and $0.75 per 100 pounds of barley. At the same time, seasonal apricot cutters made between $0.80 and $1.50 per day (Peet 1949) for considerably less effort than was required for growing 100 pounds of wheat. It is easy to see why Indian people rejected the BIA's efforts to restrict them to the reservation and to agriculture as a primary economic pursuit. As a point of comparison between wages and costs, a man's suit sold for $6.50, a mare brought between $8 and $12, and a bucket of lard sold for $0.60 (San Diego Union 1895). Income derived from agriculture alone, even during the best of years, proved woefully inadequate.

A review of Omish's journal for the 1890s reveals that he and his tribesmen regularly raised and sold grain to a widely dispersed market. Although his major outlet was Philip Sparkman, who owned a store in nearby Valley Center, Omish also sold in the more distant communities of Escondido and Vista. As was common at the time, Sparkman gave Omish and others a line of credit/debit. Like all farmers, Indian people were at the mercy of nature, and it was during the worst of times that Indians suffered most. In the drought year 1857 the local newspaper reported that the southern California Indians experienced severe crop failure (San Diego Union 1857). In 1880 east county Indians were reportedly starving because of an extended drought coupled with severe snowstorms (San Diego Union 1880). Omish's entries reveal that 1898 was a terrible year for crops in northern San Diego County and that he sold only one sack of wheat, 400 pounds of hay, and no barley that year.

In response to such vagaries of weather and crop yield, Indian people diversified their efforts. Omish reports in his journal for 1895–1897 that to supplement his income, he sold a sorrel mare for $12.00 and a white mare for $8.00 in 1896, a dozen hens for $2.75 in 1897, and a variety of other livestock including cattle and hogs. His economic acumen was not restricted to selling farm products. Understanding the importance to Anglo-Americans of having a supply of fireworks on the Fourth of July, Omish purchased a large supply in San Diego in 1890 and sold them to rural ranchers and farmers.

In the particularly bad drought years or years of crop failures such as 1898, Omish's journal clearly depicts him and his neighbors switching their efforts from farming to cutting and selling firewood and to doing other jobs that took them off the reservation. These varied efforts represent far more than production and sale of petty commodities. They reflect an understanding of the evolving marketplace and the ability to seize opportunities. In contrast to some newspaper accounts of the time and later historical accounts, the Indian people of southern California were not sitting back waiting for government assistance; they were active at a variety of economic pursuits and sought mainly land rights, not handouts. In a particularly poignant petition to the secretary of the interior, the Luiseño leaders pleaded, "We do not ask, Mr. Minister, for the Government to give us money, nor blankets, nor seeds; only some lands for us to cultivate for the support of our families, and to raise our animals to work our lands, and that we shall be protected against the whites" (Painter 1886, 13). The diaries and correspondence of the 1860s–1900 suggest how little the government was willing to do for the Indians. BIA reports for the era reveal that between 1905 and

Fig. 8.2. Juan José Warner of Warner's Ranch posed with his north-county Indian labor supervisors and vaqueros, circa 1870. (Photo courtesy of Los Angeles Public Library)

1909 only $50 were allotted for all of southern California, and those funds were earmarked for the disabled and the elderly (Shipek 1977).

AGRICULTURAL PURSUITS:
INDIANS WORKING FOR OTHERS

With the fluctuating price of crops and the uncertainties of producing for the marketplace, many Indians did what their white counterparts did: they went to work for others as wage laborers. Data from the agricultural census of the era demonstrate that Indian farmers, like white farmers, spent at least one-third of the year working for others while still farming their own land. Ted Couro, a Mesa Grande Kumeyaay born in 1890, remembers that his people regularly ignored the agricultural

Fig. 8.3. Kumeyaay baskets from Mesa Grande, circa 1924. (Photo courtesy of the Bancroft Library)

specialists provided by the government because the government men knew little about the local soils and conditions. As Couro (1975, 3) notes: "Some of them wouldn't do a thing, they'd just leave it [the reservation land] alone. They'd go get a job somewhere else." Pioneer Mary Rockwood Peet (1949) reports that in the San Pasqual Valley of northern San Diego County, among other jobs, whites and Indians worked side by side as apricot cutters for the same wages. During the 1890s they received $0.03 a tray and, if they worked fast and long, could draw a wage of $1.50 per day, although $0.80 per day was a good average.

But Native people did not work simply as farmhands or seasonal pickers; their wage labor included a wide variety of jobs. In the north county particularly, Indian men worked as highly regarded and well-paid ranch hands and vaqueros. Because of the skill and knowledge required to be a vaquero, the Indian cowboys were well respected and, in contrast to some of the more menial occupations, received payment

Fig. 8.4. Harvesting wheat at the *ranchería* Puerta de la Cruz, circa 1886. (Photo courtesy of San Diego Historical Society—Title Insurance and Trust Collection)

on a parity with their Mexican and white counterparts. Dr. George McKinstry, a rancher near Santa Ysabel, was an Indian agent who manipulated the Santa Ysabel land grant for his own purposes and took Indian vineyards, crops, and orchards as his own. McKinstry (1859–1879, for 1861) regularly used Indian vaqueros, as did his neighbor George Dyke. Robert Kelly, of the Agua Hedionda–San Dieguito area, regularly hired Indians as vaqueros in the 1880s. Kelly considered them a highly skilled, integral part of his cattle operations. Like Philip Sparkman, the storekeeper at Valley Center, Kelly (1968) would loan them money if he thought them deserving, and he especially helped the sick ones. During the same time period another rancher, John Wolfskill, told his neighbors that he could trust his cattle with Silistino, a local Luiseño, when he would not trust a white man (Bevington 1925, 25).

In a minority report arguing against the removal of California Indians to Indian Territory, Juan José Warner (1852) stated that Indians provided the main source of labor for San Diego County ranchers. Benjamin D. Wilson also noted that Luiseños "are the main source of vaqueros for the ranchos" (Caughey 1952, 129). A review of contemporary newspaper accounts, memoirs, and interviews conducted with Native American informants documents the dominance of north county Indian people as vaqueros, especially men from certain Luiseño, Cupeño, and northern Kumeyaay families who had earned the respect of white ranchers.

Besides working as vaqueros, Indian men were hired as herders and shearers, employment requiring skilled workers. In the 1870s–1880s, at a time when the hundreds of thousands of sheep outnumbered cattle in San Diego County, Indian sheepherders and shearers were common. In the Ballena Valley near Ramona, they drew a wage that varied from $0.50 to $0.75 a day for herding and $0.0450 a head for shearing (Foster 1874–1880). As an indicator of contemporary salaries, a skilled white carpenter received $1.00 per day, and unskilled workers drew a wage of $0.50 per day. Almost twenty years later Gregorio Omish reported in his 1898 journal that he earned $18.50 for an unspecified number of days shearing sheep at a ranch near the San Diego Mission.

In northern San Diego County, as Anglo-Americans continued to divert water from Indian land, Luiseño farmers hired their own ditchmaster and ditchmen to ensure that irrigation ditches were kept clean and flowing (Shipek 1977). In one instance Omish reported in his journal that the ditchmaster, or supervisor, a position of status and prestige, was a Luiseño who received $0.75 per day until the crops were harvested.

INDIANS AS NONAGRICULTURAL LABORERS

Even though a large number of San Diego County Indians worked in agriculture, either for themselves or for non-Indians, others worked at a variety of nonagricultural jobs. Often this type of work was hard physical labor, such as that performed by Istaako Alto, a Kwaaymii (a sub-sib, or sub-clan, of the Kumeyaays), who helped cut the Butterfield Stage road up Banner Grade and through the rugged east county mountains in the late 1850s. Earning tools instead of cash, Istaako used the tools to build a cabin in the Laguna Mountains for his family (Carrico 1976; Kline 1979, 113). Similarly, many Kumeyaay Indians of Campo helped cut the stage line from the desert floor to Mountain Springs, Jacumba, Campo, and National City. At about the same time in the Ballena Valley Indians were hired by the local doctor and dentist as messengers to deliver packages and medicines in the rough back country and to make adobes for white homesteads (McKinstry 1859–1879). Throughout the 1870–1890 period in a region always short on readily accessible timber, Indian woodcutters supplied much of the firewood to rural homes. In 1898 Gregorio Omish noted in his journal that he cut and sold cords of wood for prices that varied from $1.50 a cord in the hills near his Rincón home to $3.00 in the more distant town of Escondido.

Indian people in the urban environment varied in roles, wages, and status. Although north county Luiseños and Kumeyaays may have worked in the small towns and villages of that region, the bulk of documentation is for the larger city of San Diego itself. With its harbor, warehouses, and commercial districts, downtown San Diego offered economic opportunity to Native people. The relationship was, however, reciprocal: the city depended on the steady and reliable labor supply offered by local Indians.

As early as September 1853 Indians from nearby ranches were being sought as laborers to clear the San Diego River channel and to construct an ill-fated dike to divert the river. Their employment was sought because, as the *San Diego Herald* (1853b) noted, there was an insufficient labor supply available for such a large undertaking. Within two weeks the newspapers reported that 100 Indians were at work on the so-called Derby Dike and that they received $15 a month and rations (San Diego Herald 1853d). By comparison, the forty-nine white workers were paid $60 a month and rations. Consistent with the social and political system devised under the mission and Mexican rancho systems, Indian workers on the dike were supervised by traditional leaders, who were also responsible for the workers' welfare and good behavior.

Thirty years later, in 1881, the coming of the railroad to San Diego brought another labor boom to the area, one that was filled largely by local Kumeyaays from mountain *rancherías* of east San Diego and Indian settlements in National City. William and George Lyons, who were building the mountain portion of the line, noted that they paid their fifty Indian laborers $20 a month plus board (San Diego Union 1881a). William Lyons stated in January 1881 that the local Indians were the best laborers he had yet employed, and the newspaper reported that virtually all of the able-bodied men from the Conejo *ranchería* were off working on the railroad (San Diego Union 1881a). Six months later the contractor for the National City portion of the line west of the mountains said the Indians were "far superior to either white or Chinamen. He says that they work harder and more persistently during the working hours of the day and move more earth than the same number of white laborers do, all other things being equal, on any other section of the line" (San Diego Union 1881c).

The Indians also sought other kinds of nonagricultural labor. During San Diego's whaling and shipping boom of 1855–1865 local Indians worked as sailors on whalers and schooners, often with Native Hawaiians (San Diego Union 1856). In 1861 Judge Benjamin Hayes, an astute observer of the social and economic scene, wrote that Indian sailors received $15 a month to crew on the whaling ship *Ocean* and the same amount to work as blubber renderers at a whaling camp on nearby Ballast Point (Wolcott 1929, 234). These salaries were considered high, but the work was often hard, and life at sea could be dangerous. The pay was consistent with wages paid to non-Indians for the same tasks, and Captain Clark of the *Ocean* had replaced his white crew with Indians because of the Whites' drunkenness and poor work habits (Wolcott 1929, 231). Besides serving on the ships, Indian men worked as longshoremen and as general dockworkers. This form of employment at the docks and on ships continued for decades and was especially pronounced during the economic boom of the early 1880s, when the docks from San Diego to National City were manned largely by Indians (San Diego Union 1881b).

The urban labor market also offered employment for Indian women, who routinely worked as domestics, cooks, and laundresses in San Diego households. Considered more loyal and trustworthy than their Mexican counterparts, and often renowned for their hearty cooking, many of these women worked for decades for the same families, although rarely as live-in workers. In later life one white woman who grew up in such a household noted that her mother's Indian cook "was a genius at concocting mouth-watering tamales and green pepper dishes such as I have never tasted since then" (Tiffany 1973, 8).

Kumeyaay women from Campo in the southern mountains also exploited another economic opportunity. For almost a decade after the railroad linked southern California with the Arizona region, Pima and Maricopa pottery vessels from western Arizona brought a high price as California collectors entered into a Native and folk crafts period. In 1889–1890 the Southern Pacific Railway shut off the supply of pottery vessels from Arizona, which led to a doubling of their price and a scarcity of Indian wares. When made aware of this gap in trade, the women of Campo, who had a long tradition of ceramic manufacturing, switched from making utilitarian brownwares to producing vessels that closely resembled the Arizona wares. As the local newspaper noted, "They have succeeded well, and the ollas have been coming up of late by the wagon-load. The fifty or more men and squaws took up the idea of decoration with interest, and say that they will soon be able to turn out as fine an olla as any other tribe on the coast" (San Diego Union 1890, 8). A decade later the Indian women of Mesa Grande were reported to have a thriving lace-making business (Forbes 1902; Lummis 1902). Lacemaking among these people is another example of the adaptation of a skill learned under the mission system and continued on as an economic opportunity.

FIESTAS AS ECONOMIC ACTIVITIES

Of all the economic aspects of Native culture, the importance of the fiesta as an economic function is probably the least understood. Most often portrayed as social gatherings, the traditional fiestas served several cultural functions. Indian fiestas were, and continue to be, an opportunity for families and friends to get together, to share stories, to dance, and to continue traditional elements of their culture. Beyond these cultural and social aspects, fiestas also had important economic functions.

Realizing neither the social nor economic place of fiestas in Indian society, Indian agents opposed them as a pagan waste of time and resources. Actually, nothing could have been further from reality. Gregorio Omish and others routinely used fiestas for economic purposes, and they were an integral part of the Indian economic system. Southern California Indians traveled to northern San Diego County to sell their surplus crops, just as north county Indian farmers took their excess crops into other areas for sale or barter.

Interviews conducted with elders by Shipek (1977), as well as information in Omish's journal, reveal that fiestas traditionally had a strong economic base and that both men and women drew cash wages for building booths and working at various tasks. Booths, or spaces for booths, were rented to Indian vendors, thus producing a source of income for the host band. Omish noted in his journal that he and Feliz Calac regularly attended and sold beef at such fiestas throughout the county. In one 1895 journal account Omish reported that he and Calac had set up a meat market at a fiesta and had earned $34.70 from the sale of two cows. At a time when 100 pounds of wheat brought only $1.00 and daily wage labor was between $.50 and $1.00, their efforts were well rewarded. The rewards were so great that at least one Rincón leader traveled to Los Angeles and San Diego to place advertisements for the fiestas in local newspapers.

CONCLUSION

Indian labor in San Diego County differed for the Luiseños, Cupeños, Cahuillas, and northern Kumeyaays, on the one hand, and the coastal and southern Kumeyaays, on the other. But in spite of differences, San Diego County Indians maintained their cultural adaptability (Boscana 1933; Rudkin 1956), which allowed them to move into entirely new situations with ease. For example, the Luiseños continued to use specialization as a vehicle for adaptation and practiced a form of situational management characterized by flexibility. These and other mechanisms developed in the Spanish period by both groups assisted in their ability to cope with and utilize the U.S. economic system.

Such adaptation to new economic pressures is what Edward Spicer (1954, 663–678) calls adjustment patterns. Of the five dominant adjustment patterns that Spicer defines for the Southwest, the Luiseños and, to a lesser degree the other tribes, used what he calls limited selection. That is, they selected or focused on those aspects of the dominant culture that could benefit them and filtered these aspects through their own cultural values. The Luiseños in particular, and other Native people generally, were a major force in the rural San Diego County labor force and a lesser force as surplus-selling farmers. For the urban San Diego workforce, coastal Native people, especially the southern Kumeyaays, were the dominant source of unskilled labor in the 1850–1920 period and also filled a large segment of the skilled labor market. In fact, it was not until the transition period between the Great Depression and World War II that Indian workers were replaced by other minorities, notably Mexican workers from south of the border. As sailors, construction workers, domestics, and day laborers, Indians were ubiquitous in urban San Diego. Contemporary accounts clearly reflect not only their importance in sheer numbers but also the quality of their work and their good reputation.

The importance of Indian labor to both the commercial and agricultural sectors of the local economy was well understood and reported on by Anglo-Americans. In 1853 the San Diego Herald noted that San Diego lacked a steady labor force and that local Indians regularly filled the gap. Benjamin D. Wilson, an important southern California politician and business leader, clearly understood their importance in Anglo-American California during the 1840s and 1850s. Wilson wrote that the Indian laborers and servants were domesticated, "mix with us daily and hourly; and, with all their faults, appear to be a necessary part of the domestic economy. They are almost the only source of farm servants we have" (Caughey 1952, 21). The accounts presented herein of Indian workers on the railroads, the docks, and elsewhere in the labor market clearly attest to their preeminence as a steady, reliable labor force.

In their efforts to earn a living, the Native people were not passive participants in the labor picture. When the dictates of the Bureau of Indian Affairs impeded their ability to sell their wares or confined them to unproductive lands, they skirted the government, maintained self-reliance, and sought self-determination, two mainstays of Anglo-American economic and political ideals. Yet when the Indians were pushed off their land and deprived of the natural resources necessary to earn a living, they faltered. In those instances it was the elders, the sick, and the women and children who, in spite of the efforts of the others, often suffered and even starved.

When allowed to retain a land base or to compete on an equal footing, Indian people developed viable strategies for selling their labor, grew and sold crops in competitive markets, and seized opportunities. Their labor history is a reflection of adaptation and persistence. Although the specific adjustment patterns may have varied from one tribe to the next, all the San Diego Indians searched for, and integrated, new knowledge. As they dealt with successive intrusive cultures, this deep-rooted, pragmatic flexibility in knowledge systems proved beneficial. Rather than a static cultural group eventually swallowed up by Euro-American cultural and economic systems, southern California Indians were a dynamic force that sought and exploited opportunities and made the best of an ever-changing, volatile economy and three waves of economic and societal change represented by the Spanish, Mexican, and Anglo-American cultures.

9

WAGE LABOR
SURVIVAL FOR THE
DEATH VALLEY TIMBISHA

BETH SENNETT

Invasion by Euro-American immigrants brought change and destruction to the lives of many American Indians. The uninviting southern desert fringes of the Great Basin were no exception. The immigrants were determined to dominate the region. In less than fifty years technological advantages and the concept of wage labor economics made possible extensive mineral exploitation, the growth of ranching and agriculture, and the development of towns and roads connecting all population centers in the western fringes of the Great Basin. Immigrants came with the attitude that the West was a vast and empty land, free for the taking, with little or no consideration for the people living there. The earliest explorations had little impact in the region, but with the California gold rush of 1849, the inhabitants of Death Valley were swept into a changing world. The immigrants passing through Death Valley affected many aspects of the lives of the Timbisha, or Panamint Shoshones, with the greatest impact being a change from annual hunting and gathering rounds to full participation in a wage labor economic system. The Timbisha had begun to adjust and incorporate Anglo ways into their lifestyles by the 1860s. What follows is a brief discussion of aboriginal lifeways and how the sudden impact of mining and associated developments affected the Indian population in the Death Valley region and forced adaptive changes for survival in the twentieth century.

Mining and agriculture generally developed in the western United States as consequences of each other. Successful mining operations attracted miners; farms and ranches provided many needed supplies, especially food. The years from the 1860s through 1880s saw many booms and busts throughout the northern and central mountains of Nevada and California. The ore discovered in most districts, except for the Comstock area of northern Nevada, was complex, requiring extensive milling to make it pure. Consequently, many of these areas were merely high-graded, then abandoned (Elliot 1973, 98–99). High-grading was the act of mining the easiest and most readily available mineral sources, which created the boom-bust cycle typical of the mining regions around Death Valley and elsewhere. As new mining technology developed, the old mines were reopened, mined to the maximum potential economical at the time, and then closed again.

Newcomers to Death Valley, miners and farmers alike, settled in the oasis areas, bringing cattle and burros, which decimated the native plants. The precious piñon trees were cut down for fuel and use in the mines (Steward 1970, 7). Changes were necessary for the Timbisha to survive as the plants and animals they depended on for food were depleted. Their traditional annual rounds were severely constricted with the sudden increase in regional population.

Julian Steward (1970) is the most complete source of early ethnographic information for the Great Basin. He conducted his field research in the late 1920s, gathering extensive information for the entire Great Basin in a relatively short amount of time. The social and economic structure for the Death Valley Timbisha prior to extensive contact is summarized here from the introduction to Steward's publication.

ABORIGINAL LIFEWAYS

Aboriginally, the desert environment could not support large villages; instead, a lifestyle of seasonal gathering was necessary. Throughout the Death Valley region edible plants ripened at different times of the year at varying elevations. Semipermanent village locations were always near springs with seed-gathering areas in close proximity. The distances people traveled from village sites for food depended on the immediate environment, the season, and the types of edible plants available. The family groups did not live around the same village site all year but moved according to the seasonality of the food sources.

The primary foods were vegetal, with numerous seed-bearing grasses harvested during the spring and early summer. Some edible plants important to the Indians' diet only grew at specific altitudes. The fruit of the Joshua tree was collected at higher elevations, whereas mesquite beans, screw beans, various cacti, and yucca were gathered in valley floors. Generally the women gathered these various food resources, each keeping what was obtained for her own family (Steward 1970, 72–74).

Pine nuts, gathered in the fall (Dutcher 1893), were a major food source. Stored for winter, they were generally ground to use as cereals and in breads. Roasted nuts were also eaten whole. Piñon groves were used annually by individual families. Although not considered private property, their use by specific families was respected by other family groups. If the crop was not good in the area usually visited, families would travel greater distances to other groves (Steward 1970, 73–74).

Occasionally meat supplemented the diet. Organized communal hunting was not practiced except in rabbit drives. Individuals generally hunted alone. Deer were hunted wherever found but were most plentiful in the northern, more heavily forested areas. Very few antelope were available in the Death Valley region, and, unlike other places in the Great Basin, no communal drives were held. Individuals hunted mountain sheep, which were most abundant in the northern end of Death Valley on Tin Mountain and in the Grapevine Mountains. Those people living in the Coso–Little Lake area, southwest of Death Valley, periodically traveled to the Sierra Nevada Mountains, to the west, for sheep.

Communal rabbit drives were an annual fall event throughout the region (Steward 1970, 38–39). The location of the drives varied each year depending on the abundance of rabbits. Family groups from different areas gathered for these communal hunts and fall festivals because they were important social gatherings; families visited, young people socialized, and marriages were made (Steward 1970, 75).

Individual behavior was governed by kinship, so there was no need for organized political control. The position of "chief," even though sometimes inherited, was not one of power. A local leader, usually a man, was the director and spokesperson for the festivals and organized communal hunting activity (Steward 1970, 75). Warfare was virtually unheard of among these people. During the contact period with the Anglos there were a few small conflicts, but the Timbisha made no organized effort to fight off the immigrants.

Steward (1970) divided the Great Basin into districts based on village association. The family was the primary political unit, with each village comprising a family unit. The districts were related through marriage, which was to nonrelatives only. Dowry payments varied somewhat, but food was a major exchange item. Postmarital residence was usually matrilocal for the first year and then neolocal. Village exogamy was practiced, with a preference for staying within the district. On the periphery of these districts there were always intertribal marriages. Steward (1970) divided the Death Valley region into seven districts: northern Death Valley, central and southern Death Valley, Lida to the north, Saline Valley on the west, Coso–Little Lake south of Saline Valley, Panamint Valley to the southwest, and to the east the Beatty–Belted Range district (Figure 9.1).

Linguistically the groups in each district were predominantly Shoshone. However, when the areas bordered different tribal groups, multiple languages were spoken. To the north, Lida and Saline Valley had a mixture of Shoshone and Northern Paiute, whereas the Coso to the southwest was mixed with both Owens Valley Paiute and Kawaiisu. Panamint Valley and southern Death Valley showed an almost equal balance between Shoshone and Kawaiisu, with the southern portions of each area being predominantly Kawaiisu. The Shoshone people from Beatty and the Belted Range also had Southern Paiute speakers among them (Steward 1970, 68–99).

As noted previously, each district was based on associated villages, with villages throughout the Timbisha region linked by marriage. For instance, the Lida district consisted of five families and three main villages (refer to Figure 9.1). Between these villages there were marriage ties to Beatty, the Belted Range, northern Death Valley, the Kawich Mountains, and Big Pine in the Owens Valley to the west (Steward 1970, 68–70). Steward (1970, 76–80) divided the Saline Valley district into three

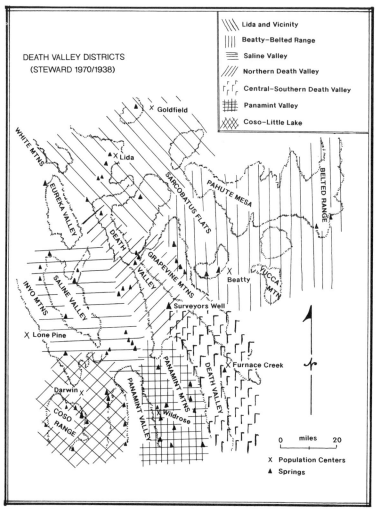

Fig. 9.1. The seven Death Valley districts defined by Steward (1970, fig. 7, facing p. 58).

subdivisions with four main villages, circa 1880. The villages were Hunter Canyon, Goldbelt Springs, Cottonwood Springs, and Waucoba Springs (Nelson 1891).

Steward's information (1970, 80–81, 91–93) concerning southern Death Valley and the Coso–Little Lake district encompassing the Panamint Valley was minimal. His data did confirm marriage ties to surrounding areas. However, he described aboriginal use of this area as seasonal, with no permanent villages. The exception to this was Hungry Bill's Ranch, located at five thousand feet in elevation on the east side of Sentinel Peak in the Panamint Mountains. It is quite conceivable that Steward was unable to locate individuals from these areas who were still living. Since the aboriginal population was part of the wage labor force by the time of his research, they were most likely in areas where work was available, which was not necessarily southern Death Valley or the Panamint Valley.

The non-Indian population in the Panamint Valley area, which dated back to the mid-1800s, was not discussed by Steward. He (1970, 84–85) mentioned briefly a few winter residents at Wildrose. Again, this may be the result of a lack of informants from the region. Nor did he mention permanent villages for southern and central Death Valley. The Timbisha appear to have spent winters at Furnace Creek and the hot summer months in the Panamint Mountains gathering seeds.

Population groups in northern Death Valley were, as all other villages, located near water sources (Steward 1970, 85–91). The three main villages in this northern district were independent for most of the year, except for communal rabbit drives and fall festivals. The villages were located at Grapevine Springs in Grapevine Canyon, Surveyors Well, and Mesquite Springs. As in other areas of the region, these villages were linked to other districts through marriage.

Mesquite Springs was a semipermanent village, where Cold Mountain Jack and Dock had ranches in postcontact times. People from Saline Valley visited the area to hunt ducks and to gather mesquite. According to Steward, Cold Mountain Jack's rather large family lived at Mesquite Springs half the year. The Dock family lived in Grapevine Canyon for most of the year but came to the springs to gather mesquite when it was available.

The Beatty–Belted Range district consisted of several camps associated with specific water sources (Steward 1970, 93–99). The overall chief of these camps, Tom Stewart's father, directed festivals and rabbit drives. Tom Stewart himself told Steward about six camps in the Beatty vicinity for the years 1875–1880.

Some of the village sites Steward reported as aboriginal were most likely chosen in relationship to where the immigrants decided to live and where work for Shoshones was available. For instance, Steward did not mention that the camps in the Beatty–Belted Range district were associated with ranches owned by immigrants and that the Indians worked seasonally as ranch hands (Cottonwood 1986; Landis 1986). Steward gave the impression that these were aboriginal campsites occupied prior to the coming of the immigrants.

Despite such historic labor-related mobility, memory of traditional family group home ranges has persisted among the Timbisha. This information was obtained by the author from older Timbisha tribal members indicating specific areas occupied by family groups (Figure 9.2). There are similarities between these geographic home ranges and Steward's districts, but they do not coincide completely (compare Figures 9.1 and 9.2). The following home ranges are associated with specific families as defined by present consultants: the Cherooty family—Goldfield, Lida areas; Shaw and Kennedy families—Lida, northern Death Valley; Patterson family—Fish Lake Valley, Lida, Grapevine Canyon; Dock family—Grapevine Canyon, northern Death Valley; Strozzi family—Beatty; Shoshone and Cottonwood families—Furnace Creek, Beatty; Boland family—Furnace Creek, Wildrose; Wrinkle family—Darwin, Lone Pine; the Bellas family—Lone Pine; and the Hunter and Sam families—Saline Valley.

Traditional family structure changed very little during the nineteenth century in comparison to the economic and subsistence changes. In brief, groups averaged fifteen to twenty people in an extended family relationship and traveled throughout their home range on annual rounds of hunting and gathering. Marriage was not allowed between cousins or those of closer relationship. Partners were sought between groups whose ranges overlapped and with which there was regular contact. This encouraged family ties over a greater area than a person's home range. During lean times families could go to other areas and receive help from

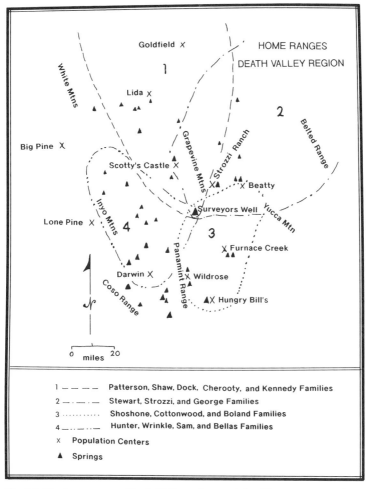

Fig. 9.2. The home ranges, Death Valley region, as defined by present consultants, with associated families (compiled by Beth Sennett, 1983–1988; adapted from Steward 1970).

people they knew. Within the areas bordering different language groups there was also intermarriage. These partnerships helped keep peaceful relationships among the different groups.

The younger Indians during the 1880s and 1890s felt the greatest conflict with the changes about them. Ike Shaw, Old Man Dock, and Tom Stewart, relatives of my present research consultants, were taught the "old ways" as children but grew up in a rapidly shrinking world. The impact of Anglo mining and ranching forced the Indians into the acculturation process on an economic level. Steward (1970, 7) pointed out that with the Indians' subsistence destroyed, they began to congregate around towns and ranches. For example, within fifteen years after the Mormons settled in Utah, circa 1865–1870, grazing had destroyed enough native grasses that the Indians were starving (Steward 1970, 14). Several of Steward's consultants (1970, 17) from throughout the Great Basin commented that areas with much rabbitbrush were areas of lush grasses prior to the introduction of cattle. With aboriginal home ranges shrinking, these people began to adapt to gardening and wage labor for economic survival. The boom-bust cycle of mineral exploitation in the Timbisha territory, however, provided the opportunity for gradual adjustment by periodically easing the impact of changing economics and the influx of non-Indians.

SPANISH AND U.S. VIEWS
OF AMERICAN INDIANS

The different perspectives of the aboriginal people held by the immigrants from the United States and the Spanish colonizers of California had a major impact on how the Indian population reacted. The Spanish came in small numbers and sought to employ the Indians, generally by force, for what the Spanish considered useful purposes. The Indians had a place in the social and economic system; they were an asset to be conserved (Cook 1951, 467). In contrast, the Anglo-Americans came in great numbers, primarily to exploit the mineral wealth. Their social and economic system excluded the aboriginal population. According to Sherburne Cook (1951, 467), if there was conflict between the Anglo-Americans and the Indians, the Indians were either eliminated by extermination or relegated to a reservation. Cook maintains that the Indians had no place or functional value in the U.S. system.

This appears to oversimplify the matter of American Indian transition from hunting and gathering to the wage labor economy. Albert Hurtado (1990) argues that the California Indians were forced to exist in a stratified society and embraced wage labor for a variety of reasons. Their traditional lifeway was not possible with the influx of immigrants, who quickly adopted the Spanish idea of forcing the Indians to work with farmers. By earning a wage, Indians could acquire the material items that revolutionized their lives. But most important, by being gainfully employed, they would be protected by their employers from those individuals who brutalized the aboriginal people and were determined to exterminate them.

The traditional lifeway of the Timbisha was also no longer possible with the influx of immigrants. However, the Timbisha were not forced to work with the Anglos, nor would being employed have offered protection to the Indians. Money made it possible to acquire material items that made life easier, thus ensuring survival.

As immigrants came to California, beginning with the Spanish, there seems to have been a shift in density and distribution of aboriginal populations (Cook 1943). The distribution and availability of a food supply no longer appeared to determine the location of aboriginal groups; rather, the density of the invading population gradually began to determine where the Indians lived and foraged. According to Cook, this was most evident between 1848 and 1860 in California. Alfred Kroeber (1925, 81) notes that immigrants settled in the most desirable environments, those areas with water. These were also places with the heaviest aboriginal population. Consequently, these Indian groups suffered the greatest decline in numbers first. With respect to Kroeber's population estimates, it appears that subsequent to the Anglo immigration the largest Indian groups developed in areas of low white population density. Cook (1943, 37) points out that the survival of aboriginal groups was dependent on their having as little contact with the immigrants as possible to ensure retention of traditional lifeways. If his assumption is correct, this change in aboriginal population density and distribution was not evident in the Death Valley region for another twenty years and was associated with areas of mineral exploration and development.

Cook's view that the aboriginal people had no place in the U.S. social system overlooks the economic role taken by the Indians. In Death Valley and elsewhere the Indians did manage to find a niche within the economic structure of the invading population (e.g., Hurtado 1988a, 1990; Knack 1987). The groups that managed to stay away from the immigrants did, as Cook infers, retain many more of their traditional lifeways. The Timbisha were one of several California American Indian groups (including the Achimawi, Northern and Southern Paiute, Eastern Mono, Tubatulabal, Washo, and Yuma [Cook 1943, 39]) untouched by the Spanish colonizers and relatively isolated geographically from Anglo-American influence. Consequently, these people retained their traditional lifeways with minimal influence from the white population for a much longer period of time than did those Indians in coastal regions or mining centers.

Cook (1943, 40) concludes from an examination of census records that whenever there were intense periods of contact between Indians and Anglos, there was an increase in emigration of young people from the aboriginal population to Anglo population centers, creating an Indian urban class in some areas. Emigration to centers of white population occurred relatively late in the nineteenth century for the Timbisha and was confined generally to the larger regional mining centers. What Cook may have overlooked was that the Indians had become part of a wage labor economic system and that in the search for employment they, like many others, migrated to the urban areas in hopes of finding a good-paying job.

Cook's theory holds up for the most part in relation to the changes that occurred for the Timbisha. It was not until the second decade of the twentieth century that the Timbisha migrated to coastal California urban areas. The Indians remaining in their home territories withstood the Anglo invasion and survived because, according to Cook (1951, 473–474), they were forced to depend totally on group adaptive powers. The most important aspect of Cook's concept of group adaptive power appears to be the ability of the entire group to adapt to a new economic system.

The Timbisha were able to shift from hunting and gathering to the wage labor economy without major changes in their social organization or structure. The group, or extended family, continued to be the basic social organization. Greater contact with other families was the most important means of keeping social values and traditions alive. Those aboriginal people protected under the Spanish mission system, unlike the Indians in Death Valley, were forced into new social roles that destroyed their traditional cultural means of survival (Cook 1943). Families and villages were separated and forced by the Spanish to work (Hurtado 1988a). They were not given the opportunity to gradually adapt to a new lifestyle.

As a group the Timbisha were able to utilize various aspects of Anglo culture and still retain their social organization and survive within their traditional home range. The mining activity in the Death Valley region did not start with one major discovery, as in northern California and Nevada. Impact during the earliest mining period, 1850–1860, was due to explorations by small geologic survey groups and mining operations encompassing limited areas. The aboriginal population was able to continue traditional lifestyles and economic patterns with little disruption.

ECONOMIC CHANGE

The 1870s saw the development of major mining centers and extensive ranching and support communities throughout the Great Basin. The traditional home ranges of the Indian groups in Death Valley were gradually restricted because of Anglo settlements. Natural resources were suddenly in short supply, and the Indians were losing in the competition for food resources with the intense influx of people and grazing animals. The indigenous animals were hunted heavily, and cattle and sheep ate the grasses the Indians depended on for survival. To compensate, they accepted those aspects of the Anglo culture that enabled them to stay in their home territories and survive. Many men herded cattle and horses for ranchers; women did domestic work (Patterson 1986; Shaw 1986). Consequently, these extended families set up semipermanent residences within close proximity to major ranches located in their home ranges. Mining communities hired the Indian men to haul wood for the mines and smelters and the women, again, to work as domestics (Landis 1986; Shaw 1986).

By the turn of the century the Timbisha territory was thoroughly saturated with Anglo settlements. To survive, the Indians adapted to a wage labor economy. A monetary income made it possible to buy food instead of depending solely on hunting and gathering. Being tied to a job for income meant having a more permanent residence. This in turn allowed for the development of horticulture to supplement food supplies and family income. Some hunting was done individually, and pine nuts were still gathered annually.

Agricultural development by immigrants came with the boom periods of mining. Myron Angel (1881, 135–140) indicates a steady increase in grain production and the number of grazing animals from 1865 to 1880 across northern Nevada. He also notes the planting of fruit trees as a positive indicator that the immigrants intended to stay and make the remote Nevada valleys their homes.

Even in Death Valley and the surrounding areas cultivation developed as a support industry to the mines. Death Valley itself had a resident farmer in 1870. Teck Bennett started the Greenland Ranch at the present site of Furnace Creek, where population is still heaviest. He supposedly claimed ownership of the entire valley. His wife and her four brothers, Leander, Philander, Meander, and Salmander, joined Bennett in 1875 (Putnam 1946, 49). George Putnam does not say how long the farm lasted, but it may have continued through the time of the Harmony Borax operation in the late 1880s.

Robert Lingenfelter (1986, 163) claims that the stories of Teck Bennett are colorful fiction, stating instead that the first farmers in Death Valley were Andy Laswell and his partner, Cal Mowery. They came during the summer of 1874 to the Panamint mining district. Having no luck with mining, they started a small farm on the west side of Death Valley near Bennett's Well. By December Mowery had moved on, and Laswell had gone to the east side of the valley near Furnace Creek. His second attempt at farming lasted until the fall of 1875, when he moved into the Amargosa Basin to the east.

The mining industry and supplemental businesses had major impacts on the environment. Wood and water were vital for mining and smelting operations, and much of the area was deforested to supply timber and charcoal. Burros, the ever-present companions of the early prospectors, were abandoned to roam wild. These animals multiplied uncontrollably for years, destroying grasses and springs throughout the Death Valley region (Rothfuss 1992, 182). By 1880 the good grazing land in Nye County, Nevada, immediately northeast of Death Valley, had been virtually destroyed by overgrazing cattle. To compensate, ranchers turned toward cultivation, especially of hay (Angel 1881, 515). The increase in cattle ranching had a severe impact on the grasses and other food sources vital to the aboriginal population and, as noted by consultants, to much of their material culture, including baskets.

The development of horticulture by the Timbisha themselves varied somewhat throughout the Death Valley region. Steward (1970, 89) suggested that farming was introduced by the Southern Paiute to the Timbisha living in the eastern portions of the territory prior to Anglo contact. The plants and cultivation patterns were similar. The western portion of the area was most likely influenced by the Owens Valley Paiute. However, the time periods Steward associated with Indian farming in and around Death Valley can be directly correlated with the arrival of Anglo settlers, who started farming as early as the 1860s to support the mining districts. Examples are Jacob Steinenger, Grapevine Canyon, circa 1880, and, as previously noted, Andy Laswell, Furnace Creek, 1875 (Lingenfelter 1986, 163; Shally and Bolton 1973, 9). Consultants remember gardening, and refer to horticulture as something their parents learned from the newcomers in the area. The similarities with Southern Paiute cultivation methods may have been the result of interaction between Native Shoshone and Southern Paiute people in the Beatty area.

William Wallace (1980, 270) notes a 1924 survey map titled "Scotty's Old Ranch" that indicated two locations for Indian gardens in Grapevine Canyon. These garden plots depended on irrigation and were family owned. Crops were planted in February and harvested in July. Plants grown included variegated corn, pumpkins, squash, two types of beans, sunflowers, watermelon, musk melon, tomatoes, some wheat, potatoes, peaches, and grapes. These crops were also grown by Steinenger in this very location prior to 1915, when Albert Johnson purchased the property to build his home, now known as Scotty's Castle.

Steward (1970, 32–33) considered farming a major food source that was introduced by the Southern Paiutes shortly after the immigrants arrived but was relegated to a secondary position by wage labor employment opportunities. He acknowledged to a limited extent that the invading economic system forced the Indians to adapt to a new lifestyle. Present consultants, however, do not agree with his claim that wage labor opportunities drew people away to work in areas outside their families' traditional home ranges or that farming was ever a major food source. According to all consultants, the Indians preferred to work within the geographic area most familiar to them. Gardening was merely a means of supplementing the food available in local community markets. The Indians' lifestyle had not become totally sedentary, however; they continued to travel in order to attend ceremonies, hunt, or visit family.

Generally the Indians did not work in the mines but were employed in related businesses, such as farming and selling food crops or gathering and hauling piñon pines to the kilns to make charcoal for the smelters. E. W. Nelson (1891) describes a borax operation in Saline Valley, to the northwest of Death Valley. Although he does not give a company name, he discusses the involvement of the Indians with the mining operation. They raised alfalfa, barley, and wheat to sell to the miners. The company paid the Indians a small royalty for using water at the time they needed it for irrigation. Some of the Indians found continual employment, at fair wages, with the borax company, which was located within one mile of the village, but Nelson provides no details on how much was paid to the Indians. This was, however, the earliest specific reference to Indians in a working relationship with mining activities.

Employment opportunities grew from 1860 to the 1930s. In addition to ranching and mining jobs, the railroad and construction industries hired Indians as laborers. With the possible exception of the early ranching jobs, all employers paid their employees, including the Indians, in cash or by check. The situation of Indians being totally indebted to their employers through a credit system, as described by Martha Knack (1987) for ranches in the Las Vegas area, did not exist for the Timbisha. In the Death Valley region credit that had to be worked off prior to receiving monetary compensation was not issued to the Indians.

After the railroad connecting northern and southern Nevada was completed and mining activities slowed circa 1915, a major economic development in the northern end of Death Valley was the Death Valley Ranch, more popularly known as Scotty's Castle. This sprawling desert castle was built by Albert M. Johnson, a wealthy Chicago businessman, aided by the miner he grubstaked, Death Valley Scotty (Shally and Bolton 1973). Johnson made many trips to Death Valley in the early years of this century, with Scotty as his guide and companion. The search for gold gradually became less important as the desire for adventure and solitude increased. They camped often in Grapevine Canyon in northern Death Valley where the Castle now sits. In 1915 Johnson acquired the former Steinenger Ranch and set up temporary camps whenever he and his wife, Bessie, came to the desert.

By 1922 Johnson had made plans for more permanent structures and three boxlike buildings were erected. He designed an elaborate complex that eventually included nine structures, electrical power generated by a Pelton waterwheel, refrigeration, and indoor plumbing. The construction began in 1925 and continued until Johnson ran out of money in 1931.

The construction of this home provided several years of employment for many Indians from the region. Between 1925 and 1931 Johnson hired a total of seventy-three Indians as general laborers (see Figure 9.3). The Indians dug all building foundations, at times having to use dynamite to get through the caliche layers. They mixed all concrete on the site and operated the gravel separator. The landscape grading and fence building were also done by the Indian laborers. The entire 1,530 acres were surrounded by a fence made of barbed wire strung between concrete posts (Shally and Bolton 1973, 10). Building this fence was, according to one consultant, a hard job because the posts weighed over four hundred pounds and were awkward to handle (Cherooty 1986).

The initial wage was $3.50 per day, dropping to $3.00 per day after the stock market crash of 1929. The steady work attracted men from eastern California and western Nevada, including Las Vegas and as far

Fig. 9.3. Indian work crew at Scotty's Castle, circa 1929 or 1930. Left to right: Ike Shaw; unknown; Joe Kennedy (?); Gilbert Landis; Johnnie Bacoch; rear, unknown; front, unknown, Death Valley Scotty; rear, unknown; Danny Mike; two in rear, unknown; Herb Kennedy; Hank Patterson; front, unknown; rear, unknown; front, unknwon; rear, unknown; Si Jack; rear, unknown; Johnnie Peavine; Bob Best; Bill Dock; Ed Fred. (NPS photo 7609, courtesy of the National Park Service, Death Valley National Monument)

north as Schurz (U.S. National Park Service 1925–1931). Bimonthly payroll records provide a detailed account of how many days were worked by each individual, with comments on what aspect of the construction he worked. Although non-Indian laborers were also hired, they were less likely to stay for long periods of time. The most consistent, long-standing employees were those Indians whose families' home ranges traditionally included Grapevine Canyon. These included the Shaw, Dock, Cherooty, Patterson, Stewart, and Kennedy families (see Figure 9.4). Non-Indian males were hired for finishing work such as tile setting, wrought iron installation, wood carving for ceilings and doors, and finishing work on interior and exterior wall surfaces. These craftsmen were not on the site for the entire work season. They were brought to the home when their particular skills were needed.

Johnson hired an Anglo by the name of Carl Schold to supervise the Indian laborers during the early years of construction. It appears this individual did not make as much of an impression on the workers as did his successor, E. M. Maxfield, who was supervisor during the last three or four years of construction. Max, as he was called, was well liked and easy to work for.

The work season began in mid-September and continued until the following August, with a one-month break during what is generally the hottest month. The total number of employees fluctuated throughout the year. The phase of construction determined how many laborers and craftsmen were needed at any particular time.

The rules for all employees, including the Indians, prohibited alcohol and gambling. Matt Roy Thompson, Johnson's construction manager, enforced these rules on everyone. Drunkenness was not tolerated and resulted in being fired. Generally the non-Indians who were fired left and did not return. The Indians, however, were the only general laborers available and were usually rehired later if there was an abundance of work (U.S. National Park Service 1925–1931).

The non-Indian laborers were housed separately from the Indians to keep them from socializing with the Indian women. All non-Indian laborers were provided with a room, but the cost of their board was taken out of their weekly paychecks. Johnson paid their transportation to and

Fig. 9.4. Indian camp at Scotty's Castle, circa 1930. Left to right, standing: Hank Patterson, Margaret Patterson (holding daughter Dorothy), Dollie Cherooty Stewart, Albert Johnson (in rear), Helen Stewart Sharp, Louis Sharp, Fred Thompson. Left to right, seated: Nellie Dock, Josephine Patterson, Tom Stewart, Ted Shaw, Warren Stewart, Pete Cherooty. (NPS photo 7613, courtesy of the National Park Service, Death Valley Monument)

Fig. 9.5. View of the Indian Camp at Scotty's Castle, looking northeast, circa 1926. The striped tent in the center belonged to Sullivan Shaw and his wife, Laura. The elongated house in the lower right was Hank Patterson's. Note the mix of traditional tule structure with modern canvas tent. (NPS photo S-0051, courtesy of the National Park Service, Death Valley National Monument)

from the construction site if they stayed until their job was complete. If the craftsmen chose to leave early, they paid their own transportation home (U.S. National Park Service 1925–1931).

Indian laborers, in contrast, occupied a specific area referred to as the "Indian Camp" south and slightly east of the construction site. This was not an aboriginal site per se because the entire canyon had been used by the Indians prior to the establishment of Steinenger's ranch (Patterson 1986). A waterline was extended to the area, and the men were encouraged by Albert Johnson to bring their families. The physical setup of the Indian Camp was a mixture of modern and traditional (see Figure 9.5). Canvas tents had rather traditional additions of tules and brush. Each house had a wood cookstove, but during the summer cooking was done outside on an open fire. The women gathered firewood and provided meals. One consultant remembers her mother collecting big knotty pieces of sage because they burned the hottest (Shaw 1986).

Going to work at Scotty's, as described by some consultants, was like being on an extended camping trip. These people were accustomed to living in houses with gardens, and several owned automobiles. Indian laborers were willing to go where the work was, even if this meant camping out for a few months. Groceries were bought in Tonopah, eighty-five miles away, or Beatty, sixty miles away. There were few gardens planted while the Indians worked at the Castle because there was not enough time to care for them. Although both men and women helped with the gardens, it was difficult to do gardening and also work for Johnson. The most accessible location for a garden near the Castle would have been the spring that fed the Castle water supply, but construction supplies were stored in the area (Hooper 1986; Shaw 1986).

One consultant remembers planting gardens as a child above what is now part of the Death Valley Ranch known as Lower Vine or Grapevine Springs. Vegetables such as tomatoes, various squashes, and melons were grown. The Indians also harvested a native cane from which they processed a sugary substance. These gardens were not maintained while they worked at the Castle, but they frequented the same area to bathe in the hot springs (Shaw 1986).

John Delphs, a man from Beatty who had a freighting business, delivered fresh meat regularly to the Indians working at the Castle and to the cook for the non-Indian laborers. His cosignature on the Indians' paychecks allowed them to cash the checks in Beatty. Thompson was upset with Delphs for paying the Indians with "booze" when he cashed all or part of their paychecks (U.S. National Park Service 1925–1931).

Life in the camp was rarely dull. Johnson's rules were usually ignored even though the Indians knew they risked being fired. There was entertainment every Saturday and Sunday evening. A large striped tent in the center of the camp belonging to Sullivan Shaw was the social center where there were always gambling games and plenty of booze. Most of the liquor came from the Burns Winery in Beatty. A variety of card games and an ever-popular hand game, a simple hiding and guessing game (Randle 1953), were the highlights of the evenings (see Figures 9.5 and 9.6). It was not unusual for $2,000 to change hands in a night (Cherooty 1986; Landis 1986; Shaw 1986). Despite the problems these

Fig. 9.6. Playing stick game in the Indian Camp at Scotty's Castle, circa 1929 or 1930. Seated on the left may be Dolly Boland's grandmother (name unknown); seated on the right is Mary Charlie; Bill Button is on the far right in the hat. (NPS photo S-0044, courtesy of the National Park Service, Death Valley National Monument)

activities created, Johnson knew he needed the Indians as laborers. He did order the camp closed periodically to put a temporary end to the problems (U.S. National Park Service 1925–1931).

A Northern Paiute woman saw the camp quite differently when she arrived with her new husband, a Shoshone from Monitor Valley, for their honeymoon. She had grown up in Fallon, Nevada, with all the modern conveniences and was shocked at having to live in tents at the Castle. She also did not speak the Shoshone language, so it took her a long time to feel partially accepted (Hooper 1986).

Bessie Johnson, Albert Johnson's wife, was an evangelist who expected everybody to go to church on Sunday. When at the Castle, she conducted worship services at the house for non-Indians (Shally and Bolton 1973, 17) and at the Indian Camp (Landis 1986; Patterson 1986; Shaw 1986). Generally, the Indians listened, took it in stride, and went about their own business when it was over. They all liked both the Johnsons and definitely enjoyed Scotty and his tall tales.

The Johnsons were concerned for the well-being of the Indians. They made an effort to get the children into the Bureau of Indian Affairs (BIA) school in Fort Mojave, Arizona, especially during 1930, although it is not quite clear why they did this. Many of the Indian children went to local public schools in every community, including Lida and Furnace Creek, with no indications of problems (Chalfant 1930; Kennedy 1986; Shaw 1986). Correspondence implied that arrangements for schooling were left primarily to Matt Roy Thompson (U.S. National Park Service 1925–1931). He seems to have used it as a means to get rid of "problem" boys. There was no reference to Timbisha girls sent to the Fort Mojave school. Those children sent to Fort Mojave generally ran away and came back to their homes in the Death Valley area (Button 1986). When the Fort Mojave school closed in the autumn of 1931, the thirteen Timbisha children then attending were transferred to Stewart Indian School in Carson City, Nevada.

Intermarriage with non-Indians extends back at least to the first influx of immigrants into the area (Sennett 1985–1986; Steward 1970, 87). As miners came to the region in full force, the rate of non-Indian marriage increased, along with the numbers of children born to racially mixed couples that never "married." Very few of the non-Indian men in the interracial marriages stayed for any length of time. The children from these unions, however, were raised with the Indian families. These children were considered part of the family and were never labeled by the Indians as illegitimate. Interracial marriages and relationships were common by the early twentieth century.

Overall, family life in the Indian Camp was structured as it had been in the past. Families continued to rely on their closest relatives and traveled to other areas for ceremonies and visits. When work was not available at Scotty's, they went to other familiar areas to look for employment. For the most part they worked ranch jobs, usually haying or herding livestock. The material culture items introduced by the immigrants made life easier on a daily basis. Money made it possible for the Indians to cope with shrinking environmental resources. Since hunting and gathering were no longer the primary subsistence pattern, foodstuffs were purchased at local markets in area communities. Money became necessary for survival. The automobile gave the Indians access to areas of the world quite possibly heard of but never seen in earlier times. Working at Scotty's was a major step for the younger generations toward total dependence on a wage labor economy.

The Indians were there, could do the job, and were willing workers. In actuality, without this workforce the progress on the Castle construction would have been extremely slow or impossible. The Indians from the area were Johnson's most reliable, consistent workforce. The non-Indians hired were generally not from the local area. Climatic extremes, in particular, were not mentioned as a reason for the relatively high turnover in the numbers of non-Indian labors. It appears from archival records at Scotty's Castle that they did not adjust to the isolation.

The employment opportunities afforded the Indians with the building of Scotty's Castle were very important; without it there was little else available, except working for local ranchers. Since the 1860s these Indians had not participated in a fully functioning hunting and gathering lifestyle. The face of the landscape, socially and physically, had changed, demanding a different economic base for them. They had become, as were the immigrants, dependent on money to buy food and supplies. Those interviewed note they did not work at the mines except possibly to haul wood for smelters. No specific reasons were given; it was just not a desirable job. By the time the Castle was under construction, the depression was beginning to hit the desert regions of the United States. Many mines were closing down, and there was rising unemployment (Elliot 1973, 182). Work on the Castle ended as Johnson's money ran out after the stock market crash of 1929. The work available for the Indians at Scotty's Castle was virtually their last reliable source of income prior to the depression years.

Albert Johnson was concerned about what would happen to the Indians in his employ. In December 1930 he wrote asking whether the government would make a reservation for the Indians bordering the ranch property. Although agents from the BIA were to write with details, they evidently never pursued the matter (U.S. National Park Service

1925–1931). As the available work lessened, the Indians gradually left the Castle, either returning to their original family locations or seeking family members in other locations. Many went back to herding cattle and horses for ranchers; most went to nearby communities and worked wherever and whenever they could. Several people with ties to families from central Death Valley congregated at Furnace Creek, living as best they could. Likewise, individuals from Ash Meadows or Lone Pine went back to their homes and families.

As the economic situation worsened, the Indians congregated in major population centers looking for work or welfare. Members of the Shaw family eventually moved to Laws, California, where Eddie Shaw worked on a cattle ranch around 1940 (Shaw 1986). Some families migrated to the newly organized reservations in the Owens Valley of California, set up through the influence of the Los Angeles Department of Water and Power, usually moving in with relatives (Kelly 1986). The census records for the early 1930s indicate that a few individuals migrated to the coastal cities of California; they were generally of the younger generation, anxious to move and find employment elsewhere.

Of all the consumer goods available to the Indians since the turn of the century, the automobile was the most sought after and prized possession (refer to Figure 9.5). With a car a person could traverse the desert regions farther and faster. As the Indian economic base changed during the early twentieth century, the automobile was a major factor in keeping families close socially even though they were dispersed geographically. This appears to have been very important for families even during the early years of the depression. It not only allowed the Indian population greater mobility but also made possible one of the greatest U.S. pastimes—tourism.

A few Timbisha women took advantage of this new sales market, creating unique items for tourists to buy. This, of course, included an elaboration of existing basketry art. With the introduction of metal cooking pots and other Anglo material culture, there was no longer a need for utilitarian baskets. The result was the development of fancy decorative baskets. Within the first two decades of the twentieth century fancy baskets were being woven by a few remaining weavers. However, even at this time basketry was a dying art in Death Valley. The younger women were not learning the technique (Landis 1986; Shaw 1986).

Changes in manufacturing techniques and basketry styles reflected changes in aboriginal lifestyles and home ranges. Gathering areas for basketry materials had been constricted or destroyed, so there was less use of indigenous materials such as juncus. The devil's claw plant was grown in gardens and used more frequently. Contact with Southern Paiute weavers resulted in a mixing of traditional designs, evident in the basket collection at Scotty's Castle (Sennett 1985–1986). New designs were also introduced in response to requests from tourists for specific styles, especially lidded baskets. Rosie Noble, from the mining center of Darwin, also made and sold baskets.

People traveling to Death Valley were the primary target for sales. Death Valley was established as a national monument in 1933 in an effort to attract tourists to boost the lagging regional economy. In 1936 the BIA and the National Park Service set aside forty acres as a village site for the Timbisha families living in Death Valley. Together these agencies provided housing at the village site in the bottom of the valley near Furnace Creek. The Park Service provided employment to the extent that it was available (U.S. Dept. of the Interior 1982, 16). The Indians earned a living by operating a branch of the Wai Pa Shone trading post and the laundry. The trading post was an Indian cooperative that operated out of Nevada to sell Indian crafts. Women in Death Valley then had a direct outlet for their baskets through the trading post (U.S. Dept. of the Interior 1982, 20).

CONCLUSION

Over the years between 1860 and 1930, with the number of immigrants increasing, the Timbisha subsistence pattern gradually shifted from hunting and gathering to wage earner–consumer methods of survival within traditional home ranges. The Indians emphasized short-term economic gain. They made money and spent it quickly; there was little planning for the future, and bank accounts were not established. Access to money enabled the Indians to have some luxury items, more free time, and the capability to travel greater distances in shorter time. As the available job market shifted, individuals adapted to alternative types of work within the vast area they called home.

In spite of the changes in the economic base, the social organization of the Timbisha remained one of loosely knit extended families covering an extensive area in annual hunting and gathering rounds. This social structure remained intact throughout the transition to a wage labor economy because it could be accommodated within the new economic framework. When the depression era began, the Indians drifted back to their traditional home ranges or joined family members in other areas. Even today kin ties cover large areas. The extended family continues to be an important part of the lives of the Death Valley Timbisha.

10

FROM LEGEND TO LAND TO LABOR
CHANGING PERSPECTIVES ON NATIVE AMERICAN WORK

PATRICIA C. ALBERS

Native Americans have been engaged in wage labor and other forms of paid work throughout much of the historic period, as the chapters in this book amply demonstrate. From indentured laborers in the mines of Mexico to commodity producers of furs in Canada, the indigenous peoples of North America were important sources of labor in early colonial development. In subsequent generations their labor contributed to the agricultural and industrial growth of the areas in which they lived. Whether they were farmworkers in Maine, bricklayers in California, lumberjacks in Michigan, or ranch hands in Nevada, their labor was an important component of local economic development. During the twentieth century thousands of Native Americans migrated to the cities, where they also gained employment in a wide range of industries from high steel to railroad work. If the scores of professional people trained in medicine, law, education, science, and business are added, Native Americans have had (and continue to have) a varied history of labor participation in the rural and urban workforces of North America.

Yet despite a long-standing and diverse history of paid employment, this feature of Native American life has been hidden especially in the United States.[1] Most information on the subject is buried in obscure government reports or mentioned only as a passing reference in scholarly publications. Even some of today's most highly publicized and revisionist-minded books (e.g., Jaimes 1992; Josephy and Limerick 1993; Trimble 1993) fail to cover wage labor as an important aspect of the Native

American experience. With few notable exceptions (i.e., Waddell 1969; Adams 1971; Mooney 1976; Knight 1978; Snipp 1980; Blanchard 1983; Jacobson 1984; MacKay 1985; Weiss 1984; Boxberger 1988; Cornell 1990), studies devoted to the historical conditions under which Native peoples performed wage labor, along with the particular ways they experienced this sort of work, hardly exist.[2]

The appearance of this book, therefore, heralds an important and much-needed change in our awareness about wage labor in the lives and livelihoods of Native Americans. Not only does the book contain a wealth of historical data on the different kinds of wage labor they performed, but it also presents solid case examples of the varied ways in which their work became incorporated into the developing (and developed) capitalist economies of the United States.

By striking a blow to various conundrums about the absence of wage labor in Native American life, this book represents a destablizing force. On the one hand, it disarms many widely accepted theories that segregate and isolate Native Americans from wider developments in political economy. It asks us to consider why Native peoples are denied a place in most accounts of labor history in the United States and, even when present, why they are relegated to a passive background position outside the flow of determinative economic movements and events (Wertheimer, Levine et al. 1989). On the other hand, it disables conventional perspectives that distance Native Americans from other Americans by viewing their work as separate and different. It challenges us to think about how a lack of coevalness, to borrow an expression from Johannes Fabian (1983), gets reinforced in discourses that categorize, operationalize, and describe Native Americans as cultural "strangers" or "others" (Krupat 1992).

This chapter represents an initial effort to rethink conventional understandings of Native American "work" in light of the compelling evidence on wage labor found in this book. This chapter calls into question standard representations that make wage labor invisible in the culture histories of Native Americans, and it argues for interpretive theory that situates this work squarely in the evolving capitalist economies of North America. Finally, a variety of questions are raised for future studies of Native American wage labor, especially their relationship to wider bodies of literature on ethnicity, capitalism, and labor force segmentation.

HISTORIC LEGENDS, CONTEMPORARY LORE

There are a series of well-established stereotypes that imply that Native Americans do not work and that when they do, their work patterns are irregular and unproductive. Part of this stereotyping results from the fact that some of the work Native Americans (and many other peoples as well) perform is defined out of existence in the U.S. economy. This usually happens when their work is not, technically speaking, a form of wage labor. It also occurs whenever particular aspects of their work are not controlled, at least directly, by a capitalist marketplace. In many conventional approaches to the economy any form of labor not aimed directly at capital accumulation is marginalized. And by extension, any work style or habit that does not feed into the "productivity" (read: profitability) of capital is dismissed (Collins and Gimenez 1990). When denied the status of "work," the unpaid, underground, and poorly compensated labor of millions of Americans (most notably minorities and women) goes unnoticed and unrecognized in the annals of economic history.[3]

But even when Native Americans engage in work that is technically considered wage labor, their paid employment is still concealed. Only now it is hidden because it does not conform to stereotypes that identify Native Americans with certain ethnically "traditional" forms of work and reciprocity. Whether their wage labor is overlooked because it does not match the conditions of capital or because it does not meet particular cultural standards, the fact remains that it is largely invisible in mainstream writings. If we are to understand how one specific kind of work, wage labor, became so obscured, we must discover how the "work" (or a lack thereof) of Native Americans gets constructed as a concept and how it is placed within a broader framework of cultural knowledge.

ETHNICITY WORK, AND STEREOTYPING

In discursive arenas where so much has been invested literally and figuratively in separating the Native American from the rest of that which is American, it is not always easy to identify, much less deconstruct, the "invented traditions" (Hobsbawm and Ranger 1983) associated with work. In popular discourse, the work that is considered a "real" expression of the Native American experience is marked and separated symbolically from most other forms of labor.[4] Woodcarving, basketweaving, and potterymaking are among several productive activities that are so isolated. Treated in legendary terms as part of a timeless, sacred tradition and ancient lore, the so-called authentic work of Native Americans is situated in a popular play of mythic images rather than in a progression of actual historic events. Privileged and elevated above all other labors, this "genuine" work is fetishized as a cultural relic and frozen in time. It becomes part of a wider body of stereotyping where Native Americans are represented as the dead chapters of history and where they are treated as symbolic mascots for everything from athletic teams to tobacco and automobiles (Berkhofer 1978; Stedman 1982).

The stereotyping of American Indian work in an ahistorical, mythical mode has implications far beyond Toronto, Hollywood, and other centers of culture production because it fundamentally affects the ways in which Native Americans as living peoples get situated in society as citizens and as workers. In this context we need to ask how the continuing use of American Indians as symbols reinforces the unreality of the lens through which the public understands their work and how it perpetuates stereotypes that deny them an authentic connection to the wage labor history of the countries in which they reside.

Among other things, popular stereotypes place Native Americans in a double bind when it comes to realizing a sense of personal and/or social identity through their own labor.[5] As an example, when Native Americans manufacture dream-catchers, even on an assemblyline, their ethnic identity is validated. When they rebuild an engine block as part of a pattern of reciprocity among kin, or when they do this as a wage laborer in a commercial garage, their ethnic identity is denied. In the first instance their work is associated with a legendary "traditionality" emblematic of the American Indian; in the second their labor occupies a liminal space because it lacks the cultural boundaries that stereotypically associate Native Americans with particular economic activities.

Imagemaking of this kind reaches beyond the realm of identity because it influences the very character of the labor Native Americans perform, encouraging them to pursue specific types of jobs while excluding them from others.

The tourist industry is one area of employment where this sort of selective process is especially evident. Throughout North America tourism has played an important part in funneling Native Americans into particular kinds of wage labor and/or petty-commodity production. From the Rockies in Alberta to the Black Hills in South Dakota, from the Smoky Mountains in North Carolina to the Dells of Wisconsin, and from the Grand Canyon in Arizona to Yosemite Park in California, Native American labor was marked by its culturally "exotic" position in local tourism. (Mekeel 1932, 1936; Albers and Medicine 1968, n.d.; Deitch 1977; Thomas 1978; Bates 1982a, 1982b; Stucki 1982; Albers and James 1983, 1985, 1987; Masayesva and Younger 1983).[6] Even though the involvement of Native Americans in tourism is well known, much of what has been written focuses on their roles as artists and performers, not as producers or laborers in a capitalist marketplace. And even though it is clear that Native Americans themselves define their creative labor in culturally specific and unique ways, the fact remains that it is not divorced from the economic dimensions of the tourist markets in which they work (Parezo 1983, 164–192). Therefore, much more needs to be known about the particular ways in which these markets appropriate Native American labor as performance.

In fact, it can be argued that the success of Native Americans in tourism is contingent on denying them any connection to a capitalist workplace and its associated wage labor. It rests on an obfuscation of the very labor conditions that support the creation of cultural productions for tourists (Albers and James 1988; Rossel 1988; Urry 1990). In this context much more needs to be understood about how their labor gets concealed in places where they are engaged in the manufacture of ethnically salient performances or products—that is, "real handmade Indian artifacts"—and how Native Americans themselves participate in the mystification of their own labor within tourist contexts. Also, how are ethnically marked jobs in the tourist industry perceived and experienced by those who perform them? How much do Native Americans invest their own personal/cultural identities in this work? And how are certain ideas about American Indian "traditionality" resistant to change because they have been located and perpetuated within a labor of tourism (Albers and Medicine, n.d.)?

Also important are the processes by which ethnically marked labor, especially when it takes place as wage work on an assembly line, becomes hidden behind mystifying hyperbole (Albers and James 1984, 1988; McLuhan 1985). How are American Indian objects made and marketed as "original," "unique," "colorful," magical," and "timeless" emblems of experience, and what consequences does this have for the character of Native American work even when it resides outside the production of stereotyped ethnic symbols? Could tourist agents and media makers appeal to the public's altern fantasies about the legendary status of Native Americans if the inherent truth of their lived-in working experiences were revealed? In short, how do the conditions of Native American labor become hidden in order to market a product/performance whose primary value resides in the character of its symbolic presentation, not in its utilitarian function?

The varying and ever-changing relationship among Native Americans, wage labor, and ethnic tourism (including the armchair varieties of consumption that can be seen on TV, at the movies, and in the tabloids) bears on some of the new and provocative theories of Jean Baudrillard (1975, 1981) and others (Foucault 1970, 1976; Williams 1980, 1982; Jameson 1983, 1984; Featherstone 1993; Wernick 1991) about the direction of work, working, and workers under postindustrial capitalism. In focusing on the rising power and play of symbolic over utilitarian forms of production, these writers present an important literature for understanding the dilemmas Native Americans face as workers whose ethnicity has been stereotyped and appropriated in various mass cultural forums (Ames 1992). More specifically, their writing offers a theoretical framework for asking a number of critical questions: Why is it troublesome to envision potato picking, uranium mining, blackjack dealing, and domestic service as essential life experiences of peoples whose "authentic" cultures the public wants to romanticize, emulate, and sanctify? How does information about such work become problematic when placed against the mass production and consumption of the American Indian as a symbolic image and illusion? Clearly, whether the American Indian stands as an idol for New Age religions, a fetish for chic interior design, or an icon for wilderness preservation, the use of this image making and its impact on the work Native Americans perform cannot be ignored either now or in the past.

ETHNICITY, LABOR MARKETS, AND THE VARIETIES OF WORK EXPERIENCE

The project of deconstructing symbolic images of American Indians in work and other contexts is interesting not simply as an effort in tracing the ideological roots and consequences of popular cultural practices (Rabinow 1986; Rosaldo 1989). Its most compelling purpose is to understand how this symbolic production becomes part of the necessary conditions that determine how Native Americans qualify as workers in various labor markets.[7] The tourist industry, when it capitalizes on ethnicity, is one of the more obvious instances where Native people are channeled into particular labor markets on the basis of their ethnic heritage, but there are others.

Another example is the long-standing practice of hiring Native Americans for certain kinds of manual work on the basis of unsubstantiated assumptions about their labor abilities, such as being endowed with superior capacities to complete repetitive tasks without boredom, lift heavy burdens without strain, and endure temperature extremes without pain.[8] Of course, these same work "traits" have been applied to other ethnic groups, including Irish Americans, African Americans, and Chinese Americans, and have been used in similar ways to justify locking minorities into unstable, poorly paid, labor-intensive jobs (Reich 1981; Glenn 1985; Brown and Philips 1991; Romero 1992). That a connection exists between the labor positions Native Americans occupy and ideological definitions of their work is clear, but it is a subject that has not been examined in any depth.

The chapters in this book, however, move in a direction that allows us to know, or at least ask the right questions about, how stereotypes come into play in reproducing ethnically segregated workforces in which Native Americans constitute a source of labor. Alice Littlefield (1993; this volume), among others (Trennert 1982; MacKay 1985, 17–20), illustrates how assimilationist ideologies were mandated and reproduced within the curricula of Bureau of Indian Affairs (BIA) boarding schools and how these socialized and trained Native Americans for particular kinds of work. What is required are more case studies like this one and others (Elias 1988; Carter 1990; Moore, this volume) that make specific connections between the conditions under which Native people labor and the ways in which their work performance is defined ideologically. Also needed are case studies that compare work ideologies surrounding Native Americans with those applied to other ethnic groups, that examine how these ideologies contribute to segregation in local labor markets, and that look at how such ideologies get used when different groups compete for the same jobs.

Although ideological characterizations of workers and their work are important, these are not sufficient for understanding the dynamics of labor market participation along ethnic and cultural lines. In contrast to other minority populations, including African Americans, Hispanic Americans, and Asian Americans,[9] little is known about the kinds of social, political, and economic forces that have drawn Native Americans into certain labor markets and excluded them from others. Therefore, much more needs to be written about the extent to which Native American wage labor has been tracked according to ethnic markers and the specific conditions under which this tracking has taken place (Forbes 1991).

In areas such as the Great Basin (Knack 1987, this volume) and California (Hurtado 1982, 1988b; Carrico and Shipek, Sennett, this volume), we find that Native American labor entered a wide range of jobs during the late nineteenth and early twentieth centuries. Among other occupations, Native Americans were farm laborers, domestics, mine workers, ranchers, masons, bricklayers, and carpenters. Wherever they were hired, however, they tended to be placed in the more unstable, unskilled, and poorly paid sectors of the workforce. In general, they entered segmented labor forces where Native peoples built the mining structures but did not generally mine, laid the flooring but did not set the tile, or performed rough carpentry but did not do finished cabinetry (Hurtado 1982, 1988b; Carrico and Shipek, Knack, Sennett, this volume).

Although the literature is clear about the kinds of jobs Native Americans performed in the California–Great Basin region, and some of the changes that took place in their labor force participation over time, it is still undeveloped regarding the "causes" of specific labor arrangements. What is not known and cannot be determined without more comparative data are the general factors of production and ethnicity that placed the labor of Native Americans in particular sectors of local and regional economies. In the mine industry, for example, why were jobs organized hierarchically by ethnic group in Nevada and California during the late nineteenth century when such segmentation did not take place in certain parts of Arizona? To answer a question like this one, much greater attention has to be given to the conditions of capital (i.e., monopoly versus competitive) and production (i.e., skilled versus unskilled) within the industries in which Native Americans worked, especially as elaborated in the theoretical work of Harry Braverman (1974) and others (Gordon, Edwards, and Reich 1982). In addition, the data on Native American labor need to be evaluated against a wider body of information that takes into consideration the presence of other minority ethnic groups in the segmentation of regional labor markets. Thus, although it is perfectly appropriate in this initial stage to limit inquiry to the descriptive specifics of wage labor among Native Americans, later research must move beyond this and consider the determinative features of the industries and labor forces within which Native peoples work.

Some of these determinative features might be located in agriculture—an industry about which there is a well-developed body of theory on patterns of proletarianization and in which Native Americans constituted a primary source of seasonal and/or migrant labor in the late nineteenth and early twentieth centuries. In places as far removed as the hop farms of Washington (Boxberger 1988), the potato fields of Maine, the cherry orchards of Michigan, the cattle ranches of Nevada, and the truck gardens of California, Native Americans were a major "reserve army of labor" for seasonal farmwork. Outside of Harald Prins's rich account in chapter 2 of Mi'kmaq potato workers in Maine, however, there are few details about the history of Native American involvement in specific agricultural industries. Prins's chapter is especially important in two respects: one, it offers unique information on patterns of labor recruitment and work crew formation; and two, it traces how shifts in productive technology (e.g., mechanization of the harvest) contributed to a reduction in Mi'kmaq labor force participation. In addition to the effects of technological change, Native American involvement in agricultural labor has been influenced by competition from other ethnic groups. In the 1920s and 1930s Mexican Americans began to replace Native American farm laborers in many areas of the country, but it was not until after World War II that such transformations in the ethnic composition of most agricultural labor forces became complete. Unfortunately, there is little published information on how or why this transition took place.

In this regard one area that needs further study is the active role the federal government played as a labor contractor of American Indians in agricultural, industrial, and domestic work. In the late nineteenth century Indian children attending boarding schools were placed in the outing system, where they were contracted to work as domestics and field laborers. Federal Indian schools also acted as employment agencies for placing students in wage work positions after graduation (Trennert 1982; MacKay 1985, 17–21, 54–58). In the early decades of the twentieth century the BIA established an employment program under the direction of Charles Dagenett and encouraged local superintendents to act as labor agents to secure off-reservation employment. In subsequent years the BIA actively recruited Indians for unskilled railway, agricultural, and reclamation work, and by World War II it was seeking positions for American Indians in the steel, shipbuilding, and automobile industries. The BIA's role in labor contracting continued into the 1950s, when it became associated with various relocation projects. In later years, however, the BIA played a diminished role in this area as many of its labor training and contracting responsibilities were shifted to other federal agencies (MacKay 1985, 25–47, 58–76, 111–224).

In the ever-changing capitalist economy of the United States ethnicity has been a major marker of job segmentation and stratification. Indeed, an important sociological and economic literature (Baron 1972; Bonacich 1972; Braverman 1974; Reich 1981; Sowell 1981; Wilkinson 1981; Gordon, Edwards, and Reich 1982) has developed around the ways in which capitalism uses the ethnicity of workers for its own ends. Theories have been developed to explain not only how ethnicity is used to define and reinforce various occupational divisions and specializations but also how it has been employed to control and limit the demands of labor. In this regard Kurt Peters's chapter describes a case in which Native American labor crews were hired by the railroads as strikebreakers. This kind of situation is well recorded in the labor histories of other ethnic minorities (Boggs 1970; Saxton 1971; Ictioka 1980; Cheng and Bonacich 1984; Yamashita and Park 1985), who were hired frequently to disrupt strikes and impede union organizing. But here, as in so many other areas of wage labor, the record is nearly blank when it comes to reports on the divisive use of Native American workers in promoting the interests of capital over labor.

In contrast to many of the cases reported in this book, in which Native American work entered the laborforce because of its generalized character, the Cheyennes' labor was appropriated because of its specialized properties. Their case shows how historically developed patterns of work within Native American communities articulated with market demands for products of "traditional" manufacture. The kind of work performed by the Cheyennes in the nineteenth century was a form of petty-commodity production rather than wage labor. And even though wage labor has been the predominant working arrangement in modern U.S. economic history, the capitalist mode of production relies on other forms of labor in its pursuit of profit. Generally speaking, situations in which Native Americans controlled, indirectly or directly, the labor, techniques, and means of production contributing to capital accumulation are much more well documented than cases in which they performed wage labor.[10] Like John Moore's important chapter on the Cheyennes, several writings on the fur trade (Ray and Freeman 1978; White 1991; Cox 1993; Klein 1983) specify the ways and conditions in which capital utilized petty-commodity production; some (Tanner 1979; Foster 1988; Sprenger 1988) look even more specifically at how the ability of Native peoples to reproduce their own subsistence sustained capital accumulation under this kind of work.

Less well documented, however, is the nature of the relations that tied together different kinds of labor in larger production processes. Moore's chapter (this volume) shows how the Cheyennes' work in hunting buffalo and processing their robes was linked through a complex production chain to the wage labor of factory workers in the leather industry. Several of the chapters in this book give examples of situations in which Native Americans worked in the specialized but unskilled stages of larger production processes. Much more needs to be written about these kinds of situations in terms not only of what they report descriptively about the particular labor histories of Native Americans but also of what they reveal theoretically about how capitalism simultaneously uses different labor arrangements to organize its production (Braverman 1974).

In other but related ways several chapters in this book describe the historical circumstances in which Native Americans maintained mixed economic strategies in their communities and formed divisions of labor among themselves to make a livelihood in their rapidly changing worlds. Martha Knack, James McClurken, Harald Prins, and Beth Sennett examine a variety of situations that supported simultaneous work in subsistence, petty-commodity production, and wage labor. In the process, the chapters also evaluate those circumstances (e.g., loss of land) that required an increasing dependence on paid employment and a movement away from more autonomous working conditions. More particularly, the chapters give evidence of the strategies that Native Americans used to achieve some independence at the point of their labor and the conditions under which this autonomy was undermined. Finally, some of the chapters shed light on when, where, and how Native Americans defined the terms of their entry into wage labor, as opposed to having this participation defined for them.

Overall, the materials presented in this book represent a very significant step toward overcoming serious empirical deficiencies in two bodies of literature, neither of which has been well informed by the evidence of Native American wage labor. On the one hand, these materials bring additional evidence to bear on questions in the general economic literature about the history of labor force segmentation, especially the role that ethnicity plays in this process. And on the other hand, they make visible an aspect of the Native American experience that has been hidden in standard ethnographic and historical writing.

ETHNICITY, COMMUNITY, AND WORK CULTURE

In an effort to gain a better understanding of the conditions and varieties of paid labor, scholars should not lose sight of the particular ways Native Americans themselves experience and speak about this work. In this context Peter's chapter on Laguna involvement in railroad work is significant not only as an attempt to chronicle a neglected aspect of Native American labor history but also as an effort to describe how Native peoples organized their own culturally distinct communities around this work. In particular, his research gives evidence of a persisting pattern of community formation among the western pueblos in an environment and work setting radically different from their home territory. The ties between the railroad communities in Richmond, California, and home villages in New Mexico appear to replicate the age-old and formally structured models of relationship between mother and daughter settlements. Historically a similar pattern appears in the links between the homeland villages of the Mohawks and the satellite communities of their wage workers in places such as Brooklyn, New York (Voget 1953; Katzer 1988).[11]

The cases of Mohawks in Brooklyn and Lagunas in Richmond are interesting not only as general instances of cultural continuity but also as specific examples of an indigenous culture's influence on aspects of labor force participation. The Mohawks' involvement in high steel, for example, has been linked to a variety of cultural features (Voget 1953; Blanchard 1983; Katzer 1988). The Lagunas' successful and extended involvement in railroad work at the Richmond yards also appears to have had cultural concomitants, and one of these may have involved (either directly or indirectly) the use of age-graded, kiva associations as models for achieving solidarity and cooperation among male work crews. To dispel the many unsubstantiated and persisting claims that Native American cultural traditions lead to failure in wage labor, scholars must address more thoroughly how capitalist labor arrangements articulate with indigenous cultural practice in compatible, as well as incompatible, ways.[12]

How connections are established between historic cultural practices in Native American communities and the characteristics of their wage labor participation need to be evaluated with great care because it is not always easy to discern which comes first in a particular causal pathway. Beth Sennett's chapter on the early wage labor history of the Timbisha from Death Valley in California is a case in point. This chapter describes their flexible and family-based social formations in association with their involvement in wage labor. There is no question that this kind of organization was well suited to the exigencies of life under wage labor in nineteenth century California and Nevada. It is unclear, however, to what extent this pattern conformed to aboriginal patterns. It might be argued, just as convincingly, that some of the characteristics that ethnographers attributed to Great Basin populations were a post-contact response to environmental degradation and the need to secure survival through wage labor. Whatever the case may be, it is clear that the flexible, family-based communities so characteristic of ethnographic description in the Great Basin need to be reexamined in light of post-contact adaptations to the atomizing effects of wage labor.

Questions about the connection between indigenous cultural practices and labor force participation are especially well suited to the skills of ethnographers and ethnohistorians. More case studies of the sort contained in this book need to focus on the kinds of situations that permit Native peoples to use their own cultural practices in recruiting, contracting, and organizing wage labor; that allow them to construct an identity as wage workers without destroying basic cultural values; and that enable them to reproduce themselves as wage laborers within an indigenous cultural framework. In fact, it is around particular people's labor lifelines, rather than an industry or a market, that anthropologists have achieved a sense of unity in much of their research on work (Wallman 1979; Romero 1992). And it is in this aspect of the wage labor experience that the research specialties of anthropologists tend to stand out and differ most from those of sociologists and economists.

In the study of relationships among capitalism, wage labor, and ethnicity, the lived-in experiences of the workers must take center stage because it is at the point of their labor that ethnic heritage intersects with capitalism in the workplace. In this regard much more oral history research needs to be completed to understand how Native Americans themselves represent and interpret their own experiences in wage labor. In the fashion of materials available on wage laborers from other ethnic groups (Willis 1981; Sacks and Remy 1984; Zavella 1987, 1991; Romero 1992), Native American workers need to give a greater voice to their own working experiences.[13] Is their own work history a subject of pride or a source of alienation? To what extent is a sense of selfhood invested in (or denied by) employment? What kinds of workplaces and employment are favored? When or under what circumstances have jobs been entered voluntarily/involuntarily? And how does this bear on the way wage labor is experienced? These are just a few of the hundreds of questions that Native Americans need to be asked, or to ask themselves, to further an understanding of their labor history.

There is a caveat here: however Native Americans come to talk or write about and record their working histories, these should not be used on behalf of generalizations that divorce their labor from other aspects of living. Whether Native Americans share their impressions about working in the timber stands of northern California, the tire factories of Ohio, the copper mines of Arizona, the cattle ranches of Wyoming, the law firms of New Mexico, or the schoolrooms of Oklahoma, these job experiences need to be interpreted within the wider flow of life events that push them into, as well as pull them away from, employment. Above all, scholars must move away from the kinds of classifications and conceptualizations that historically described Native Americans in terms of reified work identities, such as "hunters," "gatherers," and "basket weavers." Whatever else contemporary Native Americans may be, they are not simply "welders," "bank tellers," or "physicians." To describe them in such limiting terms only pigeonholes Native people and in the process produces stereotypic images used for purposes and interests beyond their own control (Deloria 1969; McNickle 1972; Vizenor 1984, 1987).

ETHNICITY, IDEOLOGY, AND LABOR FORCE PARTICIPATION

In conjunction with (and in some cases, in opposition to) the forces that bring Native Americans to certain occupations are those that block their entry into particular workplaces and/or that eliminate them entirely from the labor force. As Martha Knack and Alice Littlefield point out in chapter 1, much of what has been written about American Indian wage labor comes from the perspective of their unemployment or lack of paid work. By and large the position of Native Americans in the labor force has been approached from the standpoint of its negation. Historically this has had the conceptual and rhetorical effect of preemptively closing discussion before any details of Native American labor history have been gathered, presented, or discussed.

Unless evidence of the kind presented in this book becomes more widely known, there is nothing to counteract popular ideas about the absence of wage labor in Native American history. Challenging stereotypic legend and lore with positive bodies of evidence on the long and varied history of Native American wage labor is not enough, however. The entire ideological system within which the stereotypes are nested must be dismantled. And just as we need to know more about how cultural ideologies are implicated in selecting Native Americans for particular kinds of wage labor, we also need to understand how these prevent Native Americans from entering the workforce in general. Equally important, we need to understand how stereotypic interpretation serves ideological purposes and functions beyond the scope of work characterizations per se (Moore, this volume).

One question to ask at this point is, Where did the myth that Native Americans do not work come from? There are two possible ways of looking for an answer to this question. One way is to pursue further the consequences of discourses that stereotype Native American labor in culturally distancing terms. Any examination of work activities such as rug weaving, jewelry making, and hide painting reveals that most of the labor classified as "authentically" Native American is not really considered work. Rather, it is represented and interpreted as an artistic performance, an endeavor unsullied by any association with the mundane, workaday world.[14] Indeed, in some writing craftwork is envisioned as a kind of religious calling, and its products are elevated to the realm of the sacred.[15]

Another way to answer the question is to look at conventional representations of Native Americans as workers, especially before the twentieth century. Here the denial of Native American wage labor was achieved by the differentiation of labor along gender lines and then the declassification of it as work. Thus, whereas the labor commonly associated with American Indian men, including warfare, fishing, and hunting, was typically glorified, elevated, and given the valorous status of a "sport," much of the labor performed by American Indian women was trivialized, denigrated, and relegated to the menial status of "drudgery" (Kehoe 1983; Albers and Kay n.d.). By conceptually keeping the labor of Native peoples outside a world of commerce and manufacture, either by romanticizing it as sport or degrading it as drudgery, many early writers and later ones as well distorted the character of this work and mystified its outcome and contribution to the growth of capitalism as well.

This kind of thinking was consistent with popular notions that Native Americans should be deprived of their lands because they were unable to work them productively, as in the argument that hunters do not make good farmers (Carter 1990). Women generally did not count here. Relegated as they often were to a slavelike status, their connection to labor and landownership was often dismissed a priori (Nowak 1976; Rothenberg 1980; Poole 1988). The conceptual sleight of hand that led Euro-Americans to reason that Native forms of labor were not really "work" was a powerful one, and it was a crucial aspect of the rhetoric used to justify the expropriation of the lands on which Native Americans retained some degree of independence, either by performing their "own" work or by engaging in forms of labor viewed as "real" work in the developing capitalist economies of the New World.

In the early twentieth century the myth that Native people were ill suited to "productive" labor in the agrarian and industrial workplace continued to serve as a convenient rationale for wrestling land from them. Various decisions reached by the federal government in the early decades of the twentieth century to sell or lease Native American lands to outsiders rather than support Native self-sufficiency in farming and ranching were bolstered by additional myths about an absence of a work "ethic" among Indians. Not only was the validity of their productive skills challenged, but also questions were raised about whether they were capable of performing any work at all. And even though federal and mission schools (Littlefield 1993) faithfully trained many Native Americans in the arts and techniques of "productive" land use, knowledge of this education was conveniently dismissed when it came to expropriating their land (McNickle 1962; Meyer 1969).

In truth, Native Americans were able to work their lands successfully, but the conjunction of a variety of economic forces with federal policymaking ultimately prevented them from doing so. Once the land was alienated through lease or sale, many Native Americans in the plains region were forced to seek paid employment as workers on farms run by neighboring whites (Meyer 1969; Elias 1988; Poole 1988; Carter 1990). In some locales this created an ironic situation in which Native Americans became wage laborers on leased farmlands they technically owned (Albers 1982).

Disassociating Native American work from the larger economies in which it was nested served as a rationale to disenfranchise them from their land and sources of livelihood and also distorted their labor contributions in the economic development of the regions in which they lived. The evidence presented herein on San Diego County and Death Valley in California, as well as neighboring regions of the Great Basin, makes clear the early and vital role that Native Americans played in the development of local economies in mining, agriculture, and construction. Descendants of Euro-American colonizers in places such as Utah often stake a claim to the land on the basis of labor they invested in its settlement and development. Actually, however, much of this region's agricultural growth rested on the backs of the local Native American laborers hired by the settlers. Yet many pioneer histories perpetuate the lore that American Indians were not part of the local workplace, either as laborers or small commodity producers. As a result Native Americans are kept conceptually at a distance, denied claims to the lands they participated in developing, and deprived of rights in the very economies they helped build (Forbes 1991).

Some of the same rationalizations that were used to disabuse Native Americans of their land and its resources a century ago continue today. This occurs whenever Native American workers are blamed for failures in tribal development schemes. In the 1970s and 1980s the collapse of numerous projects sponsored by tribes in association with the Economic Development Administration (EDA) was commonly attributed to the "poor" work ethic of Native Americans.[16] Many of these failures, however, were not related to tribal labor force characteristics at all. As argued in a *Wall Street Journal* article (Koon 1978), most of the EDA-supported projects were highly risky business enterprises that, even under the best of circumstances, had less than a 50 percent chance of success. In a pattern reminiscent of the past, however, policymakers and developers on some reservations argued against further developing labor-intensive projects that used local workers in favor of investing tribal resources for other development purposes. This ultimately mystified the source of the problem and supported the interests of outside capital over those of Native labor.[17]

In areas where tribes have rich holdings of natural resources in timber, coal, and/or oil, the development of labor power has often taken a back seat to resource extraction. Since World War II many energy rich tribes have depended on their mineral/timber royalties to fund jobs in a tribal public sector rather than supporting the growth of employment in or outside the extractive industries on their trust land (Weiss 1984). For a time in the 1970s and the early 1980s this strategy was successful in building a base for tribal employment. When resource prices plummeted in the late 1980s, however, many of these tribes were faced with layoffs and a massive restructuring of their public sector employment.[18]

Some tribes lacking natural resource assets built factories in the 1970s and 1980s under joint capitalist ventures, such as those of the Devil's Lake Sioux with the Brunswick Corporation (Henderson 1979; Albers 1982, 1985; Schneider 1986; Reynolds 1990), the Mississippi Choctaws with Ford Motor Company (Peterson 1992), and the Oklahoma Choctaws with Weyerhauser (McKee 1987; Faiman-Silva 1993). Among these tribes, employment levels remained high (Peterson 1992) as long as market demands for tribal industry products continued. When these declined, as recently happened when the Pentagon reduced its spending for military equipment manufactured by the Devil's Lake Sioux, major job cutbacks became inevitable.[19]

The point to be made here is that Native Americans have been employed successfully by tribes in private and public sector work and that much of the problem tribes face in regard to employment relates to the conditions of capital rather than labor (Sorkin 1970, 1973; Burt 1977; Reynolds 1990; Peterson 1992; Faiman-Silva 1993). Notwithstanding this, Native American workers are still denigrated and scapegoated for deficiencies that reside outside the scope of their work habits, skills, and motivation. Ideological readings of Native American labor still exist because misconceptions about their work and its history dominate the public media. They also persist because there is inadequate information on the historic, much less the modern, working experiences of Native Americans to combat and challenge the stereotypes. And they continue because they may perform vital ideological functions for capitalist enterprises under certain circumstances.[20]

If the evidence of this book reveals anything, it should be the unacceptability of perpetuating false dichotomies that represent Native American economic activity as components of some legendary, distanced culture and that as a result divorce them from the economic system at large, especially from various kinds of wage labor that have contributed to the accumulation of capital by Europeans and their descendants in North America. In the future scholars must put more effort into uncovering information on the variable kinds of work Native Americans performed during the growth of capitalism in North America; scholars must also bear witness to Native Americans' diverse and continuing involvement in the workforces of Canada, the United States, and Mexico. Anything less only cloaks the work of Native Americans in a false idealism that misrepresents both the conditions of their labor and its connections to a world system of capitalism.

HISTORIC LAND, CONTEMPORARY LAW

The relationship of Native Americans to the "land" has been a pivotal defining marker of their experience in historic and modern times. It has also had a lot of stereotypic romanticism associated with it. The idea that Native Americans relate to the land primarily through some mystical dreamtime rather than as a lived, working experience is another feature of the distancing rhetoric that divorces them from a wider world of politics and economy. This is not to say that Native peoples do not have important sacred traditions associated with their land and its use. They most certainly do. Rather, the point is that the purpose for which land is put is often lost—namely, providing human labor with the means to transform itself.

Since most federal treaties and policies revolve around the sovereign relationship of Native Americans to the land, much of their own energy, and that of their advisers as well, has focused on various property-related interests, from land and water rights to hunting and fishing claims.[21] The pivotal importance of sovereignty and its relation to the land and law, especially for Native Americans who are members of federally recognized communities (and to those who are seeking this status), has done much to focus and frame the direction of contemporary writing. Whether found in the work of scholars or journalists, a primary point of departure for defining and studying Native Americans has been to understand their connection to the land.

This emphasis on the relationship of Native Americans to their land, its law, and its resources has done much in recent times to deflect scholarly attention from issues of labor. Apart from the effects of legendary thinking, there are other important ways that attention to the land has sidetracked an interest in Native American work, especially as a form of wage labor. Two of these can be singled out for the purposes of discussion.

TRUST RIGHTS, ETHNICITY, AND THE LABOR FORCE

The first problem has to do with demographics and the relation of trust land and law to the definition of who constitutes an "American Indian."[22] Conventionally, at least, most historical, ethnographic, and journalistic writing has been tied to Native Americans whose lands and communities now have (or have had) some kind of acknowledged trust relationship with the federal government or a state (e.g., the Lumbees of North Carolina). Even more specific than this, most discussions about Native Americans focus on those who live on or near their trust lands. The dominance of this kind of focus has had especially important consequences for how Native American workers and their work are reported in particular case studies as well as national statistical figures.

Accounts of the Acomas (i.e., White 1929–30; Minge 1991) in New Mexico, for example, make little mention of their work history with the railways, much less the formation of satellite communities around such employment in distant locales. Much of the published discussion about their labor is limited to employment performed on or near their reservation, as if the sum total of their job experience was bounded by their trust lands. Thinking about the working relations of Native Americans in terms of discrete groups is an extension of the closed-system tribal model and is just as problematic (Quinn 1993). In relation to wage labor, what this thinking essentially does is eliminate from examination the off-reservation places and settings in which this type of work most frequently takes place; in the process analyses of tribal involvement in broader regional and national economies are effectively truncated.

Another example of this thinking are figures the Bureau of Indian Affairs (1977–1987) compiles and publishes on labor force participation. Outside of data from the general census, these are the most complete and continuing set of figures on Native American employment. The BIA figures, however, are confined to Native Americans working on or near federal trust lands, effectively eliminating from consideration and computation thousands of tribal members working away from these areas. These figures also eliminate, of course, the scores of Native Americans who are not enrolled members of federally recognized groups. These Native Americans include the large numbers of Oklahoma Cherokees who migrated to the West Coast from the 1930s to the 1950s and who lost contact with their homeland communities (Anders 1979, 1980, 1981; Thornton 1990). As a consequence, many of the lineal descendants of these Cherokees do not have federal status. Also included are individuals from communities (e.g., Affiliated Utes) that lost federal recognition during the "termination" years of the 1950s but who continue to identify as Native American and carry on their own tribal traditions; countless Native Americans who never had this status because, unlike their cousins and even siblings, their "blood quantum" is not sufficient to meet the enrollment requirements of one or both parents' tribes;[23] and entire populations who never had trust status but nonetheless maintained their identity as Native Americans (Blu 1980). In the final analysis the Bureau of Indian Affairs, which is the primary repository of hard data on Native American wage labor, has colored our understanding of Native American labor force participation around the trust entities it represents.

Finding reliable and representative statistical figures on Native American labor force participation is not easy. In the past many Native Americans failed to get counted by the Census Bureau because of the methods this agency used for eliciting information on race and ethnicity. For a wide range of reasons elaborated on elsewhere (Kleinfield and Kruse 1982; Snipp 1986b; Thornton 1987, 1990), a large segment of the working population with acknowledged Native American ancestry was not counted as such. As a result, much of the census data gathered before 1970 (when changes in the collection of data on ethnicity went into effect) underrepresented not only the actual numbers of the Native Americans in the United States but also the actual size of their labor force participation.

Besides the impact on counts of the numbers of Native American workers, the focus on Native Americans attached to federally recognized trust groups has limited much of our understanding of wage labor to the conditions of this association. Some recent but unpublished research (Breen and Albers 1989) on the labor force participation of Native American women reveals that significant features of their work vary in measurable ways depending on whether they enter off-reservation job markets dominated by the private sector or on-reservation labor forces with public sector employment and "Indian preference" hiring. More generally, this research reveals a need to disaggregate and control the gross statistical data along regional lines and other important indices (e.g., rural versus urban, reservation versus nonreservation).

The absence of detailed and skillfully analyzed employment data comparable over extended periods of time has led to some serious misinterpretations of what has happened with Native American labor in recent times. The uncritical use of census data on Native Americans for comparative purposes (Tienda and Jensen 1986; Amott and Matthaei 1991) gives the mistaken impression that significant progress took place from 1960 to 1980 in earned incomes and in the proportion of the population engaged in wage labor. This is a statistical fluke based on the fact that very different populations made up the Native American category in each of these years. One of the tragedies of this statistical misprison is that when fine case studies such as the ones appearing in this book get published, there is not a wider screen of good statistical data against which to compare and interpret the more localized situations. Indeed, there is not even a solid foundation for making comparative generalizations about the positions of Native American workers in local, regional, and national labor markets at different points in history.

LANDOWNERSHIP, CAPITAL, RESOURCES, AND EMPLOYMENT

The second problem with restricting an understanding of wage labor to Native Americans living on or near federal trust lands is that it creates the mistaken impression that most are landholders. The fact of the matter is that even when Native Americans hold membership in a federally recognized group, most of them are landless and have been so for many generations. The cases of some Ottawas/Ojibwes in Michigan, Kumeyaays in California, and Paiutes in southern Utah exemplify the hundreds and thousands of Native Americans who have long been landless as individuals, communities, or both. And like populations elsewhere in the world, Native Americans have had to seek some form of wage labor to sustain themselves in the absence of their access to a productive land base.

There is no question that a direct correlation has existed over time between losses in land and increases in the numbers of Native Americans entering wage labor. But even though many studies have reported on these declines, their relationship to the widespread poverty in "Indian country," and a resultant need for employment, such studies rarely offer concrete information on how Native Americans have come to work for wages in the face of dwindling land assets. By contrast, several of the case studies in this book offer precise descriptions of the relationships between land losses and wage labor entry. And chapters 3 and 8 spell out in great detail how the differential loss of land among neighboring Native populations affected the contrasting character of their labor force participation.

Landholding is certainly a critical variable in defining patterns of labor force entry in Native American history. Explanations that rest on this variable alone, however, reach a point of diminishing returns very soon. Beyond a Native population's relation to the land, a host of other factors relating to the character of local/regional industries and the composition of their associated labor forces must be addressed. In this regard many of the indices that economists and sociologists customarily use to assess jobs and employment are barely evident in the literature on Native Americans. What this may reflect are the limits of the historian's and anthropologist's disciplinary expertise—the two groups of scholars most involved in Native American studies. Yet these limits can be problematic, especially if they unwittingly reproduce frameworks that segregate Native American labor from the rest of the economy and portray it in isolating terms.

From the 1960s through the 1980s, when a great deal of scholarly energy was devoted to researching Native American economies in the light of various modernization and development theories, very little effort was made to highlight employment conditions in the various trust communities anthropologists studied. And although many of the recent dependency theories helped combat earlier ideas that Native Americans stood of outside the path of global political and economic development, the focus of attention, as Knack and Littlefield argue in chapter 1, remained on the land and the appropriation of resources within a world system of "unequal exchange." Generally speaking, this research did not address, at least in any detail, how the appropriation of such diverse resources as oil, timber, coal, and uranium affected trust communities at the point of labor. With few exceptions (Lamphere 1976; Clemmer 1977; Weiss 1984; Faiman-Silva 1993), little was written on the extent to which trust community landholdings and resources influenced the labor force participation of their members or the size, composition, and structure of their own internal labor markets. Indeed, some scholars (Jacobson 1984; Snipp 1986a) have even gone so far as to maintain that U.S. capitalism benefits from Native American land rather than Native American labor.

Focusing only on land, and thereby leaving labor in the background or out of the picture entirely, is yet another way to separate Native Americans from their political economic roots. The continuing focus on land and resources in the development of Native Americans' identity and political consciousness (Olson and Wilson 1984; Jaimes 1992) is understandable, given their legal status within modern nation-states, but it does have serious policy ramifications. In the United States, many tribes have felt tremendous pressure to become involved in natural resource extraction—often in contradiction to their own cultural and environmental interests. In the face of unsubstantiated plans for generating employment, they have ventured into a wide variety of development efforts, only to find that the jobs produced are few and that most require skills their members do not possess. The track record for using trust estates to generate employment has been dismal (Weiss 1984). Part of the problem has been that tribes do not carry enough legal-political muscle to ensure that corporate developers honor agreements to hire and train local labor.

From the late 1940s to the mid-1960s members of the Hoopa Tribal Valley Business Committee raised many questions about the unfair labor practices of companies that milled timber from their vast forest estate. They questioned the failure of local companies to hire Native American labor, but they also challenged the lower rates Native Americans did receive compared to that of the European Americans who worked alongside them. Notwithstanding the fact that all timber contracts and mill leases contained Indian preference hiring clauses, the lumber companies did not uphold their contractual agreements. In responding to complaints, lumber company executives argued their discriminatory practices were justified because local Native American labor did not have adequate work skills, attitudes, and ethics. In the end, discrimination and consequent ethnic divisions in the workforce continued because the federal agencies responsible for negotiating and upholding the contractual agreements between the Hoopa Valley Tribe and various timber corporations failed to enforce the labor provisions in the contracts (Hoopa Tribal History Documents 1945–1962).

Beyond the fact that tribes do not have the legal-political clout to assert the interests of their own laborers, and in fact may act in ways that contradict these interests,[24] they may have little formal knowledge of the social relations of production within their own communities. Even though American Indian tribes throughout the United States are major employers of Native Americans across a wide variety of occupations, hardly any research has been done on the ways in which labor is arranged in these trust settings. The kinds of useful information that Sennett offers on the Timbisha and Prins presents on Mi'kmaq labor relations with employers, coworkers, and within community members are precisely what are needed for understanding wage labor in contemporary settings. More data are needed on how Native Americans organize and divide labor forces within their own communities in relation to such matters as management versus labor, skilled versus unskilled work, unionized versus nonunionized workers, and public versus private sector employment (Basset 1994). Also needed is information on the extent to which labor force characteristics vary when markets are controlled by Indian versus non-Indian enterprises.[25] As American Indian tribes expand their employment bases beyond the public sector to industrial and recreational development, especially gambling, there will be an increasing need to understand the dynamics of their internal labor arrangements as these compare with those in outside markets.

Regardless of whether attention is given to wage labor in the context of tribal trust entities, one thing is clear: scholars need to think about and apply the concept of "class" in their studies of Native American labor (Albers 1982, 1985; Weiss 1984). By and large the modern emergence of class formations within Native American communities has been ignored. Consequently, the impact of these formations on the course of economic development, especially on the ways labor markets are structured, is virtually unknown. And even though inequalities are widening in many Native American communities as a result of differential access to jobs and other resources, there is a massive refusal to acknowlede this transition and explain its origins. As with American culture more generally, where class differences are dismissed in a political rhetoric of equality and democracy, Native American communities have their own homegrown political ideologies for masking differences in access to resources and associated labor power (Lake 1991). These, as much as the ideologies of the dominant society, need to be understood in terms of the way they privilege the interests of an elite capital-controlling (or owning) class over proletarianized and unemployed sectors of the population (Sacks 1989).

CONCLUSION

The chapters in this book go a long way in forcing us to reconsider the place of wage labor in the culture and history of Native Americans. Not only do these chapters inspire more interest in the variety of ways Native Americans have been involved in wage labor; they also motivate us to find out more about where this work has been situated, how it has been structured, and what it has meant in various kinds of historic and modern economies. Furthermore, the chapters encourage us to reconsider how the increasingly capitalized economies of North America relied on the paid and unpaid labor contributions of Native peoples. Finally, they challenge us to recalibrate our interpretive paradigms to take this work into account.

Once wage labor is understood as a more pivotal and defining feature of the Native American experience, scholars will no longer be able to complacently dismiss this kind of work in their cultural and historical representations. Every time scholars divorce their understandings of Native American work from its wider political and economic moorings, they artificially separate and distance this experience and thereby deny its coevalness in the modern world. In the end they aid and abet the various mythical ploys that deny Native Americans a right to their lands and labor. It may be presumptuous to suggest that a shift in public attitude might bring about a change in the structural relationship of Native Americans to their resources and work in the U.S. economy, but at the very least such a transition would make it more difficult to mask the conditions of their work behind the mystifying language of a cultural other.

NOTES

CHAPTER 1. NATIVE AMERICAN LABOR:
RETRIEVING HISTORY, RETHINKING THEORY

1. Long after the fur trade had faded from importance, the non-Indian dynasties it founded continued to play a dynamic role in U.S. economic and political life. Many members of Detroit's contemporary corporate elite, for example, are related by descent or marriage to the important fur trading families and land grant holders of the French era, such as the Morans, Campeaus, and Godfroys (Ewen 1978, 46–77).

2. An interesting example of such work is the extensive use of BIA-trained crews to combat forest fires throughout the western United States. For example, over five hundred men and women from the Fort Peck Reservation were dispatched on twenty-seven occasions in fire-related activity in 1991, earning over $650,000 (News from Indian Country 1992).

3. Perhaps detailed study of the impact of earlier legislation, such as the Chinese Exclusion Act (1882), might show a chronological correlation with Indian entry into labor markets in the West, such as in the often mentioned railroad maintenance work.

CHAPTER 2. TRIBAL NETWORK AND MIGRANT LABOR:
MI'KMAQ INDIANS AS SEASONAL WORKERS IN
AROOSTOOK'S POTATO FIELDS, 1870–1980

1. Historically, the Mi'kmaq have been known by different names. They referred to themselves as L'nu'k (or Ulnoo), meaning "humans." In the early colonial period Europeans used different ethnonyms, including Souriquois, Gaspesiens,

274

Acadian Indians, and Cape Sable Indians. Since the late 1600s the present name began to appear in the records as Micmac, Mikemak, Miquemaque, Mukmack, Muqumawaach, Mic Mac, and Miqmaq. During the past two decades Mi'kmaq has become the preferred indigenous orthography (cf. Dickason 1992, 16), a usage I have also adopted in my forthcoming case study (Prins 1996). Other spellings are used only when referring to an established name, such as the Aroostook Band of Micmacs, or when the name appears within quotation marks.

2. Although wage labor among North American Indians did not become common until the late 1800s, the practice dates to the early colonial period. For instance, English settlers in Massachusetts employed Nipmucks and other tribespeople, among others, as farmworkers beginning in the mid-1600s. Also, the Narragansett Indians of Rhode Island hired themselves out as stone masons, servants, and laborers beginning in the 1700s (see also Gookin 1806, 162; Simmons 1978, 195).

3. The concept of commodification is based on Polanyi (1944, 73), who observes that labor (like land and money) is a "fictive commodity" (see Mingione 1991, 22, 103). In my discussion of the commodification process in Mi'kmaq culture, I rely on Italian sociologist Mingioni (1991, 96–97, 112), who notes that the persistence of various forms of self-provisioning, organized and regulated within reciprocal networks such as kinship, friendship, or local communities or regional and ethnic groupings, poses "limits to the full commodification of social life."

4. The off-reservation Mi'kmaqs and Maliseets in northern Maine organized themselves on a regional basis, forming the Association of Aroostook Indians (AAI) in 1969. In 1980 a group of Maliseets within the AAI gained federal recognition as the Houlton Band of Maliseet. In 1991 the Aroostook Band of Micmacs became federally recognized as a U.S. tribe and received funding to purchase a 5,000-acre tract to serve this 580-member community in northern Maine as a land base (Prins 1994). I served these Mi'kmaqs, who now maintain headquarters in Presque Isle, Maine, as staff anthropologist from 1981 to 1991, conducting in-depth ethnohistorical research on their behalf. For a description of their native rights quest, see, among others, Heald (1987), McBride (1987), and Prins (1988, 1990, 1996).

5. A seasonal worker is commonly defined as someone who works at a job that does not offer continuing, year-round employment, usually involving farmwork, and works 25 to 149 days per year (Goldfarb 1981, 16; Holt 1984, 20).

6. Although it is impossible to accurately estimate the number of seasonal farmworkers, including migrant laborers, a 1974 U.S. Department of Agriculture survey concluded that their number was about 927,000 (Goldfarb 1981, 16). On the East Coast the main stream of migratory farmworker movement runs northward in the spring and returns south in the fall and may have involved some 58,000 workers in 1949, most of whom were blacks with a home base in Florida and other southern states. Leaving for the summer to work in the northern states, these black migrant workers were joined by laborers from Puerto Rico, Jamaica, and the Bahamas. In addition, thousands of American Indians and French Canadians could be found in the East Coast migratory stream (Thomas-Lycklema à Nijeholt 1980, 33–36; see also Friedland and Nelkin 1971).

7. This ruling had the effect of excluding Mi'kmaqs and other "Canadian Indians" from the protections accorded "bonded" Canadians but denied domestic farm labor in the United States. A year later the U.S. Congress confirmed the validity of the 1794 Jay Treaty guaranteeing these Indians free border-crossing rights into the United States. This agreement, although challenged repeatedly since that time, continues to be upheld (Buesing 1972, 22–23; Johnston and Metzger 1974, 3–4).

CHAPTER 3. WAGE LABOR IN
TWO MICHIGAN OTTAWA COMMUNITIES

1. The Little Traverse Bay Bands Tribal Council has chosen to spell its tribal name *Odawa* rather than the more common *Ottawa*. The Little River Tribe spells its name *Ottawa*. To respect the wishes of both tribes, this chapter uses the common spelling *Ottawa* when making historical and cultural generalizations. When discussing the individual tribes, however, the chapter spells the names as the tribe members themselves would spell them.

CHAPTER 4. INDIAN EDUCATION AND THE
WORLD OF WORK IN MICHIGAN, 1893-1933

The research for this chapter was supported in part by a summer research fellowship granted by Central Michigan University, 1990, and by a Michigan Humanities Council grant to the Saginaw Chippewa Tribe, 1991.

1. The Isabella Reservation was created under the Treaty of 1855 between the United States and the Saginaw, Swan Creek, and Black River bands of Chippewa. Under the treaty's provisions the three bands agreed to cede reservations in southeastern Michigan and remove to Isabella County, where

land equal to six townships was set aside for them. The treaty also stipulated that the members of the bands would select allotments from these lands within five years and that their tribal status would thereafter end. From the point of view of members of the three bands, this arrangement was accepted as preferable to removal to areas west of the Mississippi. Of the original six townships, only a handful of allotments remain under Indian ownership today. Descendants of the bands reorganized as the Saginaw Chippewa Tribe in 1937.

2. The thirty-five former students interviewed comprised twenty women and fifteen men. All were born between 1902 and 1923, with 1916 the median year of birth for both men and women. The interviews were conducted between 1984 and 1991 in several locations in Michigan, including Allegan, Bay Mills, Benton Harbor, Charlevoix, Dowagiac, Grand Rapids, Harbor Springs, Lansing, Mecosta, Mt. Pleasant, Peshawbestown, Pestoskey, and Sault Ste. Marie.

I employed several strategies for locating former students. I began with a mailing list compiled by those who organized and attended periodic reunions of former students during the 1970s and early 1980s. Because reunion attendees may view their school experiences more positively than those not attending, I also solicited names of former students from staff of three of the federally recognized tribes and sought out places where former students were likely to congregate, such as senior citizen lunch programs in historically Indian communities. I secured many names through the snowball technique: asking those I interviewed for names of other former students.

I made an effort to enhance the representativeness of the sample by scattering the interviews geographically and trying to balance the numbers of men and women interviewed. My respondents, although representing a wide range of economic circumstances, may have been somewhat more "successful" on the average than former students in general. One index of this is their relatively high rate, for indigenous people of their generation, of high school completion: thirteen of the thirty-five. In one crucial respect, however, my sample is very skewed: all of the people I interviewed had survived at least fifty years after the Mt. Pleasant School closed in 1933. We can only speculate about the differences between the experiences and attitudes of this group of survivors and those of their school mates whose lives were shorter.

3. The lack of congruence between training and employment may be a more general phenomenon for Native Americans. Similar results are reported for Great Basin Paiutes by Knack (1978).

CHAPTER 5. THE SIGNIFICANCE OF
CHEYENNE WORK IN THE HISTORY OF U.S. CAPITALISM

An earlier version of this chapter was published in Russian in 1987 as "The Cheyenne Indians Within the American System of Hired Labor," *Soviet Ethnography* 5 (September–October): 111–118.

CHAPTER 6. NINETEENTH-CENTURY
GREAT BASIN INDIAN WAGE LABOR

1. It was precisely in the Mason Valley that the famed Ghost Dance prophet Wovoka grew up as such a laborer on the Wilson ranch, possibly acquiring there the much-debated Christian elements of his eclectic religious movement.

2. This is the first explicit mention I have seen in the Walker River documents of women working. We know, however, that women identified generally as Northern Paiutes worked in fields and used traditional burden baskets from a much earlier date, and there are even extant photographs of them doing so (e.g., Davis 1905). We know they did washing and housecleaning in towns from at least the 1880s and probably earlier (Mathews 1880, 286–291; "Jerseyman" 1886), as well as soliciting charity from railway travelers (Union Pacific Railroad 1890).

CHAPTER 7. WATERING THE FLOWER:
LAGUNA PUEBLO AND THE SANTA FE RAILROAD, 1880–1943

1. Spicer (1962, 176) comments about the impact the railroad's arrival had on pueblo employment patterns in the Southwest: "With occasional loss of crops due to floods, the necessity arose, especially after the 1880's, for finding additional means of support from time to time. Work on the railroad which was built through the Pueblo country in the 1880's became available and as the Anglo cities increased in population various kinds of jobs became available in Albuquerque, Santa Fe, Bernalillo, and the many new towns. In addition, the population of every village was slowly but steadily increasing, and there was less and less possibility of new families taking up the new land, as a result of the Mexican and Anglo population expansion through the whole Pueblo area. Outside employment was more and more relied on as a way of making at least a portion of one's living. New skills were acquired and a closer acquaintance with Anglo-American culture steadily developed."

2. For an example, see letters requesting copies of a documented contract, written by the Sacramento Agency, Bureau of Indian Affairs, on behalf of Acoma residents at the Richmond Village (Pacific-Sierra Region, Sacramento Area Office,

Coded Central Files, 1910–1958, RG 75/BIA, National Archives Branch Depositig at San Bruno, Calif., box 7, folder 039 Acoma Pueblo).

3. According to my interviews with Laguna descendants of the men in this "first group," the laborers numbered about one hundred. This and additional information were obtained through personal interviews conducted between September 1992 and May 1993 with Lagunas now residing at Richmond and San Pablo, California, and Laguna Pueblo, New Mexico (hereinafter referred to as personal interviews).

4. Data provided by the Laguna Tribal Office, Laguna, New Mexico, 23 June 1993.

5. See also the minutes of the shareholders' meeting, attached to correspondence of Charles King Holliday dated 15 September 1927, memorializing the railroad's origins (Santa Fe Collection, Kansas Historical Society, Kansas State Museum, Topeka).

6. In addition, the grant of 1863 to the Atchison, Topeka and Santa Fe was for about three million total acres along the Old Santa Fe Trail, making a land strip up to twenty miles in width along the route. An exemption was made for acreage already established as national forests, acreage claimed under prior occupancy, Indian reservations, and acreage under mining and other classifications.

7. Various railroad expeditionary surveys were conducted in 1853, and subsequent years, to determine the most economically advantageous southern route through New Mexico, linking California to Colorado and Kansas. For examples of the considerations that eventually weighted a decision in favor of the so-called thirty-fifth parallel route, see reconnaissance and survey reports submitted by H. R. Holbrook and Lewis Kingman to the executives of the Atchison, Topeka and Santa Fe (Santa Fe Collection, Kansas Historical Society, Kansas State Museum, Topeka).

8. A basic outline of the events that led to the Laguna–Santa Fe relationship has been repeated in numerous interviews with the Laguna people. Presentation in this text of the original encounter represents a compilation of the most commonly repeated testimony. The occurrence during 1880 has become incorporated inextricably in the fabric of Laguna life. For one example of the railroad's impact on accounts of other Laguna experiences, see Horr (1974, 25).

9. The Atlantic and Pacific Railroad Company signed an agreement, August 19, 1885, with the "Pueblo of Laguna, a society and community owning its lands in common, by and through its proper officers, authorized and empowered so to do by immemorial usage and custom" for the purchase of Laguna water. The

agreement was made for the purchase price of $1 and was signed by the Atlantic and Pacific president and secretary. Laguna Pueblo was represented by its governor, two lieutenant governors, three officers called "fiscals," and three war leaders. The U S. agent for the Territory of New Mexico, County of Valencia, approved the transaction. There is no mention of Laguna employment in the agreement document. See document titled "Deed. Aug 19, 1885 The Pueblo of Laguna To The Atlantic and Pacific Railroad Company" (Santa Fe Collection, Kansas Historical Society, Kansas State Museum, Topeka).

10. The narrator is referring to the inability of the Atlantic and Pacific to meet the requirements imposed by the congressional act of 1866 for retaining its land grant.

11. See archived copies of *Santa Fe Magazine*, as well as extensive photographic documentation, regarding the Reading Room system (Santa Fe Collection, Kansas State Museum, Kansas Historical Society, Topeka).

12. One Laguna interviewed recalls the year as being 1943. However, given the arrival of large numbers of workers at Richmond just prior to World War II, the vote to organize may have been made during the period between President Harry Truman's seizure of the railroads in 1946 and the work rule disputes of 1950 (see Bryant 1974, 324).

13. The word *ritual* was specifically employed by an officer of the Santa Fe Public Relations Department, during an interview in April 1993, in describing the character of the meetings held in Los Angeles to "water the flower."

14. Copies of Santa Fe documents, loaned by former employees, bear the designation of "colony" as applied to the Richmond village.

CHAPTER 8. INDIAN LABOR IN
SAN DIEGO COUNTY, CALIFORNIA, 1850–1900

1. In southern California the term *emigrant* has always been used by contemporaries of the migrations circa 1840–1870, as well as by historians, to designate those coming from other parts of the United States, whereas *immigrant* is applied to those coming from other countries.

CHAPTER 10. FROM LEGEND TO LAND TO LABOR:
CHANGING PERSPECTIVES ON NATIVE AMERICAN WORK

1. Much more exists on the wage labor of American Indian populations in Mexico than in the United States. This contrast in treatment is consistent with popular stereotypes regarding the differential working status of Native

peoples north and south of the U.S.-Mexico border. Except for Knight's pioneering study (1978) of British Columbia, the literature on Native wage labor in Canada is also weak.

2. Knack and Littlefield describe the lack of attention to wage labor in the literature on Native Americans. There is also a striking absence of information on Native American wage labor in general treatments of historic and modern U.S. labor markets (Rubery 1978; Sowell 1981; Wilkinson 1981; Gordon, Edwards, and Reich 1982; Wertheimer, Levine et al. 1989). And even where attention (Amott and Matthaei 1991) is given to their wage labor, it is often couched in discussions that culturally isolate the working experiences of Native Americans from other ethnic groups.

3. This is part of a wider trend discussed in writings on women and the economy (Sokoloff 1980; Amott and Matthaei 1991; Romero 1992). It is also evident in the historic silencing of minority contributions to U.S. economic history (Bonacich 1972; Barrera 1979; Takaki 1979; Glenn 1981; Cheng and Bonacich 1984; Hogan 1984).

4. This separation is evident in any number of popular books (Lafarge 1956; Billard 1974; Maxwell 1978) published on American Indians over the past several decades. It is also obvious in much of the contemporary arts and crafts literature, especially as represented over the past two decades in the quarterly magazine *American Indian Art*.

5. Bates (1982a, 1982b) discusses the impact of this kind of stereotyping on the Miwok in California, and Deloria (1969, 1970) writes about it in more general terms.

6. In the 1960s ethnic craftwork and participation in summer exhibitions, such as Banff Indian Days and the Calgary Stampede, were the primary sources of income for some individuals from the Blood, Piegan, Blackfoot, Cree, Sarcee, and Assiniboin bands in central Alberta. In fact, it was only during the occasion of the Calgary Stampede that Native Americans were hired locally as clerks in retail stores. Their employment in this context was part of an acknowledged effort to lend "authenticity" to the sale of "Indian handicrafts" (Albers and Medicine 1968, n.d.).

7. Willis's classic study (1981) of English working-class youths offers an intriguing model for understanding the relationships among ideology, working consciousness, and class formation.

8. These were work characteristics described in a plan entitled "Provisional Overall Economic Development Plan: Fort Totten Redevelopment Area," issued

by the Fort Totten Redevelopment Commission in the late 1960s. Other examples of this kind of thinking abound in mainstream discourse.

9. There is a large and growing literature on ethnicity, work, and labor force participation that includes writings on African Americans (Boggs 1970; Baron 1972; Lewis 1977; Reich 1981; Albelda 1985; Sacks 1988; Sokoloff 1991); Asian-Americans (Saxton 1971; Cheng and Bonacich 1984; Takaki 1979; Ictioka 1980; Glenn 1981, 1985; Yamashita and Park 1985; Woo 1985; Brown and Philips 1991); and Hispanic Americans (Barrera 1979; Garcia 1981; Deutsch 1985; Ruiz 1987; Zavella 1987, 1991; Romero 1992), along with more general discussions of the subject (Bonacich 1972; Rubery 1978; Sowell 1981; Wilkinson 1981; Gordon, Edwards, and Reich 1982; Brittan and Maynard 1984; Amott and Matthaei 1991; Kiefer and Philips 1991).

10. There is a well-developed literature on the production and marketing of furs and hides in North America (see Peterson and Anfinson's 1984 review article). The attention given by anthropologists, historians, and geographers to Native American participation in this over other types of work is not surprising since it conforms much more readily to the separatist paradigms that dominate the interpretation of tribal cultures and their histories.

11. The maintenance of formally structured relationships between home villages and immigrating ones has been reported for the western Pueblos (Connelly 1979) and the Iroquois (Konrad 1987) in historic times.

12. A good example of this is a study (Trosper 1978) on Native American ranching. Using a neoclassical (or formalist) methodology, this study demonstrates that Native American ranchers were just as efficient (and in certain instances more so) in their labor skills than neighboring Euro-Americans. Trosper concludes that it was inadequate access to sufficient capital and land that spelled failure for most Native Americans in ranching.

13. Indeed, some of the best descriptions of Native American wage labor are found in autobiographical writings (Lurie 1961; Radin 1963; Spradley 1969).

14. A quick survey of *American Indian Art* issues published over the past two decades reveals two things. First, almost nothing is mentioned about the economic conditions under which Native American artists or craftworkers produce and/or sell their objects. Second, the lack of attention to the economic underpinnings of artistic production is accompanied by lengthy reports on auction sales and glossy advertising copy hawking Native wares through chic galleries.

15. A good example of this is an article on Navajo basket weavers from Utah's San Juan County, recently published in the "Religion" section of the *Salt Lake Tribune* (Miller 1994).

16. From my own experience this is a common explanation among some Native Americans and their Euro-American neighbors for the failure of tribal motel complexes at places such as the Uintah-Ouray Reservation in Utah.

17. In the aftermath of EDA-supported business closures this has certainly been the case on the Uintah-Ouray Reservation (Wright 1983, personal communication).

18. This has clearly been the case for the Hoopa Tribe of northern California and also the Uintah-Ouray Tribe in Utah (based on a reading of various archival documents and oral histories located at American West Center, University of Utah, Salt Lake City). Large sectors of public employment on these reservations were also affected by a huge withdrawal of federal funding under the Reagan administration.

19. Personal communications (1991–1993) with former employees of the Devil's Lake Sioux Manufacturing Corporation.

20. See discussion later in this chapter on the Hoopa Valley Tribe of northern California.

21. It can be argued that the increasing importance of land issues was related to research and litigation associated with the work of the Indians Claims Commission. This, coupled with the rising value of various natural resources, has done much to focus the interest of Native Americans, and those who chronicle their experiences, on the land (Satz 1991; Satz, Gulig, and St. Germaine 1991).

22. Currently the labels *American Indian* versus *Native American* have become highly politicized. In the 1980s the National Congress of American Indians voted to sanction the use of American Indian to refer to Native Americans who are members of federally recognized tribes. Recently the issue of who has the right to claim an American Indian identity has been debated at some length in the pages of the national newspaper *Indian Country Today*. On one side are those who argue that federal trust status definitions are too exclusionary, rejecting many people with legitimate claims to an American Indian ancestry. On the other side are those who favor restrictive definitions as a way to eliminate the "fakes," people with fraudulent ancestral claims, and by extension, to protect a rapidly dwindling pie of federal funding sources.

23. It is becoming more common to find Native Americans who have spent all their lives in trust communities among family and friends but who lack enrollment status because they do not have the "one quarter," "one third," or "one half" blood quantum and/or a tribal patriline (e.g., Santa Clara Pueblo, which enrolls only through the father's line).

24. In the early 1980s the Tribal Council of the Devil's Lake Sioux Tribe actively campaigned against efforts to unionize the workforce in its manufacturing plants. In a situation in which the division between labor and capital is blurred because the workers are also owners (as enrolled members of the tribe), it is difficult to organize and amass support for labor in opposition to corporate interests. Faiman-Silva (1993) also makes a similar point with respect to the development of manufacturing enterprises among the Oklahoma Choctaws.

25. Even though a few works (i.e., Spradley 1969; Gilbreath 1973) give evidence of Native American entrepreneurship and even describe relations between Native American employers and their hired workers, most of the information has been narrative and descriptive.

REFERENCES

Abbott, John S. C.

1875   *The History of Maine, from the Earliest Discovery of the Region by the Northmen Until the Present Time.* Boston: B. B. Russell.

Aberle, David F.

1983   Navajo Economic Development. In *Handbook of North American Indians.* Vol. 10, *Southwest,* ed. Alfonso Ortiz, 641–658. Washington, D.C.: Smithsonian Institution Press.

Abler, Thomas S., and Elizabeth Tooker

1978   Seneca. In *Handbook of North American Indians.* Vol. 15, *The Northeast,* ed. Bruce G. Trigger, 505–517. Washington, D.C.: Smithsonian Institution Press.

Ablon, Joan

1964   Relocated American Indians in the San Francisco Bay Area. *Human Organization* 24: 296–304.

Adams, William

1852   Letter to Bro[ther] Richards, 9 November. *Deseret News,* 11 December.

Adams, William Y.

1963   *Shonto: A Study of the Role of the Trader in a Modern Navajo Community.* Bureau of American Ethnology Bulletin 188. Washington, D.C.: GPO.

1971   The Development of San Carlos Apache Wage Labor to 1954. In *Apachean Culture History and Ethnology,* ed. Keith H. Basso and Morris E. Opler, 116–128. University of Arizona Anthropological Papers, no. 21. Tucson: University of Arizona Press.

285

Adler, Mortimer J., and William Gorman, eds.
1980   *The Great Ideas: A Synopticon of Great Books of the Western World.*
         Vol. 1. Chicago: Encyclopedia Britannica.
Albelda, Randy
1985   "Nice Work If You Can Get It": Segmentation of White and Black
         Women Workers in the Post-War Period. *Review of Radical Political
         Economics* 17, no. 3: 7285.
Albers, Patricia C.
1982   Sioux Kinship in a Colonial Setting. *Dialectical Anthropology* 6: 253–269.
1985   Autonomy and Dependency in the Lives of Dakota Women: A Study
         in Historical Change. *Review of Radical Political Economics* 17, no.
         3: 109–134.
1991   Discussion. Symposium on Native Americans and Wage Labor,
         American Society for Ethnohistory, Tulsa, Okla., November.
Albers, Patricia, and William R. James
1983   Tourism and the Changing Image of the Great Lakes Indian. *Annals
         of Tourism Research* 10: 128–148.
1984   Utah's Indians and Popular Photography in the American West. *Utah
         Historical Quarterly* 52, no.1: 72–91.
1985   Images and Reality: Postcards of Minnesota's Ojibway People,
         1900–1980. *Minnesota History* 49: 229–240.
1987   Wisconsin Indians on the Picture Postcard: A History in
         Photographic Stereotyping. *Lore* 37: 3–19.
1988   Travel Photography: A Methodological Approach. *Annals of Tourism
         Research* 15: 134–158.
Albers, Patricia, and Jeanne Kay
n.d.   Gender and Systems of Property Ownership Among Indians of the
         Upper Middle West. Unpub. ms. in authors' possession.
Albers, Patricia, and Beatrice Medicine
1968   Patterns and Peripheries of Plains Indian Powwows. Paper presented
         at the Central States Anthropology Association, Milwaukee, Wis.,
         April.
n.d.   Exhibitions, Powwows, and Celebrations: Contemporary Cere-
         monialism in the Northern Plains. Unpub. ms. in authors' possession.
American Indian Policy Review Commission
1976   *Report on Reservation and Resource Development and Protection.*
         Washington, D.C.: GPO.

Ames, Michael
1992   *Cannibal Tours and Glass Boxes*. Vancouver: University of British Columbia Press.

Amott, Teresa, and Julie Matthaei
1991   *Race, Gender, and Work: A Multicultural Economic History of Women in the United States*. Boston: South End Press.

Anders, Gary
1979   The Internal Colonization of Cherokee Native Americans. *Development and Change* 10: 41–55.

1980   Theories of Underdevelopment and the American Indian. *Journal of Economic Issues* 40: 681–701.

1981   The Reduction of Self-Sufficient People to Poverty and Welfare Dependence: An Analysis of the Causes of Cherokee Indian Underdevelopment. *American Journal of Economics and Sociology* 40: 225–237.

Angel, Myron
1881   *History of Nevada*. Oakland, Calif.: Thompson and West.

Antoine, George
1915   Letter to Sir, 10 September. Bureau of Indian Affairs, Central Classified Files, 1907–1939. RG 75. National Archives. File CCF-MACK 99440-1915, 115.

Armitage, Merle
1948   *Operation Santa Fe: Atchison, Topeka and Santa Fe Railway System*. New York: Duell, Sloan, and Pearce.

Armstrong, Louise V.
1938   *We Too Are the People*. Boston: Little, Brown.

Arrington, Leonard J.
1966   *Great Basin Kingdom: Economic History of the Latter-day Saints, 1830–1900*. Lincoln: University of Nebraska Press.

Asbury, C. H.
1907   Letter to Commissioner of Indian Affairs, 28 May. Bureau of Indian Affairs, Irrigation Division, Correspondence of the Chief Engineer. National Archives. RG 75.

Ashworth, William B.
n.d.   Life of William B. Ashworth, by Himself. Utah Historical Society, Salt Lake City.

Bailey, Daniel
1994   Statement of Daniel Bailey, Chairman, Little River Band of Ottawa Indians. Hearing Before the Committee on Indian Affairs, U.S.

Senate, on S. 1066 to Restore Federal Services to the Pokagon Band of Potawatomi Indians and S. 1357 to Reaffirm and Clarify the Federal Relationships of the Little Traverse Bay Bands of Odawa Indians as Distinct Federally Recognized Indian Tribes. 10 February, 103d Cong. 2d sess., 41–42. Washington, D.C.: GPO.

Bailey, Garrick, and Robert Glenn Bailey

1986   A History of the Navajos: The Reservation Years. Seattle: University of Washington Press.

Bailey, Lynn R.

1966   Indian Slave Trade in the Southwest. Los Angeles: Westernlore Press.

Bailey, Mary

1975   Interview, 20 August. Unpub. transcript. Grand Rapids (Mich.) Public Library, Michigan Room Collections.

Bailey, Robert

1975   Interview, 22 August. Unpub. transcript. Grand Rapids (Mich.) Public Library, Michigan Room Collections.

Baker, William, and Stephen Graham

1981   Business. In Harbor Springs: A Collection of Historical Essays, ed. Jan Morley, 17–26. Harbor Springs, Mich.: Harbor Springs Historical Commission.

Baron, Harold

1972   Racial Domination in Advanced Capitalism: A Theory of Nationalism and Divisions in the Labor Market. In Labor Market Segmentation, ed. Richard Edwards, Michael Reich, and David M. Gordon, 173–216. Lexington, Mass.: D. C. Heath.

Barrera, Mario

1979   Race and Class in the Southwest: A Theory of Racial Inequality. Notre Dame, Ind.: University of Notre Dame Press.

Barsh, Russel Lawrence

1988   Contemporary Marxist Theory and Native American Reality, American Indian Quarterly 12, no. 3: 187–211.

Basset, Everett

1994   Gender, Social Organization, and Wage Labor Among the Apache. In Those of Little Note: Gender, Race, and Class in Historical Archaeology, ed. Elizabeth Scott, 55–80. Tucson: University of Arizona Press.

Bateman, C. A.

1871   Letter to E. S. Parker, 8 May. Bureau of Indian Affairs, Letters Received, 1824–1881. National Archives. RG 75.

Bates, Craig

1982a   Dressing the Part: A Brief Look at the Development of Stereotypical
          Indian Clothing Among Native Peoples in the Far West. *Journal of
          California and Great Basin Anthropology* 4, no. 1: 55–66.

1982b   Ethnographic Collections at Yosemite National Park. *American Indian
          Art* 7, no. 3: 28–35.

Battice, Isaac

1975   Interview, 16 October. Unpub. transcript. Grand Rapids (Mich.)
          Public Library, Michigan Room Collections.

Battiste, Marie

1977   Cultural Transmission and Cultural Survival in Contemporary
          Micmac Society. *The Indian Historian* 10 (fall): 2–13.

Baudrillard, Jean

1975   *The Mirror of Production.* St. Louis: Telos Press.

1981   *For a Critique of the Political Economy of the Sign.* St. Louis: Telos Press.

Bean, George Washington

n.d.   Diary. Typescript copy. Utah Historical Society, Salt Lake City, ms.
          no. A-68.

Bee, Robert L.

1981   *Crosscurrents Along the Colorado: The Impact of Government Policy on
          the Quechan Indians.* Tucson: University of Arizona Press.

Berkhofer, Robert Jr.

1978   *The Whiteman's Indian.* New York: Random House.

Bernstein, Alison R.

1991   *American Indians and World War II: Toward a New Era in Indian Affairs.*
          Norman: University of Oklahoma Press.

Berthrong, Donald J.

1976   *The Cheyenne and Arapaho Ordeal.* Norman: University of Oklahoma
          Press.

1985   Legacies of the Dawes Act: Bureaucrats and Land Thieves at the
          Cheyenne-Arapaho Agencies of Oklahoma. In *The Plains Indians
          of the Twentieth Century,* ed. Peter Iverson, 31–53. Norman: University
          of Oklahoma Press.

Bevington, Tamar Elizabeth Marshall

1925   As I Remember. Typescript. San Diego (Calif.) Public Library,
          California Room.

Billard, Jules, ed.
1974   *The World of the American Indian.* Washington, D.C.: National Geographic Society.

Biolsi, Thomas
1992   *Organizing the Lakota: The Political Economy of the New Deal on the Pine Ridge and Rosebud Reservations.* Tucson: University of Arizona Press.

Blackbird, Andrew J.
1887   *History of the Ottawa and Chippewa Indians of Michigan.* Ypsilanti, Mich.: Ypsilantian Job Printing House.

Blackbird, John
1892   John Blackbird (Petoskey) to President of the United States, 7 February. Bureau of Indian Affairs, Letters Received, 1881–1907. RG 75. National Archives. LROIA 7185-1892.

Blair, Emma, ed.
1911   *The Indian Tribes of the Upper Mississippi Valley and the Region of the Great Lakes.* 2 vols. Cleveland: A. H. Clark.

Blanchard, David
1983   High Steel! The Kahnawake Mohawk and the High Construction Trade. *Journal of Ethnic Studies* 11, no. 2: 41–60.

Blauner, Robert
1972   *Racial Oppression in America.* New York: Harper and Row.

Bleak, James
n.d.   Annals of the Southern Utah Mission. Typescript copy by Work Projects Administration. Utah Historical Society, Salt Lake City.

Blu, Karen
1980   *The Lumbee Problem: The Making of an American Indian People.* Cambridge: Cambridge University Press.

Bock, Philip K.
1966   *The Micmac Indians of Restigouche: History and Contemporary Description.* Bulletin 213, Anthropological Series 77. Ottawa: National Museum of Canada.
1978   Micmac. In *Handbook of North American Indians.* Vol. 15, *The Northeast,* ed. Bruce G. Trigger, 109–122. Washington, D.C.: Smithsonian Institution Press.

Boggs, James
1970   *Racism and Class Struggle: Further Pages from a Black Worker's Notebook.* New York: Monthly Review Press.

Bonacich, Edna
1972   A Theory of Ethnic Antagonism: The Split Labor Market. *American Sociological Review* 37: 547–559.

Boscana, Gerónimo
1933   Chinigchinich. In *Chinigchinich: A Revised and Annotated Version of Alfred Robinson's Translation of Father Gerónimo Boscana's Historical Account of the Beliefs, Usages, Customs, and Extravagancies of the Indians of the Mission of San Juan Capistrano Called the Acaghem Tribe,* ed. Phil T. Hanna, 19–22. Santa Ana, Calif.: Fine Arts Press.

Boserup, Ester
1970   *Woman's Role in Economic Development.* New York: St. Martin's Press.

Boxberger, Daniel L.
1988   In and Out of the Labor Force: The Lummi Indians and the Development of the Commercial Salmon Fishery of North Puget Sound, 1880–1900. *Ethnohistory* 35, no. 2: 161–190.

Bradfute, W. R.
1879a   Letter to James Spencer, 12 October. Bureau of Indian Affairs, Letters Received, 1824–1881. RG 75. National Archives.
1879b   Letter to James Spencer, 29 November. Bureau of Indian Affairs, Letters Received, 1824–1881. RG 75. National Archives.
1880   Letter to James Spencer, 3 April. Bureau of Indian Affairs, Letters Received, 1824–1881. RG 75. National Archives.
1886   Letter to W. D. C. Gibson, 22 July. Bureau of Indian Affairs, Letters Received, 1881–1907. RG 75. National Archives.

Braroe, Niels W.
1975   *Indian and White: Self-Image and Interaction in a Canadian Plains Community.* Stanford: Stanford University Press.

Braverman, Harry
1974   *Labor and Monopoly Capital.* New York: Monthly Review Press.

Breen, Nancy, and Patricia Albers
1989   Deciphering the Census for Trends in the Status of American Indian Women. Paper presented at the American Social Science Association, Chicago, Ill., December.

Brittan, Arthur, and Mary Maynard
1984   *Sexism, Racism, and Oppression.* London: Basil Blackwell.

Brooks, Edward J.
1877a   Report of Complaints of Indians Relative to Homestead Grand Traverse Land District, February. Correspondence of the Office of

Indian Affairs (Central Office) and Related Records—Letters Received. RG 75. National Archives. Microcopy M234, reel 412, frames 207–233.

1877b   Letter to J. A. Williamson, 27 December. Correspondence of the Office of Indian Affairs (Central Office) and Related Records—Letters Received. RG 75. National Archives. Microcopy M234, reel 413, frames 64–103.

1878a   Letter to Ezra A. Hayt, 4 January. Correspondence of the Office of Indian Affairs (Central Office) and Related Records—Letters Received. RG 75. National Archives. Microcopy M234, reel 413, frames 3–64.

1878b   Letter to Ezra A. Hayt, 12 January. Correspondence of the Office of Indian Affairs (Central Office) and Related Records—Letters Received. RG 75. National Archives. Microcopy M234, reel 413, frames 104–136.

Brooks, Juanita, ed.

1972   *Journal of the Southern Indian Mission: Diary of Thomas D. Brown.* Western Text Society Monograph, no. 4. Logan: Utah State University Press.

Brophy, William A., and Sophie D. Aberle

1966   *The Indian: America's Unfinished Business.* Norman: University of Oklahoma Press.

Brown, Martin, and Peter Philips

1991   Competition, Racism, and the Substitution of White Women for Chinese Men in Nineteenth-Century California Manufacturing. *Explorations in Political Economy,* ed. R. Kanth and K. Hunt, 173–199. Savage, Md.: Rowland and Little.

Brown, Thomas D.

1972   Letter to Brigham Young, 22 December 1854. In *Journal of the Southern Indian Mission: Diary of Thomas D. Brown,* ed. Juanita Brooks, Western Text Society Monograph, no. 4: 103–105. Logan: Utah State University Press.

Brumble, H. David

1988   *American Indian Autobiography.* Berkeley and Los Angeles: University of California Press.

Bryant, Keith L. Jr.

1974   *History of the Atchison, Topeka and Santa Fe Railway.* New York: Macmillan.

Buchanan, Golden

1974–1975   Interview. James Moyle Oral History Program. Typescript. Church Historian's Office, Church of Jesus Christ of Latter-day Saints, Salt Lake City, ms. no. 200/186/3.

Buesing, Gregory

1972   Maliseet and Micmac Rights in the United States. Houlton, Me.: Association of Aroostook Indians. Unpub. ms.

Bureau of Indian Affairs

1875   *Annual Report of the Commissioner of Indian Affairs.* Washington, D.C.: GPO.

1880   *Annual Report of the Commissioner of Indian Affairs.* Washington, D.C.: GPO.

1910–1932   Annual Reports of the Superintendent, Mt. Pleasant School. Superintendents' Annual Narrative and Statistical Reports from the Field Jurisdictions of the Bureau of Indian Affairs, 1907–1938. RG 75. National Archives. Microfilm publication M1011, Reel 89.

1926   Semiannual School Report, Mt. Pleasant School, 31 December. RG 75. National Archives. Entry 746.

1977–1987   *Indian Service Population and Labor Force Estimates.* Washington, D.C.: Department of the Interior.

1980   Quarterly Manpower Report. Anadarko, Okla.: Anadarko Area Office.

n.d.   Mt. Pleasant School, Michigan. Typescript. RG 75. National Archives. Entry 723, Office File of W. Carson Ryan, box 6.

Burgess, Thomas

1991   Wage Labor Lost: Silent History of the Lakota. Paper presented at the American Anthropological Association, Chicago, Ill., November.

Burt, Larry

1977   Factories on Reservations: The Industrial Development Programs of Commissioner Glenn Emmons, 1953–1960. *Arizona West* 19: 317–332.

Button, Leslie

1986   Personal communication to author. January.

California, State Legislature.

1866   Appendix to the Journals of Senate and Assembly 16th Session. Report of W. E. Lovett, Special Indian Agent to Austin Wiley, Superintendent of Indian Affairs in California.

Call, Anson

1865   Letter to George A. Smith. *Deseret Weekly News*, 18 January, p. 124, col. 4.

Campbell, Franklin

1865   Letter to H. G. Parker, 9 June. Bureau of Indian Affairs, Letters Received, 1824–1881. RG 75. National Archives. Microfilm 234, roll 538, frames 416–422.

1866   Letter to H. G. Parker, 22 August. In *Annual Report of the Commissioner of Indian Affairs*, 119. Washington, D.C.: GPO.

Campbell, Gregory R.

1993   Health Patterns and Economic Underdevelopment on the Northern Cheyenne Reservation, 1910–1920. In *The Political Economy of North American Indians*, ed. John H. Moore, 60–86. Norman: University of Oklahoma Press.

Campeau, Eliza

1975   Interview, 21 August. Unpub. transcript. Grand Rapids (Mich.) Public Library, Michigan Room Collections.

Campeau, Percy

1990   Interview, 13 October. Manistee, Mich.: Little River Band of Ottawa Indians. Unpub. transcript.

Canada

1881   *Census of Canada*. Ottawa: Public Archives of Canada. Microfilm.

Canada, Department of Indian Affairs

1880–1936 *Annual Reports of the Superintendent General*. Ottawa: Government Printing Office.

Carlson, Leonard A.

1981   *Indians, Bureaucrats, and Land: The Dawes Act and the Decline of Indian Farming*. Westport, Conn.: Greenwood Press.

Carrico, Richard

1976   Interview with Thomas Lucas, San Diego, Calif. Transcription. San Diego (Calif.) Historical Society, Research Center and Archives.

1990   *Strangers in a Stolen Land: Native Americans in San Diego County, 1850–1880*. Sacramento: Sierra Oaks.

Carrico, Susan

1985   Urban Indians of San Diego: 1880–1900. Master's thesis, University of San Diego.

Carter, Sarah
1990   *Lost Harvest: Prairie Indians and Reserve Farming.* Montreal: McGill-
        Queen's University Press.
Carvalho, S. N.
1857   *Incidents of Travel and Adventure in the Far West with Col. Fremont's
        Last Expedition.* New York: Derby and Jackson.
Cass, Lewis
1821   Letter to John Calhoun, 24 October. Records of the Michigan
        Superintendency, 1814–1851. RG 75. National Archives. Microcopy
        M1, reel 4, frames 323–332.
Castile, George Pierre
1991   Indian Sign: Hegemony and Symbolism in Federal Indian Policy.
        In *State and Reservation*, ed. George Pierre Castile and Robert L.
        Bee, 165–186. Tucson: University of Arizona Press.
1993   Native North Americans and the National Question. In *The
        Political Economy of North American Indians*, ed. John H. Moore,
        270–287. Norman: University of Oklahoma Press.
Caughey, John Walton, ed.
1952   *The Indians of California in 1852.* San Marino, Calif.: Huntington
        Library.
Chadwick, Bruce A., and Lynn C. White
1973   Correlates of Length of Urban Residence Among the Spokane
        Indians. *Human Organization* 32: 9–16.
Chalfant, William A.
1930   *Death Valley, the Facts.* Davis, Calif.: Stanford University Press.
Chandler, Margaret
1990   Interview with Margaret Chandler, Connie Waitner, and Elizabeth
        Bailey, 13 October. Manistee, Mich.: Little River Band of Ottawa
        Indians. Unpub. transcript.
Cheney, Lela
1933   Report of School Social Worker, U.S. Indian School, Mt. Pleasant,
        30 June. Typescript. RG 75. National Archives. Entry 723, Office
        File of W. Carson Ryan, box 3.
Cheng, Lucie, and Edna Bonacich
1984   *Labor Immigration Under Capitalism: Asian Workers in the United
        States Before World War II.* Berkeley and Los Angeles: University
        of California Press.

Cherooty, Pete
1986   Personal communication to author. January.
Chidester, Ida
n.d.   (Indian Tribe) Piute. Ms. in collections of Daughters of the Utah
            Pioneers, Salt Lake City.
Chittenden, Hiram M.
1935   *The American Fur Trade of the Far West*. 1902. 3 vols. New York:
            Press of the Pioneers.
Church, Gladys Mamagona
1992   Videotaped discussion. School Days Remembered: The Mt.
            Pleasant Indian School Reunion, 1991. Mt. Pleasant, Mich.: Saginaw
            Chippewa Tribe.
Churchill, Frank
1907   Letter to Secretary of the Interior, 30 August. Bureau of Indian
            Affairs, Central Classified Files, 1907–1939. RG 75. National
            Archives.
Churchill, Ward
1983   Marxism and the Native American. In *Marxism and Native
            Americans*, ed. Ward Churchill, 183–203. Boston: South End Press.
Cleaves, Robert
1980   A Betrayal of Trust: The Maine Settlement Act and the Houlton
            Band of Maliseets. *American Indian Journal* (November): 1–8.
Cleland, Charles E.
1992   *Rites of Conquest: The History and Culture of Michigan Native
            Americans*. Ann Arbor: University of Michigan Press.
Cleland, Robert Glass, and Juanita Brooks, eds.
1955   *A Mormon Chronicle: The Diaries of John D. Lee, 1848–1876*. 2 vols.
            San Marino, Calif.: Huntington Library.
Clemmer, Richard O.
1977   Hopi Political Economy: Industrialization and Alienation. *Southwest
            Economy and Society* 2, no. 2: 4–33.
Clifton, James A.
1978   Potawatomi. In *Handbook of North American Indians*. Vol. 15, *The
            Northeast*, ed. Bruce G. Trigger, 725–742. Washington, D.C.:
            Smithsonian Institution Press.
Clinton, Lawrence, Bruce A. Chadwick, and Howard M. Bahr
1975   Urban Relocation Reconsidered: Antecedents of Employment
            Among Indian Males. *Rural Sociology* 40, no. 2: 117–133.

Collins, Jane L., and Martha Gimenez
1990   *Work Without Wages*. Albany: State University of New York Press.
Confederated Historic Tribes
1992   Little River Band of Ottawa Indians Economic Needs Assessment.
            Lansing, Mich.: Confederated Historic Tribes. Ms.
Connelly, John
1979   Hopi Social Organization. In *Handbook of North American Indians*.
            Vol. 9, *Southwest*, ed. Alfonso Ortiz, 539–553. Washington, D.C.:
            Smithsonian Institution Press.
Cook, Sherburne F.
1943   Migration and Urbanization of the Indians in California. *Human
            Biology* 15: 33–45.
1951   Conflict Between the California Indians and White Civilization,
            the American Invasion, 1848–1870. In *The California Indians: A
            Source Book*, ed. Robert F. Heizer and Mary Anne Whipple,
            465–474. Berkeley and Los Angeles: University of California Press.
1976   *The Conflict Between the California Indian and White Civilization*.
            Berkeley and Los Angeles: University of California Press.
Cooney, Robert
1896   *A Compendious History of the Northern Part of the Province of New
            Brunswick and of the District of Gaspe, in Lower Canada*. Chatham,
            N.B.: D. G. Smith.
Cornell, Stephen
1988   *The Return of the Native*. New York: Oxford University Press.
1990   Land, Labour, and Group Formation: Blacks and Indians in the
            United States. *Ethnic and Racial Studies* 13, no. 3: 368–388.
Cottonwood, Ted
1986   Personal communication to author. January.
Couro, Ted
1975   *San Diego Indians as Farmers and Wage Earners*. Ramona, Calif.:
            Ramona Pioneer Historical Society.
Cox, Bruce
1993   Natives and the Development of Mercantile Capitalism: A New
            Look at 'Opposition' in the Eighteenth-Century Fur Trade. In *The
            Political Economy of North American Indians*, ed. John H. Moore,
            87–93. Norman: University of Oklahoma Press.

Cox, John R.
1911   Letter to Commissioner of Indian Affairs, 31 March. Bureau of
            Indian Affairs, Central Classified Files, 1907–1939. RG 75. National
            Archives.

Cox, Martha Cragun
ca. 1928–   Autobiography. Microfilm of manuscript. Church Historian's Office,
1930   Church of Jesus Christ of Latter-day Saints, Salt Lake City, ms.
            no. 1661.

Cutler, Morton Brigham
n.d.   Autobiography of Morton Brigham Cutler, 1853–1940. Typescript
            copy. Church Historian's Office, Church of Jesus Christ of Latter-
            day Saints, Salt Lake City, ms. no. 4515.

Daggett, Stuart
1981   *Railroad Consolidation West of the Mississippi River*. New York: Arno
            Press.

Damrell, David
1991   Class and Conflict in the Ojibwa Nation: Some Preliminary
            Findings. Paper presented at American Society for Ethnohistory
            meetings, Tulsa, Okla., November.

Davis, Sam
1905   The Nevada Piutes. *Sunset Magazine* 15 (September): 458–460.

Deitch, L.
1977   The Impact of Tourism upon the Arts and Crafts of the Indians
            of the Southwestern United States. In *Hosts and Guests*, ed. V.
            Smith, 173–184. Philadelphia: University of Pennsylvania Press.

DeLaVergne, Earl, and Stephen Graham
1981   Early History. In *Harbor Springs: A Collection of Essays*, ed. Jan
            Morley. Harbor Springs, Mich.: Harbor Springs Historical
            Commission.

Deloria, Vine Jr.
1969   *Custer Died for Your Sins*. New York: Macmillan.
1970   *We Talk, You Listen*. New York: Macmillan.

Deloria, Vine Jr., and Clifford Lytle
1984   *The Nations Within: The Past and Future of American Indian
            Sovereignty*. New York: Pantheon Books.

Dembinski, Isabell, Arthur Dembinski, and Theresa Fischer
1991   Interview, 5 May. Manistee, Mich.: Little River Band of Ottawa
            Indians. Unpub. transcript.

Deutsch, Sarah
1985   *No Separate Refuge: Culture, Class, and Gender on an Anglo-Hispanic Frontier in the American Southwest, 1880-1940.* New York: Oxford University Press.

Dickason, Olive P.
1992   *Canada's First Nations: A History of Founding Peoples from Earliest Times.* Norman: University of Oklahoma Press.

Dobson, Pamela J., ed.
1978   *The Tree That Never Dies: Oral History of the Michigan Indians.* Grand Rapids, Mich.: Grand Rapids Public Library.

Dobyns, Henry F., Richard W. Stoffle, and Kristine Jones
1975   Native American Urbanization and Socio-Economic Integration in the Southwestern United States. *Ethnohistory* 22: 155-179.

Dodge, Fredrick
1859   Letter to Jacob Forney, 4 January. In *Annual Report of the Commissioner of Indian Affairs*, 373. Washington, D.C.: GPO.

Douglas, Henry
1869   Letter to E. S. Parker, 8 December. Bureau of Indian Affairs, Letters Received, 1824-1881. RG 75. National Archives.
1870   Report to Commissioner of Indian Affairs, 27 May 1870. Bureau of Indian Affairs, Letters Received, 1824-1881. National Archives.

Downs, James F.
1966   *The Two Worlds of the Washo.* New York: Holt, Rinehart and Winston.

Dozier, Edward P.
1970   *The Pueblo Indians of North America.* New York: Holt, Rinehart, and Winston.

Dozier, Edward P., George E. Simpson, and J. Milton Yinger
1957   The Integration of Americans of Indian Descent. *Annals of the American Academy of Political and Social Science* 311: 158-165.

Driver, Harold E., and William C. Massey
1957   *Comparative Studies of North American Indians.* Transactions of the American Philosophical Society, no. 47, 163-456.

Dubay, Guy F.
1989a   Aroostook: The Military Impact. In *The County: Land of Promise: A Pictorial History of Aroostook County, Maine*, ed. Anna F. McGrath, 161-170. Norfolk, Va.: Donning.

1989b The Garden of Maine. In *The County: Land of Promise: A Pictorial History of Aroostook County, Maine*, ed. Anna F. McGrath, 153–160. Norfolk, Va.: Donning.

1989c The Land: In Common and Undivided. In *The County: Land of Promise: A Pictorial History of Aroostook County, Maine*, ed. Anna F. McGrath, 145–152. Norfolk, Va.: Donning.

Ducker, James H.

1983 *Men of the Steel Rails: Workers on the Atchison, Topeka and Santa Fe Railroad, 1869–1900.* Lincoln: University of Nebraska Press.

Duke, Donald, and Stan Kistler

1963 *Santa Fe . . . Steel Rails Through California.* San Marino, Calif.: Pacific Railroad Publications.

Dunbar, Willis F.

1965 *Michigan: A History of the Wolverine State.* Grand Rapids, Mich.: Erdmans Printing.

Dunlay, Thomas

1982 *Wolves for the Blue Soldiers: Indian Scouts and Auxiliaries with the United States Army, 1860–90.* Lincoln: University of Nebraska Press.

Dutcher, B. H.

1893 Piñon Gathering Among the Panamint Indians. *American Anthropologist*, o.s., 6: 377–380.

Elias, Peter

1988 *The Dakota of the Canadian Northwest.* Winnipeg: University of Manitoba Press.

Elliot, Russell R.

1973 *History of Nevada.* Lincoln: University of Nebraska Press.

Ellis, C. L.

1911 Letter to Commissioner of Indian Affairs, 14 July. Bureau of Indian Affairs, Central Classified Files, 1907–1939. RG 75. National Archives.

Ellis, Lambert

1894 Letter to I. J. Wootten, 19 December. Walker River Agency Files, Letter Book I. RG 75. National Archives Branch Depository, San Bruno, Calif.

Englehardt, Zephyrin

1920 *San Diego Mission.* San Francisco: James H. Barry Co.

Engels, Friedrich
1972   On Social Relations in Russia. In *The Marx-Engels Reader*, ed. Robert
            C. Tucker, 589–599. New York: W. W. Norton.
Ewen, Lynda Ann
1978   *Corporate Power and Urban Crisis in Detroit*. Princeton: Princeton
            University Press.
Fabian, Johannes
1983   *Time and the Other: How Anthropology Makes Its Object*. New York:
            Columbia University Press.
Faiman-Silva, Sandra
1993   Multinational Corporate Development in the American
            Hinterland: The Case of the Oklahoma Choctaws. In *The Political
            Economy of North American Indians*, ed. John H. Moore, 214–239.
            Norman: University of Oklahoma Press.
Farnes, Ebenezer
1920   Reminiscences, 1843–1920. Church Historian's Office, Church of
            Jesus Christ of Latter-day Saints, Salt Lake City, ms. no. 7329.
Farrow, E. A.
1935   Letter to Commissioner of Indian Affairs, 6 April. Bureau of Indian
            Affairs, Central Classified Files, 1907–1939, RG 75. National
            Archives.
Featherstone, Mike
1993   *Consumer Culture and Postmodernism*. London: Sage.
Feest, Johanna E., and Christian F. Feest
1978   Ottawa. In *Handbook of North American Indians*. Vol.15, *The
            Northeast*, ed. Bruce G. Trigger, 772–786. Washington, D.C:
            Smithsonian Institution Press.
Findlay, John M.
1992   An Elusive Institution: The Birth of Indian Reservations in Gold
            Rush California. In *State and Reservation*, ed. George Castile and
            Robert L. Bee, 13–37. Tucson: University of Arizona Press.
Finger, John R.
1984   *The Eastern Band of Cherokees, 1819–1900*. Knoxville: University
            of Tennessee Press.
Fitzpatrick, Anthony
1982   Unpublished interview by Bunny McBride.

Foote, William
n.d.   Journal. Typescript copy. Manuscript Collections. Church Historian's Office, Church of Jesus Christ of Latter-day Saints, Salt Lake City.

Forbes, A. S. C.
1902   Lace Making. *Out West* 26, no. 6: 613–616.

Forbes, Jack D.
1960   *Apache, Navajo, and Spaniard.* Norman: University of Oklahoma Press.

1969   *Native Americans of California and Nevada.* Healdsburg, Calif.: Naturegraph.

1991   Envelopment, Proletarianization, and Interiorization: Aspects of Colonialism's Impact upon Native Americans and Other People of Color in Eastern North America. *Journal of Ethnic Studies* 18, no. 4: 95–122.

Foster, J. E.
1988   The Home Guard Cree and the Hudson's Bay Company: The First Hundred Years. In *Native People, Native Lands*, ed. Bruce Cox, 107–119. Ottawa: Carlton University Press.

Foster, Joseph
1874–1880   Diary of Joseph Foster. Ms. San Diego (Calif.) Historic Society, Research Center and Archives.

Foucault, Michel
1970   *The Order of Things.* New York: Random House.

1976   *The Archaeology of Knowledge.* New York: Harper and Row.

Frank, Andre Gunder
1966   The Development of Underdevelopment. *Monthly Review* 18: 17–31.

Friedland, William H., and Dorothy Nelkin
1971   *Migrant Agricultural Workers in America's Northeast.* New York: Holt, Rinehart and Winston.

Garcia, Mario
1981   *Desert Immigrants: The Mexicans of El Paso, 1880–1920.* New Haven: Yale University Press.

George, Captain
1888   Letter to Commissioner of Indian Affairs, 13 February. Bureau of Indian Affairs, Letters Received, 1881–1907. RG 75. National Archives.

Getty, Harry
1963 *The San Carlos Indian Cattle Industry*. University of Arizona Anthropological Papers, no. 7. Tucson: University of Arizona Press.

Gibson, W. D. C.
1885 Letter to H. Price, 23 February. Bureau of Indian Affairs, Letters Received, 1881–1907. RG 75. National Archives.
1887 Letter to J. D. C. Atkins, Commissioner of Indian Affairs, 28 June. Bureau of Indian Affairs, Letters Received, 1881–1907. National Archives.
1888 Letter to J. D. C. Atkins, 25 July. Bureau of Indian Affairs, Letters Received, 1881–1907. RG 75. National Archives.

Gilbreath, Kent
1973 *Red Capitalism: An Analysis of the Navajo Economy*. Norman: University of Oklahoma Press.

Gilpin, Alex
1970 *The Territory of Michigan, 1805–1837*. East Lansing: Michigan State University Press.

Gilpin, J. Bernard
1878 Indians of Nova Scotia (1875–1878). In *The Native People of Atlantic Canada*, ed. Harold F. McGee, 102–119. Toronto: McClelland and Stewart.

Gleed, Charles
1912 The Rehabilitation of the Santa Fe System. Santa Fe Railway Collection, Kansas Historical Society, Kansas State Museum, Topeka.

Glenn, Evelyn
1981 Occupational Ghettoization: Japanese-American Women and Domestic Service, 1905–1970. *Ethnicity* 7: 352–386.
1985 Racial Ethnic Women's Labor: The Intersection of Race, Gender, and Class Oppression. *Review of Radical Political Economics* 17, no. 3: 86–108.

Glocheski, Katherine Sam
1991 Interview, 28 April. Manistee, Mich.: Little River Band of Ottawa Indians. Unpub. transcript.

Godelier, Maurice
1977 Salt Money and the Circulation of Commodities Among the Baruya of New Guinea. In *Perspectives in Marxist Anthropology*, ed. Maurice Godelier, 127–151. Cambridge: Cambridge University Press.

Goldfarb, Ronald L.
1981   *Migrant Farm Workers: A Caste of Despair.* Ames: Iowa State University Press.

Gonzalez, Nancie L. Solien
1969   *Black Carib Household Structure: A Study of Migration and Modernization.* Seattle: University of Washington Press.

Goodall, Otis
1913   Report of Inspection of Kaibab Agency, 20 September. Bureau of Indian Affairs, Central Classified Files, 1907–1939. RG 75. National Archives.

Gookin, Daniel
1806   Historical Collections of the Indians in New England (1674). *Collections of the Massachusetts Historical Society.* First Series, vol. 1, 141–229. Boston.

Gordon, David M., Richard Edwards, and Michael Reich
1982   *Segmented Work, Divided Workers.* London: Cambridge University Press.

Grand Rapids Daily Enquirer and Herald
1858   The Ottawa in Oceana and Mason Counties. 19 June, p. 2.

Graves, Theodore D.
1970   Personal Adjustment of Navaho Indian Migrants to Denver, Colorado. *American Anthropologist* 72: 35–54.
1974   Urban Indian Personality and the 'Culture of Poverty.' *American Ethnologist* 1: 65–86.

Graves, Theodore D., and Charles A. Lane
1972   Determinants of Urban Migrant Indian Wages. *Human Organization* 31: 47–61.

Graves, Theodore D., and Minor van Arsdale
1965   Perceived Opportunities, Expectations, and the Decision to Remain on Relocation: The Case of the Navajo Indian Migrant to Denver, Colorado. *Human Organization* 25: 300–307.

Green, Jere W.
1989   Aroostook Becomes a County. In *The County: Land of Promise: A Pictorial History of Aroostook County, Maine,* ed. Anna F. McGrath, 63–73. Norfolk, Va.: Donning.

Gregg, Josiah
1970   *The Commerce of the Praries.* New York: Citadel.

Gregory, James N.
1989   *American Exodus: The Dust Bowl Migration and Okie Culture in California.* New York: Oxford University Press.

Gribb, William James
1981   The Grand Traverse Bands' Land Base: A Cultural Historical Study of Land Transfer in Michigan. Ph.D. diss., Michigan State University, East Lansing.

Grobsmith, Elizabeth S.
1979   The Lakota Giveaway: A System of Social Reciprocity. *Plains Anthropologist* 24: 123–131.
1981   *Lakota of the Rosebud: A Contemporary Ethnography.* New York: Holt, Rinehart and Winston.

Guillemin, Jeanne
1975   *Urban Renegades: The Cultural Strategy of American Indians.* New York: Columbia University Press.

Gundlach, James H., Nelson Reid, and Alden E. Roberts
1977   Migration, Labor Mobility, and Relocation Assistance: The Case of the American Indian. *Social Science Review* 51: 464–473.

Hackenberg, Robert A.
1972   Restricted Interdependence: The Adaptive Pattern of Papago Indian Society. *Human Organization* 31: 113–125.

Hackenberg, Robert A., and C. Roderick Wilson
1972   Reluctant Emigrants: The Role of Migration in Papago Indian Adaptation. *Human Organization* 31: 171–187.

Hagan, William T.
1961   *American Indians.* Chicago: University of Chicago Press.

Haines, Walter W.
1983   The Myth of Continuous Inflation, 1700–1980. In *Inflation Through the Ages,* ed. Nathan Schmukler and Edward Marcus, 183–204. New York: Columbia University Press.

Hale, Douglas
1982   The People of Oklahoma: Economics and Social Change. In *Oklahoma: New Views,* ed. Anne H. Morgan and H. Wayne Morgan, 31–92. Norman: University of Oklahoma Press.

Hall, Thomas D.
1989a   Historical Sociology and Native Americans: Methodological Problems. *American Indian Quarterly* 13, no. 3: 223–238.

1989b   *Social Change in the Southwest, 1350-1880.* Lawrence: University
           Press of Kansas.

Hamblin, Jacob

n.d.   Journal, 1854-1857. Typescript. Utah State Historical Society, Salt
           Lake City.

Harris, Benjamin Butler

1960   *The Gila Trail: The Texas Argonauts and the California Gold Rush,*
           ed. Richard H. Dillon. Norman: University of Oklahoma Press.

Hart, Taylor, and Company

1876   Flyer. Missouri Historical Society, St. Louis.

Hauke, Margaret Irwin

1984   Oral History of Margaret Irwin Hauke, Council Grove, Kans.,
           Employee, Santa Fe Railway, 1924-1946. Recorded by Constance
           L. Menninger. Santa Fe Collection, Kansas State Historical Society,
           Kansas State Museum, Topeka.

Hayden, Carl

1965   *A History of the Pima Indians and the San Carlos Irrigation Project.*
           89th Cong., 1st sess., Document 11. Washington, D.C.: GPO.

Heald, Nan

1987   The Aroostook Band of Micmacs' Struggle for Tribal Recognition.
           In *Maine Bar Journal* (Sept.): 272-276.

Hechter, Michael

1975   *Internal Colonialism: The Celtic Fringe in British National Development.*
           Berkeley and Los Angeles: University of California Press.

Henderson, Al

1970   Tribal Enterprises: Will They Survive? In *Economic Development in
           American Indian Reservations,* 114-128. Native American Studies,
           University of New Mexico, Development Series, no. 1.
           Albuquerque.

Henderson, Eric

1979   Skilled and Unskilled Blue Collar Navajo Workers: Occupational
           Diversity in an American Indian Tribe. *Social Science Journal* 16:
           63-80.

Hewes, Mina, and Gordon

1952   Indian Life and Customs at Mission San Luis Rey: A Record of
           California Mission Life by Pablo Tac, an Indian Neophyte (Rome
           1935). *The Americas* 9: 87-106.

Hill, Richard
1987   *Skywalkers: A History of Indian Ironworkers.* Brantford, Ont,: Woodland Indian Cultural Educational Centre.

History of Manistee, Mason, and Oceana Counties
1882.   H. R. Page.

Hobsbawm, Eric, and Terence Ranger
1983   *The Invention of Tradition.* Cambridge: Cambridge University Press.

Hodge, William H.
1969   *The Albuquerque Navajos.* University of Arizona Anthropological Papers, no. 11. Tucson: University of Arizona Press.

Hoffman, Bernard G.
1955   The Historical Ethnography of the Micmac of the Sixteenth and Seventeenth Centuries. Ph.D. diss., University of California, Berkeley.

Hogan, Lloyd
1984   *Principles of Black Political Economy.* Boston: Routledge and Kegan Paul.

Holm, Tom
1985   Fighting a White Man's War: The Extent and Legacy of American Indian Participation in World War II. In *The Plains Indians of the Twentieth Century,* ed. Peter Iverson, 149–168. Norman: University of Oklahoma Press.

Holt, J. S.
1984   Introduction to the Seasonal Farm Labor Problem. In *Seasonal Agricultural Labor Markets in the United States,* ed. Robert D. Emerson, 3–32. Ames: Iowa State University Press.

Hoopa Tribal History Documents
1945–1962   American West Center. University of Utah, Salt Lake City, Utah.

Hooper, Mamie
1986   Personal communication to author. January.

Hornaday, William T.
1889   *The Extermination of the American Bison.* Annual Report of the National Museum. Washington, D.C.: U.S. National Museum.

Horr, David Agee, ed.
1974   *American Indian Ethnohistory: Indians of the Southwest.* New York: Garland.

Hosmer, Brian C.

1991   Creating Indian Entrepreneurs: Menominees, Neopit Mills, and
            Timber Exploitation, 1890–1915. *American Indian Culture and
            Research Journal* 15, no.1: 1–28.

Hosmer, James K., ed.

1917   *History of the Expedition of Captains Lewis and Clark.* Chicago:
            McClurg.

Houghton, Ruth

1973   Adaptive Strategies in an American Indian Reservation Com-
            munity: The War on Poverty, 1965–1971. Ph.D. diss., University
            of Oregon.

Hoxie, Frederick E.

1984   *A Final Promise: The Campaign to Assimilate the Indians, 1880–1920.*
            Lincoln: University of Nebraska Press.

Hurd, C. W.

n.d.   *Bents' Stockade.* Privately published.

Hurt, R. Douglas

1987   *Indian Agriculture in America: Prehistory to the Present.* Lawrence:
            University of Kansas Press.

Hurtado, Albert L.

1982   Hardly a Farmhouse or a Kitchen Without Them: Indian and
            White Households on the California Borderland Frontier 1860.
            Western Historical Quarterly 13: 245–270.

1983   'Saved So Much as Possible for Labour': Indian Population and
            the New Helvetia Work Force. *American Indian Culture and Research
            Journal* 6, no. 4: 63–78.

1988a   Indians in Town and Country: The Nisenan Indians' Changing
            Economy and Society as Shown in John A. Sutter's 1856 Corre-
            spondence. *American Indian Culture and Research Journal* 12, no.
            2: 31–51.

1988b   *Indian Survival on the California Frontier.* New Haven: Yale University
            Press.

1990   California Indians and the Workaday West. *California History*
            (spring): 2–11.

Husband, Mike

1969   Anonymous interviews by Mike Husband at Laguna Pueblo, 18
            November. Doris Duke Collection, General Library, Special Collec-

tions, University of New Mexico, Albuquerque, folder no. 213 (tape no. 213, side 1).

Ictioka, Yuji
1980   Japanese Immigrant Labor Contractors and the Northern Pacific and the Great Northern Railroad Companies, 1898–1907. *Labor History* 21: 132–149.

Indian Task Force
n.d.   United States Legal Rights of Native Americans Born in Canada. Boston: Office of the Indian Task Force, Federal Regional Council of New England, with the assistance of the Boston Indian Council.

Ingalls, George W.
1874a   Letter to Commissioner of Indian Affairs, 5 June. Bureau of Indian Affairs, Letters Received, 1874-I-645. RG 75. National Archives.
1874b   Letter to E. P. Smith, Commissioner of Indian Affairs, 1 October. In *Annual Report of the Commissioner of Indian Affairs*, 282–284. Washington, D.C.: GPO.

Ivins, Anthony
1893   Letter to T. J. Morgan, Commissioner of Indian Affairs, 16 January. Bureau of Indian Affairs, Letters Received, 1881–1907. RG 75. National Archives.

J. A. L.
1957   Letter to the Editor, *San Francisco Herald*, 5 September 1853. Quoted in *The Far West and the Rockies*. Vol. 5, *Central Route to the Pacific*, ed. LeRoy R. Hafen and Ann W. Hafen, 296–301. Glendale, Calif.: Arthur Clark.

Jacobson, Cardell K.
1984   Internal Colonialism and Native Americans: Indian Labor in the United States from 1871 to World War II. *Social Science Quarterly* 65, no. 1: 158–171.

Jaimes, M. Annette, ed.
1992   *The State of Native America*. Boston: South End Press

Jameson, Fredric
1983   Postmodernism and Consumer Society. In *The Anti-Aesthetic Essays on Post Modern Culture*, ed. H. Foster, 111–125. Port Townsend, Wash.: Bay Press.
1984   Postmodernism or the Cultural Logic of Late Capitalism. *New Left Review* 146: 53–93.

Jensen, Andrew, comp.
1926   *History of the Las Vegas Mission.* Nevada State Historical Society
            Papers, vol. 5. Reno.
"Jerseyman"
1886   Among the Piutes. *Newark Advertiser,* 1 July.
Johnson, Seth
n.d.   Biographical Sketch. Typescript copy. Church Historian's Office,
            Church of Jesus Christ of Latter-day Saints, Salt Lake City, ms.
            no. 4888.
Johnston, E. W., and H. B. Metzger
1974   Labor Replacement in Potato Harvesting in Aroostook County.
            Research in the Life Sciences 22, no. 5: 1–13.
Jones, E. E.
1907a   Letter to C. H. Asbury, 19 July. Bureau of Indian Affairs, Carson
            Indian School. RG 75. National Archives Branch Depository, San
            Bruno, Calif. Correspondence Box 248B.
1907b   Letter to C. H. Asbury, 16 October. Bureau of Indian Affairs,
            Carson Indian School. RG 75. National Archives Branch
            Depository, San Bruno, Calif. Correspondence Box 248B.
1907c   Letter to C. H. Asbury, 27 October. Bureau of Indian Affairs,
            Carson Indian School. RG 75. National Archives Branch
            Depository, San Bruno, Calif. Correspondence Box 248B.
1907d   Letter to W. H. Code, 7 November. Bureau of Indian Affairs,
            Irrigation Division, Correspondence of the Chief of Engineers.
            National Archives.
1907e   Letter to C. H. Asbury, 11 December. Bureau of Indian Affairs,
            Carson Indian School Files. RG 75. National Archives Branch
            Depository, San Bruno, Calif. Correspondence Box 248B.
1907f   Letter to C. H. Asbury, ca. 19 December. Bureau of Indian Affairs,
            Carson Indian School Files. RG 75. National Archives Branch
            Depository, San Bruno, Calif. Correspondence Box 248B.
Jorgensen, Joseph G.
1971   Indians and the Metropolis. In *The American Indian in Urban Society,*
            ed. Jack O. Waddell and O. Michael Watson, 66–113. Boston: Little,
            Brown.
1972   *The Sun Dance Religion: Power for the Powerless.* Chicago: University
            of Chicago Press.

1978   A Century of Political Economic Effects on American Indian Economy, 1880–1980. *Journal of Ethnic Studies* 6, no. 3: 1–82.

1990   *Oil Age Eskimos*. Berkeley and Los Angeles: University of California Press.

Jorgensen, Joseph G. et al.

1978   *Native Americans and Energy Development*. Cambridge, Mass.: Anthropology Resource Center.

1984   *Native Americans and Energy Development II*. Cambridge, Mass.: Anthropology Resource Center/Seventh Generation Fund.

Josephy, Alvin M. Jr.

1984   *Now That the Buffalo's Gone*. Norman: University of Oklahoma Press.

Josephy, Alvin, and Patricia Limerick

1993   *The Native Americans: An Illustrated History*. Atlanta: Turner.

Kappler, Charles J.

1904   *Indian Affairs: Laws and Treaties*. 4 vols. Washington, D.C.: GPO.

Katzer, Bruce

1988   The Caughnawaga Mohawks: The Other Side of Ironwork. *Journal of Ethnic Studies* 15, no. 4: 39–55.

Keesing, Felix M.

1987   *The Menomini Indians of Wisconsin*. Madison: University of Wisconsin Press.

Kehoe, Alice

1983   The Shackles of Tradition. In *The Hidden Half: Studies of Plains Indian Women*. ed. Patricia Albers and Beatrice Medicine, 53–76. Lanham, Md.: University Press of America.

Kelly, Anna

1986   Personal communication to author. January.

Kelly, Charles, ed.

1948–1949 Journal of W. D. Powell, 21 April 1871–7 December 1872. *Utah Historical Quarterly* 16–17: 257–478.

Kelly, Isabel T., and Catherine S. Fowler

1986   Southern Paiute. In *Handbook of North American Indians*. Vol. 11, *The Great Basin*, ed. Warren L. D'Azevedo, 368–397. Washington, D.C.: Smithsonian Institution Press.

Kelly, John Lincoln

1968   Life on a San Diego County Ranch. Ms., California Room, San Diego (Calif.) Public Library.

Kelly, Roger E., and John O. Cramer
1966   *American Indians in Small Cities.* University of Northern Arizona Rehabilitation Monographs, no. 1. Flagstaff.

Kelly, William H.
1957   The Economic Basis of Indian Life. *Annals of the American Academy of Political and Social Science* 311: 71–115.

Kennedy, Margaret
1986   Personal communication to author. January.

Kenner, Charles L.
1969   *A History of New Mexican–Plains Indian Relations.* Norman: University of Oklahoma Press.

Kidder, Frederic
1867   *Military Operations in Eastern Maine and Nova Scotia During the Revolution, Chiefly Compiled from the Journals and the Letters of Colonel John Allan, with Notes and a Memoir of Col. John Allan.* Albany: Joel Munsell.

Kiefer, David, and Peter Philips
1991   Explanation of Long-Term Trends in the Racial Wage Gap. In *Explorations in Political Economy,* ed. R. Kanth and K. Hunt, 137–150. Savage, Md.: Rowland and Little.

Kimball, Abraham
1867–1889   Reminiscences and Journal. Church Historian's Office, Church of Jesus Christ of Latter-day Saints, Salt Lake City, ms. no. 1778.

Klein, Alan
1983   The Political-Economy of Gender: An Eighteenth-Century Plains Indian Case Study. In *The Hidden Half: Studies of Plains Indian Women,* ed. Patricia Albers and Beatrice Medicine, 143–174. Washington, D.C.: University Press of America.

1991   Political Economy of the Buffalo Hide Trade: Race and Class on the Plains. In *The Political Economy of North American Indians,* ed. John H. Moore, 133–160. Norman: University of Oklahoma Press.

Klein, Laura F.
1978   Seasonality and the Division of Labor in a Contemporary Native American Community. Paper read at American Anthropological Association meetings, Los Angeles, November.

1980   Contending with Colonization: Tlingit Men and Women in Change. In *Women and Colonization,* ed. Mona Etienne and Eleanor Leacock, 88–108. New York: Praeger.

Kleinfeld, Judith, and John A. Kruse
1982   Native Americans in the Labor Force: Hunting for an Accurate Measure. *Monthly Labor Review* 105: 47–51.

Klett, Mark et al.
1984   *A Second View: The Rephotographic Survey Project.* Albuquerque: University of New Mexico Press.

Kline, Lora L.
1979   *The Kwaaymii: Reflections on a Lost Culture.* El Centro, Calif.: Imperial Valley College Museum Society.

Knack, Martha C.
1978   Beyond a Differential: An Inquiry into Southern Paiute Indian Experience with Public Schools. *Anthropology and Education Quarterly* 9, no. 3: 216–234.
1980   *Life Is With People: Household Organization of the Contemporary Southern Paiute Indians of Utah.* Ballena Press Anthropological Papers, no. 19. Socorro, N.M.: Ballena Press.
1982   The Effects of Nevada State Fishing Laws on the Northern Paiutes of Pyramid Lake. *Nevada Historical Society Quarterly* 25: 251–265.
1986a   Indian Economies, 1950–1980. In *Handbook of North American Indians.* Vol. 11, *Great Basin,* ed. Warren L. d'Azevedo, 573–591. Washington, D.C.: Smithsonian Institution Press.
1986b   Newspaper Accounts of Indian Women in Southern Nevada Mining Towns, 1850–1900. *Journal of California and Great Basin Anthropology* 8: 83–98.
1987   The Role of Credit in Native American Adaptation to the Great Basin Ranching Economy. *American Indian Culture and Research Journal* 11: 43–65.
1989   Contemporary Southern Paiute Women and the Measurement of Women's Economic and Political Status. *Ethnology* 28: 233–248.
1992   Utah Indians and the Homestead Laws. In *State and Reservation: New Perspectives on Federal Indian Policy,* ed. George Castile and Robert L. Bee, 63–91. Tucson: University of Arizona Press.

Knight, Rolf
1978   *Indians at Work: An Informal History of Native American Labour in British Columbia, 1858–1930.* Vancouver: New Star Books.

Konrad, Victor
1987   The Iroquois Return to Their Homeland: Military Retreat or Cultural Adjustment? In *A Cultural Geography of North American*

Indians, ed. Thomas E. Ross and Tyrel G. Moore, 191–212. Boulder, Colo.: Westview Press.

Koon, Bruce
1978 Indian Tribes Find Great White Father Is Big Loss Leader. *Wall Street Journal*, 21 April.

Koon, Jim
1975 Interview, 15 October. Transcript. Grand Rapids (Mich.) Public Library, Michigan Room Collections.

Koon, Jim [son of Jim Koon]
1990 Interview, 2 June. Manistee, Mich.: Little River Band of Ottawa Indians. Unpub. transcript.

Kroeber, Alfred L.
1925 The Native Population of California. In *The California Indians: A Source Book*, ed. Robert F. Heizer and Mary Anne Whipple, 68–81. Berkeley and Los Angeles: University of California Press.

Krupat, Arnold
1992 *Ethno-Criticism*. Berkeley and Los Angeles: University of California Press.

Krutz, Gordon V.
1971 San Carlos Apache Wage Labor in 1970. In *Apachean Culture History and Ethnology*, ed. Keith H. Basso and Morris E. Opler, 129–134. University of Arizona Anthropological Papers, no. 21. Tucson: University of Arizona Press.

Kunitz, Stephen J.
1977 Economic Variation on the Navajo Reservation. *Human Organization* 36: 186–193.

Kvasnicka, Robert M., and Herman J. Viola
1979 *The Commissioners of Indian Affairs, 1824–1977*. Lincoln: University of Nebraska Press.

LaFarge, Oliver
1956 *A Pictorial History of the American Indian*. New York: Crown.

Lake, Randall
1991 Between Myth and History: Enacting Time in Native American Protest Rhetoric. *Quarterly Journal of Speech* 77: 123–151.

Lamphere, Louise
1976 The Internal Colonization of the Navajo People. *Southwest Economy and Society* 1, no. 1: 6–14.

Landis, Juanita
1986   Personal communication to author. January.
Las Vegas Review-Journal
1931   [No title]. 28 July, p. 1, col. 2.
1983   Reagan Has Cut Funding to Indians by a Third. 29 September,
            p. 8A.
Latorre, Felipe A., and Dolores L. Latorre
1991   The Mexican Kickapoo Indians. 1976. Reprint, New York: Dover.
Lauber, Almon Wheeler
1913   Indian Slavery in Colonial Times Within the Present Limits of the United
            States. Studies in History, Economics, and Public Law, vol. 54, no.
            3. New York: Columbia University Press.
Lavender, David
1954   Bent's Fort. Garden City, N.Y.: Doubleday.
Leacock, Eleanor, and Helen I. Safa, eds.
1986   Women's Work: Development and the Division of Labor by Gender.
            South Hadley, Mass.: Bergin and Garvey.
Lecompte, Janet
1978   Pueblo, Hardscrabble, Greenhorn. Norman: University of Oklahoma
            Press.
Lee, George
1878a   Letter to Commissioner of Indian Affairs, 1 April. Bureau of Indian
            Affairs, Letters Sent by the Mackinac Agency, 1865–1868,
            1877–1885. RG 75. National Archives. Entry 1133, 195–201.
1878b   Letter to Commissioner of Indian Affairs, 1 September. In Annual
            Report of the Commissioner of Indian Affairs, 570–572. Washington,
            D.C.: GPO.
Lee, John D.
1852   Letter to Brother Richards, 7 August. Deseret News, 4 September.
1853   Letter to Brigham Young. Journal History of the Church of Jesus
            Christ of Latter-day Saints, entry for 6 March. Church Historian's
            Office, Church of Jesus Christ of Latter-day Saints, Salt Lake City.
1854   Letter to Brigham Young, 24 January. Deseret News, 16 February.
Lempke, Anna Sam, and Katie Sam Glocheski
1990   Interview, 29 July. Manistee, Mich.: Little River Band of Ottawa
            Indians. Unpub. transcript.

Leupp, Francis E.
1910   *The Indian and His Problem.* New York: Charles Scribner's Sons.

Lewis, Diane
1977   A Response to Inequality: Black Women, Racism, and Sexism. *Signs* 3: 339–361.

Lieberman, Paul
1991   Indian Gaming. *Las Vegas Review-Journal,* 13 October, 10B, 11B, 13B; 20 October, 9B, 11B; 27 October, 4–5B; 3 November, 3–4B; and 10 November, 3B.

Lincoln County Record
1903   Death Sentence. 13 November, p. 4, col. 2.

Lindquist, G. E. E.
1933   Letter to Samuel Eliot, Board of Indian Commissioners, 7 April. Bureau of Indian Affairs, Central Classified Files, 1907–1939. RG 75. National Archives.

Lingenfelter, Robert E.
1986   *Death Valley and the Amargosa.* Berkeley and Los Angeles: University of California Press.

Little, James A.
1945   *Jacob Hamblin Among the Indians.* Juvenile Instructor's Office, Church of Jesus Christ of Latter-day Saints, Salt Lake City.

Littlefield, Alice
1989   The B.I.A. Boarding School: Theories of Resistance and Social Reproduction. *Humanity and Society* 13, no. 4: 428–441.
1991   Native American Labor and Public Policy in the United States. In *Marxist Approaches in Economic Anthropology,* ed. Alice Littlefield and Hill Gates, 219–232. Society for Economic Anthropology, Monographs in Economic Anthropology, no. 9. Lanham, Md.: University Press of America.
1993   Learning to Labor: Native American Education in the United States, 1880–1930. In *The Political Economy of North American Indians,* ed. John H. Moore, 43–59. Norman: University of Oklahoma Press.

Lockwood, Daniel
1872   Report to George M. Wheeler, 28 February. In *Preliminary Report Concerning Explorations and Surveys Principally in Nevada and Arizona,* by George Wheeler, App. A. Washington, D.C.: GPO.

Look Magazine, editors of
1946   *The Santa Fe Trail.* New York: Random House.
Lovegrove, R. A.
1907a   Letter to C. H. Asbury, 27 October. Bureau of Indian Affairs,
            Carson Indian School. RG 75. National Archives Branch Deposi-
            tory, San Bruno, Calif. Correspondence box 248B.
1907b   Letter to Supt. Asbury, 1 November. Carson Indian School Files.
            RG 75. National Archives Branch Depository, San Bruno, Calif.
            Correspondence box 248B.
1907c   Letter to Supt. Asbury, 3 November. Carson Indian School Files.
            RG 75. National Archives Branch Depository, San Bruno, Calif.
            Correspondence box 248B.
Luebben, Ralph A.
1964   Prejudice and Discrimination Against Navajos in a Mining
            Community. *Kiva* 30: 1–17.
Lummis, Charles
1902   Two Days at Mesa Grande. *Out West* 26(6): 602–612.
Lund, Sarah
1987   How I Remember. *Aroostook Micmac Council Newsletter* (November):
            3–5.
Lunt, Henry
n.d.   Journal. Typescript copy. Southern Utah State College (Cedar City),
            Special Collections.
Lurie, Nancy O.
1978   Winnebago. In *Handbook of North American Indians.* Vol. 15, *The
            Northeast,* ed. Bruce G. Trigger, 690–707. Washington, D.C.: Smith-
            sonian Institution Press.
Lurie, Nancy O., ed.
1961   *Mountain Wolf Woman.* Ann Arbor: University of Michigan Press.
Lyman, Amasa
1857–1863   Journal, no. 16. Typescript copy. Utah State Historical Society, Salt
            Lake City.
MacKay, Kathryn
1985   Warrior into Welder: A History of Federal Employment Programs
            for American Indians, 1879–1972. Ph.D. diss., University of Utah.
Madsen, Brigham D.
1980   *The Northern Shoshoni.* Caldwell, Idaho: Caxton Printers.

Magleby, Grant
1953   Memorandum to Ralph Gelvin, 23 November. Bureau of Indian
               Affairs, Phoenix Area Office Central Classified Files, 1937–1974.
               RG 75. National Archives Branch Depository, Laguna Niguel, Calif.
               Box 31.
Mallett, R. D.
n.d.   City and State Abstracts by R. D. Mallett and Co. Manistee (Mich.)
               Historical Museum.
Malouf, Carling
1966   Ethnohistory in the Great Basin. In *Current Status of Anthropological
               Research in the Great Basin: 1964*, ed. Warren d'Azevedo, Wilbur
               Davis, Don Fowler, and Wayne Suttles, 1–38. Desert Research
               Institute (Reno) Social Sciences and Humanities Publications, no. 1.
Malouf, Carling, and A. Arline Malouf
1945   The Effects of Spanish Slavery on the Indians of the Intermountain
               West. *Southwestern Journal of Anthropology* 1: 378–391.
Mangum, David Newton
1939   History of David Newton Mangum, 17 March. WPA Writer's Project
               Files, Utah State Historical Society, Salt Lake City.
Manistee County
1916   *Plat Book of Manistee County*. Chicago: Fred Wild.
1930   *Plat Book of Manistee County*. Rockford, Illinois: W. W. Hixson.
Manypenny, George
1880   *Our Indian Wards*. Cincinnati: Robert Clarke.
Marx, Karl
1906   *Capital*. Reprint, New York: Modern Library.
1972   Manifesto of the Communist Party. In *The Marx-Engels Reader*, ed.
               Robert C. Tucker, 331–362. New York: W. W. Norton.
Masayesva, Victor, and Erin Younger
1983   *Hopi Photographers/Hopi Images*. Tucson: Sun Tracks/University of
               Arizona Press.
Mathews, Mary McNair
1880   *Ten Years in Nevada: Or, Life on the Pacific Coast*. Buffalo, N.Y.: Baker,
               Jones.
Maxwell, James, ed.
1978   *America's Fascinating Indian Heritage*. Pleasantville, N.Y.: Reader's
               Digest Association.

Maxwell, Joseph
1913   Letter to Commissioner of Indian Affairs, 25 November. Bureau of Indian Affairs, Central Classified Files, 1907–1939. RG 75. National Archives.

McBeth, Sally J.
1983   *Ethnic Identity and the Boarding School Experience of West-Central Oklahoma American Indians.* Washington, D.C: University Press of America.

McBride, Bunny
1983   A Special Kind of Freedom. *Down East: Magazine of Maine 29*, no. 11: 88–93, 114.
1987   The Micmac of Maine: A Continuing Struggle. In *Rooted Like the Ash Trees: New England Indians and the Land*, ed. Richard G. Carlson, 35–39. Naugatuck, Conn.: Eagle Wing Press.

McBride, Bunny, and Harald E. L. Prins
1983   In Their Own Words: Oral Histories of Six Contemporary Aroostook Micmac Families. Unpub. ms. on file with the Aroostook Band of Micmacs, Presque Isle, and with authors.
1991   Micmacs and Splint Basketry: Tradition, Adaptation, and Survival. In *Our Lives in Our Hands: Micmac Indian Basketmakers*, ed. Bunny McBride, 3–23. Gardiner, Maine: Tilbury House.

McClurken, James M.
1988   We Wish to Be Civilized: Ottawa-American Political Contests on the Michigan Frontier. Ph.D. diss., Michigan State University, East Lansing.
1991   *Gah-Baeh-Jhagwah-Buk, The Way It Happened: A Visual Culture History of the Little Traverse Bay Bands of Odawa.* East Lansing: Michigan State University Museum.
1992a   Personal communication to Alice Littlefield.
1992b   Videotaped discussion. School Days Remembered: The Mt. Pleasant Indian School Reunion, 1991. Mt. Pleasant, Mich.: Saginaw Chippewa Tribe.
1993   Ethnohistorical Report on The Little River Band of Ottawa Indians. Unpublished ms., Little River Band Of Ottawa Indians, Manistee, Michigan.

McDonald, James A.
1994   Social Change and the Creation of Underdevelopment: A Northwest Coast Case. *American Ethnologist 21*: 152–175.

McEwan, J. Richard
1988   *Memories of a Micmac Life*. Fredericton, N.B.: Micmac-Maliseet Institute, University of New Brunswick.

McGerr, Michael
1993   The Persistence of Individualism. *The Chronicle of Higher Education*, 10 February, p. A48.

McKee, Jesse O.
1987   The Choctaw: Self-Determination and Economic Development. In *A Cultural Geography of North American Indians*, ed. Thomas E. Ross and Tyrel G. Moore, 173–190. Boulder, Colo.: Westview Press.

McKinstry, George
1859–1879   Diary of George McKinstry. Ms., San Diego (Calif.) Historical Society, Research Center and Archives.

McLuhan, T. C.
1985   *Dream Tracks: The Railroad and the American Indian, 1890–1930*. New York: Abrams.

McMaster, Joseph
1882   Letter to Commissioner of Indian Affairs, 29 August. In *Annual Report of the Commissioner of Indian Affairs*, 117–119. Washington, D.C.: GPO.

1884a   Letter to Commissioner of Indian Affairs, 15 August. In *Annual Report of the Commissioner of Indian Affairs*, 126–128. Washington, D.C.: GPO.

1884b   Letter to Commissioner of Indian Affairs, 22 September. Bureau of Indian Affairs, Letters Received, 1881–1907. RG 75. National Archives.

McNickle, D'Arcy
1962   *The Indian Tribes of the United States: Ethnic and Cultural Survival*. London: Oxford University Press.

1972   American Indians Who Never Were. In *The American Indian Reader: Anthropology*, ed. J. Henry, 23–28. San Francisco: Indian Historian Press.

1973   *Native American Tribalism: Indian Survivals and Renewals*. London: Oxford University Press.

Medacco, Moses K.
1930   Letter to Commissioner of Indian Affairs, 3 March. Bureau of Indian Affairs, Central Classified Files, 1907–1939. RG 75. National Archives. File CCF-Mt. Pleasant, 71953-1931, 013.

Medacco, Steve, and Dorothy Medacco
1991   Interview, June. Manistee, Mich.: Little River Band of Ottawa Indians. Unpub. transcript.

Meggitt, Mervyn J.
1962   *Desert People: A Study of the Walbiri Aborigines of Central Australia.* Sydney: Angus and Robertson.

Mekeel, H. Scudder
1932   A Discussion of Culture Change as Illustrated by Material from a Teton-Dakota Community. *American Anthropologist* 34: 274–285.
1936   The Economy of a Modern Teton Dakota Community. Yale University Publications in Anthropology, no. 6. New Haven: Yale University Press.

Meriam, Lewis et al.
1928   *The Problem of Indian Administration.* Baltimore: Johns Hopkins University Press.

Meyer, Roy W.
1969   *History of the Santee Sioux.* Lincoln: University of Nebraska Press.

Michigan County Atlas.
1977.   Lansing, Mich.: Universal Map Enterprises.

Michigan Commission on Indian Affairs
1992   *1990 and 1991 Biennial Report.* Lansing: Michigan Commission on Indian Affairs.

Micko, Charity, and Theresa Micko
1975   Interview, 12 September. Unpub. transcript. Grand Rapids (Mich.) Public Library, Michigan Room Collections.

Miller, Layne
1994   Clan Keeps Traditional Navajo Basket Weaving Alive. *Salt Lake Tribune,* 19 February, p. D1.

Miller, Susan
1975   Interview. Unpub. transcript. Grand Rapids (Mich.) Public Library, Michigan Room Collections.

Minge, Ward Alan
1991   *Acoma: Pueblo In the Sky.* Rev. ed. Albuquerque, N.M.: Pueblo of Acoma.

Mingione, Enzo
1991   *Fragmented Societies: The Sociology of Economic Life: Beyond the Market Paradigm.* London: Basil Blackwell.

Mitchell, J. Clyde
1966   Theoretical Orientations in African Urban Studies. In *The Social Anthropology of Complex Societies*, ed. Michael Banton, 37–68. London: Tavistock.

Mitchell, Joseph
1959   The Mohawks in High Steel. In *Apologies to the Iroquois*, by Edmund Wilson, 1–36. New York: Farrar, Straus and Cudahy.

Mooney, James
1903   Manuscript 2213. National Anthropological Archives, Washington, D.C.

Mooney, Kathleen
1976   Urban and Reserve Coast Salish Employment: A Test of Two Approaches to the Indian's Niche in North America. *Journal of Anthropological Research* 32: 390–410.

Moore, John H.
1987   *The Cheyenne Nation*. Lincoln: University of Nebraska Press.
1989   The Myth of the Lazy Indian: Native American Contributions to the U.S. Economy. *Nature, Society, and Thought* 2, no. 2: 195–215.
1991   Discussion. Symposium on Native Americans and Wage Labor, American Anthropological Association, Chicago, Ill., November.
1993   How Giveaways and Pow-Wows Redistribute the Means of Subsistence. In *The Political Economy of North American Indians*, ed. John H. Moore, 240–269. Norman: University of Oklahoma Press.

Morris, C. Patrick
1992   Termination by Accountants: The Reagan Indian Policy. In *Native Americans and Public Policy*, ed. Fremont J. Lyden and Lyman H. Legters, 63–84. Pittsburgh: University of Pittsburgh Press.

Munsell, Marvin R.
1967   Land and Labor at Salt River: Household Organization in a Changing Economy. Ph.D. diss., University of Oregon.

Nash, Gary B.
1992   *Red, White, and Black: The Peoples of Early North America*. Rev. ed. Englewood Cliffs, N.J.: Prentice-Hall.

Nagata, Shuichi
1970   *Modern Transformations of Moenkopi Pueblo*. Illinois Studies in Anthropology, no. 6. Urbana: University of Illinois Press.

1971   The Reservation Community and the Urban Community: Hopi Indians of Moenkopi. In *The American Indian in Urban Society*, ed. Jack O. Waddell and O. Michael Watson, 114–160. Boston: Little, Brown.

National Indian Association
1906   Indian Labor. *The Indian's Friend*. Rpt. June. New Haven, Conn.

Neils, Elaine M.
1971   *Reservation to City: Indian Migration and Federal Relocation*. University of Chicago Dept. of Geography Research Paper, no. 131.

Nelson, E. W.
1891   The Panamint and Saline Valley (California) Indians. *American Anthropologist* 4: 371–372.

Nespor, Robert
1984   The Evolution of the Agricultural Settlement Pattern of the Southern Cheyenne Indians in Western Oklahoma, 1876–1930, Ph.D. diss., University of Oklahoma.

News from Indian Country
1991   Tribes, Communities Mobilize to Support Indian Troops. Vol. 5, issue 4 (late February): 2. Hayward, Wisconsin: Indian Country Communications.
1992   Native Firefighters Battle Blazes in Montana and Across the Nation. Vol. 6, issue 14 (late July): 10. Hayward, Wisconsin: Indian Country Communications.

Nicholas, Andrea B., with contributions by Harald E. L. Prins
1989   The Spirit in the Land: The Native People of Aroostook. In *The County: Land of Promise: A Pictorial History of Aroostook County, Maine*, ed. Anna F. McGrath, 19–38. Norfolk, Va.: Donning.

Nichols, Roger L.
1965   *General Henry Atkinson*. Norman: University of Oklahoma Press.

Nietfeld, Patricia K. L.
1981   Determinants of Aboriginal Micmac Political Structure. Ph.D. diss., University of New Mexico, Albuquerque.

Norris, Joseph
1910a   General Investigation of Conditions at the Shivwits Agency, 25 July. Bureau of Indian Affairs, Central Classified Files, 1907–1939. RG 75. National Archives.
1910b   Report to Secretary of the Interior, 5 November. Bureau of Indian Affairs, Central Classified Files, 1907–1939. RG 75. National Archives.

Nowak, Barbara
1976   Women's Roles and Status in a Changing Iroquois Society. In *Sex Roles in Changing Cultures*, ed. Ann McElroy and C. Matthiasson, 95–111. Occasional Papers in Anthropology, no. 1. Buffalo: Dept. of Anthropology, State University of New York.

Nybroten, Norman
1964   *Economy and Conditions of the Fort Hall Indian Reservation*. University of Idaho (Moscow) Bureau of Business and Economic Research Research Report, no. 9.

Officer, James E.
1971   The American Indian and Federal Policy. In *The American Indian in Urban Society*, ed. Jack O. Waddell and O. Michael Watson, 9–65. Boston: Little, Brown.

Ogabegijigokwe, Margaret (Boyd)
1877   Margaret Ogabegijigokwe to President Grant, 7 January. Correspondence of the Office of Indian Affairs (Central Office) and Related Records—Letters Received. RG 75. National Archives. Microcopy M234, reel 412, frames 468–471.

Olexer, Barbara
1982   *The Enslavement of the American Indian*. Monroe, N.Y.: Library Research Associates.

Oliver, Jay
1990   Interview, 27 March. East Lansing: Anthropology Division, Michigan State University. Unpub. transcript.

Olson, Edwardine
1928   Letter to Director of Indian Reservation, 12 November. Bureau of Indian Affairs, Central Classified Files, 1907–1939. RG 75. National Archives. File CCF-Mt. Pleasant 55390-1928, 115.

Olson, James S., and Raymond Wilson
1984   *Native Americans in the Twentieth Century*. Urbana: University of Illinois Press.

Omish, Gregorio
1893–1910   Journal of Gregorio Omish. In the possession of Florence Shipek, San Diego, Calif.

Ong, Aihwa
1991   The Gender and Labor Politics of Postmodernity. *Annual Review of Anthropology* 20: 279–309.

Opler, Morris E.
1983   Mescalero Apache. In *Handbook of North American Indians*. Vol.
            10, *Southwest*, ed. Alfonso Ortiz, 419–439. Washington, D.C.:
            Smithsonian Institution Press.
Painter, Charles
1886   *A Visit to the Mission Indians of Southern California*. Philadelphia:
            Indian Rights Association.
Papin, T.
1831   Letter to P. M. Papin, 24 February. Chouteau Collection, Missouri
            Historical Society, St. Louis.
Parezo, Nancy
1983   *Navajo Sandpainting: From Religious Act to Commercial Art*.
            Albuquerque: University of New Mexico Press.
Parker, H. G.
1869   Letter to E. S. Parker, Commissioner of Indian Affairs, 20 September
            1869. In *Annual Report of the Commissioner of Indian Affairs*, letter
            36. Washington, D.C.: GPO.
Parman, Donald L.
1971   The Indian and the Civilian Conservation Corps. *Pacific Historical
            Review* 40 (February): 39–56.
Patterson, Hank
1986   Personal communication to author. January.
Paybame, et al.
1869   Proceedings of a Council Held at Paybawme, Oceana County, State
            of Michigan, 24–26 July. Correspondence of the Office of Indian
            Affairs (Central Office) and Related Records—Letters Received. RG
            75. National Archives. Microcopy M234, reel 408, frames 781–808.
Peet, Mary
1949   *San Pasqual: A Crack in the Hills*. Privately published, San Diego.
Pego, George
1991   Interview, 11 May. Manistee, Mich.: Little River Band of Ottawa
            Indians. Unpub. transcript.
Perry, Richard J.
1993   *Apache Reservation: Indigenous Peoples and the American State*. Austin:
            University of Texas Press.
Peters, Grace
1975   Interview. Unpub. transcript. Grand Rapids (Mich.) Public Library,
            Michigan Room Collections.

Peters, Ike
1991   Interview, 22 July. Manistee, Mich.: Little River Band of Ottawa
            Indians. Unpub. transcript.
Peterson, Jacqueline
1985   Many Roads to Red River: Métis Genesis in the Great Lakes Region.
            In *The New Peoples: Being and Becoming Métis in North America*,
            ed. Jacqueline Peterson and Jennifer S. H. Brown, pp. 37–71.
            Manitoba Studies in Native History, no. 1. Lincoln: University of
            Nebraska Press.
Peterson, Jacqueline, and Jennifer S. H. Brown, eds.
1985   *The New Peoples: Being and Becoming Métis in North America.*
            Manitoba Studies in Native History, no. 1. Lincoln: University of
            Nebraska Press.
Peterson, Jennifer, and John Anfinson
1984   The Indian and the Fur Trade: Review of Recent Literature. In
            *Scholars and the Indian Experience: Critical Reviews of Recent Writing
            in the Social Sciences*, ed. William R. Swagerty, 223–257.
            Bloomington: Indiana University Press for D'Arcy McNickle Center
            for the History of the American Indian, Newberry Library.
Peterson, John H.
1992   Choctaw Self-Determination in the 1980s. In *Indians of the
            Southeastern United States in the Late Twentieth Century*, ed. J.
            Anthony Paredes, 140–161. Tuscaloosa: University of Alabama Press.
Phillips, George Harwood
1980   Indians in Los Angeles, 1781–1875: Economic Integration, Social
            Disintegration. *Pacific Historical Review* 49, no. 3: 179–193.
Phillips, Paul C.
1961   *The Fur Trade.* 2 vols. Norman: University of Oklahoma Press.
Pikyavit, Robert
1909   Letter to Commissioner of Indian Affairs, 6 December. Bureau of
            Indian Affairs, Central Classified Files, 1907–1939. RG 75. National
            Archives.
Pioche Daily Record
1875   Pine Nut Gathering . . . . 1 September, p. 3, col. 1.
Pioche Weekly Record
1885a   The New Pine-Nut Crop . . . . 29 August, p. 3, col. 1.
1885b   In Demand. 10 October, p. 3, col. 1.

1889   The Iron Roof over . . . . 19 January, p. 3, col. 2.

1891a   [No Title]. 21 May, p. 3, col. 3.

1891b   The River Is Depended on for Drift Wood . . . . 21 May, p. 3, col. 3.

Piute Company of California and Nevada, The.

1870   San Francisco: Edward Bosquie.

Plessis, Joseph-Octave

1903   *Journal des visites pastorales de 1815 et 1816 par Monseigneur Joseph-Octave Plessis Eveque de Quebec.* Quebec: Tetu.

Polanyi, Karl

1944   *The Great Transformation.* New York: Rinehart.

Poole, Carolyn

1988   Reservation Policy and the Economic Position of Wichita Women. *Great Plains Quarterly* 8: 158–171.

Porter, Andrew

1855   Letter to Walter Lowrie, 26 March 1855. Presbyterian Historical Society Collection, American Indian Correspondence: Collection of Missionaries' Letters, 1833–1893. Library of Congress. Microfilm, box 7, vol. 1: 154.

Powdermaker, Hortense

1962   *Copper Town: Changing Africa.* New York: Harper and Row.

Pratt, Richard Henry

1964   *Battlefield and Classroom: Four Decades with the American Indian, 1867–1904,* ed. Robert M. Utley. New Haven: Yale University Press.

Price, John A.

1968   The Migration and Adaptation of American Indians to Los Angeles. *Human Organization* 27: 168–177.

Prins, Harald E. L.

1982a   Genesis of the Micmac Community in Maine and Its Intricate Relationship to Micmac Reserves in the Maritimes. Unpub. report on file with the Aroostook Band of Micmacs, Presque Isle, Maine, and with author.

1982b   Unpub. fieldnotes of visit to Micmac Reserves in Canada.

1983   Social and Economic Profile of the Aroostook Micmac Band in Northern Maine, as based on the A.M.C. Census. Unpub. report on file with the Aroostook Band of Micmacs, Presque Isle, Maine, and with author.

1986a   The Aroostook Micmac Band in Maine: An Ethnohistorical View. Document Prepared for the Federal Acknowledgment Petition to the Bureau of Indian Affairs. Unpub. report on file with the Aroostook Band of Micmacs, Presque Isle, Maine; with Pine Tree Legal Assistance, Augusta, Maine; and with author.

1986b   Micmacs and Maliseets in the St. Lawrence River Valley. *Actes du dix-septieme congres des Algonquinistes*, ed. William Cowan, 263–278. Ottawa: Carleton University Press.

1988   Tribulations of a Border Tribe: A Discourse on the Political Ecology of the Aroostook Band of Micmacs (Sixteenth–Twentieth Centuries). Ph.D. diss., New School for Social Research, New York.

1990   The Aroostook Band of Micmacs: An Historical Anthropological Review. In *Hearing Before the Select Committee on Indian Affairs on S. 1413 to Settle All Claims of the Aroostook Band of Micmacs Resulting from the Band's Omission from the Maine Indian Claims Settlement Act of 1980.* 101st Cong., 2d sess. March 28. Washington, D.C.: GPO.

1994   Micmac. In *Native America in the Twentieth Century: An Encyclopedia*, ed. Mary B. Davis, 339–340. New York and London: Garland Publishing.

1996   *The Mi'kmaq: Resistance, Accommodation, and Cultural Survival.* Fort Worth, Texas: Harcourt Brace.

Prucha, Francis Paul

1975   *Documents of United States Indian Policy.* Lincoln: University of Nebraska Press.

1984   *The Great Father: The United States Government and the American Indians.* 2 vols. Lincoln: University of Nebraska Press.

Putnam, George P.

1946   *Death Valley and Its Country.* New York: Duell, Sloan, and Pearce.

Quinn, William

1993   Intertribal Integration: The Ethnological Argument in *Duro* v. *Reina*. *Ethnohistory* 40: 34–69.

Rabinow, Paul

1986   Representations Are Social Facts: Modernity and Post-Modernity in Anthropology. In *Writing Culture: The Poetics and Politics of Ethnography*, ed. James Clifford and George E. Marcus, 234–261. Berkeley and Los Angeles: University of California Press.

Radin, Paul
1963   *The Autobiography of a Winnebago Indian.* New York: Dover.
Randle, Martha C.
1953   A Shoshone Hand Game Gambling Song. *Journal of American
            Folklore* 66, no. 260: 155–159.
Ray, Arthur, and Donald Freeman
1978   *Give Us Good Measure: An Economic Analysis of Relations Between
            Indians and the Hudson's Bay Company Before 1763.* Toronto:
            University of Toronto Press.
Reddy, Marlita A., ed.
1993   *Statistical Record of Native North Americans.* Detroit: Gale Research.
Redfield, Robert
1953   *The Primitive World and Its Transformations.* Ithaca: Cornell
            University Press.
Redfield, Robert, Ralph Linton, and Melville Herskovits
1936   Memorandum on the Study of Acculturation. *American
            Anthropologist* 38: 149–152.
Reese, John
1861   Letter to Utah Territory Superintendent of Indian Affairs, 3
            February. Bureau of Indian Affairs, Letters Received, 1824–1881.
            RG 75. National Archives.
Reich, Michael
1981   *Racial Inequality.* London: Macmillan.
Reynolds, Jerry
1990   Devil's Lake Wins in Corporate Struggle. *Lakota Times* 27
            November, pp. A1, A7.
Richards, Audrey I.
1961   *Land, Labour and Diet in Northern Rhodesia.* Oxford: Oxford
            University Press.
Ritterbush, Lauren
1990   Culture Change and Continuity: Ethnohistoric Analysis of Ojibwa
            and Ottawa Adjustment to the Prairies. Ph.D. diss., University of
            Kansas, Lawrence.
Robbins, Lynn A.
1968   Economics, Household Composition, and the Family Cycle: The
            Blackfeet Case. In *Spanish-Speaking People in the United States,* ed.
            June Helm, 196–215. Seattle: University of Washington Press.

1978   Navajo Labor and the Establishment of a Voluntary Workers Association. *Journal of Ethnic Studies* 6, no. 3: 97–112.

Roberts, John M.

1965   *Zuni Daily Life.* New Haven: Human Relations Area Files Press.

Roe, Frank Gilbert

1951   *The North American Buffalo.* Toronto: University of Toronto Press.

Rogers, Barbara

1980   *The Domestication of Women: Discrimination in Developing Societies.* London: Tavistock.

Romero, Mary

1992   *Maid in the U.S.A.* New York: Routledge.

Rosaldo, Renato

1989   *Culture and Truth: The Remaking of Social Analysis.* Boston: Beacon Press.

Ross, P. S., and partners

1974   An Economic Development Study for the Restigouche Indian Reserve, Restigouche, 1966. Unpub. report cited in Claude Audet, *Les indiens de Ristigouche,* 46–47. Rimouski, Que.: College de Rimouski.

Rossel, Pierre, ed.

1988   *Tourism: Manufacturing the Exotic.* Copenhagen: International Work Group for Indigenous Affairs.

Rothenberg, Diane

1980   The Mothers of the Nation: Seneca Resistance to Quaker Intervention. In *Women and Colonization: Anthropological Perspectives,* ed. Mona Etienne and Eleanor Leacock, 63–87. New York: Praeger.

Rothfuss, Edwin L.

1992   Death Valley Burros. In *Proceedings Third Death Valley Conference on History and Prehistory,* ed. James Pisarowicz, 182–206. Death Valley, Calif.: Natural History Association.

Rothstein, Frances A.

1992   What Happens to the Past? Return Industrial Migrants in Latin America. In *Anthropology and the Global Factory,* ed. Frances Rothstein and Michael L. Blim, 33–46. New York: Bergin and Garvey.

Rothstein, Frances A., and Michael L. Blim, eds.

1992   *Anthropology and the Global Factory.* New York: Bergin and Garvey.

Rowe, Eugene
1965   Maine's Potato Empire and How It Grew. *Produce Marketing* (October): n.p.
Rubenstein, Bruce Alan
1974   Justice Denied: An Analysis of American Indian–White Relations in Michigan, 1855–1889. Ph.D. diss., Michigan State University.
Rubery, Jill
1978   Structured Labor Markets, Worker Organization, and Low Pay. *Cambridge Journal of Economics* 2: 14–36.
Rudkin, Charles, trans. and ed.
1956   *Observations on California 1772–1790 by Father Luis Sales O.P.* Los Angeles: Dawson's Book Shop.
Ruiz, Vicki
1987   *Cannery Women, Cannery Lives: Mexican Women, Unionization, and the California Food Processing Industry, 1930–1950.* Albuquerque: University of New Mexico Press.
Runke, Walter
1907   Letter to Commissioner of Indian Affairs, 10 December. Bureau of Indian Affairs, Central Classified Files, 1907–1939. RG 75. National Archives.
1908   Letter to Commissioner of Indian Affairs, 7 April. Bureau of Indian Affairs, Central Classified Files, 1907–1939. National Archives.
Ruonavaara, Lois Jane, and Judy Rodgers
1981   Homesteading. In *Harbor Springs: A Collection of Essays*, ed. Jan Morley, pp. 11–16. Harbor Springs, Mich.: Harbor Springs Historical Commission.
Rusco, Elmer
1991   Indian Reorganization Act in Nevada: Creation of the Yomba Reservation. *Journal of California and Great Basin Anthropology* 13: 77–94.
Sacks, Karen
1988   *Caring by the Hour.* Urbana: University of Illinois Press.
1989   Toward a Unified Theory of Class, Race, and Gender. *American Ethnologist* 16, no. 3: 534–550.
Sacks, Karen, and Dorothy Remy, eds.
1984   *My Troubles Are Going to Have Trouble with Me: Everyday Trials and Triumphs of Women Workers.* New Brunswick: Rutgers University Press.

Saginaw Chippewa Indian Tribe
1992   School Days Remembered: The Mt. Pleasant Indian School
            Reunion 1991. Videotape.
Salt Lake Tribune
1951   Letter to Officials Requests Indian Worker Screening. 1 February.
Sam, Alex
1990   Interview, 30 July. Manistee, Mich.: Little River Band of Ottawa
            Indians. Unpub. transcript.
Sam, Rose
1990   Interview with Rose Sam, Connie Waitner, and Katie Sam
            Glocheski, 31 July. Manistee, Mich.: Little River Band of Ottawa
            Indians. Unpub. transcript.
San Diego Herald
1853   [No title]. 23 September, p. 2.
1853b   [No title]. 24 September, p. 2.
1853c   [No title]. 7 October, p. 2.
1853d   [No title]. 8 October, p. 2.
San Diego Union
1856   [No title]. 9 February, p. 2.
1857   [No title]. 5 May, p. 2.
1880   [No title]. 1 February, p. 4.
1881a   [No title]. 30 January, p. 4.
1881b   [No title]. 5 May, p. 4.
1881c   [No title]. 3 June, p. 4.
1890   [No title]. 6 November, p. 8.
1895   [No title]. 12 November, pp. 4–5.
Santa Fe Pacific Railroad Co.
1897   Approval by Dept. of Interior of Capital Stock Transfer, 29 June.
            Santa Fe Collection, Kansas Historical Society, Kansas State
            Museum, Topeka.
Satz, Ronald
1991   Chippewa Treaty Rights: The Reserved Rights of Wisconsin's Chip-
            pewa Indians in Historical Perspective. Wisconsin Academy of
            Sciences, Arts, and Letters. *Transactions* 79, no. 1:1–251.
Satz, Ronald, Anthony Gulig, and Richard St. Germaine
1991   *Classroom Activities on Chippewa Treaty Rights.* Madison: Wisconsin
            Dept. of Public Instruction.

Saxton, Alexander
1971   *The Indispensible Enemy: The Anti-Chinese Movement in California.*
             Berkeley and Los Angeles: University of California Press.
Schneider, Mary Jane
1986   *North Dakota Indians: An Introduction.* Dubuque, Iowa: Kendell
             Hunt.
Schoolcraft, Henry R.
1839   Ottawa and Chippewa Annuity Roll. Henry Rowe Schoolcraft
             Papers. Library of Congress. Microfilm, reel 8, frame 41828.
Scott, Mel
1985   *The San Francisco Bay Area: A Metropolis in Perspective.* Berkeley
             and Los Angeles: University of California Press.
Sears, S. S.
1889   Letter to John Oberly, 11 June. Bureau of Indian Affairs, Letters
             Received, 1881–1907. RG 75, National Archives.
1890   Letter to Thomas J. Morgan, 15 February. Bureau of Indian Affairs,
             Letters Received, 1881–1907. RG 75. National Archives.
Selkrig, James
1855   Letter to Henry Gilbert, 30 June. Bureau of Indian Affairs, Letters
             Received by the Michigan Superintendency and Mackinac Agency,
             1849–1869. RG 75. National Archives. Entry 1131.
Sennett, Beth
1985–1986   Fieldnotes in possession of the author.
Shally, Dorothy, and William Bolton
1973   *Scotty's Castle.* Yosemite, Calif.: Flying Spur Press.
Sharp, William
1903   Letter to Commissioner of Indian Affairs, 26 January. Bureau of
             Indian Affairs, Letters Received, 1881–1907. RG 75. National
             Archives.
1904   Letter to Commissioner of Indian Affairs, 15 August. In *Annual
             Report of the Commissioner of Indian Affairs*, 244–245. Washington,
             D.C.: GPO.
1907   Letter to Commissioner of Indian Affairs, 1 July. Bureau of Indian
             Affairs, Central Classified Files, 1907–1939. RG 75. National
             Archives.
Shaw, Ivy
1986   Personal communication to author. January.

Shifferd, Patricia A.
1976   A Study in Economic Change: The Chippewa of Northern Wis-
            consin, 1854–1900. *Western Canadian Journal of Anthropology* 6, no.
            4: 16–41.
Shipek, Florence C.
1977   Strategy for Change: The Luiseño of Southern California. Ph.D.
            diss. University of Hawaii.
1982   Kumeyaay Socio-Political Structure. *Journal of California and Great
            Basin Anthropology* 4, no. 2: 293–303.
1986   The Impacts of Europeans upon Kumeyaay Culture. In *The Impact
            of European Exploration and Settlement on Local Native Americans*,
            pp. 13–25. Cabrillo Festival Historic Seminar. San Diego: Cabrillo
            Historical Association.
1988   Research notes and interviews on file with the author, San Diego,
            Calif.
1991   Docket 80-A, United States Court of Claims.
Shorten, Lillian Negake
1992   Videotaped discussion. School Days Remembered: The Mt.
            Pleasant Indian School Reunion, 1991. Mt. Pleasant, Mich.: Saginaw
            Chippewa Tribe.
Simmons, William S.
1978   Narragansett. In *Handbook of North American Indians*. Vol. 15, *The
            Northeast*, ed. Bruce G. Trigger, 190–197. Washington, D.C: Smith-
            sonian Institution Press.
Simonds, John C., and John T. McEnnis
1887   *The Story of Manual Labor*. Chicago: R. S. Peale.
Smith, Gavin
1991   Writing for Real: Capitalist Constructions and Constructions of
            Capitalism. *Critique of Anthropology* 11, no. 3: 213–232.
Smith, George A.
1852   Letter to Samuel Richards, 7 November. *Millennial Star*, p. 188.
1855   Letter to Editor, 18 May. *Deseret News*, p. 92.
Smith, Jesse Nathaniel
1970   *Six Decades in the Early West: Journals of Jesse Nathaniel Smith*. Provo,
            Utah: privately published.
Smith, Richard
1871   Report of Richard M. Smith to H. R. Clum, 18 September. In *Annual
            Report of the Commissioner of Indian Affairs*, 924–927. Washington,
            D.C.: GPO.

Smith, Titus
1974   Extract from 1801–1802 Journal. *Micmac News,* 4 no. 10: 4.
Snipp, C. Matthew
1980   Determinants of Employment in Wisconsin Native American Communities. *Growth and Change* 11: 39–47.
1986a   The Changing Political and Economic Status of the American Indians: From Captive Nations to Internal Colonies. *American Journal of Economics and Sociology* 45, no. 2: 145–158.
1986b   Who Are American Indians? Some Observations About the Perils and Pitfalls of Data for Race and Ethnicity. *Population Research and Policy Review* 5: 237–252.
1989   *American Indians: The First of This Land.* New York: Russell Sage Foundation.
Snyder, Peter Z.
1968   *Social Assimilation and Adjustment of Navajo Migrants to Denver, Colorado.* University of Colorado Navajo Urban Relocation Research Report, no. 13.
Sokoloff, Natalie
1980   *Between Money and Love: The Dialectics of Women's Home Work and Market Work.* New York: Praeger.
1991   *Black Women and White Women in the Professions: Occupational Segregation by Race and Gender, 1960–1980.* New York: Routledge.
Sorkin, Alan
1970   Trends in Employment and Earnings of American Indians. In *Toward Economic Development for Native American Communities: A Compendium of Papers Submitted to the Subcommittee on Economy in Government of the Joint Economic Committee, Congress of the United States,* 107–118. Reprint, New York: Arno Press.
1973   Manpower Programs for American Indians. *Journal of Economics and Business* 26: 49–57.
Sowell, Thomas
1981   *Markets and Minorities.* New York: Basic Books.
Spicer, Edward H.
1954   Spanish-Indian Acculturation in the Southwest. *American Anthropologist* 56: 663–678.
1962   *Cycles of Conquest: The Impact of Spain, Mexico, and the United States on the Indians of the Southwest, 1533–1960.* Tucson: University of Arizona Press.

1971 Persistent Cultural Systems: A Comparative Study of Identity Systems That Can Adapt to Contrasting Environments. *Science* 174, no. 19: 798.

Spindler, George, and Louise Spindler

1971 *Dreamers Without Power: The Menomini Indians.* New York: Holt, Rinehart and Winston.

Spindler, Louise S.

1978 Menominee. In *Handbook of North American Indians.* Vol. 15, *The Northeast,* ed. Bruce G. Trigger, 708–724. Washington, D.C.: Smithsonian Institution Press.

Spradley, James, ed.

1969 *Guests Never Leave Hungry: The Autobiography of James Sewid, a Kwakiutl Indian.* New Haven: Yale University Press.

Sprenger, Herman

1988 The Métis Nation: Buffalo Hunting Versus Agriculture in the Red River Settlement, 1810–1870. In *Native People, Native Lands,* ed. Bruce Cox, 120–135. Ottawa: Carleton University Press.

Spriggs, Fred

1906 Letter to Commissioner of Indian Affairs, 15 September. In *Annual Report of the Commissioner of Indian Affairs,* 271–272. Washington, D.C.: GPO.

Spruce, Albert

1992 Videotaped discussion. School Days Remembered: The Mt. Pleasant Indian School Reunion, 1991. Mt. Pleasant, Mich.: Saginaw Chippewa Tribe.

Stanley, Sam, ed.

1978 *American Indian Economic Development.* The Hague: Mouton.

Stedman, Raymond

1982 *Shadows of the Indian: Stereotypes in American Culture.* Norman: University of Oklahoma Press.

Steele, John

n.d. Reminiscences and Journals, 1846–1898. Typescript copy. Church Historian's Office, Church of Jesus Christ of Latter-day Saints, Salt Lake City, ms. no. 1847.

Steward, Julian

1970 *Basin-Plateau Aboriginal Sociopolitical Groups.* Bureau of American Ethnology Bulletin 120. 1938. Reprint, Salt Lake City: University of Utah Press.

Stewart, Helen J.
n.d.   Account books. Helen J. Stewart Papers. Nevada State Historical Society, Las Vegas.

Streeper, Mary Amelia
1867   Letter to Mary Ann, 12 December. Microfilm copy. Church Historian's Office, Church of Jesus Christ of Latter-day Saints, Salt Lake City, ms. no. 9430.

Strong, John A.
1994   The Imposition of Colonial Jurisdiction over the Montauk Indians of Long Island. *Ethnohistory* 41, no. 4: 561–590.

Stucki, Larry R.
1982   Will the "Real" Indian Survive?: Tourism and Affluence at Cherokee, North Carolina. In *Affluence and Cultural Survival*, ed. R. Salisbury and E. Tooker, 53–73. Washington, D.C.: American Ethnological Society.

Sunder, John E.
1965   *The Fur Trade on the Upper Missouri, 1840–1865.* Norman: University of Oklahoma Press.

Szasz, Margaret Connell
1974   *Education and the American Indian: The Road to Self-Determination Since 1928.* Albuquerque: University of New Mexico Press.

Tabeau, Pierre A.
1939   *Tabeau's Narrative of Loisel's Expedition to the Upper Missouri.* Norman: University of Oklahoma Press.

Takaki, Ronald
1979   *Iron Cages: Race and Culture in 19th-Century America.* New York: Random House.

Talbot, Steve
1981   *Roots of Oppression.* New York: International Publishers.
1985   Native Americans and the Working Class. In *Ethnicity and the Work Force*, ed. Winston Van Horne and Thomas V. Tonnesen, 65–95. Ethnicity and Public Policy Series. Milwaukee: University of Wisconsin System, American Ethnic Studies Coordinating Committee.

Tanner, Adrian
1979   *Bringing Home Animals.* New York: St. Martin's Press.

Tawney, Ella, and Eli Thomas
1975   Interview, 14 May. Unpub. ms., Grand Rapids (Mich.) Public Library, Michigan Room Collections.

Taylor, Garth
1986   Assiginac's Canoe. *The Beaver* 66, no. 5: 50–53.

Thomas, David H.
1971   Historic and Prehistoric Land-Use Patterns at Reese River. *Nevada Historical Society Quarterly* 14: 3–10.

Thomas, Dianne H.
1978   *Southwestern Indian Detours.* Phoenix: Hunter.

Thomas, H. A.
1866   Letter to Franklin Campbell, 28 August. In *Annual Report of the Commissioner of Indian Affairs*, 120–121. Washington, D.C.: GPO.

Thomas-Lycklema à Nÿeholt, G.
1980   *On the Road for Work: Migratory Workers on the East Coast of the United States.* The Hague: Martinus Nijhoff.

Thornton, Russell
1987   *American Indian Holocaust and Survival: A Population History Since 1492.* Norman: University of Oklahoma Press.
1990   *The Cherokees: A Population History.* Norman: University of Oklahoma Press.

Tienda, Marta, and Leif Jensen
1986   Poverty and Social Policy: The Minority Experience. IRP Conference Paper. Madison: University of Wisconsin.

Tiffany, Susan Davis
1973   Interview. Typescript. Bancroft Library, Berkeley, Calif.

Trelease, Allen W.
1960   *Indian Affairs in Colonial New York: The Seventeenth Century.* Ithaca: Cornell University Press.

Trennert, Robert A. Jr.
1982   Educating Indian Girls at Nonreservation Boarding Schools, 1878–1920. *Western Historical Quarterly* 13: 271–290.
1983   From Carlisle to Phoenix: The Rise and Fall of the Indian Outing System, 1878–1930. *Pacific Historical Review* 59: 267–291.
1988   *The Phoenix Indian School: Forced Assimilation in Arizona, 1891–1935.* Norman: University of Oklahoma Press.

Trimble, Stephen
1993   The People: Indians of the American Southwest. Santa Fe: School of American Research.

Trosper, Ronald
1978   American Indian Relative Ranching Efficiency. The American Economic Review 68(4): 503–516.

Turner, J. G.
1857   Letter to Walter Lowrie, 10 September. Presbyterian Historical Society Collection, American Indian Correspondence: Collection of Missionaries' Letters, 1833–1893. Library of Congress. Microfilm, box 7, vol. 2, 30.

Tyler, S. Lyman
1973   A History of Indian Policy. Washington, D.C.: Bureau of Indian Affairs.

Uchendu, Victor Chikezie
1966   Seasonal Agricultural Labor Among the Navaho Indians: A Study in Socio-Economic Transition. Ph.D. diss. Northwestern University.

Union Pacific Railroad
1890   Utah and the Mountain West: Sights and Scenes. Omaha: Union Pacific.

United States
1859   Ottawa and Chippewa Annuity Payroll. RG 75. National Archives.
1872   An Act for the Restoration to Market of Certain Lands in Michigan, 5 July. U.S. Statutes at Large 11, 621.
1875   An Act to Amend the Act Entitled 'An Act for the Restoration of Homestead Entry,' 3 March 1875. U.S. Statutes at Large 18, 516
1876   An Act Extending the Time Within Which Homestead Entries upon Certain Lands in Michigan May Be Made, 23 May 1876. U.S. Statutes at Large 19, 55.
1894   Report on Indians Taxed   dndians Not Taxed in the United States at the Eleventh Census, 1890. Department of the Interior. Washington, D.C.: GPO.

United States, Civil Rights Commission
1973   The Southwest Indian Report. Washington, D.C.: GPO.

United States, Congress, Joint Economic Committee, Subcommittee on Economy in Government.
1969   Toward Economic Development for Native American Communities. 2 vols. Washington, D.C.: GPO.

United States, Department of the Interior
1982   Technical Reports Regarding the Death Valley Timbisha Shoshone
              Band of Death Valley, CA. Prepared in Response to a Petition
              submitted to the Secretary of the Interior for Federal Acknowledg-
              ment that the Death Valley Timbisha Shoshone Band Exists as
              an Indian Tribe. Washington, D.C.: National Park Service.
1984   *American Indians.* Washington, D.C.
1986   *Report of the Task Force on Indian Economic Development.* Washington,
              D.C.: Office of Policy Analysis.
United States, National Park Service
1925-1931   Construction Files, Indian Affairs, Payroll Records. Scotty's Castle,
              Death Valley National Monument, Calif.
Upton, Leslie F. S.
1979   *Micmacs and Colonists: Indian-White Relations in the Maritimes,
              1713-1867.* Vancouver: University of British Columbia Press.
Urry, John
1990   *The Tourist Gaze.* London: Sage.
Van Kirk, Sylvia
1980   *Many Tender Ties: Women in Fur-Trade Society, 1670–1870.* Norman:
              University of Oklahoma Press.
Vizenor, Gerald
1984   *The People Named the Chippewa: Narrative Histories.* Minneapolis:
              University of Minnesota Press.
1987   Socioacupuncture: Mythic Reversals and the Striptease in Four
              Scenes. In *The American Indian and the Problem of History,* ed. Calvin
              Martin, 180–191. New York: Oxford University Press.
Voget, Fred
1953   Kinship Changes at Caughnawaga. *American Anthropologist* 55:
              385–395.
Vogt, Evon Z.
1951   *Navaho Veterans: A Study of Changing Values.* Harvard University
              Peabody Museum of American Archaeology and Ethnology Papers,
              no. 41. Cambridge, Mass.
Waddell, Jack O.
1969   *Papago Indians at Work.* Tucson: University of Arizona Press.
Waitner, Connie
1990   Interview with Connie Waitner and Katie Sam Glocheski, 30 July.
              Unpub. transcript. Manistee, Mich.: Little River Band of Ottawa
              Indians.

Wallace, Anthony F. C.
1969   *The Death and Rebirth of the Seneca.* New York: Vintage Books.
Wallace, William J.
1980   Death Valley Indian Farming. *Journal of California and Great Basin Anthropology* 2: 269–272.
Wallerstein, Immanuel
1974   *The Modern World-System: Capitalist Agriculture and the Origins of the European World-Economy in the Sixteenth Century.* New York: Academic Press.
Wallis, Wilson D., and Ruth S. Wallis.
1953   Culture Loss and Culture Change Among the Micmac of the Canadian Maritime Provinces, 1912–1950. Kroeber Anthropological Society Papers, nos. 8–9, 100–129. Berkeley: University of California.
1955   *The Micmac Indians of Eastern Canada.* Minneapolis: University of Minnesota Press.
Wallman, Sandra, ed.
1979   *Social Anthropology of Work.* Association of Social Anthropologists Monograph 19. New York: Academic Press.
Ward, Ralph A.
1910   Letter to Commissioner of Indian Affairs, 31 January. Bureau of Indian Affairs, Central Classified Files, 1907–1939. RG 75. National Archives.
Warner, Juan José
1852   Minority Report to the Senate and Assembly of the State of California. *Journal of the Third Session of the Legislature of California.* Sacramento: G. K. Fitch and Company, State Printers.
Warner, Charles C.
1891   Letter to Commissioner of Indian Affairs, 13 February. Bureau of Indian Affairs, Letters Received, 1881–1907. RG 75. National Archives.
1893   Letter to Commissioner of Indian Affairs, 8 April. Bureau of Indian Affairs, Letters Received, 1881–1907. RG 75. National Archives.
Washburn, Wilcomb E.
1975   *The Indian in America.* New York: Harper Colophon.
Washburn, Wilcomb E., ed.
1988   *History of Indian-White Relations.* Vol. 4, *Handbook of North American Indians.* Washington, D.C.: Smithsonian Institution Press.

Waters, Lawrence L.
1950   *Steel Trails to Santa Fe*. Lawrence: University Press of Kansas.

Watson, William
1959   Migrant Labour in Africa South of the Sahara: Migrant Labour and Detribalisation. *Bulletin of the Inter-African Labour Institute* 6: 8–33.

Wax, Murray L.
1971   *Indian Americans: Unity and Diversity*. Englewood Cliffs, N.J.: Prentice-Hall.

Weaver, Sally M.
1978   Six Nations of the Grand River, Ontario. In *Handbook of North American Indians*. Vol. 15, *The Northeast*, ed. Bruce G. Trigger, 525–543. Washington, D.C.: Smithsonian Institution Press.

Weibel, Joan
1976   The American Indian Family in Los Angeles: A Comparison of Premigration Experience, Postmigration Residence and Employment Mobility, and Coping Strategies. In *Geographical Perspectives on Native Americans: Topics and Resources*, ed. Jerry McDonald and Tony Lazewski, 121–146. Association of American Geographers Committee on Native Americans Publications, no. 1.

Weibel-Orlando, Joan
1991   *Indian Country, L.A.: Maintaining Ethnic Community in Complex Society*. Urbana: University of Illinois Press.

Weiss, Lawrence David
1984   *The Development of Capitalism in the Navajo Nation*. Minneapolis: Marxist Educational Press.

Welton, H. S.
1887   Letter to Commissioner of Indian Affairs, 2 November. Bureau of Indian Affairs, Letters Received, 1881–1907. RG 75. National Archives.

Weppner, Robert S.
1967   The Economic Adjustment of Navajo Indian Migrants to Denver. Ph.D. diss., University of Colorado, Boulder.
1971   Urban Economic Opportunities: The Example of Denver. In *The American Indian in Urban Society*, ed. Jack O. Waddell and O. Michael Watson, 245–273. Boston: Little, Brown.
1972   Socioeconomic Barriers to Assimilation of Navajo Migrants. *Human Organization* 31: 303–314.

Wernick, Andrew
1991   *Promotional Culture: Advertising, Ideology, and Symbolic Expression.*
            London: Sage.
Wertheimer, Barbara, Bruce Levine et al.
1989   *Who Built America? Working People and the Nation's Economy, Politics,*
            Culture, and Society: From Conquest and Colonization Through Recon-
            struction and the Great Uprising of 1877. New York: Pantheon Books.
Wheeler, George M.
1872   Preliminary Report Concerning Explorations and Surveys
            Principally in Nevada and Arizona. 42d Cong., 2d sess., Senate
            exec. doc. 65, serial set no. 1479.
Wherry, James D.
1979   The History of Maliseets and Micmacs in Aroostook County,
            Maine: Preliminary Report Two. In *Hearings Before the Select*
            Committee on Indian Affairs on S. 2829 to Provide for the Settlement
            of the Maine Indian Land Claims. 96th Cong., 2d sess., 506–609.
            Washington, D.C.: GPO.
1980   Of Maliseets and Micmacs: Maine's Other Indians. *Indian Truth,*
            no. 231 (April): 1, 3.
White, Leslie
1929–1930   *The Acoma Indians.* Forty-Seventh Annual Report of the Bureau
            of American Ethnology. Washington, D.C.: Smithsonian Institution.
White, Richard
n.d.   Ethnohistorical Report on the Grand Traverse Ottawas. Unpub.
            ms., Suttons Bay, Mich., Grand Traverse Bay Ottawas and
            Chippewas.
1991   *The Middle Ground: Indians, Empires, and Republics in the Great Lakes*
            Region, 1650–1815. New York: Cambridge University Press.
Whitehead, Ruth H.
1980   *Elitekey: Micmac Material Culture from 1600 A.D. to the Present.*
            Halifax: Nova Scotia Museum.
1987   I Have Lived Here Since the World Began: Atlantic Coast Artistic
            Traditions. In *The Spirit Sings: Artistic Traditions of Canada's First*
            Peoples, 17–51. Glenbow-Alberta Institute. Toronto: McClelland and
            Stewart.
Wilkinson, Frank, ed.
1981   *The Dynamics of Labour Market Segmentation.* London: Academic
            Press.

Williams, Raymond
1980   *Problems in Materialism and Culture.* London: Verso.
1982   *The Sociology of Culture.* New York: Schocken Books.
Willis, Paul
1981   *Learning to Labor: How Working-Class Kids Get Working-Class Jobs.* New York: Columbia University Press.
Willis, William S.
1962   Divide and Rule: Red, White, and Black in the Southeast. *Journal of Negro History* 48: 157–176.
Wilson, Charles M.
1937   Potato Race. *Country Gentleman* (January): 12–13, 64–65.
Wilson, Terry P.
1985   *The Underground Reservation: Osage Oil.* Lincoln: University of Nebraska Press.
Wolcott, Margaret Tisdale
1929   *Pioneer Notes from the Diaries of Judge Benjamin Hayes.* Los Angeles: Privately printed.
Wolf, Eric R.
1982   *Europe and the People Without History.* Berkeley and Los Angeles: University of California Press.
Woo, Deborah
1985   The Socioeconomic Status of Asian-American Women in the Labor Force: An Alternative View. *Sociological Perspectives* 28, no. 3: 307–338.
Wootten, I. J.
1894   Letter to Commissioner of Indian Affairs, 17 August. Bureau of Indian Affairs, Letters Received, 1881–1907. RG 75. National Archives.
1895   Letter to Commissioner of Indian Affairs, 23 August. Bureau of Indian Affairs, Letters Received, 1881–1907. RG 75. National Archives.
1896   Letter to Commissioner of Indian Affairs, 3 August. Bureau of Indian Affairs, Letters Received, 1881–1907. RG 75. National Archives.
Work, Laura B.
1898a   Letter to W. A. Jones, Commissioner of Indian Affairs, 5 July. Bureau of Indian Affairs, Letters Received, 1881–1907. RG 75. National Archives.

1898b   Letter to Commissioner of Indian Affairs, 8 October. Bureau of Indian Affairs, Letters Received, 1881–1907. National Archives.

1906   Letter to Commissioner of Indian Affairs, 20 February. Bureau of Indian Affairs, Letters Received, 1881–1907. National Archives.

Wright, William

1983   Personal communication to Patricia Albers, August 14.

Wurttenberg, Jonas

1822   Letter of 23 November. Chouteau Collection, Missouri Historical Society, St. Louis.

Yamashita, Robert, and Peter Park

1985   The Politics of Race: The Open Door, Ozawa, and the Case of the Japanese in America. *Review of Radical Political Economics* 17, no. 3: 135–156.

York, Dena W.

1989   Heading for the Aroostook. In *The County: Land of Promise: A Pictorial History of Aroostook County, Maine*, ed. Anna F. McGrath, 49–58. Norfolk, Va.: Donning.

Zavella, Patricia

1987   The Impact of "Sun Belt Industrializations" on Chicanas. In *The Women's West*, ed. S. Armitage and E. Jameson, 291–304. Norman: University of Oklahoma Press.

1991   Mujeres in Factories. In *Gender at the Crossroads of Knowledge: Feminist Anthropology in the Postmodern Era*, ed. Micaela di Leonardo, 312–336. Berkeley and Los Angeles: University of California Press.

Zimmerman, William Jr.

1957   The Role of the Bureau of Indian Affairs Since 1933. In *American Indians and American Life*, ed. George E. Simpson and J. Milton Yinger. *Annals of the American Academy of Political and Social Science* 311: 32–40.

CONTRIBUTORS

PATRICIA C. ALBERS received her Ph.D. at the University of Wisconsin, Madison. She is professor of anthropology and associate director of the American West Center at the University of Utah, Salt Lake City. Her publications include an edited book, *The Hidden Half: Studies of Plains Indian Women* (1983), and numerous articles on ethnicity and intergroup relations. Currently she is writing a book on popular postcard images of American Indians.

RICHARD L. CARRICO holds an M.A. in history from the University of San Diego and has taught in the American Indian Studies Department at San Diego State University and at Mesa Community College. He is currently the cultural resources manager for Ogden Environmental and Energy Services, San Diego. Active in local Native American affairs and research, he has authored numerous articles in ethnohistory and archaeology. His book *Strangers in a Stolen Land: Native Americans in San Diego County, 1850-1880* (1990) won an Award of Merit from the San Diego Historical Society. His current research focuses on Native American life and interaction at Mission San Diego from contact to 1830.

MARTHA C. KNACK has done extensive ethnographic and ethnohistoric research on economics and social organization, women's roles, and political rights involving several groups in the Great Basin, including Southern Paiutes, Shoshones, and Northern Paiutes. Her books include *Life Is with People: Household Organization of Contemporary Southern Paiute Indians* (1980) and *As Long as the River Shall Run: An Ethnohistory of Pyramid Lake Indian Reservation* (1984), with Omer C. Stewart. Her articles appear in such scholarly journals as *Ethnohistory*,

American Indian Culture and Research Journal, Ethnology, Nevada Historical Quarterly, and *Prologue: Quarterly Journal of the U.S. National Archives*. Her doctorate is from the University of Michigan, and she is professor of anthropology and ethnic studies at the University of Nevada, Las Vegas.

ALICE LITTLEFIELD holds a Ph.D. from Michigan State University and is currently professor of anthropology and chair of the Department of Sociology, Anthropology, and Social Work at Central Michigan University, Mt. Pleasant. Her articles on craft production in Mexico, the race concept in anthropology, and Native American education have appeared in the *American Ethnologist, Journal of Peasant Studies, Current Anthropology*, and several other journals and books. She is coeditor, with Hill Gates, of *Marxist Approaches in Economic Anthropology* (1991). Currently she is researching the history of Native American labor in Michigan.

JAMES M. McCLURKEN holds a Ph.D. from Michigan State University and is an ethnohistorical consultant in East Lansing. He has conducted extensive research with Michigan Ottawas and is the author of several books and articles, including *Gah-baeh-jagwah-buk (The Way It Happened): A Visual Culture History of the Little Traverse Bay Odawa* (1991), and he is coauthor of *People of the Three Fires* (1987). He has also conducted extensive ethnohistorical research on Chippewa tribes in Minnesota, Wisconsin, and Michigan on topics related to treaty rights litigation and federal acknowledgment.

JOHN H. MOORE is professor and chair of the Anthropology Department at the University of Florida, Gainesville. He has worked with Native American people since 1969 and is the author of over fifty articles, monographs, and books, including *The Cheyenne Nation: A Social and Demographic History* (1987). He also edited *The Political Economy of North American Indians* (1993). He is currently serving on the Ethics Committee of the Human Genome Diversity Project. He has served as an expert witness for Indian people in many cases involving treaty rights, land claims, and civil rights. He currently serves as a consultant to the Sand Creek Massacre Descendants Association.

KURT M. PETERS received a Ph.D. in ethnic studies from the University of California, Berkeley, in 1994. His research focuses on twentieth-century Native American history, including published studies on Natives as wage earners and several essays on Native American railroad laborers. He is a postdoctoral fellow in the American Indian Studies Center, University of California, Los Angeles.

HARALD E. L. PRINS studied anthropology and history at the University of Nijmegen in the Netherlands, receiving his doctoral degree. He then served as research and teaching fellow in comparative history at Nijmegen's History Department. Elected as list fellow in 1978, Prins came to New York's New School for Social Research, earning his Ph.D. in anthropology. After fieldwork in the Argentine pampas, he worked a decade for the Aroostook Band of Micmacs in Maine as staff anthropologist and helped them gain federal recognition. He has produced *Our Lives in Our Hands*, a documentary film on the Mi'kmaq basketmakers and potato pickers in Maine, co-edited *American Beginnings: Explorations, Culture, and Cartography in the Land of Norumbega* (University of Nebraska Press, 1994), and published over sixty articles and chapters. His case study of Mi'kmaq tribal history, *The Mi'kmaq: Resistance, Accommodation, and Cultural Survival* (Harcourt Brace), is in press. He has taught anthropology at Bowdoin College and Colby College and, since 1990, at Kansas State University, Manhattan.

BETH SENNETT has a master of arts degree in anthropology from the University of Nevada, Reno. She has worked as a professional archaeologist in cultural resource management and museums since 1979. At present she is the principal investigator for her own company, P2F2. Her professional emphasis is on the care and preservation of archaeological artifacts and documents. She lives in Rock Springs, Wyoming, with her husband, Randall Porter, and family.

FLORENCE C. SHIPEK holds a Ph.D. from the University of Hawaii and is the author of numerous articles and books, including *Pushed into the Rocks: Southern California Indian Land Tenure, 1769–1986* (1988). Since 1954 she has conducted ethnohistorical research with and for several southern California bands, also serving as an expert witness. She was the first Costo Professor of American Indian History, University of California, Riverside, and has been honored as a distinguished scholar by the Southwestern Anthropological Association. She retired from full-time teaching in 1989 and holds professor emeritus rank at the University of Wisconsin, Parkside.

INDEX